MARTIN LUTHER

MARTIN LUTHER

VISIONARY REFORMER

SCOTT H. HENDRIX

YALE UNIVERSITY PRESS

NEW HAVEN AND LONDON

Published with assistance from the foundation established in memory of Oliver Baty Cunningham of the Class of 1917, Yale College.

For information about this and other Yale University Press publications, please contact:
U.S. Office: sales.press@yale.edu   www.yalebooks.com
Europe Office: sales@yaleup.co.uk   www.yalebooks.co.uk

Typeset in Minion Pro by IDSUK (DataConnection) Ltd
Printed in Great Britain by Gomer Press Ltd, Llandysul, Ceredigion, Wales

Library of Congress Cataloging-in-Publication Data

Hendrix, Scott H.
   Martin Luther: the man and his vision/c Scott H. Hendrix.
      pages cm
   ISBN 978-0-300-16669-9 (cl: alk. paper)
1. Luther, Martin, 1483–1546.   2. Reformation—Germany—Biography.   I. Title.
   BR325.H37 2015
   284.1092—dc23
   [B]

                                                                 2015017636

A catalogue record for this book is available from the British Library.

10 9 8 7 6 5 4 3 2 1

FOR
AMELIA, ZOE, and MAYA

What a wee little part of a person's life are his acts and his words! His real life is led in his head, and is known to none but himself. . . . Biographies are but the clothes and buttons of a man—the biography of the man himself cannot be written.
— Mark Twain 1906

CONTENTS

PREFACE

In 2014 a digital mapping project at the Massachusetts Institute of Technology measured human cultural production across the centuries from 800 BCE to 1950 CE. The project, named Pantheon, selected all the prominent people whose Wikipedia pages appeared in twenty-five or more languages. Pantheon found 4,002 such individuals who made significant contributions to the arts and sciences prior to 1950. The digital program then ranked the accomplishments of each candidate against others in categories such as their field of endeavor, and their dates and places of birth.[1] To my surprise, Martin Luther ranked number five out of 518 notable people in the category of religion and number four out of 746 candidates born in Germany.[2] Among religious figures, only Jesus, Moses, Muhammad, and Abraham ranked higher than Luther; in line behind Luther were St. Paul, King Solomon, Mary, and St. Peter. Among people born in Germany, only Einstein, Bach, and Beethoven ranked higher; Martin Luther beat out the father of communism, Karl Marx, the literary genius, Johann Wolfgang von Goethe, the artist, Albrecht Dürer, and the printer of the Gutenberg Bible.

According to these results, the reformation ignited in 1517 by Martin Luther resulted in lasting contributions to the field of religion and human culture in general. The broadest impact was made by the translation of the complete Bible into German, which quickly led to translations in other vernacular languages. Putting the Bible into the hands of laity and allowing it to penetrate European culture diversified Christianity to an extent not seen in hundreds of years. Owing to expansive colonization by European powers, the impact of the reformation spread across continents and is still felt by both Protestants and Roman Catholics. In the 1500s the Roman

Church lost its dominance over European Christianity but gained a strong presence in the Americas and parts of Africa and Asia.

Not all historians view a diversified Christianity as a cultural contribution. Some see it rather as a detrimental consequence for which Martin Luther is largely to blame. Nevertheless, even those who regret the divisions and expansion of Christendom acknowledge that the reformation's impact on religion, culture, and political upheavals was immense. Luther owes his reputation to that impact, but for biographers of Luther it poses a problem. The reformation became such a big story that its initiator is easily lost among the other characters that carried reforms down roads never trodden or imagined by Luther himself. Biographers of Luther, therefore, face this dilemma: We cannot tell the story of his life separately from that of the early reformation, but neither can we allow the reformation to overwhelm the person. Histories of the reformation say a lot about what Luther did but very little about who he was.

Even apart from what he accomplished, however, Martin Luther was an intriguing person. Luther lived what is now called a "full" life. His daily existence was filled with colorful and emotional hours among friends, colleagues, relatives, and critics. He rejoiced and he mourned, he was healthy and sick, he spoke tenderly and lashed out in anger, he believed and he doubted, he was courageous and afraid, he cursed and he prayed, he was thrilled and disappointed. The reformation was started not by a heroic robot but by a dynamic human being leading a vigorous life. This biography offers as many glimpses of that life as possible while following Luther's unconventional public career as a university professor, heretic, renegade monk, political outlaw, provocative thinker, and religious visionary.

In 1983, the German Luther scholar, Helmar Junghans, cautioned: "Writing a thoroughly accurate and fitting biography of Martin Luther is too much to ask of a single historian."[3] Junghans was reviewing a group of biographies that appeared in celebration of Luther's 500th birthday. More biographies will appear around 2017, which is the 500th anniversary of Martin Luther's ninety-five theses—the traditional beginning of the reformation—and none of them will be perfect. Junghans was right: no biography can be thoroughly accurate and suitable for every reader; but I believe a biography is better written by a single author than patched together by a committee.

My reason for attempting the unattainable is simple. From time to time I was asked for the name of a "good Luther biography" in English. To me, a good Luther biography covered his entire life and was both free of Luther lore and based on the latest research. If I wanted to assign such a book for my courses, it also had to be a reasonable length and readable. Older biographies, short and long, were available, as were good recent books that dealt with special themes or specific periods of Luther's life. While I was still teaching, however, I could not find a biography that satisfied me, and to attempt it myself seemed too daunting.

A biographer of Martin Luther faces manifold challenges, but lack of material is not one of them. The challenge lies in having more material than any single biographer can read. The scholarly edition of Luther's writings in German and Latin occupies over 120 thick tomes. The American edition of Luther's works, initially "complete" at fifty-five volumes, is now being extended. Other challenges are numerous: Recent research questions accepted dates, such as the year of Luther's birth; for some crucial events we have no sources—for example, how and when Martin Luther and Katharina von Bora decided to marry. High on the list remains the uncertain authenticity of juicy snippets from Luther's conversations at meals with family, boarders, friends, and colleagues. Those conversations were recorded in German or Latin (or a mix of both) and comprise six volumes of the so-called *Table Talk*. It was compiled from collections of notes taken by at least eleven different guests who were present at intervals during the last fifteen years of Luther's life.[4] The reliability of the *Table Talk* is contested, but I have chosen to use some excerpts that bear on Luther's life and appear consistent with his flair for bluntness and drama.

Other challenges for the biographer are the patchwork of cities and states that made up sixteenth-century Germany, the commingling of church and state, and the temptation to identify pre-reformation Christianity with modern Roman Catholicism, or to confuse early Protestants, who called themselves evangelicals, with modern evangelical Christians. More hurdles arise: the parade of popes, cardinals, bishops, monks, and nuns who marched through Luther's life; the unclear motives of politicians who made decisions that either put Luther in danger or kept him from harm; unfamiliar theological terms that require explanation but not extensive analysis;[5] and archeological digs that may or may not offer reliable clues to daily life in Luther's time.

Challenges, however, are not excuses. I navigate my way through and around them by keeping in mind three touchstones. First, Luther was neither a hero nor a villain, but a human being with both merits and faults. "At the same time saint and sinner," a key theological principle of his own, fits no one better than Luther himself. I have tried to show both sides of the man while allowing for his extraordinary qualities. Second, Luther was not a reformer in isolation. He lived and worked closely with relatives, friends, colleagues, and political advisors without whom the reformation would not have been possible. They are identified in the cast of characters at the front of this book along with many others who played significant roles in Luther's story. Third, I strive to present the characters and events as they were in the sixteenth century and not judge them by modern criteria. No historian can do that perfectly. Every historian has a point of view, and I have interspersed my opinions, based on the sources I read, about who Martin Luther was and what he wanted. I hope, however, that those readers who disagree with my opinions can still enjoy the story of his life. I remain fascinated by that story and wish that I could know the man and the people in his life better than intensive investigation allows. The past can be studied but not relived. That is the attraction and the frustration of history.

Although the Pantheon project ranked Martin Luther near the top of past contributors to the fields of religion and culture, in our time he may be worth knowing for what he envisioned more than for what he accomplished. He is best understood not as a reformer of the church but as a reformer of religion, who strove to replace bad religion with a faith that valued freedom and justice instead of narrow orthodoxy and moralism; religion that opened minds instead of closing them; religion that opened hearts with "mutual consolation" (his words) rather than closing them with bitterness and exploitation. Religion was not a crusade and Luther was wary of endorsing campaigns that applauded or practiced violence. Luther himself was hardly free of egotism, but the religion he desired was not based on self-seeking that fueled the pursuit of happiness either here or in the hereafter. Luther would not endear himself to promoters of faith who promise healing and success if people believe and pray hard enough. For him faith was a gift, not a commodity to be grown, and a little of it went a long way. Faith was not merely a private opinion but entailed a public commitment to the welfare of others.

Luther was, however, a realist about the human condition. His evil triumvirate, "sin, death, and the devil," caused believers and non-believers alike to mistreat, exploit, and kill one another. Evil could not be eliminated by human reason and optimism or, for that matter, by religion that deluded people with the promise of miracles, which Luther often dismissed as superstitions. He did not expect the world to become perfect through religion, but he did believe the religion he advocated provided comfort, strength, and compassion until the fight against evil was won. For Luther,

God was indeed a harsh judge of evil, but God was also merciful, trust-worthy, and committed to his creation, regardless of the extent to which it was corrupted.

Whether one believes in God or not, religion remains a powerful force for good and evil in human affairs and does not appear to be losing its potency. Luther would not be surprised, nor would he try to explain why God does not jump in and fix the world. The mystery and otherness of God were precious to him, and the faith that captured his heart sustained him when his mind found no easy answer for the suffering and disappoint-ment that touched his own life. According to Luther, faith was hard, but it was the only sure foundation of a religion that was both humble and hopeful: humble about its own power to remake the world and yet hopeful about a power—greater than that of religion itself—to save us from ourselves.

*   *   *

Luther's life divides nicely into two parts: before and after he became a reformer. Part one ends at the point (1521) when Luther states for the first time his calling to oversee the remaking of medieval religion according to his vision of what Christianity should be. Before 1521, Luther proposed many reforms but did not see himself as the leader of a popular movement as comprehensive as the reformation turned out to be. Part two is the story of Luther the reformer, in the true sense of his leading a movement that took action on what until then was only proposed—albeit proposed so broadly and forcefully that Luther was declared an outlaw in Germany and a heretic by the church. The movement he took over in 1522 started in the small German town of Wittenberg, where Luther had lived and taught for eleven years. The radical reforms he suggested in writing were first attempted by his colleagues at the university and by fellow monks at the monastery. Only upon his return from political exile did Luther become the leader of a reforming movement. Even then, no master plan for a refor-mation existed. Luther and his colleagues had to proceed by trial and error, and adjustments were still being made after his death in 1546.

Titles of chapters are taken from Luther's words quoted at the head of each chapter. I have not been rigid about giving the English equivalents of German or Latin names. For example, I use the familiar Nuremberg for Nürnberg, but I have kept Braunschweig instead of changing it to Brunswick, which is not a well-known equivalent of Braunschweig. Martin Luther's first name poses no problem, and Katharina, the popular name of

Martin's wife and other women in the story, does not need to appear as
Katharine or Catherine. The name Jerome, however, is more common in
English than the Latin Hieronymus. For the sake of simplicity I have also
changed Johannes and Johann to John. A member of the nobility, such as
Johann von Staupitz, becomes John Staupitz unless the noble status needs
emphasis. Estimating the value of sixteenth-century money poses a special
difficulty. In this case the best solution is to compare a sum in one context
to a different sum in a similar or contrasting setting. For example, it is
impossible to determine today's value of Luther's salary as a university
professor, but comparing it to the salary of a colleague or a skilled craftsman
is meaningful.

*   *   *

It may be true that a biography is best written by one person, but behind
and alongside the author stand teachers, friends, and colleagues whose
knowledge and suggestions over the years have shaped the finished book.
Since it is impossible to name them all, I will mention those who, over the
past four years, have contributed, perhaps unknowingly, to this project. I am
especially grateful to the institutions in Germany that invited me to use
their rich resources: the University of Frankfurt Center for Research in the
Humanities, located in Bad Homburg; and the Herzog August Library in
Wolfenbüttel. For the ideal living and working environment at Bad
Homburg I owe special thanks to Professor Luise Schorn-Schütte and the
gracious personnel at the institute under managing director Ingrid Rudolph.
Dr. Jill Bepler encouraged me to spend two months at the library in
Wolfenbüttel, where I was assisted by its expert staff and enriched by inter-
action with other guests. The holdings of the Leibniz-Institut für
Europäische Geschichte in Mainz were made available to me courtesy of
its director, Professor Irene Dingel.

My appreciation also goes to the following friends and colleagues for
clarifying my direction with their knowledge and questions: Ilya Adronov,
Ronald Asch, Ulrich Bubenheimer, Hauke Christiansen, Mona Garloff,
Elizabeth Harding, Sigrun Haude, Bridget Heal, Luka Illic, Henning
Jürgens, Robert Kolb, Ulrich Kopp, Austra Reinis, and Gerhild Scholz
Williams. In Wittenberg, Martin Treu devoted three days to answering my
questions, explaining the recent archeological digs, and bringing me up to
date about the town as Luther knew it. Scott Moore escorted me around
Erfurt and connected me with recent research on Luther's student years. At
the library of the Augustinian cloister, Michael Ludscheidt guided me to

resources about the cloister and its books that were available to Luther. I am also grateful for questions from the unnamed listeners who responded to my presentations at Bad Homburg, the Dulwich Picture Gallery in south London, and in Münster. My visit to Münster was arranged by the coordinator of the interdisciplinary program on religion and politics, Iris Flessenkämper. She also found time to discuss my unfinished book and to reacquaint me with the city and its notorious attempt at reform.

For her invitation to take on this project and her persistent encouragement thereafter I am especially grateful to my editor, Heather McCallum, Samantha Cross and Tami Halliday at the London office of Yale University Press. I received feedback on the early draft of this book from anonymous readers and from Stan Frick and Robert Harriman, whom I thank for their comments and suggestions. Finally, my wife, Emilee, read every chapter as it was written and then focused her critical eye on the entire manuscript. Martin Luther was hardly new to her; but she put that aside and complied with my request to be brutally honest, as only a caring spouse can. She pointed out the spots where I assumed more than I should; and if this book is both readable and understandable, much of the credit belongs to her.

Scott H. Hendrix
Fearrington Village, North Carolina
February 18, 2015

PEOPLE

Mansfeld Luther Household

Hans Luder	Martin's father, d. 1530
Margaret Lindemann	Martin's mother, d. 1531
Martin Luder/Luther	1483/84–1546
Barbara Luder	Martin's sister, d. 1520
Dorothy Luder	Martin's sister, married Mackenrot
Margaret Luder	Martin's sister, married Kaufmann
? Luder	Martin's sister, married Polner
Jacob Luder	Martin's brother, d. 1571

Wittenberg Luther Household

Katharina von Bora	Martin's wife, 1499–1552
"Hänschen" Luther	First son, 1526–1575
Elisabeth Luther	First daughter, 1527–1528
Magdalena "Lenchen" Luther	Second daughter, 1529–1542
Martin Luther	Second son, 1531–1565
Paul Luther	Third son, 1533–1593
Margaret Luther	Third daughter, 1534–1570
Magdalena von Bora	Aunt of Katharina
Wolfgang Sieberger	Housekeeper

Von Bora Family

Hans von Bora	Father of Katharina, d. before 1523
Katharina von Haugwitz/Haubitz	Mother of Katharina, d. 1504/05

Hans von Bora   Brother of Katharina, d. 1542
Florian von Bora   Nephew of Katharina

Eisenach Connections

John Braun   Priest, humanist, mentor
Antonius Lindemann   Uncle of Martin's mother
Caspar Lindemann   Physician related to Martin's mother
Heinrich Schalbe   Wealthy citizen, provided board to
                                     Martin

Augustinian Contacts

Bartholomew Arnoldi von Usingen   Philosophy professor in Erfurt
Robert Barnes   Prior in Cambridge, envoy of
                                     Henry VIII to Germany, executed
                                     1540
John Lang   Martin's contemporary in Erfurt,
                                     prior and reformer
Wenzel Linck   Prior in Wittenberg-vicar general,
                                     reformer in Altenburg and
                                     Nuremberg
John Nathin   Theology professor in Erfurt
Jacob Propst   Prior in Antwerp, reformer in
                                     Bremen
John Staupitz   Vicar-general, Martin's superior,
                                     chief mentor and promoter

Wittenberg Colleagues and Friends

John Agricola ("Master Eisleben")   Luther's assistant, principal and
                                     preacher in Eisleben, superintendent
                                     in Brandenburg
Nicholas Amsdorf   Professor, reformer in Magdeburg,
                                     bishop of Naumburg
Matthew Aurogallus   Professor of Hebrew, co-translator of
                                     the Old Testament
John Bugenhagen   Pastor at Town Church, professor,
                                     church organizer

Lucas Cranach the Elder	Court painter, apothecary, wealthy citizen, mayor
Caspar Cruciger	Professor, recorder, daughter married Hänschen Luther
Veit Dietrich	Assistant, recorder, editor, reformer in Nuremberg
Justus Jonas	Dean at Castle Church, professor, reformer in Halle
Andrew Karlstadt	Professor, reformer, dissenter, professor in Basel
Philip Melanchthon	Professor, layman, exceptional scholar and theologian, Luther's chief co-reformer
George Rörer	Deacon at Town Church, recorder, editor
George Spalatin	Secretary and chaplain to Elector Frederick, historian, reformer in Altenburg

Dukes of Saxony

Frederick "the Wise"	Elector 1486–1525, Luther's protector, Catholic
John "the Steadfast"	Frederick's brother, Elector 1525–1532, Lutheran
John Frederick "the Magnanimous"	Son of John, Elector 1532–1547, Lutheran
George "the Bearded"	Duke of Saxony, 1500–1539, Catholic
Henry "the Pious"	Brother of George, Duke 1539–1541, Lutheran
Maurice of Saxony	Son of Henry, Duke 1541–1547, Elector 1547–1553, Lutheran

Other Rulers in the Holy Roman Empire

Charles I of Spain	Emperor Charles V 1519–1556, Catholic
Ferdinand I	Brother of Charles, Archduke of Austria, Emperor 1558–1564

Albert of Prussia	Duke 1525–1568, Lutheran
Philip "the Magnanimous"	Count (Landgrave) of Hesse 1519–1567, Lutheran
Albert of Brandenburg	Archbishop of Mainz and Magdeburg 1514–1545, Archchancellor of Germany, Cardinal
Joachim I of Brandenburg	Brother of Albert, Elector 1499–1535, Catholic
Joachim II of Brandenberg	Nephew of Albert, Elector 1535–1571, Lutheran
Ernest the "Confessor"	Duke of Lüneburg 1520–1547, nephew of Elector Frederick of Saxony, Lutheran
Henry II ("Hanswurst")	Duke of Braunschweig-Wolfenbüttel 1514–1568, Catholic

European Sovereigns

Christian II	King of Denmark and Norway 1513–1523, nephew of Elector Frederick, Catholic/Lutheran
Christian III	King of Denmark and Norway 1534–1559, Lutheran
Francis I	King of France 1515–1547, Catholic
Henry VIII	King of England 1509–1547, Catholic/Protestant
Suleyman "the Magnificent"	Sultan of the Ottoman Turkish Empire 1520–1566, Muslim

Popes during Luther's Lifetime

Innocent VIII	1484–1492, Italian
Alexander VI	1492–1503, Italian
Pius III	1503–1503, Italian
Julius II	1503–1513, Italian
Leo X	1513–1521, Italian
Adrian VI	1522–1523, Dutch
Clement VII	1523–1534, Italian
Paul III	1534–1549, Italian

Catholic Literary Opponents

Alveld, Augustine	German Franciscan, *The Apostolic See* 1520
Cajetan, Thomas	Italian Dominican, Aquinas expert, cardinal, papal legate, interrogated Luther 1518 at Augsburg
Catharinus, Ambrose	Italian Dominican, *Defense of Catholic Truth* 1520
Cochlaeus, John	German humanist and priest, *Seven-headed Luther* 1529, biography of Luther 1549
Eck, John	German theologian at Ingolstadt, debated Luther at Leipzig 1519, *Enchiridion . . . against Luther* 1525
Emser, Jerome	German humanist, secretary to Duke George, *New Testament . . . Emended* 1527
Erasmus	Dutch, leading humanist, *Freedom of the Will* 1524
King Henry VIII	*Assertion of the Seven Sacraments* 1521
Latomus, Jacob	Flemish theologian at Louvain, defended condemnation of Luther 1521
More, Thomas	English humanist, Lord Chancellor, *Response to Luther* 1523, executed 1535
Murner, Thomas	Alsatian satirist & poet, *The Great Lutheran Fool* 1522
Prierias, Silvester	Italian papal theologian, *The Power of the Pope* 1518

Protestant Reformers

John Brenz	Schwäbisch Hall, Duchy of Württemberg, d. 1570
Martin Bucer	Strasbourg, Cambridge, d. 1551
Henry Bullinger	Zurich, d. 1575
John Calvin	Strasbourg, Geneva, d. 1564

Wolfgang Capito	Basel, Mainz, Strasbourg, d. 1541
Argula von Grumbach	Bavaria, Franconia, d. 1554
Thomas Müntzer	Wittenberg, Prague, Thuringia, d. 1525
John Oecolampadius	Basel, d. 1531
Andrew Osiander	Nuremberg, Königsberg (Prussia), d. 1552
Urban Rhegius	Augsburg, Lüneburg, d. 1541
Paul Speratus	Austria, Wittenberg, Prussia, d. 1551
William Tyndale	English Bible translator, executed 1536
Katharina Schütz Zell	Strasbourg, d. 1562
Ulrich Zwingli	Zurich, died in battle 1531

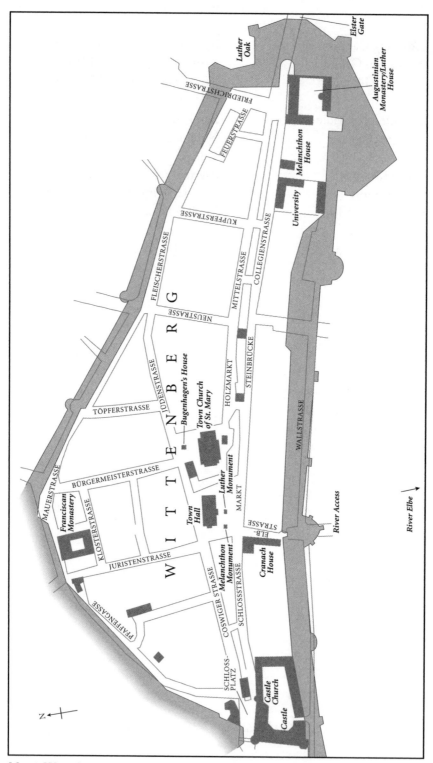

Map 1. Wittenberg.

Map 2. Central Europe during the Reformation.

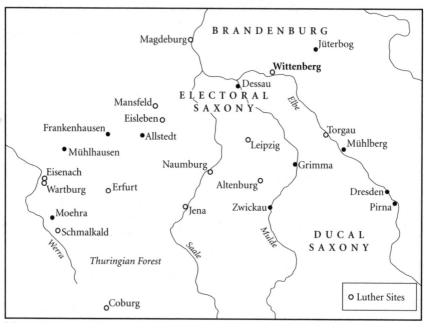

Map 3. Saxony and Surrounding Territory.

PART ONE

PATHWAYS TO REFORM
1483/84–1521

CHAPTER ONE

MY HOMELAND
1546

Eisleben—Mansfeld—Wittenberg—Rome

"Your Grace knows that I am a native of the territory of Mansfeld and have therefore loved my homeland in accord with all the ancient books that say children should love their fatherland."[1]

The last letter sent by Martin Luther to his wife, Katharina von Bora, was composed on Valentine's Day, 1546. Four days later Luther died in Eisleben, the same town in which he was born. It was not a romantic letter, because in medieval Germany Valentine's Day was not a celebration of love. It was instead, for Martin and Katharina, a religious occasion: the feast day of St. Valentine, which in 1546 happened to fall on a Sunday. Katharina, a former nun, would have known the letter was written on February 14, and therefore Luther signed off matter-of-factly: "At Eisleben on the Sunday of Valentine 1546."[2] About 2,600 authentic letters written by Martin Luther are extant,[3] and most of them, like the letter to Katharina, are dated according to the nearest festival on the ecclesiastical calendar in use for centuries. The church calendar was not a day planner or a preview of the month's events. It was a universal timekeeper, which tapped out the rhythms that governed the lives of most sixteenth-century Europeans. The calendar fixed them in the flow of a biblical history that began with Adam and would end with the Last Day. The flow was relived each year in a journey that began with preparation for the birth of Jesus (the Advent Sundays before Christmas), reached its high point in the Easter season, which ended in spring, and counted the Sundays of Pentecost through summer and autumn until Advent came round again.

Martin Luther, the former Augustinian friar, knew that calendar by heart. He learned it in elementary school with the help of a poetic memory device that identified the saints' days within each month. During the twenty years between entering the monastery (1505) and marrying Katharina (1525), Luther lived in two cloisters that celebrated not only major festivals such as Easter but also commemorations of the apostles, saints, and martyrs. A saint was assigned to almost every day, and that day reminded the faithful where they were in the year of sacred time. Four days before his last letter, Luther dated one to Katharina on the day of St. Scholastica (February 10) and another on the Sunday after St. Dorothy, whose feast day was February 6. Initiating the Protestant Reformation, excommunication from the Roman Church, and living as an outlaw in the Holy Roman Empire did not alter the way Luther marked his days. For him, the reformation was not the beginning of a modern era that kept time with numbers, but a harbinger of the world's end when time no longer mattered. A final struggle would bring in the long-sought kingdom of God. We know that did not happen, but Luther did not. The long-term impact of his life was unknown to Luther and everyone around him. When he died, the survival of the reformation was in doubt, and Luther himself was ambivalent about the job he had done.

The last letter to Katharina contained other clues to Luther's world. Although he lived most of his life in Saxony, where the reformation began, Luther remained attached to the county of Mansfeld in Thuringia, which he called "my homeland."[4] Eisleben, where Martin was born, was only ten miles (sixteen kilometers) from the village of Mansfeld in which his childhood was spent; and Wittenberg, the Saxon university town in which Luther worked, was close enough to Mansfeld (sixty-five miles; 100 kilometers) for him to maintain regular contact with relatives. Since the 1200s the county of Mansfeld had expanded its wealth by extracting copper and other minerals from the shale on the eastern side of the Harz mountains. In the early 1500s Luther's family and friends were involved in this business by owning franchises granted by the counts. The franchises entitled them to own and operate smelters, the small furnaces for melting ore before the metal was extracted. Martin's brother, Jacob Luder, inherited their father's smelters. Other smelters belonged to his brothers-in-law and to the family of Hans Reinicke, with whom Luther attended school. A family friend, Dr. Philip Drachstedt, who once owned the Eisleben house in which Luther died, also had furnaces.

In 1546, however, there were too many middlemen between the copper mines owned by the counts and the retail market, and Luther's relatives were in danger of losing their franchises. They needed an advocate to negotiate with the counts and settle their quarrels. Luther's friends and relatives chose him, and in the last week of his life, Luther found himself in Eisleben trying to settle a dispute among the counts. At first, the prospect of success was poor. In the letter of February 7, Luther told Katharina the sides were so deadlocked that no devils could be left in hell because they were all in Eisleben trying to thwart his efforts. A week later, however, his last letter reported so much progress that Luther invited Counts Albert and Gebhart to dine with him so they could reconcile face-to-face. In appreciation, Count Albert's wife made Luther a gift of trout, which he promised to Katharina.[5]

Letters were the primary means of conveying news about matters both important and trivial. Rarely did Luther send a letter that failed to contain such reports. From his last letter to Katharina we learn that their younger sons, who had traveled to Eisleben with their father, had continued to Mansfeld to visit their uncle Jacob. Luther also noted a leg injury had been sustained by Justus Jonas, his former colleague in Wittenberg, who had accompanied the reformer to Eisleben. Jonas had remained a close friend and told the reformer he wanted Luther to be present at his deathbed. In Eisleben it happened the other way around; but before Luther died, the wound to Jonas' leg had caused small holes to form in his shin, and Luther asked Katharina to report Jonas' condition to their friends in Wittenberg. The friends were the colleagues who in 1546 made up Luther's inner circle: Philip Melanchthon, John Bugenhagen, and Caspar Cruciger. Before Jonas left Wittenberg he belonged to that circle. Luther's selection of those colleagues to receive the report of Jonas' condition was not serendipitous; it expressed the collegial leadership of reform which Luther had always espoused, even though he was the first among equals.

Finally, as he often did, Luther passed along hearsay. In Eisleben and elsewhere, it was rumored he had been kidnapped. Luther teased his wife about it by blaming the rumor on his enemies around Meissen, which was near Katharina's birthplace. Luther also heard that the Catholic emperor, Charles V, and his army were not far away, planning perhaps their long-postponed attack on the German Protestants. Although Luther dismissed the report with his usual confidence that God would take care of the matter, one year later (1547) Catholic forces did defeat the Protestants and forced Wittenberg to capitulate. Luther was spared that humiliation, having died on February 18, 1546, four days after writing to Katharina: "We hope to come home this week if it is God's will."[6]

Except for the exposure caused by Luther's fame, his personal relationships were not unlike those of contemporaries. Even before he became a notorious hero, Luther had relatives and friends, colleagues and enemies, all of whom in one way or another brought joy, sorrow, pleasure, or irritation into his life. Our awareness of those relationships has been eclipsed by the monumental role given to him in most accounts of the reformation. It had hardly begun when Luther was hoisted onto a pedestal by his family and other fans. Moreover, after his years in the cloister, where he was Brother Martin, Luther was scarcely on first-name terms with anyone apart from his brother Jacob. Even Katharina, at least in public, addressed him as "Herr Doktor." Nevertheless, his correspondence and table conversations show that relationships were essential to Luther's work and well-being. He was seldom isolated, except for the ten months of friendly exile (1521–1522) at the Wartburg fortress; even there he received visitors, wrote several letters a day, and managed a brief, incognito visit to Wittenberg. His daily routines were almost always performed in the company of others. During his last twenty years, the Luther residence was more like a hostel than a home. Almost every word he spoke in the lecture hall, from the pulpit, and at mealtime was recorded by a secretary or a guest. Nor did Martin Luther die alone. In addition to Justus Jonas, his two younger sons, servants, and several others were present at his death.

His horizons, though broader than those most people of his era enjoyed, were by modern standards narrow. Luther made many short journeys but only one trip that took him outside Germany. The date and purpose of that trip have recently been revised by a persuasive piece of detective work and puzzle solving.[7] In October of 1511 (not 1510), soon after Luther had moved to Wittenberg for good, he and another friar were entrusted with a mission to the headquarters of the Augustinian order in Rome. Taking a route that covered almost 900 miles (1,450 kilometers), Luther and his colleague passed by Liechtenstein and Chur, crossed the Alps through the Septimer pass, and arrived in Rome by way of Milan and Florence before the end of November 1511. In all likelihood they lodged at the monastery of St. Augustine, saw Pope Julius II from a distance, conferred with the general of the Augustinian order, and set out on their return as the year 1511 ended. Luther's colleague was ordered to report directly to their superior in Salzburg, but Luther returned to Wittenberg by a different route to ensure that one of them reached home safely. Instead of retracing his path through the Swiss Alps, Luther might have followed the Italian coastline west along the Gulf of Genoa into France, then turned north along the Rhône river to Lyon, and traveled northeast through western Switzerland into Germany. By taking that route he would have skirted the armed hostilities taking place in northern Italy and avoided the Alps at their wintry worst. For Brother Martin it was the trip of a lifetime but, compared to a well-traveled scholar like Erasmus of Rotterdam, who spent time in Holland, Belgium, France, England, Italy, Switzerland, and Germany, Martin Luther was a local.

Luther identified only one stop on the journey back to Wittenberg. Two excerpts from Luther's table conversations indicate that he stayed briefly in Augsburg. In both sources Luther says he met and conversed with a woman known as Ursel of Augsburg who was reputed to be a prostitute. Ursel's real name was Anna Laminit, and for longer than sixteen years she had lived in Augsburg, claiming that she was unable to eat or digest regular food. Whether or not she was a whore, her miraculous existence deceived many people until she was exposed by the emperor's sister. She had Anna secluded in a convent and watched secretly through holes drilled into the walls of her cell. Anna was spied hiding food in her clothing and disposing of her waste through a window. When they met, Luther asked Anna if she was ready to die. "Oh no," she responded, "here I know how things work, but there I don't know what will happen."[8] Anna Laminit was hoping the miracle of her survival would qualify her for sainthood; however, she was banished from Augsburg and was later arrested in Switzerland for fraud and executed by drowning.[9] For Luther, who told the story many years afterward, Anna's deception illustrated the work of the devil that prevailed under papal rule.

The return from Rome took a month longer than the outbound segment of the journey. Once back in Wittenberg, Luther scarcely had time to repack before heading to Cologne for the quadrennial convention of the German Augustinians. Although it could not be compared to the trip he had just completed, the journey to Cologne was no mere excursion. It took Luther and his companions at least a week to cover the 290 miles (463 kilometers). After that he undertook no long trips outside Saxony until 1518, when his theology was debated at the Augustinian conclave in Heidelberg. Later that year he was interrogated by Cardinal Cajetan at Augsburg, forty-five miles (seventy-two kilometers) west of Munich, and in 1521 he was summoned to appear before Emperor Charles V at Worms on the Rhine river, forty-five miles south of Frankfurt. The rest of his life, which he passed as a condemned heretic and outlaw, was spent almost entirely in Saxony under the protection of its influential and supportive princes. Nevertheless, he remained attentive to the diplomatic jockeying and political strife in Europe. The German Reformation was in the middle of this turmoil—geographically and tactically—and would not have survived if France and the Turkish Ottoman Empire had not kept the aspirations of Emperor Charles in check.

The Holy Roman Empire of the German nation had become the major power in Central Europe before Charles, scion of the House of Habsburg, was elected emperor at the age of nineteen. In addition to Austria and Hungary, the Habsburgs had gained control over the Low Countries and Spain through strategic marriages that made Charles the grandson of Spain's rulers, Ferdinand and Isabella. After Charles was crowned Holy Roman Emperor in 1519, he was so preoccupied with Italy and Spain that he returned to Germany only once during the next eleven years. At Worms in 1521 Charles presided over the governing convention of the empire, called a diet, attended by the rulers of German cities and territories: lands that belonged to the church (such as Mainz), states that were secular (such as Saxony), and imperial cities that enjoyed independence from the states surrounding them. At the Diet of Worms, which condemned Luther, he and Emperor Charles V met face-to-face for the only time. Soon thereafter Charles ceded the rule of Austria to his younger brother, Archduke Ferdinand, and made him the emperor's representative in Germany.

It was a bad time for the emperor to be absent. The aggressive Ottoman rulers of the Islamic state in Turkey, known to Europeans simply as "the Turks," became a serious threat to Central Europe. A clever and ambitious new sultan, Suleyman, only four years older than Charles, had consolidated his rule of the Balkans by taking Belgrade. In 1522, a brutal six-month siege enabled Suleyman's army to overrun the citadel of the Knights of St. John at Rhodes, the last bastion of Christendom in the eastern Mediterranean. Then, four years later, after the king of France requested Suleyman's support against his archrivals Charles and Ferdinand, the Turkish sultan marched westward toward Austria and Germany. In the summer of 1526, at Mohács on the plains of the Danube, Ottoman forces cut down King Louis of Hungary, the brother-in-law of Ferdinand and Charles, and his vastly outnumbered troops. Ten days later, Suleyman was in Buda taking possession of the royal palace and enjoying the view from high above the Danube. It would now be up to Austria to repel the Turks, while the fate of Germany hung in the balance.

The Turkish threat gave Luther and the German Reformation breathing room. By 1526 large territories and important cities had become Lutheran and demanded the right to stay that way. When Ferdinand asked them for money and troops to stop the Turks, the Lutheran rulers realized they had leverage: their support could be exchanged for legal recognition of the reformation. Emperor Charles (if he had returned to Germany) and Archduke Ferdinand, both loyal Catholics, could have nipped the Lutheran movement in the bud, but now it was too late. They needed Lutheran support and, in 1526, the diet of the empire voted to allow each city and territory temporarily to set its own religious policy, Lutheran or Catholic. Luther did not, however, celebrate the Turkish victory or its favorable impact on German Protestantism. While he doubted that the Hungarian king had died at Mohács, he presumed that if it was true, it was another portent of the Last Day.[10] The Turks did not overrun Germany and the Last Day did not arrive; but the Turkish threat and other pressures made Emperor Charles hesitant to attack the Lutherans and weaken his empire. It would take almost thirty years to settle the fate of the Lutheran movement but, during the critical decade of the 1520s, Martin Luther and the German Reformation owed their survival to the Islamic threat and to the neglect of Germany by Emperor Charles.

When Luther was in his mid-forties, about nine million people lived in the Germany that lies within the boundaries set at the reunification of East and West Germany in 1990. Thus the population of Luther's Germany was about equal to the number of residents estimated to live in New York City in 2013.[11] Until the Thirty Years' War (1618–1648), the population steadily increased, even though death was a visitor more familiar to sixteenth-century families than to people born in the northern hemisphere after World War II. During Luther's lifetime, the average life expectancy at birth was less than forty years because so many infants and children died. In the family of Martin and Katharina, two of six children died before turning fourteen, and only two of the remaining four reached the age of forty.

Although he lived in the age of exploration, Martin Luther knew little about the world beyond Europe. Only a few times did he mention the Americas, describing them as "newly discovered islands in the West" and the source of a "new disease" (syphilis) that had been introduced into Europe. The pox, he commented, was named by some after the French and by others after the Spanish, but for Luther it was another token of the Last Day, like other "great signs" that had recently appeared.[12] This comment appeared in a chronological chart of world history made for his own use and printed not long before his death.[13] The chart was divided into the traditional six millennia and Luther reckoned that the year 1540, where it stopped, corresponded to the year 5500 in world history. It was high time for the world to end because, in his judgment, the full term of 6,000 years would not be completed. With similar pessimism, Professor Luther told his students that "the world was deteriorating from day to day."[14] For him the European discovery of the Americas was not the beginning of a new age but one more sign that the old age was nearing its end.

The Orient was a different matter. The trade routes to India and China had existed for centuries, and Luther adeptly incorporated them into his biblical views of time and space. Commenting on the four rivers that emerged from one stream in the Garden of Eden,[15] he equated the first (Pishon) with the Ganges, and the rich land around it with India. We still see, he asserted from afar, that India abounds in emeralds, rubies, sapphires, turquoise, and diamonds. The second river (Gihon) was identified by Luther as the Nile, but that presented a problem. Although the headwaters of the Nile were not yet known to Europeans, Luther was aware that the Nile flowed north while many rivers flowed south. How, therefore, could all four rivers emerge from a single stream in the Garden of Eden? Because, concluded Luther, the entire surface of the earth had been altered by the flood that only Noah's ark survived.[16] Hence "one must not imagine that the source of these rivers is the same today as it was."[17] If we could see the Nile and other rivers in their original state, speculated Luther, they would present a far more beautiful sight than they do now. The Ganges was singled out for censure: "If you had known its attractiveness, its produc- tivity, and its course, you would see there is almost nothing left of this noble river."[18]

Luther did not live to see the best new maps of the Orient or the Occident that appeared after 1550. The well-known cartographer, Gerard Mercator, was born in 1512, the year that Luther returned from Rome and received his doctorate. While Luther was compiling his chart of world history, Mercator was publishing his first map of the world (1538), but it is unlikely that Luther ever saw it or would have paid much attention to the map of 1569 based on Mercator's new projection. Mercator, however, paid attention to Luther: a world chronology of his own design mentioned Luther and other reformers. Like Luther's writings, Mercator's chronology ended up on the Vatican's index of banned books.[19]

Luther's conception of the world had much more in common with a splendid map drawn and colored in the thirteenth century and named after the German village of Ebstorf, where it was discovered. The Ebstorf map made no pretense at geographical accuracy but offered instead an artistic rendering of the world as perceived by religious north Germans in the late Middle Ages.[20] It was more like an historical atlas than a map of the world.

A large camel dominated the center of a circular design that was marred by two holes on its edges. One square piece was neatly excised from the upper right curve and long ago a second piece on the lower left edge fell victim to mice, the damp, or both in the storage area of a Benedictine convent. The convent is still standing at Ebstorf, in the heathland south of Hamburg, but after the reformation made the area Protestant, it was occupied by a community of Lutheran women. In 1830, one of them stumbled on the map and for the first time in centuries fully exposed it to daylight. Eventually, the community entrusted it to experts in the city of Hannover, who wisely made copies of the original before it was destroyed during World War II. Those old copies preserved the map's features, and techniques available after the war enabled the production of five new and improved copies, one of which was returned to the women at Ebstorf.[21]

While Mercator's maps were concerned mainly with geographical perspective, the Ebstorf map melded geography with history, both of which relied heavily, but not exclusively, on the Bible. The earth was a disc surrounded by the ocean and the firmament. Undergirding the disc was a cosmic Christ, whose head appeared, with paradise, at the top, and whose feet protruded from the bottom. The arms and hands extended from each side so that his risen body supported the earth in all directions. Such support might have signified a redemption of the world rather than the catastrophic Last Judgment that was typical of medieval piety. The four primeval rivers flowed out of paradise and diverged into a remarkable network of 162 streams (such as the Ganges, Nile, Rhine, Danube) and seas (Black, Dead, Caspian, Persian Gulf). The earth was full of identifiable landmarks: 534 cities, sixty mountain ranges, more than sixty islands, and those parts of Asia and Africa that were nearest the Mediterranean Sea. At its center was Jerusalem, depicted as a walled square inside which Jesus rises from the tomb. And turned away from Jerusalem was the curiously oversized camel with two humps. Camels were prized for their ability to discover water in the wasteland and, for that reason, this camel may (or may not) have pointed to Jesus as the water of life.[22]

Although Luther did not know the Ebstorf map, he envisioned the past through a similar lens. In school he learned Ptolemy's earth-centered cosmology, and both classical and biblical authors had familiarized him with the map's content. In the decade before he died, a sun-centered model of the universe was being discussed in Wittenberg four years before the work of Nicolaus Copernicus was published. In 1539 the subject must have arisen in the circle of Luther and his companions. According to an excerpt from the *Table Talk*, Luther rejected the theory of "a certain astrologer who wanted to prove that the earth moved and not the sky, the sun, and the moon."[23] That astrologer was Copernicus, the cleric and astronomer whose heliocentric theory enjoyed support from the twenty-two-year-old mathematician and Wittenberg professor, G. J. Rheticus. A month or two before Luther made his remark, Rheticus took a leave of absence (official or not) in order to visit Copernicus in Frauenburg on the Baltic Sea. He remained two years with Copernicus and became his eager disciple. Together they carried out observations, and Rheticus published a first account of their research. Copernicus then invited Rheticus to collaborate on a fuller presentation of his ideas: the famous *Revolutions of the Heavenly Bodies*. Two years before it was published in 1543, Rheticus carried a copy of the manuscript back to Wittenberg. Although received with caution, the theories of Copernicus were taken seriously by Luther's colleague, Philip Melanchthon, who encouraged the teaching of mathematics and astronomy.[24] Rheticus, an impulsive character it seems, soon left Wittenberg and to the end of his life claimed that he alone deserved credit for making Copernicus known.

Luther was more concerned with the earth than the heavens, but he was fascinated by unusual phenomena on both planes. When Halley's Comet reappeared in 1531, Luther decided it was an evil portent for Emperor Charles and his brother Ferdinand, because its tail changed direction from north to south.[25] Melanchthon was captivated by astrology, which was not sharply differentiated from astronomy, and he cast horoscopes for all sorts of people, including Luther and his family. Known both to Melanchthon and Luther were the prognostications of John Lichtenberger (d. 1503), a prominent fifteenth-century astrologer, who published them in 1488. After they were translated into German at Wittenberg in 1527, Luther supplied the book with a preface that summarized his views on prophetic predictions and astrology. Only those prophets who were inspired by the Holy Spirit could make authentic predictions and, he judged, Lichtenberger was not one of them. By relying on the stars he was practicing an old pagan art that was unproven even though, admitted Luther, Lichtenberger occasionally hit the mark. The existence of false prophets and the pagan origin of stargazing did not mean, however, that comets, eclipses, and freaks of nature had no meaning. In fact, said Luther, they were often sent by God, who alone ruled the world, in order to threaten the godless and warn them of what was in store. The faithful, however, because they had no need of such warnings, should pay no attention and rest easy. Moreover, in Luther's opinion, care had to be taken because portents sent by God mingled with signs sent by the devil and it was hard to tell the difference.[26]

That difficulty did not stop the reformer from offering interpretations of his own while rejecting those of his opponents. In 1523 Luther and Melanchthon collaborated on an illustrated anti-Roman pamphlet based on the alleged appearance of two monstrosities. One, dubbed the "pope-donkey," was washed up on the banks of the Tiber river in Rome, and the other, called the "monk-calf," was born only a few miles from Wittenberg. The pope-donkey was pictured in front of the papal castle at Rome. It was a standing figure with a donkey's head, a skin of fish scales, female breasts, a hoof and claw for feet, and the end of an elephant's trunk for its right hand. The head of a dragon protruded from its rear. Luther deemed it a sign of God's wrath against the papacy and warned that more omens would appear. Relying on a medieval treatise on the Antichrist,[27] Melanchthon offered a similar reading in which, for example, the head protruding from the donkey's rear signified the decline and demise of the papacy. The "monk-calf" fared no better. The actual calf, if it existed, was probably born with an abnormally large fold of skin behind the neck. It reminded Luther of a monastic cowl which, he extrapolated, was "without doubt" proof that the monastic life in its entirety would soon be exposed as the fraud he deemed it to be.[28]

Why would Luther and Melanchthon point such ugly fingers at the papacy and monasticism? First of all, because niceness was not a virtue in their day; and second, because, by 1523, they had been the butt of similar satire from their opponents. However, they also had more profound reasons, which went to the heart of the reformation. Luther was convinced that laity were being hoodwinked by the medieval church, which taught them that pious practices earned them a place in heaven. The two buttresses of the Roman system were the papal claims to divine authority and the monastic claims to the perfect or nearly perfect Christian way of life that laity ought to emulate. This living was an unattainable goal; but to simulate it and improve their chances, some prominent laity were buried not in their finery but in monastic garb. For Luther the pope-donkey and the monk-calf symbolized the futility of trusting in a religious authority that sanctioned the pursuit of perfection as the right way to heaven. On the contrary, claimed Luther, a less demanding and more merciful Christianity would liberate people from anxiety about reaching heaven and redirect their concern toward others in place of themselves. Beginning in 1518, an astounding number of people agreed with Luther, left behind the religion of their ancestors, and rallied to his side.

Rome, however, did not buckle, and what ensued from 1520 to 1525 was a war of words and images on a scale never previously imagined. The war was made possible by a new, cheaper, and faster technology—printing with movable type. Luther's facility with words, combined with the artistic skill of Lucas Cranach and his journeymen in Wittenberg, fed a burgeoning printing industry that gave Luther a distinct advantage in the competition to sway religious opinion. In those five years, around sixty Catholic writers produced more than 200 pamphlets and books against Luther and other Protestant authors. Many of these were theological essays of good quality, but they were written in Latin and thus inaccessible for most laypeople. In contrast, Luther wrote in a lively German style that explained clearly and directly the changes he wanted to make and the theological basis for them. It was not a fair fight. Protestant pamphlets outnumbered Catholic publications five to one; Luther alone published twice as many as all his Catholic opponents combined.[29] His adversaries did, however, get in their licks. In 1522 an impressive verse satire by the imperial poet laureate, Thomas Murner, pilloried Luther as the "Great Lutheran Fool." One illustration depicted the reformer as a renegade monk interred head-down in a privy while a cat that hunted fools wailed a requiem.[30]

Such mockeries are easily dismissed as naïve, vulgar, and slanderous, but in the sixteenth century coarse polemics were standard fare. They were not products of a primitive mentality,[31] unless they are measured against Victorian refinement and the scientific method. On the one hand, Martin Luther rejected a good deal of medieval superstition, but on the other he was a child of his age, who accepted the symbolic meaning of natural phenomena that suited his campaign against Rome and his agenda of reform. Did he dabble in the occult? No, not in the way that sorcerers, soothsayers, or witches claimed to have magical powers they could manipulate. Was he disposed to believe rumors and to interpret events in a way that might promote a favorable outcome for the reformation and the defeat of his opponents? Yes. Moreover, he was convinced that the devil was an ever present threat that justified harsh polemics against adversaries whom he regarded as Satan's agents. To protect themselves, however, Christians need not pray to saints. They were blessed with guardian angels who watched over them at all times. Martin Luther's world may have been small, but it was rife with useful signs and spiritual beings that allowed people to make sense of the randomness that haunted them and to feel a semblance of control.

One year before Luther died, he received the German translation of an Italian tract that described strange events surrounding his alleged death.[32]

The tract claimed that during a last illness, Luther asked for his corpse to be placed on an altar and worshiped as a god. As soon as his body was placed in the grave, however, a terrible uproar was heard "as if the devil and hell had crumpled." Everyone raised their eyes to the sky, and when they spied the host, the sacramental wafer transformed by the mass into the body of Christ, the noise subsided. The next night an uproar worse than the first erupted over the spot where Luther was buried. At daybreak the grave was opened and found to be empty except for a "sulphurous odor" that made the bystanders sick. That omen, claimed the tract, forced many people to clean up their lives and strengthen their faith to the glory of the Roman Church, the "pillar of truth." Luther had the tract published with an afterword, in which he claimed not to "take it seriously to heart that the devil and his retinue, pope and papists, were so sincerely hostile" to him.[33]

To counter similar fabrications that were certain to appear after Luther really died, Justus Jonas and Michael Coelius, the court chaplain at Mansfeld, were asked by Luther's prince, Elector John Frederick of Saxony, to write a factual account of the reformer's last hours. Both Jonas and Coelius had been present at the deathbed and made notes on which they could rely. At four o'clock in the morning of February 18, 1546, about two hours after Luther died, Jonas dictated a report to the secretary of Count Albert of Mansfeld and had it forwarded to the elector, who sent it from his residence to Wittenberg. It arrived there early on February 19, and later that morning, when Melanchthon, Bugenhagen, and Cruciger broke the news of her husband's death to Katharina, they brought the report with them. Melanchthon also read from the report when he announced Luther's death to the audience that arrived as usual for a lecture. Before Luther's body was returned to Wittenberg, it lay in state in the Church of St. Andrew at Eisleben. Sermons were preached by Jonas on February 19 and by Coelius one day later before the cortège began its journey. The official account of Luther's last hours was published on or shortly after March 15, 1546.[34] By then, the reformer had been interred in Wittenberg and not in Mansfeld, the place he preferred to call home.

CHAPTER TWO

ALL THAT I AM AND HAVE
1483/84–1501
Mansfeld—Magdeburg—Eisenach

"Today Hans Reinicke wrote me that my very dear father, Hans Luder the elder, departed this life on Exaudi Sunday at one o'clock. This death has plunged me into deep sadness not only because he was my father but also because he loved me very much. Through him my creator has given me all that I am and have."[1]

Blame it on the parents! That tactic was applied to Luther by psychoanalyst Erik Erikson in his book *Young Man Luther,* published in the 1950s. Erikson proposed that resentment of both parents and ambivalence toward the father predisposed his adult son to rebel against the pope in place of the father he could not safely defy.[2] Erikson's book, though popular, was weak on several counts.

First, by choosing the monastic life the twenty-one-year-old Martin defied his father Hans, who had paid for a university education in order to prepare his son to study law. Hans Luder was deeply disappointed by Martin's decision and expressed his anger after attending Luther's first mass. At the same time, Hans made a handsome donation to the monastery, and Martin, though initially distressed, successfully pursued a monastic career.

Second, Martin did not rebel against the pope. Although Luther's reproaches of the papacy became harsher with age, in his early years evidence suggests he questioned papal authority in mainly three matters: the scam of indulgences, the absence of pastoral concern in the Roman hierarchy, and the lack of historical and biblical evidence for papal supremacy.

Third, Luther did not leave the monastic life, as Erikson suggested, in order to please his father. Martin acknowledged that his father's disapproval was well founded and that he should have obeyed Hans. But Martin's rejection of monasticism was theological and personal. The monastic pursuit of holiness and perfection fundamentally contradicted the essence of Christian freedom that Martin discovered for himself and shared with his followers. Erikson's analysis offered some insight into Luther's complex psyche, and he gave the mature Luther credit for becoming not only a great figure but, as it were, his own man. In the end, however, Erikson's diagnosis of the young Luther remains speculative.

Analyzing young Martin is tempting because we have more information about him than we do about most public figures of the 1500s. Some of this material, however, is uncertain and none of it comes from young Martin himself except as reminiscence and recall. The uncertainty begins with designating 1483 as the year in which Martin was born.[3] According to a brief chronology of his life by Luther himself, he was born in 1484,[4] and on one occasion the reformer claimed "for certain" he was born in 1484 at Mansfeld.[5] Nevertheless, a 1483 birth date has prevailed since Luther's close colleague, Philip Melanchthon, published the first biographical sketch soon after Luther died. Melanchthon was told by Martin's brother Jacob that the family was agreed on 1483. As long as Luther was alive, however, Melanchthon himself adhered to 1484 and reported that the horoscope cast by a famous Italian astrologer confirmed 1484 for Luther's birth.[6] In 1542, when Melanchthon and Luther were arguing over his age, Luther said he was sixty and thus born in 1482; but in that conversation Melanchthon claimed that Luther's mother told him her son was fifty-eight and that placed his birth in 1484.

More questions about his birth are raised by Luther's grave marker in the Castle Church at Wittenberg. It claims that on the day Luther died, February 18, 1546, the reformer had lived sixty-three years, two months, and ten days. Although the accepted date of his birth is November 10, 1483, according to the grave marker he was born in December of 1482. To complicate matters, it was possible for age to be calculated from the person's next birthday instead of from the last. When evaluating Luther's life and career the exact year of his birth is insignificant, but for casting horoscopes, writing biographies, and celebrating anniversaries of his birth the correct date is desirable. Not knowing it, however, can also serve a purpose. It cautions us against accepting too quickly other assumptions about his early life that have become part of Luther lore.

Evidence for the day and place of Luther's birth is stronger than for the year, but it is not watertight. Martin was probably born in the town of

Eisleben on November 10, but only barely on that day, since his mother remembered giving birth to Martin one hour before midnight. The next day, at the Church of Saints Peter and Paul, the baby was baptized and named after St. Martin of Tours, whose feast day was November 11. A fire that consumed Eisleben in 1689 burned the birth house to the ground, but some artifacts survived and were placed in the new building that served as a museum. Among them was a posthumous portrait of the reformer. It identified the original house as the site of Luther's birth and the neighborhood church as the place of his baptism. The undamaged portrait gave rise to the legend of an "incombustible Luther" that elevated him to a status resembling sainthood.[7] In fact, the painting was no longer in the house when it burned. It had been removed by one of the town magistrates because he found it unsuitable for the taproom that opened on the premises. All in all Luther lived in Eisleben less than a year, if indeed he was born there at all. An excerpt from the *Table Talk* reports he was born in Mansfeld after his father "with wife and son" had moved there.[8] The son, if he existed, was not Martin of course, but an older brother who must have died very young.

Whether in Eisleben or in Mansfeld, Luther's mother, Margaret Lindemann, was in her early twenties when Martin was born. The Lindemanns came from the town of Neustadt on the Saale river in northern Bavaria, 135 miles (215 kilometers) southwest of Mansfeld and Eisleben. A branch of her family moved to Thuringia and settled in Eisenach, where Margaret grew up and may have been born. One of her nephews, named John like her father, later studied theology and was ordained in Wittenberg. Caspar, another Lindemann cousin, studied and taught medicine in Leipzig and became a personal physician to the Saxon electors. In 1532 Caspar joined the medical faculty in Wittenberg and briefly served as rector of the university. Caspar's wife was the godmother of Martin's son Paul and was present at his birth in 1533.[9] In later life Luther was rarely able to avoid his Lindemann cousins, especially after spending several years at school in Eisenach.

In the *Table Talk*, Margaret is portrayed as hard working and strict, especially when she whipped Martin until he bled for stealing a single nut.[10] Corporal punishment was not, however, unusual in Luther's day, since most parents believed there was no proper child rearing "without whippings."[11] Luther later claimed that punishment during his childhood had made him faint hearted, but the adult Luther rarely, if ever, showed signs of timidity. In Luther's correspondence Margaret seldom made an appearance. One noteworthy exception was a letter of consolation Luther sent to Mansfeld shortly before his mother died. Informed by his brother Jacob of her illness, Luther assured her that death itself was now "quite dead" and that her faith in Christ, the true comforter, had liberated her from the "papistic error" that Christ was a severe judge to be feared. Before signing off as "your dear son," Luther wrote: "All your children and my Kate pray for you; some weep, others say at dinner: 'Grandmother is quite sick.'"[12] When she died on June 30, 1531, the Luthers had only two living children: Hans, who had just turned five, and Magdalena, aged two. Katharina was pregnant with their second son, Martin, who was born in November of that year. Father Martin himself was in his late forties and had lost his father just one year earlier. We are not told how the death of his mother affected the reformer; but after his childhood schoolmate, Hans Reinicke, informed Luther that his father had died, the bereft son held nothing back. "Seldom if ever," he wrote, "have I despised death as much as I do now." Then, recalling his father's love, Luther declared that "through him my creator has given me all that I am and have."[13]

Luther's father, Hans, was the eldest son in his own family, but tradition did not allow him to inherit the farm of his father. Forced to rely on his own devices, Hans took advantage of the regional mining boom and was looking for opportunities in Eisenach when he met Margaret. In all likelihood Hans was assisted by Margaret's uncle, Antonius Lindemann, who prior to 1500 was a prosperous smelter-master in Eisleben and was able to advise Hans how best to obtain his own smelting franchise. After moving to Mansfeld Hans became a small businessman who had bills to pay and was vulnerable, like his friends and relatives, to the whims of the counts of Mansfeld, who owned the mines, the greed of the trading companies from which he borrowed capital, and the fluctuation of copper prices. Nevertheless, Hans' business thrived. In addition to his smelter, Hans earned an annual stipend from the counts for overseeing mines in the county. He was able to send Martin to the university and, despite indebtedness toward the end of his life, left an estate that exceeded the assets of his brother, who had inherited the family farm.[14]

In Mansfeld Hans moved up the social and political ladder, first as one of four men who represented the citizenry, then as a founder of the Marian brotherhood (a lay religious association), which endowed an altar in the Church of St. George. Although never a member of the Mansfeld elite, Hans was respected as a citizen who could afford to buy property and merited election to the town council. Archeological findings from the large homesite he purchased suggests that during Martin's childhood the Luther family lived comfortably. Among the remains were marbles with which young Martin might have played, silver pennies, and bones of animals and fish that indicated how well the family ate.[15]

Nothing, not even the strict discipline, implies that Martin's childhood was abnormal or that he was reared in a dysfunctional family.[16] It makes little sense to apply such labels to families of the past or to ask anachronistic questions about the relationship between Luther's parents. According to the *Table Talk*, for example, Luther once offered his parents as proof that marriage was not evil. They were godly people, he said, even though they must have slept together and had sex, a phrase that Luther rendered with the German word for "joked," a euphemism for fondled or copulated.[17] On that slim basis, however, we can no more deduce that Luther's parents had a happy marriage than we can conclude that Luther's family was poor because one excerpt from the *Table Talk* describes his parents as needy. Instead, during Luther's childhood the family was comfortable, stable, and religious in the customary manner. After Martin left the house, however, financial worries beset his parents. Their strain showed in the portraits of Hans and Margaret painted by Lucas Cranach shortly before they died.

The children we know about received the names of saints: Martin, Barbara, who died when Martin was thirty-six,[18] Dorothy, Margaret, and Jacob. Dorothy and Margaret married into local families and Jacob took over his father's business. A fourth daughter married a man named Polner, also from Mansfeld, and they had a son who lived on and off with his Uncle Martin and Aunt Katharina while studying in Wittenberg. Luther once chastised Hans Polner for drinking to excess and failing to control his temper. Polner's conduct reflected badly on the reformer, who by that time was under constant scrutiny by his enemies. Over the years Martin remained in contact with his siblings and their children, as he did with his Lindemann cousins and nephews. In 1529, Luther reported a family visit from his father, brother Jacob and his wife, and his brother-in-law Kaufmann, whose sons would study in Wittenberg.[19] When Hans Luder's estate was settled in 1534, present were his sons Martin and Jacob, one son-in-law, Paul Mackenrot, and a nephew, George Kaufmann. In 1520 Luther reported that his parents and sisters honored the wedding of Philip Melanchthon with their presence in Wittenberg.[20]

Both Martin and his father were examples of economic and professional advancement in a rural society that was fast becoming urban and mercantile. While Hans owed success to his own enterprise and to the prosperity made possible by the mining boom, Martin owed his accomplishments to the education that was encouraged and financed by his father. Luther testified to the value of that education in a pamphlet, published soon after Hans died, that urged parents to keep their children in school:

> My dear father lovingly and faithfully kept me at the university in Erfurt and by his bitter sweat and labor helped me to get where I am. I have come so far by means of the pen ... that I would not exchange all my skill and knowledge for the wealth of the Turkish Sultan or for all the world's treasure many times over. Without any doubt, I would not have come to this if I had not gone to school and become a writer.[21]

Much has been made of the discipline to which Luther was subjected at home and at school; by the same token, too little attention has been paid to what Luther learned in school that prepared him for a notable career as professor, teacher, writer, and reformer. True, the mature Luther paid his teachers few compliments and called those school days "hell and purgatory."[22] By the time he wrote those words, however, Luther held two advanced degrees and was proposing a solid reform of public education. In other words, his standards were unrealistically high and his opinion of teachers was low: "Now, however, anyone can apply [to be a teacher], and those who have only themselves for supervisors get the jobs. Alas, it has come to the point that institutions in which one should learn the right things properly are nothing but schools for rogues."[23] Those words can be taken in two ways: "now" either includes Martin's own schooling or implies that his own teachers were better than the current lot. The second interpretation is more likely since Luther had high praise for his teacher in Eisenach.

Professor Luther was an engaging preacher and teacher because of skills gained during his long training in languages and rhetoric. In Mansfeld, school started at age seven, although some parents wanted to send their children earlier, as one source reports, in order to make nannies out of the teachers.[24] The school sat next to the Church of St. George. It was a "trivial" school because three subjects—grammar, logic, and rhetoric—were taught, but mainly the pupils learned Latin grammar from the books of Aelius Donatus, who lived in the fourth century (CE) and was the teacher of St. Jerome, the Christian ascetic who translated much of the Bible into Latin. The grammar of Donatus became a mainstay of medieval schools, as did the moral maxims of Cato, now attributed to a certain Cato who lived in the third or fourth century (CE). In Mansfeld, young Martin studied Cato's anthology in order to polish his Latin and imbibe practical wisdom from its maxims. In 1524, when he advocated the establishment of public schools in German towns, Luther rejected medieval curricula in which "boys slaved away at their Donatus."[25] Four years later, however, he endorsed Melanchthon's plan of study that required pupils to study Donatus and to expound Cato in order to "build up a vocabulary of Latin words for writing and speaking."[26] Melanchthon's plan also required children to read and explain the fables of Aesop. Luther first read these as a child in Mansfeld and retained a lifelong interest in them. Eventually he prepared his own edition. It was by God's providence, he said, that Aesop and the maxims of Cato had survived and were still being taught. Then came greater praise: "After the Bible, the writings of Cato and Aesop are in my judgment the best, better than the mangled opinions of the philosophers and jurists, just as Donatus is the best grammarian."[27]

Like many adults, Luther advocated for the younger generation a basic education similar to his own because it turned out to be more valuable than a child could foresee. Even though he remembered the parts that were unpleasant, he and Melanchthon had no intention of discarding the foundation in classical studies that bolstered the reformation and would enable a learned ministry and educated laity to maintain it. Before Luther entered the university at Erfurt, he was required to read selections from classical authors, mainly in Latin. Once in Erfurt, however, and perhaps already in Eisenach, he was exposed to the innovative pedagogy of the renaissance. Its agents were renaissance scholars called humanists, who had rediscovered classical literature from antiquity and were reading and editing those writings in the original languages. In addition to Latin, they were teaching Greek and Hebrew and publishing grammars for use in schools.

In Erfurt Luther added some Greek and Hebrew to the Latin he knew well and began to read the classical authors for fun and profit, although he complained there was never enough time to read all the books that appealed to him. Still, Luther became well enough acquainted with many classical works to cite or at least mention them in his writings. The list includes the Greek writers Homer, Plato, Aristotle, and Epicurus; the Romans Cicero, Virgil, who wrote the *Aeneid*, Horace and Ovid, Terence known for his comedies, the younger Seneca, and Tacitus the historian.[28] Upon entering the cloister, Luther took with him only the writings of Virgil and Terence; and two days before he died, he left a note that appealed to Virgil and Cicero in support of his argument that no one should think they could "taste the scriptures" until they had governed the churches "with the prophets" for a hundred years.[29] Unfortunately, Luther had been unable to follow his own advice. Caught in the throes of religious controversy during his late thirties, he was forced to savor the scriptures in much less time. Or so he recalled in his fifties, when he maintained that the Bible was best understood when read under duress.[30]

Around the age of thirteen Luther was sent to school in Magdeburg, the largest city in Saxony. When he arrived from Mansfeld with his friend Hans Reinicke, two village boys were seeing the big city for the first time. Luther spent just one year in Magdeburg and later mentioned only that it was rich. However, it introduced him to the world of religion and politics that would later engulf him on a much larger scale. Magdeburg was an archdiocese and home to the first Gothic cathedral built in Germany. Construction started in the year 1209, but the steeples were not yet finished when Luther arrived almost 300 years later. At the time, the archbishop of Magdeburg was Ernest, a brother of the Saxon rulers Frederick and John, who would later protect and support Luther. Ernest was succeeded by Albert of Brandenburg, who became a staunch opponent of the reformation. On one occasion, Albert wished Luther well in his heart,[31] but they remained adversaries until their deaths only a year apart. Shortly before they died, Luther said that, despite all their quarrels, he did not wish his kidney stones on Albert.[32]

The Magdeburg school that Luther attended has never been identified with certainty, but it was probably at the cathedral. Teachers were usually members of the cathedral chapter, a resident community of bishop and priests with pastoral duties and offices within the archdiocese. A prominent member of the chapter, Dr. Paul Mosshauer, came from Mansfeld and may have persuaded the Luther and Reinicke families to send their sons to Magdeburg. Luther was an occasional guest in Mosshauer's home and reported that his schooling had a connection with the Brethren of the Common Life. Since the Brethren, a monastic-like community that provided lodging and tutoring for pupils, had no school of their own in Magdeburg, several brothers may have instructed Martin in the cathedral school and both he and Hans may have resided at their house.[33] At school Martin may have met Wenzel Linck, a lifelong friend who joined the Augustinian order and became Luther's colleague in Wittenberg.[34] Although Martin left Magdeburg after one year, as an adult he made two visits to the city: ten years later as an Augustinian friar and eight years after that as a well-known reformer. The city never saw him twice in the same role.

Martin was then sent to Eisenach, a pretty town nestled in the hills on the edge of the Thuringian forest and home to his mother's relatives. The

Lindemanns were in close contact with two other Eisenach families, the Schalbes and the Cottas, themselves connected by the marriage of Ursula Schalbe to Konrad Cotta. Both were mentioned favorably by Luther, and he may have found board and lodging with them but not necessarily in the structure now designated the "Luther house."[35] During the three or four teenage years Martin spent in his "beloved town of Eisenach," he could have resided in several places, but none would have been very far from the school he attended in St. George's parish.

In Melanchthon's opinion, the St. George Latin school was better than most owing to Martin's teacher, Wigand Güldenapf, whose skill Luther praised and for whom Luther later sought a pension from a town that Güldenapf served as pastor.[36] After he was ordained a priest in Erfurt, Luther invited Güldenapf to be present for the first mass he was about to celebrate.[37] The Eisenach curriculum was an advanced version of the grammar, rhetoric, and logic that Luther had learned in Mansfeld and Magdeburg; and, since the school provided singers for church services, Luther intensified the musical training he had begun at the Magdeburg cathedral. He developed a decent tenor voice and studied musical theory, both of which were later useful for writing hymns and arranging tunes for the reform of worship. Recalling their university days at Erfurt, the humanist poet Crotus Rubeanus said that Luther was already then "a learned musician and philosopher."[38] During the early years in Erfurt, while convalescing from a wound to his thigh, Martin passed the time by teaching himself the lute.[39]

Following the custom in Eisenach, Luther and other pupils sometimes went door to door singing for bread,[40] but by itself that gives a false impression of his life as a student. Outside school Martin had contact with religious and intellectual circles comprised of educated clerics and laypeople. Eisenach was full of clerics: one priest or monk for every ten residents. They belonged to an array of religious institutions: Dominican, Franciscan, and Benedictine monasteries; a church and chapter of clergy dedicated to the Virgin Mary; the parish Church of St. George (where in 1685 Johann Sebastian Bach was baptized); and churches dedicated to St. Anne, St. Nicholas, and St. Elisabeth. For ten percent of residents to be clergy was not atypical of German towns in 1500; nor was it unusual for prominent families such as the Schalbes to be benefactors of churches and cloisters. They might endow an altar that was dedicated to one or more saints in order to support a priest who would say prayers and hold private masses for the family. The Church of St. Mary, for example, had twenty altars, each one dedicated to three saints. At these altars mass was said daily by the priests in its clergy chapter, one of whom was a Schalbe. And there were many relics of saints on or around these altars. They had allegedly belonged to Mary Magdalene, Luke the Evangelist, the martyrs Stephen and Lucy, and Pope Leo the Great. The collection included a piece of the very arms that, according to Luke 2:28, held the child Jesus.[41]

Luther was familiar with St. Mary's Church because he developed a respectful friendship with the priest, John Braun. Braun was much older than Luther and opened his home to students for evenings of music and discussion. After leaving Eisenach Luther corresponded with Braun, and the invitation he penned in 1507 is the oldest authentic letter from Luther's hand. It was sent after he was ordained and encouraged Braun, whom he addressed as "his dearest friend in Christ," to be present in Erfurt for the first mass Luther would celebrate. The letter, though formal and deferential, recalled the kindness Braun had shown him and his ongoing concern for Luther's welfare. Luther's letter also suggested one of his own relatives in Eisenach as a travel companion and requested Braun to convey his appreciation to members of the "Schalbe collegium," whom he had decided not to invite. The members of that collegium, Luther said, were exceptional men who should not be burdened by the wishes of a mere monk who had now "died to the world." The collegium, not otherwise mentioned, may have resembled the gatherings of humanist scholars who met in larger towns such as Erfurt and Nuremberg to read the classics and share their ideas.[42] These scholars, including the clergy among them, were excited about the renewal of classical learning and its impact on the world around them. Luther, having apparently abandoned that world for the religious life, was perhaps embarrassed and too unsure of their reaction to invite them directly.

In 1501 Luther left Eisenach to enroll at the university in Erfurt, less than forty miles (sixty-four kilometers) away. If he was born in 1484, Martin was seventeen and embarking on an educational adventure that should culminate in the legal career planned by his father. Academically he was ready, but the robust religious environments in Magdeburg and Eisenach held out the possibility of a life other than one teaching law or serving on retainer as a legal advisor to princes and town councils. Luther's decision to become a monk, whether or not provoked by a storm, as is popularly held, was not a bolt from the blue. His letter to Braun hinted at an internal struggle between opting for a secular career and "dying to the world," a battle that may have taken root in Eisenach. If so, Luther's conflict came to a head after he began to study law, but then decided, against his father's wishes, to enter the cloister. The education Martin had received to that point prepared him to take either road, and Erfurt provided the advanced resources he needed to make that decision. The young Latin scholar and musician left Eisenach with no inkling that the road he finally chose would after twenty years lead him, a heretic and imperial outlaw, back to Eisenach, his "beloved town." However, that time, between 1521 and 1522, he was sequestered high above Eisenach in the Wartburg fortress, where, among other pursuits, he translated the New Testament into German using skills he had once polished in the town below.

CHAPTER THREE

HOLY FROM HEAD TO TOE
1501–1511
Erfurt—Wittenberg

"The greatest holiness one could imagine drew us into the cloister.... We fasted and prayed repeatedly, wore hair shirts under woolen cowls, led a strict and austere life. In short, we took on a monkish holiness. We were so deeply involved in that pretentious business that we considered ourselves holy from head to toe."[1]

To travel the thirty-five miles (fifty-seven kilometers) from Eisenach to Erfurt by foot might take a sturdy walker two days, with an overnight in the town of Gotha. Unless Luther first went home to Mansfeld, he made that journey in April of 1501 in order to enroll at the university in time for the summer semester. If the early spring weather was pleasant, he would have enjoyed the greening of the countryside as he strode alongside lush meadows that climbed to the tree line or slipped down to rows of bushes providing escort for a nearby stream. Were he thirsty or in need of a rest, clusters of tiny white blossoms in the bushes told him how far he was from that stream. The leaves, just making their appearance, were barely large enough for him to detect the different shades of green that added variety to nature's palette. It was springtime, Thuringia was at its best, the university was straight ahead, and Luther had every reason to be optimistic about the future.

Thuringia is the geographical center of Germany, and its capital, Erfurt, was founded in the eighth century by Boniface, the storied missionary to Germany. In the late Middle Ages the city became a prosperous commercial center because it stood at the intersection of vital north-south and east-west trade routes. One road was the old king's highway that connected Western and Eastern Europe. Outside the city wall, bountiful fields produced so much woad, a desirable source of blue dye, that Luther called the area a "very fertile Bethlehem."[2] Its prosperity enabled Erfurt in 1392 to found an institution of higher learning that has become the oldest public university on the current territory of Germany—not, however, without a long interruption. After Erfurt was taken over by Prussia in 1816, the school was closed and not reopened until after the reunification of Germany in 1990.

When Luther arrived in 1501, Erfurt counted 19,000 inhabitants and about eighty religious institutions, thus bestowing upon it the nickname "Rome of the North." Viewed from the Petersberg, a flat-topped hill with an elevation of 800 feet (284 meters), the churches and their towers gave the city a sharp profile dominated by the cathedral and the spires of St. Severi church. Among the other churches and cloisters were three that belonged to orders regularly found in German cities—Dominicans, Franciscans, Augustinians—and each institution had a claim to distinction. In 1300 the prior of the Erfurt Dominicans was Meister Eckhart, a prominent preacher and theologian whose sermons and tracts were the quintessence of German mysticism. The Franciscan church was partially destroyed in World War II, but two thirteenth-century stained-glass scenes from the life of St. Francis were spared and can be viewed in the windows of the restored choir. The Augustinian church and cloister—repaired, refurbished, and expanded for tourists and conferences—owes its fame to Martin Luther. Four years after he arrived in Erfurt, Luther chose to join the Augustinians, for reasons he never disclosed.

Luther's name was entered into the ledger of the university three times: in 1501, when he matriculated and paid the tuition in full; in 1502, after completing requirements for the Bachelor of Arts degree; and in 1505, after passing the Master of Arts exam. In all three entries, the oldest documentary evidence for Luther's life, he was identified as "Martinus Luder" from Mansfeld.[3] Every student was required to wear distinctive garb and to take board and lodging in a residential college or *bursa*, a Latin word meaning "sac" or purse and denoting the cost of room and board. In Erfurt five or six bursas accommodated fewer than 1,000 students, and it seems likely that Luther lived in two of them. A relative from Eisenach, Dietrich Lindemann, who visited Luther in Erfurt, recalled that he was hosted in the bursa of St. George.[4] Other evidence indicates that Luther resided in the larger Amplonian College, which was endowed in the early 1400s by the second rector of the university. The donor's exceptional library, still intact, was housed in the college, which was also called Heaven's Gate.

Another resident was Crotus Rubeanus, Luther's comrade, who became a famous scholar and later recalled their time as students.[5] According to Justus Jonas, who also studied in Erfurt, the farewell meal before Luther entered the monastery was held at Heaven's Gate.[6]

In all the bursas, student life was regimented and subject to the oversight of a professor and his associates. At Heaven's Gate the day began at four o'clock with devotions and preparation for the academic exercises that started at six. One meal was served mid-morning and another in the afternoon. The library door was unlocked one hour before the afternoon meal. At eight o'clock in the evening the doors to the outside were shut. When students were allowed to go out, dens of potential iniquity were off limits. Private prayer was encouraged, attendance at mass was monitored, and on Saturdays the residents of the college had to wash their heads.[7] The house rules were clear, but to what extent they were followed is not. Thirty years later Luther alleged that Erfurt students had learned two subjects, whoring and drinking, because the city was nothing but a "whorehouse and a beer house."[8] Luther himself was scarcely an angel, but there is no record of serious mischief. Presumably he enjoyed beer as much then as he did in later years, when his wife Katharina brewed it for the household. He liked music, played the lute, and presumably enjoyed good times with other students. Like them he carried a dagger, but nothing from his Erfurt years indicates that he ran wild.

For the bachelor's degree students were required to expand and intensify what they had previously learned in their Latin schools. Besides reading, they attended formal lectures and debated propositions assigned by their teachers. Although he failed to place near the top, Luther passed his baccalaureate exams with a group that included Christian Beyer, who became a mayor of Wittenberg and counselor to the electors of Saxony. In 1530 Beyer read aloud the Lutheran *Augsburg Confession* in the presence of Emperor Charles V.[9]

Straightaway Luther began to study for the master's degree to which only a few students aspired. This time, at the age of twenty, he performed much better, placing second in a class of seventeen candidates who took the exam in January of 1505. Exams, disputations, and lectures were usually held in the "great college," which was the oldest bursa and home to the philosophy department in which Luther was enrolled. With the master's degree he became part of the teaching staff that delivered lectures and participated in disputations.[10] Luther liked to do both, and as Professor Luther in Wittenberg he was still doing both until shortly before he died.

Erfurt was a high-powered academic town: it was home to a top-level university, a college of liberal arts, and three professional schools, as well as three monastic houses with their own theology programs integrated into the university. Erfurt also boasted a distinct circle of humanists, many of them connected to the university. The arts curriculum was heavily weighted in favor of the Greek philosopher, Aristotle, who lived in the fourth century (BCE). Among scholars in Western Europe his writings became widely known during the 1100s after they were translated from Greek and Arabic into Latin. Aristotle's writings covered the range of human thinking, perception, and behavior (articulated as logic, psychology, and ethics), while attempting to grasp and categorize both the natural world (physics) and whatever reality transcended nature (metaphysics). Aristotle's thought also became the foundation of theology as it was taught and debated in medieval schools.

After 1400, however, the dominance of Aristotle was gradually eroded by the renaissance and its new patterns of scholarship. Humanist scholars preferred the study of grammar, rhetoric, mathematics, and music. Those subjects were also familiar to Luther. The university library in Erfurt holds a two-volume encyclopedia printed in 1501 at Venice and bound in Erfurt before 1505. Markings and marginal notes, called glosses, in Luther's hand are found in both the chapter on logic and the chapter on geometry.[11] An old volume held by the Herzog August Library in Wolfenbüttel has additional marginal glosses in Luther's hand from his years in the Erfurt Augustinian monastery (1505–1511). In a chronicle of emperors Luther found mention of St. Elisabeth of Thuringia, who was revered in his homeland, and he inserted her birth and death dates into the chronicle. A different booklet bound into the volume contains verse by the late medieval Italian poet, Baptista Mantuanus.[12] The margin next to the word "faith" shows a phrase in Luther's hand from chapter one of Paul's Letter to the Romans: "The just live from faith." This gloss, discovered in 2013, was elaborated by Luther and became a pillar of his theology.[13] These marginal notes demonstrate that the young Martin, both before and during his time in the monastery, was reading material normally associated with his humanist contemporaries. Luther is often contrasted with other reformers, such as Ulrich Zwingli and John Calvin, whose humanist credentials are better known; but each new discovery of Luther's familiarity with non-theological sources, and their frequent mention throughout his writings, weaken the argument that Luther was less subject than other reformers to humanist influence.

Many professors were open to humanism, even while they were trans-mitting Aristotle's thought and its impact on medieval philosophy. That was true of Luther's teachers, Jodocus Trutvetter and Bartholomew Arnoldi von Usingen, both of them prominent members of the Erfurt faculty. In 1501 Trutvetter, a native of Eisenach, was rector of the university during the summer semester for which Luther enrolled. He and Usingen were experts on Aristotle and wrote textbooks on logic, grammar, and natural philosophy. They were also respected by the Erfurt humanists, who provided introductory poems for Trutvetter's books and hailed Usingen's campaign to expand the study of languages. As a result, Luther not only learned Aristotle from his teachers, but through them he became aware of the humanist agenda. As Luther began his studies, the leading humanist in Erfurt was Nicholas Marschalk. As well as lecturing at the university, Marschalk opened a print shop that published classical texts in their ori-ginal languages. To facilitate the correct use of those languages, he made available grammars for Hebrew, Greek, and classical Latin. Marschalk's guide to Greek orthography was the first Greek textbook published in Germany and may have been used by Luther.[14]

It is unlikely that Luther and Marschalk ever met, but Erfurt humanism became a seedbed of support for the reformation through figures like George Spalatin, who became Luther's liaison at the court of Elector Frederick in Wittenberg. Spalatin came to Erfurt from Bavaria and earned his Bachelor of Arts degree in 1499. Marschalk was one of his teachers and invited Spalatin to become his assistant and accompany him to Wittenberg in 1502. When Marschalk left Wittenberg in 1505, Spalatin returned to Erfurt and became a protégé of Marschalk's better-known successor, Conrad Mutian. Theology was not Spalatin's first love; he preferred history and later in life published chronicles of Saxony and the reformation. But he also needed a job. With Mutian's help he landed a teaching post in a Cistercian monastery not far from Erfurt and a small pastorate for which he had to be ordained. Spalatin's ordination took place in 1508 at Erfurt's cathedral and was administered by the same bishop who ordained Martin Luther the year before.

Soon thereafter Mutian recommended Spalatin to Elector Frederick as a tutor for the elector's nephew. Spalatin occupied this post for two years in Torgau,[15] one of several locations where the electors resided. Frederick then made Spalatin the tutor of two additional nephews, who were enrolling at the university in Wittenberg. For that task, and to build the library that Frederick had long desired, Spalatin moved to Wittenberg in 1511, the same year that Luther became a permanent resident of the town. Since Spalatin was also assigned to manage university affairs for the elector, within three years he had met Brother Martin and was in a position to secure the political backing that later spared the heretic Luther from execution.

In Mutian's circle Spalatin met other Erfurt humanists who became supporters of Luther. Among them was the poet Eoban Hessus and the knight Ulrich von Hutten—the latter a harsh critic of the papacy who attempted to organize military support for the reformation.[16] Two additional Erfurt humanists became Luther's lifelong friends: John Lang and Justus Jonas. Spalatin knew both of them well. Lang, a Greek scholar, was born in Erfurt and studied at the university. One year after Luther joined the Augustinian order, Lang entered the same Erfurt cloister and the two friars became close. When both were transferred to Wittenberg in 1511, Lang earned the Master of Arts degree and began teaching Greek and using Greek texts in his courses. True to his humanist principles and much like Luther, Lang rebuked teachers who accorded more authority to recent medieval theologians than to church fathers such as Augustine, Jerome, and Ambrose.[17] In 1516 Lang returned to Erfurt and was made prior of the same Augustinian cloister in which he and Luther had taken their vows.

Lang may also have met Justus Jonas in Erfurt. Between 1506 and 1511 Luther and Lang were living in the Erfurt cloister while Jonas, who was younger, was earning his bachelor's and master's degrees at the university. It was a tumultuous time. 1509 went down in Erfurt's history as the "mad" year. Because of heavy debts the city council imposed new taxes, which incensed the citizenry. Their protests turned violent and led to the execution of a prominent councillor. After wealthy students sided with the council, the resentment of the populace erupted in violence that damaged college buildings and threatened to shut down the university. In 1511 the unrest resurfaced and Jonas left Erfurt for Wittenberg to study law. It happened to be the same year that Lang and Luther were transferred to the Wittenberg cloister. In early 1515 Jonas returned to Erfurt to complete his law degree, but he had lived almost four years in the small town of Wittenberg at the same time that Luther and Lang were teaching at the university there. Exactly when these reformers met one another is unknown, but by 1517 Luther, Lang, and Spalatin were well acquainted with one another and at least knew about Justus Jonas.

Acknowledging these Erfurt-Wittenberg connections is the first step in demythologizing notions of Luther as an isolated hero and learning to appreciate the networks that influenced him. The popular version of his Erfurt years mentions only the following: Luther was a student who played the lute; was so frightened by a storm that suddenly he vowed to enter a monastery; scarcely left his Erfurt cell; and was constantly counting his sins, despairing of forgiveness, and fighting off the devil. The story line hardly changes after 1512, when Luther becomes a professor in Wittenberg. His early courses might be mentioned, but not his regular duties and contacts within the university and the Augustinian order. Again, suddenly and alone, he had a "reformation discovery" that led him to post the ninety-five theses and willy-nilly ignite the conflict with Rome. The result is a myth of Luther the hero who single-handedly started the reformation. Nothing could be further from the truth.

By the time Luther the student decided to become Brother Martin, he had a full four years of university life, new relationships, and intense study behind him. Then came the storm, but did a storm alone convince Luther suddenly to become a monk? It is unlikely. The fullest account we have, recorded in the *Table Talk* thirty-four years after it happened, says that Luther vowed to St. Anna to become a monk; but it also reports that Luther regretted the vow and that "many people" tried to deter him during the two weeks between the storm and his entering the cloister. Some of those people were his "best friends," who tried to dissuade him at the farewell dinner hosted by Luther. Moreover, his father was irate when he learned that Luther had entered the monastery.[18] That was understandable. Hans Luder had just bought for his son an expensive textbook of jurisprudence and was sure that Martin was on the way to a high-flying legal and diplomatic career. Apparently Luther did not warn Hans that he was considering the monastic life. The account in *Table Talk* is also the first time that St. Anna is mentioned, perhaps to make the vow seem more binding and thus explain why Luther persisted in spite of so much opposition.[19] The storm and vow story was first mentioned only after 1517, by Crotus Rubeanus, Luther's college friend, who compared it to the conversion of St. Paul in order to give Luther quasi-divine sanction for resisting Rome.[20] After the reformer had renounced both monasticism and the papacy, the story was too good for Crotus and others to resist when explaining why Luther became a monk in the first place.

However the story was subsequently used, a storm and vow of some kind may well have precipitated Luther's decision to alter not only his field of study but his entire life, in the face of undoubted paternal disapproval. To become a monk was a giant step he must have pondered for some time.

Perhaps he so disliked studying law that he was looking for an exit but could not bring himself to act. Embarking on the monastic life was as hard, perhaps, as later leaving that life. In 1533 he sympathized with a friar who still adhered to the monastery and could not tear himself away. Having lived almost twenty years as an Augustinian, Luther wrote: "I was thoroughly immersed in the same opinion, and unless God had snatched me out with manifest force, words alone would not have pulled me out. I speak as one who has experience and therefore I readily believe you."[21] At both ends of his monastic career, in addition to his own deliberation, Luther needed what he perceived as divine intervention.

But why the Augustinians? Simply because they were nearby? If Luther was living in the bursa of St. George, it took less than ten minutes to zigzag his way to the cloister. He and his friends walked out the door, turned left for twenty yards, turned right for a block, turned left to cross over a small arm of the Gera river, turned right for a block, and turned left into the Comthurgasse, where the high wall of the cloister quickly guided them to the gate. If Luther was living instead at Heaven's Gate, it would have taken only a few minutes longer, since most of the university buildings, including the "great college," were closer to the Augustinian house than to other monasteries.

Aside from this proximity, other factors may have led Luther to choose the Augustinians. He might have been attracted by their reputation for adhering strictly to their rule. Fifty years earlier the Erfurt Augustinians had become one of the so-called "observant" houses that submitted to an earnest reform of monastic life. They were also closely connected to the university through theological courses taught by their own brothers who were members of the faculty. The venerable bishop and scholar, Augustine of Hippo (d. 430 CE), who was the order's namesake, chose after his conversion to remain celibate and live in a religious community. Augustine became Luther's favorite theologian and easily could have served as a model for the holy scholar that Luther, always the idealist, hoped to become. His own words declare that he and others were drawn to the monastery by the greatest holiness one could imagine. Great holiness was also claimed by other strict orders, such as the Carthusians and the observant branch of the Franciscans, but it did not endear them to everyone. The parish clergy viewed them as competitors, especially since the friars, who were not strictly cloistered, attracted laypeople through their own preaching and charitable work. True monks and nuns, who secluded themselves, were also resented by parish clergy for avoiding the demands of public ministry in order to cultivate their holiness.

Whatever drove his decision, on July 17, 1505, Luther took leave of the distraught friends who accompanied him to the modest entrance of the cloister. According to the Augustinian constitution, the porter on duty was to notify the prior when a guest desired entrance. Luther was led by the prior to the chapter room, the gathering place of the monastery, where they knelt in prayer before the prior inquired about his intentions. When the prior was satisfied with the response, Luther was allowed to stay and given a room in the guest house that was acquired by the Augustinians in 1277 and remains the oldest building in Erfurt.[22]

Admission as a novice was granted to a supplicant only at the end of a waiting period and after exhaustive confession. Hence Luther found himself again in the chapter room, but this time all the brothers were present to witness his plea for mercy while prostrate on the tiled floor, which is still there. The prior assured the community that Martin was neither married nor burdened by other worldly obligations. He then asked Luther if he was willing to undergo the arduous demands of monastic life. Luther said yes and was granted a year's probation, known as the novitiate. While the brothers sang a hymn that extolled St. Augustine, Luther's head was carefully shaved so that the distinctive tonsure, a circle of hair on top, remained visible. Then he was dressed in the Augustinian habit: a woolen undershirt; linen leggings; a short woolen tunic covered by a long black cowl or gown and topped by a hood; leather straps for a belt; and finally the scapula, a shoulder-length white collar with an opening for his head. For the trial year he was granted personal use of a red-bound Bible, from which daily readings were assigned to every novice. When the year ended, the Bible had to be returned.

As a novice Luther participated in the rituals of the monastery and received regular instruction from the novice master. It was a demanding routine that pivoted around the Divine Office or daily hours: ancient liturgies sung seven times a day, which altogether resulted in the chanting of all 150 psalms every week. The routine also included a daily mass, two meals eaten while listening in silence to an edifying text read aloud, more periods of enforced silence, chores, study, and instruction. Once a week the friars disclosed to the prior how they had broken the Augustinian rule or noticed another brother doing the same. When the year was up, Luther was assigned a cell for study and prayer, a place to sleep in the common dormitory, and a stall in the chancel for worship. He also received a personal copy of the rule and a new habit that had been consecrated with incense and holy water. Monastic garb, deemed superior to the baptismal gown, symbolized the new person the monk had become, the old person having died to the world. Years hence Luther would reject the claim that taking monastic vows was a second baptism more powerful than the first. One hallmark of his theology was to restore the first and only baptism to preeminence in Christianity.

After taking his vows, Luther's monastic career took off. It started with preparation for the priesthood, which required the postgraduate study of theology. The prerequisites posed no obstacle for Luther, since he had earned the master's degree that made him a desirable candidate. Monastic houses in university towns functioned like modern divinity schools and theological colleges at American and British universities. In Erfurt the Augustinians, like the Franciscans and Dominicans, had their own in-house schools, but their students were also enrolled in the university and degrees earned by them were university degrees. The primary link between the monastery and the university was the professor, who was both a teacher in the order and a member of the university's faculty. Luther's professor was John Nathin, who had joined the Augustinians in 1472 and earned his doctorate twenty years later.[23] He was so impressed by Luther's conversion that Nathin, like Luther's friend Crotus, praised him as a "second Paul."[24]

Under Nathin's tutelage Luther studied a commentary on the canon of the mass by the late medieval theologian Gabriel Biel.[25] The canon was the ancient prayer of thanksgiving, which contained the words of consecration that turned bread and wine into the body and blood of Christ. Coming as it did so late in the Middle Ages, Biel's commentary on this sacred text was by no means the first nor was it wholly original. He allowed himself to use material, some taken verbatim, from earlier commentaries, one of which was written by a theologian whom Biel befriended while studying in Erfurt. The year that Luther was born Biel joined the faculty of the seven-year-old university at Tübingen in southwestern Germany. When Biel arrived in Tübingen, John Nathin was living in the Augustinian cloister and beginning his doctoral studies in theology. In all likelihood Nathin heard some of the lectures that became Biel's commentary on the canon.[26] It was only natural that Nathin later assigned that commentary to his students. At the time, reminisced Luther to a colleague, he thought Biel's book was so good that his heart overflowed.[27] By 1516, however, Luther had changed his mind. Biel, he said, expressed himself well on all topics except those that truly mattered: grace and the virtues of love, hope, and faith.[28]

Because it contained numerous references to earlier scholars, Biel's commentary acquainted Luther with a smorgasbord of medieval sources and prominent theologians: Augustine, Bernard of Clairvaux, Thomas

Aquinas, Duns Scotus, Bonaventure, William Ockham, and Jean Gerson. His teachers in the philosophy faculty, Usingen and Trutvetter, not only taught Aristotle but were known to favor the way Aristotle was used by Ockham and Biel. For that reason, once Luther became critical of Aristotle and scholastic theology, he referred to the Erfurt scholars who first taught him the material—Usingen and Trutvetter—as "Gabrielists."[29] It was not a compliment; by that time Luther had rejected Biel's Ockhamist approach to theology. Four years later, however, Luther was still calling the Ockhamist method his own "sect" and "faction."[30]

In addition to understanding the mass he celebrated, Luther learned how a priest should respond to sins revealed to him in the confessional. To that end, he studied a textbook, informally named the Angelic Digest, which prescribed how cases of conscience should be handled. This preparation was crucial to Luther's development, because he struggled with his own guilty conscience. Although he diligently confessed his sins, he could find no assurance that God was forgiving them. Once he began to hear the confessions of others, he realized that priests like himself were giving people an easy way out. Instead of taking their sins earnestly, being contrite, and then receiving forgiveness, people were ordered to perform routine rounds of penance (almsgiving, fasting, saying the rosary, making a pilgrimage). In some cases, they were allowed to forgo penance. It was a mechanical system that did not encourage people to change their behavior or give them genuine assurance. The system remained a problem for Luther in Wittenberg, where he not only heard confessions, but also lectured, preached, and celebrated mass.

For help with his own struggles Luther appealed to his confessors; but they responded that he was too scrupulous about counting his sins. God's justice, they said, according to which sins deserved to be punished, was always tempered by God's mercy. That was not consolation enough, and Luther sought stronger solace, not only from Biel and the Bible, but also from earlier theologians such as Augustine, Bernard of Clairvaux, and Jean Gerson. The sermons of Bernard, a celebrated Cistercian abbot, were highly prized for their spirituality and widely read in late medieval cloisters.[31] Gerson, nicknamed the "teacher of great consolation," was a reform-minded academic who appreciated the mystical tradition and based theology more on experience than on speculation and logic.[32] Even though both had supported the monastic life and papal authority that he finally rejected, Luther praised them: Bernard, because he preached Christ more beautifully than Augustine and other theologians; and Gerson, for offering the first glimmer of hope to conscientious believers burdened by the mandates of the church.[33]

In early April of 1507, probably in the company of other candidates, Luther was ordained to the priesthood in the chapel of St. Kilian at Erfurt cathedral. On May 2 he celebrated mass for the first time. It took place in the Augustinian church where he worshiped every day, but he was nervous nonetheless. After mass, Luther heard from his disappointed father the reproaches that still hurt fourteen years later. "Let us hope," Hans told his son, "that your vow was not an illusion"; and "Have you not heard that parents are to be obeyed?" Recalling the encounter, Luther also realized how cocky he had been, "so sure of my own righteousness that in you [his father] I heard only a man and boldly ignored you."[34] In 1507, however, Luther went back to his books and the life to which he felt sure God had called him.

Advancement came quickly. In 1508 Luther was chosen to fill a temporary position as lecturer in philosophy at the new university in Wittenberg. He remained there one year and probably lived in the Augustinian house that was still under construction. During that year he lectured on the *Ethics* of Aristotle and satisfied the first requirement of his doctoral program, which obligated him to comment on books from the Old and New Testaments. The next requirement was to lecture on the four "books" of *Sentences* by Peter Lombard (1100s), a standard textbook of scholastic theology that every aspiring professor had to master. Each "sentence" was phrased as a debatable question or thesis for which Lombard sought the right answer from reasoning, scripture, or from earlier theologians. In book one, which deals with the nature of God, Lombard asked: "Can we say that God is all-powerful when we humans are able to do things that God cannot?" For example, God cannot walk or speak since it would diminish His divine nature for God to have a mouth and legs. Not at all, countered Lombard. We speak and walk because God created us with these abilities. God's power is the force behind what all creatures are able to do and therefore God can be described as all-powerful. Lectures on book one of the *Sentences* discussed all the questions devised by Lombard; the remaining books likewise required thorough and time-consuming treatments.

Luther was qualified to begin this task when he returned to Erfurt in 1509, but his credentials were challenged. For the doctorate Luther was supposed to satisfy all the requirements in Erfurt, but the first one had been fulfilled in Wittenberg. The Erfurt brothers had a legitimate grievance, but politics were also involved. In Wittenberg, the vicar-general of the strict

Augustinians, John Staupitz, was organizing a program of theological study that would compete with Erfurt. Luther's flouting of the rules, with the permission of Staupitz, gave the Erfurters a perfect opportunity to express their displeasure and justify their resistance to Staupitz. In the end, after promising not to complete his doctorate at another university, Luther was allowed to deliver in Erfurt his inaugural lecture on the *Sentences,* a festive occasion that took place at the cathedral. When he gave the first lecture on the third book of the *Sentences,* he was awarded another degree, which marked his progress toward a professorship.

Since Luther's academic achievements are usually dwarfed by his religious trials, it may seem as if the future reformer leapt over these academic hurdles quickly and with ease. According to university statutes, however, lecturing on Lombard's *Sentences* normally required two years at the rate of three lectures per week. Luther chose that schedule instead of the accelerated one-year option. Why? Because he wanted to prepare the lectures carefully, even meticulously, by consulting other sources and making notes in his own copy, which had been printed twenty years earlier. Luther accessed two more editions of the *Sentences,* compared his 1489 text to these, and made not just notes about the text but corrections in the text itself, which, although not numerous, correspond to the methods of modern textual criticism.[35] In Erfurt he was able to examine manuscripts and, in some cases, to check references that Lombard made to Augustine by looking up the passage in Augustine's own works. Luther also made notes in other books between his return to Erfurt in the spring of 1509 and his reassignment to Wittenberg in the summer of 1511. The list of authors is short but the number of writings consulted is sizable: the topical works of Anselm of Canterbury; the shorter writings of Bonaventure; and many works of Augustine, including the *Confessions, On the Trinity,* and the *City of God.* Luther also read Ockham's treatise on the sacrament of the altar, and he consulted earlier commentaries on the *Sentences* by Bonaventure, Scotus, Ockham, and Biel.

During the summer of 1511, about the time Luther was scheduled to complete his lectures on the *Sentences,* he and John Lang, his Augustinian brother and friend, were summoned to Wittenberg. Five years later Lang would return to Erfurt, but the twenty-six-year-old Luther would never move from his new home despite the turmoil that lay ahead. That turmoil, called the beginning of the reformation, did not result from, as the cliché has it, a monk's desperate search for a gracious God. Martin Luther did not leave Erfurt as a troubled monk who quivered in his sandals while occasionally

reading a theology book. Quite the contrary. The nine years in Erfurt and
the one year in Wittenberg had turned him into a skillful young scholar who
also happened to be a conscientious Augustinian friar. During the next six
years in Wittenberg, before he questioned the validity of indulgences, Luther
matured rapidly in both roles.

CHAPTER FOUR

NOT ONE OF THOSE
1511–1517
Wittenberg—Rome

"I was all alone and one of those who, as Augustine says of himself, have become proficient by writing and teaching. I was not one of those who from nothing suddenly rose to the top, though such people actually remain nothing. They have not labored, nor been tempted, nor spoken from experience, but after one glance at the scriptures they exhaust their entire spirit."[1]

In 1511 the road from Erfurt to Wittenberg was little changed from three years earlier when Brother Martin traveled it the first time. The route started in Thuringia, which was graced with rolling hills and rich vegetation; but the farther north he walked, the less diverse and colorful it became. The landscape leveled out until it was flat, and the ground became sandy as northern Germany gradually descended to the Baltic Sea. Wittenberg lies halfway between Erfurt in the south and the coast directly north. Most visitors approached Wittenberg from the south, as Luther did in the summer of 1511. One visitor in 1535 was a papal nuncio named Peter Paul Vergerio, who wanted to meet Luther and negotiate with him in person. As Luther himself did on occasion when heading home, Vergerio's party spent the night in Bitterfeld, where they were formally welcomed and given rooms.[2] The next day, after heading north through several villages and then crossing the Elbe river, they saw Wittenberg's small but distinctive skyline. Then as now it was marked by two strikingly different towers, one belonging to the castle and the other to the city church. On a clear day in summer, the tan, white, and grey towers offer a picturesque contrast to the blue sky above them and the green landscape below.

On that late summer day in 1511, Luther crossed the Elbe on a wooden bridge and entered the familiar town that was to become his permanent home. Wittenberg had just over 2,000 residents and a main street that was only one mile long. At the west end of the street, Collegienstrasse, stood the rather plain residence of Elector Frederick and the "Castle Church" (officially the Church of All Saints), which was attached to the residence. It was completed just two years earlier when the massive northwest tower, usually called the church tower, was finished. At the east end of town was the site of a new cloister for the observant Augustinians, although in 1511 very little of it was constructed. One eyewitness, Frederick Myconius, who saw the property around that time, reported that only a dormitory and the foundation of a church were completed. Within the outline of the foundation, according to Myconius, stood a small, rundown chapel that could hold at most twenty people and was still in use. From its pulpit, claimed Myconius, Luther preached his first sermons.³ Myconius was right. Located originally on the property were the almshouse, outbuildings, and the Chapel of the Holy Spirit. The Augustinians were allowed to raze the almshouse but had to pay for it to be erected elsewhere in town. They planned for a new church to replace the chapel, but the church was never built and the chapel remained a place of worship until 1542. Archeologists have not located the church foundation that Myconius saw.⁴ After the chapel was removed, Luther saw hogs rooting at the site. "Here stood a sacred edifice," he recalled. "I first preached in that church."⁵

After Luther became the most famous cleric in town, he was invited to preach at the Castle Church when the Elector and his court were entertaining important visitors. Most of the time, however, Luther delivered his sermons in Wittenberg's parish church. It is situated mid-town, just off the main street about halfway between the Elector's residence and the Augustinian cloister. Built in the late 1200s, it was dedicated to the mother of Jesus and has remained the Church of St. Mary. On the west façade Mary is portrayed twice in stone. Above the rose window she is the Madonna and in the tympanum below she holds the Christ child while seated and is flanked by St. Paul and St. Peter. Carved into the tympanum beneath Mary and the two apostles are five saints: Dorothy, John the Disciple, Sigismund of Burgundy, Nicholas, and Catherine. Sigismund, who drowned in 524, was the object of popular devotion in towns near water because he offered protection against fevers. Like other sacred buildings in the late Middle Ages, St. Mary's Church was built with the help of proceeds from the sale of indulgences.⁶

In 1511 the young university of Wittenberg was recovering from a rocky start. In its first four years new admissions dwindled quickly, especially after well-known professors such as Nicholas Marschalk departed and the town was struck by an epidemic. In 1507, however, Christoph Scheurl, a doctor of jurisprudence, arrived from Nuremberg and was appointed rector. He rewrote the statutes, changed the curriculum to make room for more lectures by humanist scholars, and rebuilt the faculty. His roster for 1507 listed five professors of theology; among them were Staupitz and Trutvetter, Luther's former philosophy teacher from Erfurt. Scheurl bragged to friends in Nuremberg that Wittenberg outshone neighboring schools and noted that the Augustinians were building a new domicile in town.[7] For a time Luther and Lang lived in the unfinished dormitory with Staupitz and a growing number of brothers. Trutvetter, however, had returned to Erfurt by the same revolving door through which Luther, Spalatin, Jonas, Lang, and others had passed or would pass again.

The official who summoned Luther and Lang to Wittenberg was John Staupitz, vicar-general of the strict Augustinians and professor of theology at the nine-year-old university. His influence on Luther was partly pastoral: he soothed Luther's doubts about obtaining divine forgiveness. After the reformation began, Luther attributed to Staupitz an anecdote that taught him the futility of pleasing God by striving for perfection: "More than a thousand times I have vowed to God that I would improve, but I have never performed what I vowed. Hereafter I shall not make such vows because I know perfectly well that I shall not live up to them."[8] Staupitz did more for Luther, however, than serving as the wise, avuncular counselor suggested by his portrait. Even though he never left the Roman Church, Staupitz set the stage for Luther's development into a reformer. After Staupitz departed Wittenberg, they stayed friends and exchanged letters, although not with the frequency Luther desired.

Born in Saxony about twenty years before Luther, Staupitz came from a noble family, which lived only eight miles (thirteen kilometers) from the town of Grimma where a young Frederick the Wise attended school in the Augustinian cloister. The friendship between Staupitz and Frederick, who was about the same age, probably began in Grimma. Around 1490, unknown circumstances led Staupitz into the Augustinian order in Munich. Seven years later he was sent to the university at Tübingen in order to study theology. In 1500, after three years in Tübingen, Staupitz was awarded the Doctor of Theology degree. Returning to Munich he was elected prior of his home cloister, but Frederick soon invited him back to Saxony to teach at the elector's new university in Wittenberg. From there it was a fast ride to the top: Staupitz was made dean of the theology faculty and, on May 7, 1503, he was elected vicar-general of the observant Augustinians. Within the order they formed a tight network of thirty observant or strict cloisters known as the Reformed Congregation, which became a favorite of Saxon electors.[9] The observant cloisters at Erfurt and Wittenberg belonged to the Congregation, as did the strict cloisters at Munich and Tübingen. Elector Frederick was kept well informed about them all and selected Staupitz for Wittenberg since they could both benefit from the arrangement. Frederick gained a prominent Augustinian for his faculty, and Staupitz gained Frederick's support for his plan to make Wittenberg the hub of theological studies for the Reformed Congregation. The plan succeeded splendidly. In its first eighteen years (1502–1520) the university at Wittenberg enrolled 120 Augustinian brothers. In contrast, by 1520 only forty Augustinians are known to have studied at Erfurt.

Luther and Lang's 1511 transfer from Erfurt to Wittenberg was part of Staupitz's plan. He first met Luther in 1506, when visiting the Erfurt cloister in his capacity as vicar-general of the Reformed Congregation.[10] In 1508 he summoned Luther to Wittenberg for one year to lecture on Aristotle and allowed him to complete one requirement for the doctorate. By 1511 Staupitz was planning to give up his professorship in theology in order to devote himself to the Reformed Congregation of strict Augustinians. Who should succeed him other than Martin Luther, whom Staupitz had groomed for the job? Lang's expertise in Greek was also a key element in Staupitz's plan. In effect, he robbed the Erfurt cloister of two bright young scholars in order to carry out his intentions in Wittenberg.

That was not all Staupitz did for Brother Martin. In Erfurt Luther had delivered his lectures on the *Sentences* and was ready to receive the Master of Theology degree, which, by itself, qualified him to teach. Staupitz, however, pressured Luther to acquire the doctorate in Wittenberg. It would add status and the academic privileges that made him a fitting candidate to succeed Staupitz in the Augustinian chair of theology. Luther resisted the plan and gave fifteen reasons why it was a bad idea. Among them was his exhaustion and the premonition that he did not have long to live. That was not a good reason, countered Staupitz. If you die soon, God will admit you to the heavenly advisory board, and anyhow the board needs more doctors.[11] Luther had also promised to acquire the doctorate in Erfurt, but he finally agreed to Wittenberg in a conversation with Staupitz under the pear tree in the grounds of the cloister.[12] Since promotion (as it was called) to the doctorate was expensive, Staupitz persuaded the Elector to pay the fifty florins and promised Frederick that Luther would remain in Wittenberg for his entire career. That promise was fulfilled, but not in the way either Frederick or Staupitz imagined. Luther himself wrote out the receipt for the fifty florins. It is the oldest extant German document in his handwriting.[13]

The decision to endorse Luther as the replacement for Staupitz at Wittenberg was ratified by the quadrennial convention of the Reformed Congregation at Cologne in May of 1512. Luther had just returned from Rome, but he attended the meeting and was named director of theological studies for the congregation. Like Staupitz before him, Luther would lead a professional life divided between his responsibilities in the Augustinian order and his academic duties as professor of theology. He was very busy and sometimes complained about it. After Lang had returned as prior to the Erfurt monastery, Luther described for his friend the "lazy" life he led in Wittenberg:

> I could almost occupy two scribes or secretaries. All day long I do nothing but write letters. . . . I preach at the monastery, I am a lector during meal-times, I am asked daily to preach in the city church, I have to supervise the program of study, and I am vicar, i.e., prior of eleven cloisters. Plus: I am warden of the fish pond at Leitzkau, and at Torgau I am involved in a dispute with the Herzbergers.[14] . . . I lecture on Paul and I am still collecting material on the Psalms. . . . I have little uninterrupted time for the daily [monastic] hours or for celebrating mass. Besides, I have my own struggles with the flesh, the world, and the devil. See what a lazy man I am![15]

As recounted to Lang in 1516, Luther's monastic duties consumed more time than his teaching at the university. He was not spending all day preparing and delivering lectures, because the office of vicar was demanding—more so than historians previously thought. When Luther said he was "vicar" of eleven monasteries, he was referring to his election in 1515 as vicar of the observant houses throughout Saxony and Thuringia. Although once or twice he called the office "district vicar," it was not a minor assignment and, as Luther implied, it required travel away from Wittenberg. The proper title was "provincial vicar," and there was one for each of the two provinces into which the German Reformed Congregation was divided. Luther's province covered Saxony and Thuringia; the other province covered Bavaria, Swabia, and the Rhineland. The top three men in the German Congregation were the vicar-general, the office Staupitz had held, and two provincial vicars. For three years, the period from May 1515 to April 1518, Martin Luther was one of those three men. When the ninety-five theses made their splash, their author was not an insignificant Augustinian monk. Rather, Brother Martin belonged to the senior management of the Reformed Congregation.[16]

The provincial vicars were elected by the congregation, not appointed by their boss; so Luther was not merely an assistant to the vicar-general. Luther and the other provincial vicar had the power to select and remove the priors of local cloisters in their provinces.[17] In the spring of 1516, Luther visited at least nine cloisters. They included Dresden and Erfurt, his home cloister, where his friend Lang was now the prior. From an Augustinian house near Erfurt, Luther reported that he had found no cloisters in better shape than those in Gotha and Langensalza.[18] The tour included a new Augustinian cloister in Eisleben, where Luther was born. He probably visited the Eisleben monastery as provincial vicar in 1515, when the counts of Mansfeld endowed it in favor of the Augustinians, and again in 1516 for the dedication, which Luther attended with both Lang and Staupitz.[19] On both occasions Luther could easily have visited family in nearby Mansfeld.

Back in Wittenberg Luther had to deal with routine matters: requesting the return of an Augustinian monk who had run away to Mainz; ordering that expenditures for the guest houses be properly recorded so that a monastery would not become "a tavern or a hotel"[20]; keeping up with personnel matters; advising a course of action when a monk from a different order desired to become an Augustinian. Because of the demands, some things had to be done at the last minute. On the morning of August 24, 1516, the feast day of St. Bartholomew, Luther asked Spalatin, who was the Elector's librarian, to rush him material on Bartholomew because Luther was preaching on the apostle at twelve noon![21] He took more time with pastoral matters, such as the letter he wrote to George Spenlein, an Augustinian brother who was transferred from Wittenberg to a cloister in southern Germany. Spenlein left behind two books and asked Luther to sell them and use the proceeds to settle a debt Spenlein owed Staupitz. The sale, reported Luther, was half a florin short of covering the debt, but he encouraged Spenlein to ask Staupitz to forgo full payment. The rest of the letter made Spenlein sound like an earlier version of Luther himself. The problem was a conscience that was too scrupulous, and Luther knowingly offered the following advice:

Now I should like to know if your soul, tired of its own righteousness, is learning to be revived by and to trust in the righteousness of Christ. . . . Beware of aspiring to such purity that you will not wish to be looked upon as a sinner, or to be one. For Christ dwells only in sinners. On this account he descended from heaven, where he dwelt among the righteous, to dwell among sinners. Meditate on this love of his and you will see his sweet consolation.[22]

It was an eloquent statement adapted from Staupitz's counsel and Luther's own experience. It also drew on the mystical tradition of a "marvelous exchange," in which Jesus the Christ exchanged his righteousness for the believer's sins and thereby undercut the necessity for sinners to become perfect, or holy enough, to merit divine forgiveness and salvation. Since the reformation had not begun, Luther did not consciously write those words as a reformer. Nonetheless, they echoed theological and personal insights that emerged from his struggle to understand Paul's letter to the Romans. When Luther wrote to Spenlein in the spring of 1516, he happened to be lecturing on that very epistle.

Although Luther was busy with his duties as provincial vicar, his job as university professor also required attention. It had started in late 1512 after he received the doctorate and was inducted into the faculty. The promotion to Doctor of Theology in Wittenberg was a festive affair that lasted two days and required the candidate to be sponsored by a colleague. Luther's sponsor was Andrew Bodenstein von Karlstadt, who had risen through the academic ranks in Wittenberg and earned his own doctorate two years earlier. Karlstadt did not belong to a monastic order, but he was a priest and had recently been named the archdeacon of the clergy community that served the Church of All Saints at the castle. Karlstadt's position required him to preach and celebrate mass at the Castle Church, but he also lectured at the university and was dean of the faculty during the semester preceding Luther's promotion. Their relationship would later turn out to be crucial to the course of the reformation.

The 1512 ceremony began on October 18 with the usual academic debates and speeches, one of which Karlstadt had to deliver. The awarding of the degree followed the next day in the Castle Church, where the oath was administered to Luther. It was one of several oaths taken by Luther at the end of his academic journey and all together he would have promised the following: to eschew "vain doctrines condemned by the church and offensive to pious ears," to remain obedient to the Roman Church, and to uphold the honor and statutes of the theological faculty. Luther was then presented with three symbols of his office: a closed and open Bible, the academic hat, and a gold ring designed in honor of the Trinity. It was a memorable day, but not everybody was happy. Luther's promotion in Wittenberg kindled so much resentment in Erfurt that two years later he tried to exonerate himself in a formal letter to the Erfurt faculty.[23]

The vow itself was ambiguous. After Luther came under attack for criticizing papal authority, he justified his stand by calling himself a "sworn doctor of holy scripture" and claiming he had vowed "to his beloved holy scripture to preach and teach it faithfully and purely."[24] Scant evidence exists for such a promise.[25] Instead of referring to a specific vow, Luther was expressing the way his professorship obligated him to the university and to the Roman Church. In medieval universities, to teach theology was by definition to teach scripture. During his academic career of thirty-three years, Luther only lectured on books of the Bible, but not because he occupied a specific chair for biblical studies, as they exist in modern theological schools. He was following the medieval tradition and university statutes that equated professors of theology with teachers of the "sacred page": the Bible.[26] To teach theology meant to explain the texts of scripture and to discuss theological questions and their relevance as they arose from those texts. As a result, academic lectures might sound like sermons or Bible studies, and Luther's lectures, all delivered in Latin, were often punctuated by the Latin word meaning "today" (*hodie*) because teaching theology also called for the timely application of a biblical text. When that application challenged the authority of the pope and his theologians, Luther's defense was simple: his doctorate mandated him to expound the "sacred page" as he understood it, regardless of the consequences.

His early lectures were in no way designed to challenge the authority of Rome. They were, however, carefully prepared and Luther never had more time to prepare than for his first course—on the Book of Psalms. In late spring of 1512, after Luther returned from Rome and from the convention of strict Augustinians in Cologne, he settled into their house at Wittenberg and pondered what it would mean to lecture week after week, semester after semester, were he to agree to obtain the doctorate and become the successor to Staupitz. It entailed, he realized with a jolt, a mountain of work, especially because he was so particular and thorough. From countless weeks of singing through the psalms, he knew them by heart, but lecturing on all 150 was a different and daunting prospect. He decided therefore to have the text of the psalms printed in a special way so that his students could take notes between the lines and in the margins of the biblical text. He chose a Latin version of the Psalter that had been printed in Leipzig, made some corrections, and with instructions for the layout gave it to the printer Grünenberg, whose press, according to one old source, may have been within the grounds of the cloister.[27] The text of the psalms, printed as ordered, came off the press on July 8, 1513, and was put to use when the new semester began.

Luther now had a printed text of the psalms for his students, but where should he turn for material for his lectures? The answer was obvious: to previous commentators on the psalms. By 1513, the invention of movable type and the editorial skill of humanist scholars had made available at least a half-dozen printed commentaries on the psalms. Most of the commentaries were published between 1490 and 1512, and the Erfurt library held a few of them. For his lectures in Wittenberg two sources had special significance: first, the "established commentary" (*Glossa ordinaria*), which contained the biblical text and interpretive notes gleaned from early Christian commentators and recent medieval authors. A block of psalm text was set in the middle of the page, spaced in such a way that short annotations were printed between the lines and longer comments around the block. The psalms text Luther ordered for himself and his students had a similar format, but the space that held printed annotations in the *Glossa* was left blank for lecture notes.

The second important source was the fivefold Psalter edited with annotations by Faber Stapulensis, the Latin moniker of a French scholar, who published the first edition in 1509 and a second in 1513. Faber printed the Latin text of the psalms in five different versions and added his own comments, some of which noted differences between one version and another. Luther paid special attention to the so-called Hebrew Psalter, which was a Latin translation of the Hebrew text. In 1885 a researcher discovered a 1509 edition of Faber's Psalter that contained marginal notes in Luther's handwriting.[28] The notes are sporadic but nevertheless substantial. They indicated Luther's willingness to consider earlier interpretations as well as to deviate from them and offer his own.

Luther's written preparations are extant in two sets: one has short notes to individual words and lines of text, and the other contains longer comments on complete verses. The manuscript of the first set is held by the Herzog August Library in Wolfenbüttel, Germany. The manuscript of the second set existed in Dresden until it was destroyed in World War II. Before the bombing, someone made a copy of that manuscript, and both sets are now available in modern editions.[29] In August of 1513 Luther delivered in Wittenberg his first lecture on the psalms—possibly in the only new building on the Augustinian property. It had cells for about forty monks and one or more common rooms on the ground floor that could be used for lectures. By 1513, however, two university buildings also existed in the Collegienstrasse near the Black Cloister, a nickname derived from the black habits of the Augustinians. These buildings had lecture rooms and lodging to accommodate the rising number of students, but soon more housing became necessary, so that bursas like those in Erfurt were provided. Between 1507 and 1520 the enrollment at Wittenberg doubled to more than 1,700 students. Luther may have delivered his earliest lectures in the cloister; but owing to the growing student body his courses were probably moved to a university building just up the street. It was but a short walk from the cloister to any place in town where brother Martin was lecturing or preaching.

For his next three courses Luther chose the New Testament books named Romans (1515–1516), Galatians (1516–1517), and Hebrews (1517–1518). For these lectures Luther depended less on earlier commentaries, in part because he had less time to consult them. In the first place, these courses coincided with his busy three-year term as provincial vicar of the observant Augustinians. In the second place, the professor of theology had other duties, for example, presiding at disputations and writing theses for candidates to defend. In 1517 Luther mentioned he was preparing six or seven brothers to be examined for the Master of Theology degree.[30] One year earlier, two disputations had taken place while Luther was lecturing on Romans. Theses that he prepared for the second disputation signaled a sharp turn in his theology. They took a provocative stand on a sticky issue that had occupied theologians for at least a thousand years: Were human beings, hampered by original sin, able in any sense to obey the commandments of God without the aid of grace?

The classic debate of that question was the fifth-century controversy between Augustine and his Pelagian opponents. Pelagius was an austere Christian teacher from Britain who caused a stir in Rome in the late 300s (CE). His teaching minimized the potency of original sin and argued that moral progress for believers was possible without God's grace. Pelagius was allegedly incensed by an appeal that Augustine, in his *Confessions*, addressed to God: "There can be no hope for me except in your great mercy. Give me the grace to do as you command and command me to do what you will!"[31] To Pelagius the words of Augustine implied that he could do nothing of what God commanded without divine grace. That made grace into a crutch that discouraged believers from doing by themselves what God required to overcome sin. Pelagius believed in human willpower and reduced grace to learning from Jesus what the human will should and could do on its own. For Augustine, however, grace was a divine gift that empowered the will to obey the commandments. As described in the *Confessions*, grace was also the power that gave Augustine the courage to change his self-important and self-indulgent life.

The conflict between Augustine and Pelagius lived on in the theological schools of medieval Europe. Some theologians, like Staupitz, took the Augustinian view that every change of heart and subsequent act of love depended on God's grace. Other theologians, like Gabriel Biel, retained the spirit of Pelagianism. Biel argued that human beings could merit grace and use it to supplement human willpower in order to obey God's commandments. Luther called that theology Pelagian, but exactly when he came to that conclusion is hard for historians to document.

Luther himself offered a clue in a revealing flashback that twentieth-century scholars identified as Luther's "reformation discovery." In 1545, the year before he died, Luther wrote a preface to the first volume of his collected Latin works. It recounted the conflict that led to the reformation and told a convincing personal story. While preparing his lectures, Luther was struggling with the meaning of Romans 1:17, in which Paul said that the justice (or righteousness) of God was revealed in the gospel (good news of unmerited redemption) and not in the law. For Luther, God's justice had been defined by the Ten Commandments, which set an intimidating standard of conduct that was difficult, even impossible, to meet. The justice of God implied punishment for not obeying the law and that was bad news for sinners. If, however, God's justice was revealed in the gospel, then it was good news since, as Paul defined it, the gospel was the power of God that saved believers (Romans 1:16). In other words, God's justice was bad news if it was defined by the law and God's power to punish; but it was good news if it was defined by the gospel, God's power to save.

But how did one access that saving power? By exercising human willpower or by receiving a divine gift? After banging his head on the verses and meditating "day and night," Luther comprehended what Paul meant: God's justice was a gift received in faith, not a product of human willpower. The solution was not only satisfying to Luther theologically. It also filled him with keen personal relief and seemed like a new birth: "I began to understand that God's justice meant that people who were just in God's sight lived by a divine gift. It is the passive justice by which God justifies us through faith, as it is written: 'They who through faith are just shall live' (Habakkuk 2:4). I felt I was altogether born again and had entered paradise through open gates!"[32] The faith in question was trust in God's mercy. God's justice was passive not because it was inactive but because it was a divine gift, God's grace, and not earned even in part by human strength or performance.

The theses prepared by Luther for the 1516 disputation made the same point. It was neither possible nor necessary for human willpower to earn God's grace; nor did the human will have to cooperate with grace to earn salvation. God's grace was the gift of faith that came through the gospel and only this faith was necessary. The 1516 theses were a direct challenge to the scholastic theology Luther had learned by reading Gabriel Biel, and it was no surprise when the theses elicited a sour reaction from Erfurt. His friend Lang reported that Luther's teachers were astonished by the attack on Biel; but Luther shrugged it off and declared he knew Biel as well as they did and knew even better where Biel was mistaken.[33]

The date of Luther's rebirth or his reformation discovery cannot be determined with exactitude. He was unable to tweet its time and location, and therefore scholars have dated it as early as 1512 and as late as 1518. Luther's discovery has also been called his tower experience, because one entry in the *Table Talk* identifies Luther's new grasp of God's justice as an inspiration received in the lavatory of the monastery's tower.[34] While the small tower, with or without a lavatory, may have contained a study area, better written evidence suggests that Luther's insight came gradually during the year 1515, when he was preparing and delivering his lectures on Romans.[35] Those lectures contained the earliest explicit criticism of scholastic theologians who advocated a Pelagian stance such as the following: Some grace was necessary during the process of salvation, but it was mainly a bonus for what really counted—obeying the commandments through the exercise of one's own knowledge and strength. Luther's criticism minced no words. To him such thinkers were "fools and pig-theologians," and he challenged them to prove they could obey the commandments fully without grace.[36] Moreover, the meaning of Romans 1:16–17 reported in the flashback written in 1545 corresponded to the interpretation given by Luther in the lectures on Romans: "For the justice of God is the cause of salvation. . . . By the justice of God we must not understand the justice by which God is just in himself but the justice by which we are made just by God. This happens through faith in the gospel."[37] The shorthand of this statement is "justification by faith," the theological innovation associated with Luther's name.

But was it new and did it cause the reformation? The answer to both questions is yes and no. Answering the second question is reserved for the next chapter. Answering the first, a question about which essays and books have been written, can be done here. In Luther's opinion justification by faith was not new. Once he discovered it, Luther claimed it was exactly what Paul taught and that Paul's meaning had been adopted by Augustine in his contest with the Pelagians. While preparing for the lectures on Romans Luther was reading Augustine's book entitled *The Spirit and the Letter*. What he found in the book was, by his own later admission, "unexpected": Augustine had also interpreted God's justice as a gift "with which God clothes those whom he justifies."[38] Moreover, in the 1515 lectures Luther referred explicitly to chapters nine and eleven of *The Spirit and the Letter* to support the same definition: "It is called the justice of God because by imparting it God makes people just, in the same way that 'Deliverance belongs to the Lord' (Psalm 3:8) refers not to God's possession but to those whom God delivers."[39] Luther would find a similar emphasis on God's grace in a treatise published by Staupitz in 1517. In the spirit of Augustine, Staupitz argued that grace was not given to believers to make them pleasing to God but to make God pleasing to them.[40] God was not to be feared but to be loved and trusted.

Justification by faith was, however, obviously new to Luther. Otherwise, his search would not have been so agonizing and its confirmation by Augustine so unexpected. It had not been taught by Biel or by any theologian Luther had read directly or read about in Biel. He had studied hard to find it. At the end of his 1545 preface, Luther asserted that he was "not one of those who rose immediately to the top" but one who, like Augustine, became proficient by writing and teaching.[41] Whom did he have in mind? Scholastic theologians like Biel? Perhaps. But by 1545, he could have named a host of theological adversaries whom he had accused of reading scripture superficially. More importantly, Luther's words indicate that his new theological insight developed gradually as he did his job—studying and preparing lectures on the Bible.

Luther was not the only Wittenberg professor to work hard like Augustine and make a discovery. Andrew Karlstadt, who had sponsored Luther for the doctorate, at first rejected Luther's reliance on Augustine; and to prove Luther wrong he purchased and began to read a recently published edition of Augustine's works. Karlstadt was stupefied, however, to discover that he agreed with Augustine and with Luther's criticism of scholastic theology. Wasting no time, Karlstadt scheduled a course on Augustine's *The Spirit and the Letter*. When the lectures were published, he dedicated them to John Staupitz, who, he said, compelled him to focus on the sweetness of Christ.[42]

The coming conflict with Rome would make Luther a host of enemies, but what bothered him more was the fear of losing Staupitz, the man who first taught him to rely on God's mercy instead of recoiling from God's judgment. When his conflict with Rome was under way, Luther sent Staupitz a revision of his lectures on Galatians and ended the letter with a poignant note: "Last night I had a dream that you were about to leave me. I was begging you not to go and crying bitter tears, but you put out your hand and said I should be at peace and that you would return to me."[43] Absent the reformation, Luther and Staupitz would have remained Augustinian brothers and possibly renewed their order through a revival of Augustine's thought. It did not turn out that way. The religious upheaval created more distance between the two friends and caused changes far more drastic than any monastic reform they together might have devised.

CHAPTER FIVE

QUIET NO LONGER
1517–1518
Wittenberg—Augsburg

"Once they acquire indulgence letters, the poor souls believe they can be sure of their salvation. . . . Good God! Souls that are instructed thus under your care are being sent to their death, and it will be harder and harder for you to account for all this. Therefore I could keep quiet no longer."[1]

Keeping quiet was never Martin Luther's strength. He offered his opinion, sought or unsought, on most matters that crossed his desk. In so doing he failed to comply with his own description of a Christian as "a person of few words and many deeds."[2] This description was inspired by the shepherds of the Christmas story, who not only said "let us go and see" what has happened in Bethlehem, but actually went and saw the newborn. Luther's point was this: Although believers do not have to talk a lot, they should do what they say and more. Luther was not a man of few words, but he seldom failed to put his words into action even when trouble was the result. Indulgences were a case in point.

As 1517 dawned, Luther had no inkling that indulgences would cause a reformation. He was busy preaching, lecturing on Paul's epistle to the Galatians, writing, and attending to his duties as provincial vicar of the strict Augustinians. For instance, after a meeting with Staupitz ninety miles (140 kilometers) west of Wittenberg, Luther alerted John Lang, the prior in Erfurt, that Staupitz was sending him six or seven students for tutoring.[3] In March his first book, a German commentary on the seven penitential psalms, was published.[4] (The title page failed to show his name—a flagrant omission for a person who allegedly restyled the German language.) In Wittenberg, the highlights of Luther's days were treks up and

down the main street: to the west end if he had to converse with Spalatin
or preach in the Castle Church; about halfway if preaching at the parish
church; and less than halfway if he was delivering lectures in the university.
Busy keeping up with all his duties, Luther was seeking anything but fame.
Responding to a letter from Christoph Scheurl, the former Wittenberg
professor who was now legal adviser to the city of Nuremberg, he declared:
"God's approval declines at the same rate that human approval increases."[5]

At the university Luther and his colleagues renewed their attack on
scholastic theology. By early 1517 the group comprising Luther, Nicholas
Amsdorf, and Karlstadt—supported by Lang in Erfurt and Spalatin at the
court of Elector Frederick—lobbied successfully for more lectures on the
Bible and early Christian writers. Lectures on scholastic theologians were
now drawing only a few students. A substantial reform was under way, and
it was happening where reform is seldom substantial: a university curriculum. In May of 1517, Luther updated Lang:

> Our theology and Augustine are progressing well and with God's help rule
> at our university. Aristotle is falling from his throne and his final doom is
> only a matter of time. It is amazing how lectures on the *Sentences* are
> disdained. Indeed, teachers cannot expect any students unless they teach
> this theology, that is, lecture on the Bible, St. Augustine, or another famous
> teacher of the church.[6]

Up to now Luther was involved in a spiraling academic dispute which
concerned merely a handful of scholars. His unwillingness to keep quiet,
however, would soon draw him, his colleagues, and Elector Frederick into
a controversy that riled church officials and caused a public stir. It all began
with a building project in Rome. In 1506 the cornerstone for a new basilica
of St. Peter was laid and Pope Julius II authorized an indulgence to finance
its construction. In exchange for a contribution to the building fund, a
papal indulgence might offer huge benefits, such as the forgiveness of
future sins and the release of loved ones from purgatory.

At first the indulgence was not offered in Germany, but in 1515 Pope
Leo X extended its market and one year later designated Archbishop Albert
of Brandenburg, at age twenty-seven the highest-ranking prelate in
Germany, to promote the indulgence in the archdioceses of Mainz and
Magdeburg. Albert selected John Tetzel to lead the campaign. In early
1517, Tetzel arrived in Jüterbog, only twenty-four miles (forty kilometers)
northeast of Wittenberg, and went about the task that made him infamous

to generations of Protestants. Tetzel was, however, not the villain that Protestant propaganda made him out to be. He was a Dominican friar, born in Saxony, and licensed to teach theology; he was a veteran promoter of indulgences before he was tapped for the action that brought him to Luther's attention.[7] That happened in a roundabout way. Wittenbergers could not acquire the St. Peter's indulgence in Saxony because Elector Frederick had declared his territory off-limits; but after they heard about the extravagant benefits conferred by the indulgence, local folk were not to be denied. A fifty-mile (eighty kilometers) round trip to Jüterbog and a silver coin or two were a small price for a free pass to heaven.

Indulgences were not new. They had appeared centuries earlier when the sacrament of penance became a private rite administered by a priest. In its simplest form an indulgence did not remit sins, rather it set aside part or all of the penalty that was required to pay for those sins. That penalty, or penance, consisted of religious actions such as giving alms, saying prayers, visiting shrines, viewing relics, and fasting. Performing those actions paid the penalty for sin even though the guilt incurred had been removed by the death of Christ. An indulgence, therefore, did not forgive sin or its guilt but exempted the sinner from some or all of the penalty. The original intention was compassionate. The word *indulgence*, which means favor or relaxation, was not pejorative in the modern sense of self-indulgence or indulging to excess.

The granting of indulgences derived its power from a treasury filled by the endless merits of Christ and the saints who had no need of them. Those merits could be transferred to ordinary believers in order to cover the penalty owed for their sins. Strictly speaking, indulgences were not sold or bought, but in reality they were acquired in exchange for money designated for a purpose like the building of St. Peter's. After 1476 the faithful were allowed to purchase indulgences for souls in purgatory, who were still working off the penalties left unfinished at their death. After that became possible, who would not wish to speed the exit of a parent or spouse from purgatory? In Germany the indulgence business boomed. Between 1486 and 1503 three campaigns led by the papal legate Peraudi raised over half a million guilders for a crusade against the Turks.[8]

By 1517, however, the boom was over and the proceeds from eight additional campaigns were dwindling. Germany had been overworked and extravagant claims were necessary to bring out new buyers. A guide for preachers of the St. Peter's indulgence, named the *Summary Instruction* and sanctioned by Albert, guaranteed recipients full remission of their sins now and in purgatory and the same for their deceased relatives. It also bestowed on recipients full participation in all the "goods" of the church; i.e., they and their deceased relatives benefitted from all the prayers, almsgiving, fasting, and pilgrimages performed anywhere in the universal church. To obtain these privileges, recipients did not have to be contrite or confess their sins.[9] Tetzel and his preachers made more outrageous claims: the cross and papal coat of arms, displayed when indulgences were offered, had power equal to the cross of Christ; indulgences would absolve a person who had violated the Virgin Mary; even St. Peter, if he were now pope, could not grant greater graces than indulgences; and "when the coin in the coffer rang, the soul from purgatory sprang."[10] In addition, potential buyers were made to feel guilty if they did not seize the opportunity: "Do you not hear the voices of your parents and ancestors clamoring for help: 'Have mercy on me, please! We are suffering unbearable punishments and torments! You can buy our release with just a few alms, but you will not?'"[11]

Tetzel's campaign and its claims may have reached Luther's ears by May of 1516. As provincial vicar Luther was conducting a visitation of Augustinian houses near Meissen and Leipzig. According to a local chronicle, he met Staupitz at Grimma and heard from his superior about Tetzel's preaching in a nearby town. The chronicle concludes that Luther began to write against Tetzel in Grimma or, as Brother Martin himself phrased it: "I'll put a hole in that drum."[12] Preaching at the Wittenberg Town Church in late 1516, Luther urged listeners to cultivate genuine sorrow for their sins and not to avoid the penance they owed by acquiring indulgences. By accepting the penance they would take up their own crosses and become truly contrite.[13] In late February of 1517, he warned worshipers that indulgences taught them how to escape the penalty of sin but not how to avoid sin itself. He ended with a dramatic outburst: "Alas, the dangers of our time! Oh, you snoring priests! Oh, darkness worse than the Egyptian![14] How secure we are in the midst of the worst of all our evils!"[15]

As yet, however, Luther did not truly know the worst. The St. Peter's indulgence not only deceived people, it also misappropriated their money. Some income from the sale did end up in the building fund for St. Peter's Basilica; however, part of the revenue would repay the loan granted to Albert by the Fugger banking enterprise in Augsburg. Albert had used that loan to pay the Roman curia for elevating him to the archbishopric of Mainz. Luther did know, however, that his own prince, Elector Frederick, believed in the power of indulgences. Frederick and his cousin, Duke George, who ruled the other half of Saxony, were deeply devout. They chose monks as confessors, attended mass regularly, made pilgrimages, and offered indulgences of their own. Their indulgences were not tied to the building of St. Peter's in Rome but to the relic collections they had amassed in Saxony. In 1493 Frederick brought home relics from a pilgrimage to the Holy Land, and he continued to acquire them until 1510, when his collection contained 5,005 pieces. Forty-five of them belonged to the Elector's patron saint, Bartholomew; they outnumbered the relics of every other saint except the Virgin Mary. One receptacle contained particles of bone from Bartholomew's left hand, one from his jaw, two teeth, a piece of one more tooth, and six skull fragments.[16] By 1520 the indulgences attached to this vast quantity of relics, so went the claim, would reduce time spent in purgatory by 1,900,000 years.[17] Luther was not the first to question such numbers. In his popular *Praise of Folly*, published six years earlier, the humanist Erasmus had already ridiculed that kind of fanciful math: "What should I say of them that have measured purgatory by an hourglass and can without the least mistake demonstrate its ages in years and months, days and hours, minutes and seconds, as if they were in a mathematical table?"[18]

Faced with Frederick's passion for relics and indulgences, Luther had to be cautious about criticizing them. He and his colleagues needed Frederick's endorsement of the reforms under way at the university. In late 1516 Luther assisted the Elector's campaign to have the remains of Ursula and 11,000 virgins moved from Cologne to Wittenberg. Ursula, a reputed fourth-century British princess who was Christian, took 11,000 virgins on a pilgrimage to Rome, but during the return they were murdered by the Huns at Cologne. In 1106 relics were unearthed from a burial ground near the church of St. Ursula in Cologne; and, although the detection and assembly of so many virgins in fourth-century Britain or Rome was unlikely, the bones were assigned to the martyred women. Their popularity swelled during the late Middle Ages and attracted the interest of wealthy collectors such as Elector Frederick. Twenty-three years before Frederick attempted to acquire the relics, Christopher Columbus named the Caribbean chain now called the Virgin Islands after Ursula and her 11,000 companions.

At the risk of displeasing Frederick, Luther finally prepared ninety-five theses "on the power and efficacy of indulgences" and sent them to Archbishop Albert. In the cover letter, dated October 31, 1517, Luther declared he "could keep quiet no longer." Why no longer? Because, he wrote, people were being given the false assurance that indulgences would save them—and those indulgences were being offered under Albert's name.

"For all these souls," he told Albert, "you have the heaviest and a constantly increasing responsibility."[19] Albert had indeed authorized Tetzel and the other preachers to make extravagant and misleading claims for the St. Peter's indulgence. Those claims, which Luther admitted not to have heard in person, were based in part on the *Summary Instruction*. Luther was familiar with this document and requested Albert to replace its claims with a "different kind of preaching," namely, with the gospel that Jesus actually commanded to be preached.[20] Luther issued no ultimatum nor was he in a position to do so; but if nothing changed, he warned, somebody less respectful than Luther would refute the *Instruction* and insult the Archbishop openly. Luther also reminded Albert that a pope had never clarified the theology behind indulgences. To remedy that, he was calling for a debate and had prepared ninety-five theses and an essay on indulgences. Both documents were enclosed and Albert should refer to them for details.

Archbishop Albert, himself a lover of relics, did not take it well when he finally received these documents. At first he brushed off Luther's request: The defiant action of that monk, he said, had little to do with him.[21] Albert could have reacted differently. Unlike many bishops, he was enlightened by tutoring in philosophy, rhetoric, law, and music. Albert soon realized, however, that the ninety-five theses could affect him personally. He would be unable to repay his loan to the Fuggers if the St. Peter's indulgence did not sell. A political issue also loomed. Albert was the younger brother of Elector Joachim I of Brandenburg, a neighbor and rival of Elector Frederick of Saxony. Frederick was offering indulgences of his own and was therefore competing with Albert. Were Luther's theses instigated by Frederick's advisors in order to discredit Albert and his brother? This speculation was so loud and insistent that Luther had to assure Spalatin that Frederick knew nothing about the theses before they became public.[22]

Albert asked his advisors and the scholars at Mainz to evaluate the "conclusions," as Luther and others called them. Ignoring Luther's critique of indulgences, Albert's counselors seized on a more provocative issue: A Wittenberg professor had audaciously challenged the pope's authority to define the benefits of indulgences. Consequently, only the pope could decide what action should be taken. Anticipating their judgment, Archbishop Albert forwarded the ninety-five theses to Pope Leo X and the Roman curia. That action by Albert, more so than a posting of the ninety-five theses on church doors, launched the conflict between Luther and the Roman hierarchy.

Suppose Luther had not written to Archbishop Albert but had instead convened in Wittenberg the scholarly debate announced by his theses. In that case, the issue might have remained academic and not have raised hackles in Mainz or Rome. Disputations and preparing theses were commonplace in Wittenberg. Between 1516 and 1521 Luther prepared twenty sets of theses, and his colleague Karlstadt almost thirty. Earlier in 1517, on April 26, Karlstadt announced and may have posted 151 theses— perhaps because Frederick's relics were also displayed on that day as well. For his announcement on October 31, 1517, Luther may have taken Karlstadt's action as a model. In both cases, however, very few pilgrims entering the Castle Church to view the relics could have read the Latin theses or would have bothered. Pictures of a defiant Luther with hammer in hand as if he were starting a popular revolt are pure make-believe. Such pictures turned up for the first time in the nineteenth century. If the ninety-five theses were posted on the eve of All Saints, it was merely an invitation to qualified debaters, not a call to arms.

Since Luther himself never mentioned it, the ninety-five theses may not have been posted at all. On the Tuesday after All Saints, November 3, 1517, Luther recalled being in nearby Kemberg with Jerome Schurf, a supportive colleague and advisor to Elector Frederick. Luther told Schurf he had decided to write against "the crass errors of indulgences." By doing so, warned Schurf, Luther would also be writing against the pope, and Rome would not take that lying down. If Luther's recollection was accurate and if the theses had been posted three days earlier, Schurf must have known about the theses and realized they had already criticized both indulgences and the pope.[23] Better evidence for a posting is found on a handwritten note, which was rediscovered in 2007 and was originally written between 1541 and 1544 by Luther's secretary, George Rörer. It says outright that on October 31, 1517, Luther posted theses concerning indulgences on the doors of the churches in Wittenberg.[24] It is also possible that a 1517 posting of the theses was witnessed by fifteen-year-old George Major, who years later became a theology professor in Wittenberg and mentioned the posting in a letter he wrote in 1553.[25] Either way, nailed to church doors or mailed only to Albert, the ninety-five theses brought Luther unwanted notoriety. His letter to Albert, together with the ninety-five theses, altered the course of Luther's life and he never forgot them. In 1541 Luther still knew where to find a copy of that letter.[26]

Luther's life did not change immediately. While he was lecturing on the New Testament book of Hebrews,[27] the ninety-five theses reached other hands, although not at the speed Luther later suggested when he claimed: "They went throughout the whole of Germany in a fortnight."[28] Too few copies of the theses had been printed for them to saturate Germany in two weeks. As an announcement of the disputation the theses were printed in placard form, but none of the placards has survived. The copy sent to Albert was printed in a smaller format, and copies from that edition found their way to other parties. On November 11, 1517, Luther himself sent a copy to John Lang in Erfurt and noted that "everyone, everywhere" was accusing him of audacity.[29]

By the end of 1517, two months after they were or were not posted, the Latin theses were printed three times: in Leipzig and Nuremberg as placards, and in Basel as pamphlets more suitable for individual readers.[30] Together those printings produced no more than several hundred copies. In Nuremberg, the theses were translated into German by Caspar Nützel, who belonged to the humanist circle named after Staupitz. That circle included Christoph Scheurl, the painter Albert Dürer, the city clerk Lazarus Spengler, and Luther's Augustinian brother Wenzel Linck.[31] They recognized the significance of the theses and forwarded them to Conrad Peutinger, a humanist and diplomat in Augsburg,[32] and to John Eck, a theologian at the University of Ingolstadt.[33] By early January, therefore, a few copies of the ninety-five theses might have reached Hamburg in northern Germany and Augsburg in the south; but the transit required two months rather than two weeks, and in no way did they blanket the country like snow.

The ninety-five theses were effortlessly understood by well-educated clergy and laity such as the Nuremberg humanists, but for others they were not easy. Albert's advisors may have seized on Luther's criticism of the pope because they were baffled by his denunciation of the indulgence preachers. For example, theses 39 and 40 claimed that not even the best-trained theologians could reconcile the benefits of indulgences with true contrition. Why not? Because "true contrition loves and seeks out punishment, whereas indulgences relax punishment and cause it to be hated." Theses 36 and 37 argued that indulgences served no purpose at all, because "every Christian who is truly contrite has full remission of guilt and punishment without indulgence letters." Rather than selling indulgences, according to theses 53–55, the good news of faith and unmerited redemption should be preached. Even the pope wished for that gospel to be proclaimed with one hundred times more pomp and ceremony than indulgences enjoyed. Archbishop Albert and his advisors certainly balked at thesis 80. It demanded that "bishops, curates and theologians" should answer for allowing outrageous claims to be spread among the people.

The indulgence preachers were an easy target, but it was trickier for Luther to defend the intention of the pope. Thesis 81 admitted as much by declaring that indulgences made it difficult for theologians to "save the pope's reputation from the slander and shrewd questions of the laity." Luther knew those questions well enough to list eight of them. They included: "Why doesn't the pope, wealthier than the Roman Crassus,[34] build St. Peter's Basilica with his own money instead of money taken from poor believers? Why doesn't the pope free pious souls from purgatory purely out of love instead of allowing someone else, not nearly so pious, to buy them out?" These and other questions were raised not only by astute laity; they must have been raised by Luther and his colleagues as well. The questions could be debated, but the answers were obvious, and listing them was a blatant censure of papal conduct.

In theses 58–66 Luther also rejected the notion of a treasury filled with the merits of Christ and the saints from which indulgences received their power. The poor, asserted Luther, were the treasure of the church, not the extra merits earned by Christ and the saints. Those merits could not be credited through indulgences to believers who still owed penance and time in purgatory. Instead, the merits of Christ and the saints were dispensed only through the gospel, which is "the true treasure of the church." Moreover, through the gospel the merits of Christ conveyed grace "even without the pope." Popes had power to cancel penalties only in certain cases reserved to their judgment; they did not have power to cancel all penalties through indulgences. Schurf was right. If Luther openly criticized indulgences, he could not avoid writing against the pope. His assertions did not merely question the poor judgment of popes, they also placed limits on papal power. Albert's advisors noticed it right away and recommended sending the theses to Rome.

The ninety-five theses were not a battle cry, but neither were they benign suggestions for reform. Luther was a devout, earnest, and high-ranking Augustinian friar for whom contrition and repentance were essential to faith. To claim they were unnecessary if you bought an indulgence was to him preposterous. He was outraged that the highest officials of the church allowed that claim to be made and asked them to stop the abuse. Why were contrition and repentance so important? Because Luther was steeped in monastic and mystical traditions in which the path to eternal life did not detour around contrition but plowed straight through it—just as

Jesus did not avoid the cross but accepted it as the path to resurrection. When Jesus said to repent, declared Luther, he intended that repentance be a constant attitude not restricted to a sacrament. Repentance was deep sorrow for one's sin and the acceptance of all the crosses that made human life unpleasant and sometimes unbearable. This repentance required more than going to confession and paying a penalty, and it was thoroughly undermined by indulgences. Nor did repentance guarantee peace, comfort, and happiness. The ninety-five theses ended on a sober note: "Christians should be exhorted to be diligent in following Christ their head through penalties, death, and hell, and thus be confident of entering heaven through many tribulations rather than through the false security of peace."[35] That was anything but the comfortable ride promised by indulgences.

Attempts to restrain Luther began in 1518, after the ninety-five theses arrived in Rome. Pope Leo X, who was probably told that Luther was a senior member of the observant Augustinians, asked the order's new vicar-general to pacify Luther and settle the matter internally. In Germany, however, John Tetzel did not let matters lie. He collaborated with Konrad Wimpina, a Dominican professor in Brandenburg, to accept Luther's invitation to a long-distance debate. Wimpina was a favorite of Elector Joachim of Brandenburg and had delivered the homily when Joachim's brother, Albert, to whom Luther sent the ninety-five theses, celebrated his first mass in Mainz. By collaborating with Wimpina, Tetzel was not only attacking Luther, he was also fanning the flames of political rivalry between Brandenburg and Saxony. The attack was delivered from a distance. Before his fellow Dominicans in Brandenburg, Tetzel defended 106 theses that declared Luther's statements erroneous and reasserted all the powers for papal indulgences that Luther had challenged. The Wimpina-Tetzel theses were then published and offered for sale in Wittenberg, of all places; no wonder that in mid-March 1518 indignant students set 800 copies on fire. For the first time Luther was alarmed. He realized the controversy was heating up and feared he might be blamed. I do not know what will happen, he told Lang in Erfurt, but my predicament can only become more perilous.[36]

To show that he did not mean to attack the pope, Luther published, in German, *A Sermon on Indulgence and Grace*, which did not mention papal authority. Its twenty articles refuted certain points made by Tetzel's 106 theses and presented Luther's own ideas to the public in language they could understand. Nonetheless, it closed with a barb. Some people, wrote Luther, wanted to label him a heretic because the truth about indulgences was bad for business. The brains of those people, charged Luther, were muddled because they had "never sniffed a Bible, never read Christian teachers, and never understood their own teachers."[37] This sermon enjoyed much wider circulation than the ninety-five theses themselves and was comprehended by more readers. John Tetzel immediately recognized its accessibility and appeal. As soon as he read the *Sermon*, Tetzel published a rebuttal to each of the twenty articles. On one vital point they seemed to be in agreement: the necessity of supporting assertions cogently with scripture and the writings of reliable theologians.[38] Luther refused to recant because no one had disproven his censure of indulgences by using convincing arguments based on those sources. The contest was not between scripture cited by Luther versus non-scriptural texts cited by his Roman opponents. Luther refused to recant because his opponents did not interpret scripture to his satisfaction.

After receiving a copy of the ninety-five theses, Tetzel had threatened to "throw that heretic Luther into the fire."[39] So far no accusation of heresy had been raised, but theologians loyal to Rome were lining up against Luther and preparing an official charge. In late April or early May, 1518, Tetzel authored a second set of theses, which accused Luther of attacking papal authority. Tetzel's first thesis laid down the rule that Luther allegedly broke: "Christians are to be taught that, since papal power is supreme and instituted by God alone, it can be restricted or amplified by no one but God."[40] On his copy of the ninety-five theses, John Eck, a prominent professor at Ingolstadt, marked with daggers the theses he considered "erroneous" and "frivolous" and inserted his repudiation of each. Eck did not publish the *Obelisks*, his word for the daggers, but forwarded them to Luther through Wenzel Linck. Luther was incensed because Eck, who had offered Luther his friendship, went behind his back and repudiated the theses as if, wrote Luther, Eck considered himself the only competent theologian.[41] Luther retaliated by marking the objections of Eck with asterisks, adding his rejoinders, and returning them privately to Eck by way of Linck. However, the private interchange became public little more than a year later when Eck and Luther faced each other in a historic debate at Leipzig.

Meanwhile in Rome, Silvester Prierias, a Dominican friar and theologian, was ordered to prepare a refutation of the ninety-five theses as part of the legal case against Luther. Born about 1456 and called Prierias after his Italian birthplace, he joined the Dominican order and immersed himself in the theology of Thomas Aquinas. In 1516 Pope Leo X appointed Prierias master of the sacred palace, a title that made him the papal court theologian and censor of books. It was the job of Prierias to find the errors that prevented books from being published, and the ninety-five theses struck his eye immediately as an attack upon papal authority rather than a protest against excessive claims for indulgences. Prierias cast his refutation as a dialogue, but it was not a dialogue between equals. Instead it was *A Dialogue against Martin Luther's Presumptuous Theses concerning the Power of the Pope*. Luther presented his theses and Prierias, operating as the superior theological authority, delivered rebuttals that demonstrated Luther's errors and inferiority. Dedicating the *Dialogue* to Pope Leo X, Prierias depicted himself as a shield in a battle for the honor of the Roman Church. Anyone who did not accept the infallible truth taught at Rome was a heretic.[42] Luther's first three theses, crowed Prierias, contained four mistakes.[43]

By Easter of 1518, Luther realized that he was dealing with adversaries "filled with hatred," and he reckoned with a trial that he might lose. With tongue in cheek he described his adversaries as "very sweet," but at the same time "more zealous for money than for souls." Because those adversaries were unable to refute his theses, he wrote, they cunningly went on the offensive and pretended that Luther had violated papal authority. He had decided, therefore, to explain his theses in writing and to send these *Explanations* to Staupitz to be forwarded to Pope Leo. Luther was hoping they would convince the pope and his theologians that he had no intention of attacking papal authority. Beyond that Staupitz was not to get involved in Luther's cause. "I prefer to take all the risk myself," wrote Luther. He had nothing to lose except his "poor, worn body, which was already exhausted by constant hardships."[44]

His words sounded defeatist, but Luther was not giving up. He dedicated the *Explanations* to Pope Leo and claimed that, by the pope's own authority, a doctor of theology like himself had the right to debate publicly the power of indulgences. The theses were intended for a discussion; they were not doctrines or dogmas. Besides, it was too late to recall them from circulation. To mollify his adversaries and to fulfill "many requests," he told Leo he was sending the *Explanations* to Rome. "Prostrate at your feet," wrote Luther, "I offer you all that I am and have. Whatever you decide, I will treat your voice as the voice of Christ speaking and presiding in you." Luther admitted that he also might err, but he would not be judged a heretic, no matter how madly those who wished otherwise raged against him.[45]

Luther meant those words in earnest; otherwise he would not have written between 100 and 200 pages[46] of explanations in Latin and sent them by way of Staupitz to the pope. However, the odds were against a favorable response from Pope Leo X. He was Giovanni de' Medici, a son of Lorenzo the Magnificent of Florence. Through his father's influence, Giovanni became a cardinal at the age of thirteen, and in 1513, at the age of thirty-seven, he was elected pope. Upon assuming the office, Leo allegedly said: "God has given us the papacy; let us now enjoy it."[47] True or not, Leo was a patron of the arts; he enjoyed lavish displays and spending money—on occasion more money than he had. As pope he was given to processing around Rome atop his white elephant, Hanno, given to him by King Manuel I of Portugal. At the same time, Leo presided over most of the Fifth Lateran Council, which sought reform of the clergy and the papal court. New rules governing the rights and duties of bishops were passed, but they were undermined by the habitual largesse, nepotism, and the granting of favors. Unexceptional for his time but better than some earlier popes, Leo was offered the last pre-reformation opportunity to enforce a renewal of the Roman Church. Before he died, on December 1, 1521, Leo thought he was snuffing out a dangerous heresy by quelling the unpleasantness caused by Luther. The friar himself had not been seen in public, that was true, but in Wittenberg major changes were under way without him.

CHAPTER SIX

THE BEST THEOLOGIANS
1518–1519
Wittenberg—Heidelberg—Leipzig

"I thank God that I hear and find my God in the German tongue, whereas I and others failed to do so in the Latin, Greek, or Hebrew tongues. God grant that this little book will become better known. Then we shall discover that German theologians are without a doubt the best theologians."[1]

As Luther composed his explanations of the ninety-five theses for Pope Leo, he was under attack from two directions. First, he was accused of condemning traditional religious practices to the point of tearing up a rosary.[2] Luther dismissed that accusation as silly, but during Lent of 1518 he denounced customary prayers and chants as "yammering and yapping."[3] Second, critics reproached Luther for preferring the Bible and early Christian theologians to medieval teachers of scholastic theology. Supported by his colleagues, Luther had been publicly demonstrating that preference since 1515, when his Roman lectures called the scholastics "fools and pig-theologians."[4] Therefore, destroying a rosary aside, both accusations were true and indicated that Luther was pushing reform on two fronts: academic theology and popular piety. Later, "by accident" as he put it, the two-front campaign started by Luther also reformed the structure of the church. However, that was not his original goal. Before he became a reformer of the church, Brother Martin was a reformer of theology and religious practice. His initial goal was to teach people that God was beneficent instead of punitive and that Christianity was about trusting God and loving others instead of earning a ticket to heaven. In 1518 Luther summarized in one sentence the essence of his reforming agenda: "I teach that people should put their trust in nothing but Jesus Christ alone, not in their prayers, merits, or their own good deeds."[5]

Luther's first opportunity to defend the reform of theology to an audience beyond Wittenberg came in April of 1518. As one of two provincial vicars, Brother Martin was obligated to attend the triennial convention of the strict Augustinians in Heidelberg. It would be a long journey and friends in Wittenberg advised against it. Despite the warning, Luther and one Augustinian companion left Wittenberg on April 11, 1518, and headed southwest until they reached Würzburg—a distance of 260 miles (400 kilometers) which they covered in nine days. For the journey, Elector Frederick supplied his professor with a safe conduct, one official escort, and letters of introduction. Spring was struggling to show itself as the party of three crossed the Thuringian terrain, which Luther knew well from his years in Erfurt and his recent visits to Augustinian houses in the region.

At Würzburg he joined Augustinian brothers from the Erfurt cloister, and together they rode the remaining 100 miles (160 kilometers) to Heidelberg. The Erfurt delegation included Bartholomew Arnoldi von Usingen, one of Luther's teachers before he entered the monastery. Usingen had subsequently joined the Augustinians, and, like Luther, he was headed for Heidelberg. Usingen and his Erfurt colleague, Jodocus Trutvetter, had introduced Luther to Aristotle's philosophy and its importance for scholastic theology. By 1518, however, Luther and his Wittenberg colleagues were attacking Aristotle and eliminating lectures on scholastic theologians. They expected support from Erfurt, but aside from John Lang, the Augustinian prior in Erfurt, the Wittenbergers had made no converts. In 1517, Luther offered to debate his theses against scholastic theology with the Erfurt faculty, but his offer was declined. The Erfurt theologians were no doubt put off by Luther's utter rejection of Aristotle. "The whole of Aristotle," Luther had declared, "is to theology as darkness is to light."[6]

By order of Staupitz, who was still Luther's superior in the Reformed Congregation, the Heidelberg convention was to host a disputation demonstrating the new theology in Wittenberg. Accordingly, Luther prepared forty theses on the subjects of sin, free will, and grace—topics that were central to the reform of theology. First of all, Luther identified the authorities that had replaced Aristotle in the Wittenberg curriculum: the apostle Paul and St. Augustine. Using them instead of Aristotle, Luther illustrated how the Wittenberg approach to sin and grace contradicted the scholastic approach. The issue was: How did sinful human beings become lovable enough in the eyes of God to receive grace and forgiveness. On the one hand, Aristotle taught that people became good by doing good deeds. Scholastic theologians built on that foundation and taught that sinners had to perform virtuous actions or meritorious works before God found them lovable enough to forgive. On the other hand, Paul and Augustine taught that God was pleased with sinners before they performed good works. They were forgiven by trusting God's promises, and only then did their actions, performed in faith and gratitude, become good in God's sight. Three years earlier Luther had noted this new sequence while lecturing on verse 147 of Psalm 119: "I came before the dawn and I cried, because I very much hoped in your words." Luther explained:

> Indeed I come before the dawn, before grace is given and no matter how unworthy I am, because you, God, promised to forgive me. I do not come early and cry because you owe me anything, or because I have earned or become worthy of so great a reward. If I had earned it, I would not come early (as the psalm says), but I would come afterwards, demanding what you rightly owed me. No, I come early and cry because I have hoped in your words. Your mercy, the mercy of a God who promises, has made me bold to pray out of season, as it were, before I have any merits.[7]

In Heidelberg, a lecture hall at the prestigious university was chosen for the second day of the disputation instead of the Augustinian cloister where the first day of debating took place and where Luther was staying. The festive occasion opened with a procession led by the marshal carrying the scepter and insignia of the faculty.[8] If the recently unsung professor from Wittenberg was intimidated by the setting, he left no record of it. One spectator was Martin Bucer, a Dominican friar studying at Heidelberg, who later became the chief Protestant reformer in Strasbourg. Bucer was so impressed by Luther that he wrote enthusiastically to an acquaintance in Basel: "Luther's sweetness in answering is remarkable; his patience in listening is incomparable; in his explanations you would recognize the acumen of Paul, not of Scotus;[9] his answers, so brief, so wise, and drawn from scripture easily turned all his hearers into admirers."[10] The impact on Bucer was profound, but not everyone admired Luther's rejection of scholastic theology. As Luther remembered them, his Heidelberg opponents debated him fairly but found his theology "something foreign."[11]

Nor did all the Augustinians present agree with Luther. On the way home, Luther rode in the same wagon as his teacher Usingen and tried to win him over. The effort appeared to fail. When Luther left him in Erfurt, Usingen was "astonished and still pondering" what he had heard.[12] A discouraged Luther reported to Spalatin: "My theology is like rotten food to the people in Erfurt."[13] Those "people" included his other Erfurt teacher, Trutvetter, whom he tried to visit before resuming the journey to Wittenberg. Luther walked to his house but was turned away. The next day, writing to Trutvetter, Luther stated the point he intended to make in person: He was neither the first nor the only Wittenberger to reject scholastic theology. Except for one teacher, the "whole university" felt that way. Luther named the colleagues who agreed with him: Andrew Karlstadt, Nicholas Amsdorf, the jurist Jerome Schurf, Bartholomew Bernhardi (rector of the university), John Dölsch,[14] and Peter Lupin.[15] The "whole university" was an exaggeration, but his supporters included professors of theology, law, and philosophy. The new method of teaching theology was not Luther's alone, nor did he want it to be. It was a Wittenberg theology. Beyond the university, claimed Luther, he was supported by Elector Frederick and by a chorus of astute minds, who avowed that until now they had neither known nor heard Christ and the gospel.[16] In the letter to Trutvetter Luther also recommended a radical curricular reform:

> I believe it is impossible for the church to be reformed unless church law, with its rules and decrees, scholastic theology, philosophy, and logic—as they are now taught—are eradicated and replaced by other studies. Daily I ask the Lord that the pure study of the Bible and the church fathers might be summoned back as soon as possible.[17]

As far as we know, the second front of reform, religious practice, was not discussed in Heidelberg. Sources for the disputation do not mention, for example, the controversy over indulgences, but it had not died down. Was it put on the agenda for a closed meeting of the Augustinians? Had Staupitz heard from Augustinian headquarters in Rome that he should silence Luther? While in Heidelberg Luther was relieved of his duties as provincial vicar and replaced by John Lang, his old friend and prior of the Erfurt Augustinians.[18] Was the replacement a result of Luther's outspokenness or did he request it? We do not know, but after he returned to Wittenberg in late May or June of 1518, a preliminary investigation of his writings was opened in Rome. About the same time, coincidentally or on purpose, Luther sent his explanations of the ninety-five theses to Pope Leo by way of Staupitz.

For the next two months—June and July of 1518—Luther was unaware of events in Rome, but there was work aplenty in Wittenberg. The summer semester was under way, and he resumed lecturing on the book of Hebrews. Luther also came across a manuscript that he had published in shorter form two years earlier. The title of the 1518 version was *A German Theology*, and it was written by an anonymous member of the Teutonic Order. In his preface, Luther confessed that no books, except the Bible and St. Augustine, had taught him more about God, Christ, humanity, and all things.[19] It was a resounding endorsement of a short tract that echoed a German mystic named John Tauler, whose sermons Luther had read and annotated. Luther cannot accurately be called a mystical theologian, but elements of mystical theology appear in his writings. For example, Luther maintained that faith created a union with Christ, but that union was not a rapturous experience of losing oneself to the degree that medieval mystics described.[20] For Luther, the union with Christ empowered believers to look outward instead of inward, relaying divine love from themselves to others in need.

In 1518 the language of *A German Theology* impressed Luther as much as its content. He warned its readers not to be irritated by the simple German vocabulary because "brilliant and pompous preachers" were never chosen to spread God's word. And, for the first time, Luther presented himself as a German theologian: "I thank God that I hear and find my God in the German tongue."[21] From that point on, Luther wrote many devotional and instructional tracts in German for a popular audience. Although he was supported by academic colleagues with whom he corresponded in Latin, Luther's German writings enjoyed a wider circulation and galvanized public support for the Wittenberg professor.

It was not long before Luther needed that support. In August of 1518 he was summoned to a hearing in Rome. It prompted him to contact Spalatin, who was in Augsburg with Frederick for the annual diet of the empire. Luther was hoping the hearing could be moved to Germany; and Frederick agreed, since no prince wanted to lose control over religious conflicts at home by having them settled in Rome. Besides, as Luther pointed out, at stake was not only his own orthodoxy but the reputation of Frederick's university in Wittenberg. As they often did, the political stars aligned themselves in Luther's favor. Emperor Maximilian wanted the German princes to elect his grandson, Charles of Spain, to succeed him, but the pope was opposed. To gain the pope's support, Maximilian promised to enforce a conviction of Luther for heresy; and the pope, seeing his chance to settle the Luther matter quickly, designated his legate to the Augsburg Diet, Cardinal Thomas Cajetan, to handle the matter in Germany.

Cajetan was the ideal man for the job: a former general of the Dominican order and an expert on Thomas Aquinas, whose first name he took after becoming a friar at sixteen. He was elevated to the rank of cardinal only fifteen months before he encountered Luther. According to Luther, Cajetan had a winsome manner: the good will and mildness, which the cardinal had promised to show Luther, "was certainly extraordinary and demonstrated in abundance."[22]

Luther's party arrived in Augsburg on October 7, 1518. The journey from Wittenberg had taken twelve days and Luther walked all but the last three miles. Stomach aches had forced him finally to climb on the wagon that carried Wenzel Linck, who had joined him in Nuremberg. Linck, about the same age as Luther, had been a faculty colleague and prior of the Augustinian house in Wittenberg. Although Augsburg was home to a cathedral and at least fifteen churches and cloisters, it had no Augustinian monastery. Luther was given quarters in the Carmelite cloister where the prior was John Frosch, who had recently studied in Wittenberg.

Four days passed before the hearing began. Pope Leo had ordered Cajetan not to debate Luther but to demand a withdrawal of his heretical statements. If Luther refused to recant, Cajetan was to take him into custody and deliver him to Rome. Fearing that outcome, Elector Frederick had designated two of his advisors to support Luther. They did not allow Luther to meet Cajetan until a safe conduct was granted by the emperor. It took several days to find the emperor, who had left Augsburg with a hunting party as soon as the diet ended. Finally, Luther was able to meet Cajetan in his quarters at the opulent house of the Fugger banking family.[23] Luther must have realized the irony: the family had lent Albert of Mainz money to pay Rome for his cardinal's hat. Albert in turn was paying the Fuggers back with money earned from selling the St. Peter's indulgence that Luther criticized. Now Luther was forced to defend himself against heresy in the very house where the loan to Albert originated. Politics, money, patronage, and power had created a vortex that threatened to sink the outspoken friar and professor.

On October 12, Luther was escorted to the first meeting by three monks from the Carmelite monastery and by Wenzel Linck, whose nicer cowl Luther had borrowed for the occasion. Having been instructed how to behave, Luther prostrated himself before the cardinal, who immediately asked him to stand and said: "You shook Germany with your theses on indulgences; if you wish to be an obedient son and please the pope, then recant. Nothing bad will happen to you, for I hear that you are a doctor of theology with many disciples." Instead of agreeing to recant, Luther briefly offered to remain silent if his adversaries would also refrain from attacking him.[24]

After that offer was rejected, Luther asked to be shown his errors and Cajetan named two: 1) Luther's denial that the treasury of the church from which indulgences drew their power contained the merits of Christ and the saints; and 2) Luther's assertion that faith brought certainty of forgiveness even before a penitent received absolution from a priest. For Luther the second issue was more important than the first, and Cajetan's repudiation caused Luther "much grief, for I would not have feared anything more than having that doctrine called into question."[25] In the background, Cajetan's retinue snickered as Luther struggled to absorb the charges against him. After regaining his composure, Luther defended himself by appealing to scripture. On the first point, the existence of a treasury of merits earned by Christ and the saints, Luther argued that no such treasury was mentioned in the Bible. Cajetan countered by appealing to a papal decree from the year 1343 that confirmed the treasury's existence. On the second point, that faith brought certainty of forgiveness, Luther appealed to biblical passages cited by him in the ninety-five theses and his explanations. He was astounded by Cajetan's response: papal authority was superior to the authority of scripture and of church councils. In those absolute terms, uttered Luther, papal authority was new to him and he rejected it outright.

The hearing threatened to turn into a long debate and Luther asked for a recess. Staupitz had now arrived from Nuremberg to lend his support to Frederick's advisors, who were deliberating the next step. They decided that Luther should present a written response to the errors identified by Cajetan and to the cardinal's demand that Luther recant those errors. At first Cajetan denied Luther's request to submit a written defense, but he relented after Staupitz supported it. Behind the scenes, however, Cajetan pushed Linck and Staupitz to make Luther recant. Staupitz replied that convincing Luther to retract his statements was Cajetan's job, not theirs. On the last day of the hearing Luther submitted his defense in the presence of his Saxon counselors. Cajetan's response was blunt. He dismissed Luther with the ultimatum: "Either recant or do not show your face again."

After serving notice that he intended to appeal directly to Pope Leo, Luther prepared to leave Augsburg. Staupitz had procured a horse from "a certain prior," and Luther, concealing his monastic habit under a borrowed hat and cloak, mounted the horse late on October 20 and followed a single bodyguard out of Augsburg.[26] They headed northeast toward Nuremberg, a trip of eighty-five miles (135 kilometers). Luther usually walked or rode in a wagon, as he did on the journey to Heidelberg; he was not an experienced horseman. Moreover, it was late October. Darkness came early and it was already cold if not yet freezing. Altogether it was an unpleasant trip—more like a flight than a dignified departure. Forty-eight hours or more later, Luther and his bodyguard arrived in Nuremberg saddle-sore and exhausted.

Luther finally reached Wittenberg on October 31, 1518, exactly one year after the ninety-five theses were mailed to Albert of Mainz and affixed, perhaps, to the church doors. One year earlier Luther was a provincial vicar of the observant Augustinians and a university professor in good standing with his prince and the church. Now he was no longer a high official in his order and, much worse, he was in trouble with other high officials both in Germany and in Rome: the pope, at least two cardinals, experts on canon law, and a growing number of sharp Roman theologians. Luther had reason to be filled with "hope and fear" while wondering why his struggle seemed so important to many prominent persons.[27] The hope was based on a formal appeal made soon after leaving Augsburg. A friar left behind by Luther was to inform Cajetan that Luther was appealing from an ill-informed pope to a pope better informed.[28] In Luther's mind, however, Pope Leo X was hardly better informed than his predecessor Julius II, who had convened the recent Fifth Vatican Council (1512–1517). Pope Julius was certain that a council would never threaten his power: "It can do me no harm," declared Julius; "I summon it and remain above it."[29]

Luther's fear was caused by a sentence of heresy anticipated to arrive any day. To avoid putting Elector Frederick in the tight spot of harboring a condemned heretic, Luther was prepared "to go away as Abraham went, not yet knowing where but most sure of the way because God is everywhere."[30] At the beginning of December, however, Luther was still in Wittenberg. The people around him were showing so much solicitude that he could hardly bear it: "I am in the hands of God and of my friends."[31] Even John Staupitz, now living in Salzburg and seeing nothing ahead for Luther but a cross, invited him to Salzburg so that the two old friends could live and die together.[32] Luther finally decided to leave Saxony and organized a farewell dinner in the cloister. While they were eating, reported one source, a note from Spalatin informed Luther that Elector Frederick wanted him to stay.[33] The next day Luther still felt like leaving but decided that Frederick and the university could be trusted to stick by him.

For Luther's life and for the reformation that lay ahead, this was a crucial moment in yet another way. Staying in Wittenberg meant that Luther gained his most important ally, Philip Melanchthon, who just two months earlier had arrived in town to become professor of Greek. Born

Philipp Schwartzerdt in Bretten, between Stuttgart and Heidelberg, Melanchthon was twenty-one years old and had never left southwestern Germany. He was recommended for the position by the noted humanist and Hebrew scholar, John Reuchlin, who was related to the family through marriage. By any measure Melanchthon was a child prodigy. From age seven he studied Latin with a tutor who required him daily to analyze the syntax of twenty or more verses of Latin poetry. For every mistake young Philip earned a whack. After his father and grandfather died, Philip was sent to the acclaimed Latin school in nearby Pforzheim. In less than a year he was so proficient in Greek that his kinsman Reuchlin presented him with a Greek grammar and dubbed him Melanchthon, the Greek equivalent of Schwartzerdt, which means black earth.

The renaming was Philip's initiation into the world of humanist scholars, many of whom also adopted Greek or Latin names. In 1509, at the age of twelve, Melanchthon entered the university at Heidelberg and earned the bachelor's degree in two years. In spite of that achievement, he was not allowed to pursue the master's degree owing to his "youth and boyish appearance."[34] Following the advice of Reuchlin, he transferred to a university in the picturesque town of Tübingen, which lay on the Neckar river seventy-five miles (120 kilometers) to the south. In Tübingen, at age sixteen, Melanchthon earned the master's degree that entitled him to teach Greek, Latin, and rhetoric to students barely younger than himself. Five years later he was a professor in Wittenberg and the colleague of a friar who was under suspicion of heresy and headed to Augsburg to be reprimanded by a prince of the church.

Regardless of what Melanchthon thought about the Luther affair, he fit perfectly into the reforming atmosphere of the university. A scant four days after arriving, he delivered in formal Latin an inaugural lecture on educational reform entitled "Correcting the Studies of Youth." After apologizing for his own youth as the rules of rhetoric dictated, Melanchthon urged students in the audience to give extra effort to their study of Greek language and literature. Enriched by a solid knowledge of Greek, they would not have to depend on Latin translations of ancient texts but could draw wisdom and inspiration directly from sources such as the New Testament. Luther heard the lecture in person and told Spalatin that, as long as he lived, he desired no other Greek instructor. He was afraid, however, that Melanchthon's constitution was "not sturdy enough for the rough way of life in our region." Moreover, Melanchthon's salary was small and the faculty at Leipzig, which gave him a royal reception as he passed through on his way to Wittenberg, was already trying to lure him away.[35] Luther immediately took advantage of his new colleague in order to improve his own Greek; and Philip in turn, as if under a spell, absorbed evangelical theology so quickly and thoroughly that within three years he published its first organized and comprehensive textbook. Neither scholar ever left Wittenberg to teach elsewhere; they died at the same age and lie entombed across from each other, if not quite side by side, in the Castle Church.

As soon as 1519 dawned, the pope and his officers renewed efforts to bring the stubborn friar to Rome, but on January 12 the political wind again shifted in Luther's favor. The Holy Roman Emperor, Maximilian I, died in Austria. He wanted to die sooner—ever since falling from his horse and mangling his leg—and for the previous five years an empty coffin had accompanied him on every journey. The death of Maximilian made choosing his successor paramount, and Pope Leo was counting on Elector Frederick of Saxony to vote for the papal candidate. To sweeten the deal, Pope Leo decided to award Frederick the Golden Rose, an ornately gilded floral arrangement bestowed on exceptional servants of the Roman Church. To present the rose, the curia chose a papal chamberlain, Karl von Miltitz, who came from Saxon nobility and whose father had connections to Elector Frederick. Under Cajetan's authority and carrying a satchel full of generous papal privileges, Miltitz arrived in Wittenberg soon after Christmas 1518. After presenting to Frederick a papal letter requesting his cooperation, Miltitz started to negotiate with the Elector's advisors. It was the first of a series of futile meetings that on three occasions involved Luther himself.

Although Miltitz was not a skilled politician, he was no buffoon and his mission was taken seriously in Saxony because the stakes had been raised. In November 1518 Pope Leo had issued a decree that upheld Tetzel's claims about indulgences, claims which Luther had ridiculed in the ninety-five theses. The decree also conceded to popes the authority over indulgences that Luther had questioned. He could no longer claim that the church lacked a definitive judgment on these matters. Luther either had to recant what he had written about indulgences or stand trial for heresy in Rome. Time, however, remained on Luther's side. In Rome the case against him dragged, and in Germany the spotlight moved onto an academic debate that involved Luther and his shrewdest and most tenacious opponent.

This opponent was John Eck, who had already rejected Luther's ninety-five theses. Born Johann Maier in the Swabian village of Egg, southeast of Ulm, Eck was three years younger than Luther. He had been a precocious student and, like Melanchthon, earned a Master of Arts at the university in Tübingen. Not long afterward he was ordained a priest, awarded a doctorate in theology, and, on his twenty-fourth birthday, installed as professor of holy scripture at the university in Ingolstadt north of Munich. By 1517 Eck had honed his debating skills by defending the right to charge interest on loans even though it was prohibited by church law. His voice was resonant and Luther himself conceded that Eck's memory was excellent and his mind incisive.[36] Like Luther he preached frequently and was fond of music. The two men were introduced by Christoph Scheurl, who had known them both for several years and thought they were compatible, and so they were until Eck read the ninety-five theses. Instead of the favorable response that Luther expected, Eck declared he would gladly walk ten miles in order to debate Brother Martin.

The disputation that finally took place in July of 1519 was originally arranged as a debate between Eck and Luther's colleague, Andrew Karlstadt. It would take place in Leipzig, even though it was unfriendly territory for the Wittenbergers. The city was located in the "other Saxony", ruled by Duke George, who did not inherit the title of Elector and remained loyal to Rome. Eck had chosen Leipzig because he expected to find more support for himself than for Karlstadt.

The debate turned into a spectacle.[37] Eck arrived in time to participate in the festival of Corpus Christi, which in 1519 fell on June 23. Luther and Karlstadt, arriving the next day in separate wagons, got off to a less festal start. The first wagon, carrying Karlstadt and a large pile of books, lost a wheel and overturned in front of the Church of St. Paul. Karlstadt was dumped in the mud and visibly shaken. Under way again, the wagons were escorted into the city by 200 Wittenberg students, who later demonstrated at Eck's quarters in the mayor's house. Not to be outdone, the Leipzigers assembled an honor guard for Eck. Besides Karlstadt, four of Luther's associates made the trip from Wittenberg to Leipzig: Melanchthon, Nicholas Amsdorf, John Agricola, and the university's rector. Before stepping down from their wagons, the Wittenbergers were alerted to notices prohibiting the debate. They had been issued by the chancellor of the university, but he was overruled by Duke George, who was eager for the debate to take place. "If the theologians at Leipzig," he wrote, "cannot stomach these debates and are afraid of losing them, they should be replaced by old women who are paid to sing and spin yarn for us."[38]

The disputation opened on June 27 with a ceremony at the Church of St. Thomas. It featured a twelve-part mass composed by the church's cantor and sung by its choir. The company then processed to the Pleissenburg castle where the debate was held in a large space furnished and decorated for the occasion. Tapestries hung from the lecterns and tables. The debaters faced each other at the lecterns while the clerks and notaries sitting nearby recorded the proceedings. The Wittenbergers' lectern sported the image of St. Martin while Eck's lectern showed the image of St. George.[39] The disputation convened each morning at seven o'clock and lasted more than two weeks.

The first session, as originally planned, featured Eck and Karlstadt. Then it was the turn of Eck and Luther, whom Eck had drawn into the debate by challenging an earlier claim by Luther that Rome had not always ranked first among Christian churches. Eck and Luther argued back and forth for nine days. The last two days belonged to Eck and Karlstadt. At that point, the disputation was cut short because Duke George expected a visit from Elector Joachim of Brandenburg, who was returning from the election of Emperor Charles V at Frankfurt. More time, however, would not have satisfied Luther. He called the debate a tragedy because he had expected it to be the long-sought opportunity to argue his case against indulgences. Instead, the nine days allotted to Eck and Luther were nearly up before they discussed indulgences, penance, and purgatory. As it happened, claimed Luther, Eck mostly agreed with him on those topics and, as a result, the debate over indulgences "fell completely flat."[40]

Indulgences would never again be the focal point of the conflict between Luther and Rome. Papal authority was made the main issue, not by Luther but by opponents like Eck, who argued that St. Peter was the first bishop of Rome and that his successors, the popes, were the supreme heads of Christendom. Luther met Eck's declaration head-on: the eastern Orthodox churches in the old Roman Empire had never recognized the Roman bishop as their head. Only the popes themselves, in decrees they had issued during the last four hundred years, claimed to be the head of all Christians. Those recent papal decrees, declared Luther, were trumped by scripture and the Council of Nicea (325 CE), which the Orthodox churches acknowledged as supreme authorities.[41]

Eck was prepared to counter Luther's argument that scripture had greater authority than papal decrees. If Luther wanted proof of papal superiority from scripture, then Eck was ready to give it: the words of Jesus to Peter in Matthew 16:18: "You are Peter and on this rock I will build my church." Peter had just confessed Jesus to be the son of God and therefore the words of Jesus gave divine authority to the actions and decrees of Peter and his successors. This interpretation of Matthew 16:18 was much older than Eck. In fact, as he and Luther debated, the words of Jesus in their

Latin translation were about to be emblazoned around the base of the dome in the new St. Peter's Basilica. Luther objected that papal primacy was not a divine mandate based on scripture but a human arrangement that developed mainly in Western Europe, where the medieval papacy arose. Christianity in the eastern Mediterranean and beyond, which he called the Greek churches, had never accepted the Roman bishop as their superior. To back up his view, Luther gave the words of Jesus a different interpretation: the rock on which Jesus built his church was the faith of Peter, not his person. Luther again pointed out that no evidence from scripture indicated that Peter ever visited or resided in Rome. That historical point gave Luther a certain advantage, but there was no way for either man to prove his interpretation of what Jesus meant by calling Peter the rock.

The unofficial outcome was decided not by the force of their arguments but by Eck's rhetorical skill—his ability to sway the audience and afterward tout himself the victor. He scored the most points by associating Luther with the Bohemian heretics, the followers of John Hus, who denied the divine origin of papal authority and was burned to death in 1415 by the Council of Constance. Hus and the Bohemians were anathema in Leipzig because its university was founded by German professors who had protested against Hus by leaving Prague and moving to Leipzig. Luther did not help himself by affirming that several statements of Hus condemned at Constance were thoroughly Christian. Duke George called Luther's statement "the plague" and abandoned the neutrality expected of a host. Eck charged it was heresy to assert that a general council of the church, like Constance, had made mistakes. Luther offered a more picturesque summary of Eck's reaction to his partial defense of Hus: "Then Eck stamped about with much ado as though he were in the arena, holding up the Bohemians before me and publicly accusing me of supporting the Bohemian heretics. For he is a sophist, no less impudent than rash. These accusations, more than the debate itself, tickled the Leipzig audience."[42] Luther exaggerated Eck's behavior, but Eck was known as a skilled debater who knew how to manipulate his audience.

The official outcome of the Leipzig disputation was to be decided by theologians at the universities of Erfurt and Paris. Erfurt, however, declined to render a verdict, and Paris, under pressure from Duke George, finally condemned Luther's writings in 1521. Paris was not the first university to take this step. In 1519, a list of erroneous statements in Luther's writings was already condemned by the universities at Cologne and Louvain and published in 1520. No official winner of the Leipzig debate was ever named, but Catholic theologians present were certain the victory belonged to Eck. Happy to accept that honor, Eck continued his campaign to have Luther tried for heresy. When he asked Luther's prince to surrender the heretic, he got nowhere. But in February of 1520, after contacting Pope Leo and requesting favors for himself, Eck traveled to Rome in order to light a fire under the papal court.

Luther left Leipzig disappointed that the disputation was not the debate he had sought. As it ended, Luther's Augustinian colleagues, Staupitz and Wenzel Linck, were visiting cloisters in the region and Luther, anxious to report on the debate and perhaps seeking solace, hurried to meet them at the monastery in nearby Grimma. After two days he returned home to acclamation from the Wittenberg city council and other well-wishers. Otherwise, for Luther, the consequences of the disputation took shape only gradually. He gained the support of reform-minded humanists; but the debate hardened the opposition of Roman theologians, such as Jerome Emser, who served as chaplain and secretary to Duke George.

For the rest of his life Luther would engage high-minded opponents in Latin, but crucial to attracting more followers was his emergence in 1519 as the most prolific and published author of German pamphlets. Intended for laypeople, they explained the basics of Christian faith from Luther's point of view in language they could understand. Typical was a tract entitled *A German Explanation of the Lord's Prayer for Ordinary Layfolk*,[43] which was published in April of 1519 and reprinted in eleven editions. One pamphlet, which appeared in twenty-one editions, instructed readers how to meditate on the suffering of Christ, and another, in sixteen editions, advised readers how to prepare for death. Most important were three pamphlets that appeared in November of 1519. For the first time German laity could read about the new meanings given by Luther to the sacraments. All together about 150 editions of these German pamphlets were published in 1519 alone. A bolder estimate claims that one year later 250,000 copies of his writings were in circulation.

By the end of 1519, Luther's pamphlets had been published in Wittenberg, Leipzig, Nuremberg, Basel, Augsburg, Strasbourg, Erfurt, and a few unidentified locations. Printers were making money and were happy to produce as many copies as they could. Representative of this surge was the Leipzig printer, Melchior Lotther, with whom Luther lodged during the debate. They must have spoken about Lotther's plan to establish a branch of his business in Wittenberg. For his courses Philip Melanchthon wanted a printer who was able to prepare texts in Greek type. Lotther seized the opportunity and entrusted the new operation in Wittenberg to his sons Michael and Melchior Jr. Melanchthon was satisfied, and in December of 1519 Luther reported to Lang: "Lotther from Leipzig is establishing a publishing house here with typefaces for printing in three languages (German, Latin, and Greek)."[44] The branch office in Wittenberg was a smart move for another reason. After 1519 Duke George blocked the printing and sale of Luther's pamphlets in his part of Saxony.

Less than a month after the disputation ended, John Tetzel died and was interred in the Dominican church at Leipzig. When Luther heard of his illness, he told Tetzel not to blame himself for starting the indulgence controversy. This child, said Luther, had many parents and, he could have added, unforeseen consequences, such as the debate over papal power. Tetzel's death also signified that the indulgence controversy had been superseded by a dispute over papal primacy. And it left little doubt that Eck had replaced Tetzel as the chief adversary who would press the charge of heresy until Luther was excommunicated. Eck should not, however, be judged solely by his campaign against Luther between 1519 and 1521. He realized that abuses in the Roman Church shared the blame for the reformation and for Luther's refusal to soften his opposition to the papacy. In 1523 his memorandum to the papal court argued that Luther's cause should be handled in regional synods, which were able to correct abuses, instead of larger church councils, which were too slow and clumsy when it came to reform.[45]

Luther's best defense, it turned out, was not a good lawyer but a host of clerical and lay supporters who were galvanized by his German writings to form a popular movement so robust that neither church nor civil authorities were able to stop it. Luther's critics who read the pamphlets also took notice. Before their private conversation in Leipzig, Duke George must have scanned Luther's German explanation of the Lord's Prayer. He informed Luther that many conscientious people were so confused by what he wrote that now the Lord's Prayer was hard for them to say.[46] Those conscientious readers probably stumbled over Luther's first point because it contradicted all they had been taught about prayer. Luther's point was: "The fewer the words, the greater the prayer; the more words, the poorer the prayer."[47] People around Duke George may have been confused by what Luther wrote, but other readers, who were frustrated by lengthy and tedious prayers, were happily surprised and ready for change.

CHAPTER SEVEN

THE SAILS OF MY HEART
1520
Wittenberg

"This tribulation frightens me not at all but inflates the sails of my heart with an astonishing wind."[1]

As 1519 came to a close, Martin Luther, now thirty-five years old, was not yet a reformer. His criticisms were confined mainly to books and pamphlets, which he published in Latin in order to restrict the sharpest debates to theologians. One tract, however, was written in German: a short correction of the misinformation being spread about his teaching.[2] After explaining his objections to invoking saints, purgatory, indulgences, and good works, he declared that no defect in the Roman Church, grievous though it might be, justified leaving it: "The worse it gets, the faster we should run and cling to it; tearing oneself away or spurning it will not make it better."[3]

Despite this declaration of loyalty, the pressure on Luther was growing. Eck had gone on the offensive, claiming that he had won over the people in Leipzig who had been *Lutherani*, a term he might have coined.[4] He went on tour to publicize his victory, then returned home to renew the written attack. Luther dismissed Eck's charges, but the accusation that Luther agreed with the Czech heretic, John Hus, refused to die. Luther felt it necessary to prove that neither he nor his parents had any Bohemian relatives,[5] but he appeared to validate the charge by recommending in December of 1519 that both bread and wine be offered to all who attended mass. One century earlier John Hus had defended the same practice, and his followers, the Hussites or Bohemian Brethren, were still offering both elements to all communicants. It did not help that visitors from Prague brought Luther a book written by Hus. After reading it, Luther decided to wear the Hussite badge with pride and share it with his mentor and superior, John Staupitz:

"Up to now I have taught and held all the teachings of John Hus. Staupitz has taught them equally unawares. In short we are all Hussites without knowing it. Even Paul and Augustine were in reality Hussites."[6]

As the calendar turned over to 1520, Luther expressed both weariness and euphoria. Everything was against him, he told Spalatin, and he longed to be released from lecturing. Instead of scaring him, however, Luther said the conflict inflated the sails of his heart with an astonishing wind. He explained: "We are completely unaccustomed to suffering and evil, that is, to the Christian life. Let it be. The more strongly they rise up, the more securely I laugh at them. I am determined to fear nothing and to scorn everything."[7] That was a far cry from what he had told Staupitz the year before:

> You take your leave of me much too often. Today I was as sad as I could be—like a child that is weaned from its mother. I beg you praise the Lord in me, sinner as I am. I hate this miserable life. I am afraid of death, and I am void of faith although full of other gifts.[8]

For the rest of his life, Luther oscillated between euphoria and dejection but not to the point of dysfunction. The next two years, 1520 and 1521, proved, among other things, that the adult Luther was resilient. Within twelve months he produced, in both German and Latin, one bold text after another as the conflict intensified.

On January 9, 1520, Luther's case was reopened in Rome. Pope Leo appointed a commission headed by Cardinal Cajetan, who had questioned Luther in Augsburg, to pass judgment on his writings and recommend further action.[9] John Eck arrived in Rome soon after, uninvited but in time to view Pope Leo celebrate the Marian feast of the Annunciation on March 25. The pope led a parade that, by Eck's count, included thirty-one cardinals, fifty-two bishops, and 736 donkeys and horses.[10] A furlough from his university enabled Eck to make the trip and present to Pope Leo his new book on papal primacy. Eck also claimed to be the only person with sufficient information to catch all of Luther's errors.[11] For those reasons, perhaps, he was added to the small group that prepared an indictment. The group excerpted forty-one erroneous propositions from Luther's writings and threatened him with excommunication. Cajetan, who may have resented Eck's presence, argued that the propositions should be judged and labeled one by one, but Eck insisted on condemning them all together as both scandalous and heretical. Eck got his way. After the college of cardinals approved it, the document was officially published on June 15, 1520, as the papal edict known by its first two Latin words, *Exsurge Domine* ("Arise, O Lord"). Alluding to verses from the psalms, the edict depicted Luther's supporters as foxes and Luther himself as a wild boar, all of whom were ravaging God's vineyard, the Roman Church. The wild boar was suggested by the hunts observed by Pope Leo near his summer castle.[12]

In Wittenberg the edict came as no surprise but it was taken seriously. Not only Frederick, whom one Roman official denounced as an "enemy of the Christian religion,"[13] but all of electoral Saxony could suffer a general interdict that curtailed the celebration of sacraments and imposed other penalties. Frederick's advisors had already decided on their defense in case he was denounced for not surrendering Luther: Frederick had nothing to do with the matter and would not send Luther to Rome because the pope's own envoy, Karl von Miltitz, was attempting to arrange a hearing for him in Germany. Moreover, Frederick had never defended Luther's sermons or writings. He was unable to determine whether or not they were Christian, although learned readers had assured Frederick they were. Luther had not yet received a fair hearing and therefore, implied Frederick's defense, the papal edict was premature. In Rome, of course, *Exsurge Domine* was considered not at all premature but long overdue. The next move belonged to the Saxon court and Luther. Either he recanted or was convicted of heresy. The reputation of Elector Frederick and Saxony's fate depended on that decision.

Instead of waiting passively for the bull, Luther wielded his best weapon, the quill. Throughout 1520 he published five books that offered a platform for reforming Christendom. Like most of his writings, they were instigated by other people or events; yet they were not mere responses, rather they were assertions of Luther's convictions. The first treatise redefined the actions or good works that were expected of believers. The second proposed a broad definition of Christendom without the pope at its head. The third booklet appealed to the nobility of Germany as Christian laity to carry out reforms that the pope and bishops refused to initiate. The fourth treatise redefined the sacraments and argued for their reduction from seven to two. The fifth treatise, intended for Pope Leo X, defined Christian freedom and explained how it upheld the proper relationship between faith and good works.

The first of the five books owed its origin to Luther's friend and contact at court, George Spalatin, who reminded him of a promise to publish a sermon on good works. Luther dragged his feet. A month went by before

Luther suddenly reported his progress: "It will not be a sermon but rather a small book, and if my writing progresses as well as it has, this book will be the best work I have published so far."[14] Best work or not, he and Spalatin knew it was necessary. People were confused by Luther's claim that salvation came by faith alone and not by works. The claim contradicted what the church had taught for centuries: Good works earned salvation. The sixth-century *Rule of St. Benedict,* the most influential monastic text in western Christendom, made good works the "tools of the spiritual craft," the essence of holiness: "If we have used these tools without ceasing day and night and returned them on judgment day, our wages will be the reward God has promised: 'No eye has seen, nor ear heard, nor the human heart conceived what God has prepared for those who love him.'"[15] A theological dictionary, which appeared in the same year as the ninety-five theses, divided good works into two categories that clarified what was expected of every believer: "Certain works are directed toward our neighbor and pertain to love of neighbor, while others are directed toward God alone and pertain to divine worship and adoration."[16]

Luther's claim that salvation came from faith alone and not good works was based on biblical verses such as Ephesians 2:8–9, but many parishioners who heard "faith not works" thought Luther was wrong or, if they were glad to hear it, assumed they did not have to do anything at all. The latter response was noted by a Lutheran preacher in south Germany who summarized what he heard: "If we do not need to perform good works, all the better. We will gladly take faith alone. And if praying, fasting, holy days, and almsgiving are not required, then we will lie near the stove, warm our feet on its tiles, turn the roasting apples, open our mouths, and let grilled doves fly into them."[17] Luther did not mean that praying, fasting, observing holy days, and almsgiving were taboo. He objected to the claim that believers could merit or earn salvation by doing those things and others: collecting relics and acquiring indulgences, venerating and praying to saints, making pilgrimages to their shrines, endowing masses to be said by priests in private, and prohibiting priests, monks, and nuns to marry. According to Luther, those deeds were the wrong kind of good works and should be distinguished from the right kind of good works—those that followed faith. What were they? Luther found an answer in the Ten Commandments. The first commandment ("You shall have no other gods") was fulfilled by faith because trusting in God alone excluded other gods. That faith ensured salvation and led spontaneously to the right kind of good works defined by the remaining commandments. For example, if God alone were trusted for every need, we would help others obtain what they needed instead of stealing from them or cheating them to obtain more for ourselves. The same sequence—faith then works—applied to all the commandments: the last nine followed the first just as the right kind of good works followed the right kind of faith.

The book *Good Works* sold well. The first edition was printed by Melchior Lotther at his new press in Wittenberg and appeared near the beginning of June. Before 1520 ended, *Good Works* was reprinted eight times and another six printings appeared in 1521. The book was dedicated to Elector Frederick's brother, Duke John, who had asked for a sample of Luther's writing. Luther used the dedication to issue a feisty rejoinder to critics of his popular German tracts: "I hear daily that many people belittle my poverty and say I produce only little pamphlets and sermons in German for the uneducated laity. That does not bother me. I will be satisfied if I work my whole life for the improvement of one layperson. I will give thanks to God and then let all my little books turn to dust."[18]

In April of 1520 Luther was warned about a threat to his life. A rumor alleged that a doctor who could make himself invisible would soon arrive in Wittenberg to assassinate him.[19] Two weeks later Luther admitted that he sometimes worried: "My ship is tossed about; now hope, now fear rules me, but I am not concerned."[20] Not concerned perhaps because his mind was occupied with an immediate challenge at the university: how best to attract a professor of Hebrew to the faculty. The committee was juggling two candidates, waiting for one to reply while pondering salary and housing demands from another. Rising enrollment at the university was making it difficult to find lodging in town. With just over 2,000 residents, Wittenberg could barely find enough rooms for 500 or 600 students, much less apartments for a growing faculty.

Luther's mind was also on a new book entitled *The Papacy at Rome*—not an auspicious subject when Pope Leo was about to charge him with heresy. It was a reply to the Leipzig Franciscan Augustine Alveld, who attempted to prove from the Bible that the papacy was a divine institution.[21] Having already debated the issue with Eck, Luther at first dismissed Alveld's book and assigned the reply to his assistant for practice. After Alveld published a German version of his book, Luther reconsidered and in less than two weeks completed his own response to "the celebrated Romanist in Leipzig," a sarcastic reference that Alveld did not deserve. The substance of Luther's reply was nonetheless sensational. He not only rejected the argument that God established the papacy but asserted that

Christendom needed no pope at all. The essence of Christendom was an "assembly of hearts in one faith,"[22] a spiritual communion without borders that becomes visible in every place that a local group of those believers gather: in a house or church, in Germany, or Rome, or elsewhere. Luther called their local gathering a physical assembly that required no foreordained structure or head. It might have a bishop, or a leader with a different title, but no head of a local or regional church could be the earthly head of all Christendom: "The head must instill life; on earth there can be no head of spiritual Christendom other than Christ alone."[23] John Hus had written very similar words prior to his execution in Constance: "Having Christ Jesus for its head, faithful Christendom exists without a pope, who is a mere man."[24] Luther's position did not rule out the label of pope. The title of his book, *The Papacy at Rome,* which seems redundant, means there could be no "papacy" except in and around Rome. The bishop of Rome, or pope, had no wider jurisdiction or divinely-based authority, and therefore (although he did not say it) the pope had no power to declare Luther a heretic.

Luther went further. Drawing on a medieval tradition, he publicly suggested that the pope and his minions were the Antichrist, a term taken from the Bible and used to denote a person or movement that perverted the Christian faith. Around 1400 the English reformer John Wyclif accused the papacy of specific crimes that qualified it to be the Antichrist: the buying and selling of clerical rank, known as simony; excommunicating people who did not pay their tithes; bringing lawsuits; exercising civil in additional to religious authority; robbing the poor; and deceiving people with indulgences.[25] For his audacity Wyclif had to face two prosecutions and three condemnations, which forced his retirement from the faculty at Oxford. He died of a stroke instead of burning at the stake, but in 1428, long after his death and after John Hus was immolated at the Council of Constance, Wyclif's bones were disinterred by order of Pope Martin V and cast into the River Swift.

Luther knew the risk of calling the pope the Antichrist. Before debating Eck, he suggested it privately to Spalatin: "Confidentially, I do not know whether the pope himself is the Antichrist or his apostle, so miserably do the pope's decrees corrupt and crucify Christ."[26] One year later he dared to say it publicly, even though he knew an indictment for heresy was looming. In *The Papacy at Rome* Luther applied the title of Antichrist to the pope and other "Romanists" who were exploiting the German laity. Luther illustrated how the pope's greed contrasted with the modest means of the high priest in ancient Israel: "The old high priest was not allowed to own any piece of Israel's land but lived instead from contributions by the people. Why then is the pope intent on possessing the whole world? Why does he ordain and dismiss as he pleases every ruler as if the papal court were the Antichrist?"[27] So far that was just name-calling; more ominous was Luther's call for action. It was up to princes and other nobility to stop the Roman exploitation of Germany. If they did not summon their courage and act, Germany could end up desolate.[28]

As he wrote those words, Luther was already being courted by members of the nobility. Foremost was Ulrich von Hutten, a knight, humanist scholar, and champion of German nationalism, who was fueled by anti-Roman sentiment. He came to Luther's attention in early 1520 after Hutten published proof that the so-called *Donation of Constantine* was an early medieval forgery. The *Donation* alleged that the fourth-century emperor Constantine had granted imperial rule over the West to Pope Sylvester. It was a spurious argument for the papal domination of church and state, but its exposure strengthened Luther's suspicion that the pope was the Antichrist.[29] Hutten saw in Luther a potential ally and offered him the armed protection of a more bellicose knight, Franz von Sickingen, whose fortress, the Ebernburg, would soon shelter other reformers. As Luther was finishing *Good Works* and *The Papacy at Rome*, the imperial knight, Silvester von Schaumberg, also volunteered to defend Luther against his enemies.

Luther never accepted those overtures, but they boosted his confidence and encouraged him to publish a general appeal to the German nobility. He mentioned the book, the *Address to the Christian Nobility of the German Nation*, to Spalatin on June 7, 1520, one week before the bull *Exsurge Domine* threatened him with excommunication. The appeal, which takes up seventy packed pages in one modern edition, was completed by him in two weeks while he was also lecturing on the psalms. It was published in mid-August and was addressed specifically to the emperor and to the Christian nobility of the German nation. He dedicated the book to his "special friend" and colleague, Nicholas von Amsdorf, the son and grandson of noblemen who had served at the electoral court. Amsdorf and Jerome Schurf, a distinguished professor of canon law and counselor to Elector Frederick, urged Luther to write the book and offered advice and material as it progressed.

The dedication opened with a paraphrase of Ecclesiastes 3:7: "The time for silence has passed and the time to speak out has come."[30] Luther had turned a corner and, having given up on the clergy, appealed to the nobility as Christian laity to help the church. References to the book often omit the word "Christian," but it is essential for understanding Luther's purpose. The goal was not to foment a German uprising against Rome but to reform the practice of religion in Christendom. Because the clergy were shirking their duty, the only recourse was an appeal to laypeople in authority who could twist arms and force change. At first Luther feigned modesty by calling himself a court jester or a fool to offer advice to the powers that be. But, he continued, sometimes a fool can speak wisdom and this fool, Luther himself, is a sworn doctor of holy scripture, who can now make good on his oath to uphold it.[31]

The appeal to the nobility was also addressed to Emperor Charles V, who was returning to Germany from Spain for the traditional coronation in Aachen. This ancient town near Cologne had been the residence of Charlemagne, whose crowning by the pope in 800 (CE) established the Holy Roman Empire. By virtue of being emperor, Charles V was the highest-ranking nobleman in Germany and the ideal leader of an anti-Roman campaign. For it to be successful, argued Luther, three walls erected by the Romanists against reform had to be breached: the dominance of laity by the clergy on grounds that only members of the priesthood belonged to the spiritual class; the claim that only the pope could interpret scripture correctly; finally, the supremacy of the papacy over church councils, two of which in the 1400s had enacted significant reforms. In 1518, Luther had already scaled the second and third walls by appealing to a church council and declaring to Cajetan that scripture was lord over the pope. Breaking down the first wall was also necessary before rehabilitation of the entire fortress could begin. To accomplish that, Luther unleashed the theological weapon that made the reformation politically possible: the priesthood of baptized believers. Invoking passages from scripture,[32] Luther declared that all baptized Christians were priests and belonged to the spiritual class by virtue of their baptism, the gospel, and their faith. Some of them served in pastoral offices and were therefore *ordained* priests. Other members of the common priesthood occupied civil offices. Their duty was to ensure the well-being of the entire Christian community, which in Luther's society included the pure worship of God. If that worship needed to be cleansed and the ordained priests or clergy were unwilling to act, the lay priests who exercised civil authority, like the Christian nobility, had the right and obligation to mandate changes. Otherwise, no substantial reform was possible.[33]

Luther's grounds for toppling the second and third walls were equally shocking. If all Christians were equally spiritual, then any Christian with a better understanding of scripture should be given preference over a pope. Moreover, if the better interpretation was accepted by a council of the church, then that council had more authority than the pope. To bolster his argument, Luther cited a word of Paul that gave "the spiritual person" authority "to judge all things and be judged by no one."[34] Supporters of papal supremacy claimed the pope was that "spiritual person" and that his interpretation of scripture was immune from human judgment. Luther drew a different conclusion from Paul's words: Every baptized believer was the "spiritual person" and could potentially judge anything more fittingly than the pope was doing. Luther's manifesto:

> We ought to become bold and free on the authority of these texts and many others. We cannot allow the Spirit of freedom, as Paul calls it,[35] to be intimidated by the fabrications of popes but march boldly forward and test all that they do or leave undone by a faithful understanding of the scriptures.[36]

These were courageous words but they would come back to haunt Luther; for who among all the baptized was to decide what that faithful interpretation of scripture should be? A council of the church, a single theologian or pastor, a small group of like-minded believers, or one layperson standing against the crowd?

Part two of the *Address* attacked the excess wealth and ostentatious style of the pope and cardinals, which was financed in collusion with the Fugger banking enterprise. To reduce the cost of maintaining the papal household Luther recommended abolishing ninety-nine percent of it; and to curb the extravagance of the cardinals, he suggested the pope create fewer of them and support them at his own expense.[37] Elevating clergy to the rank of cardinal was lucrative business for the papacy. On July 1, 1517, Pope Leo X reportedly received between 300,000 to 500,000 ducats from the creation of thirty-one cardinals.[38] Luther also wanted to cut legal ties between Germany and the papacy. The goal was not the complete separation of church and state but the liberation of Germany from the papal domination that was corrupting Christendom: "All I seek is to arouse and set to thinking those who have the ability and inclination to help the German nation become free and Christian again after the wretched, heathenish, and unchristian rule of the pope."[39]

A divorce from Rome cleared the way for revamping the religious beliefs and actions that Luther addressed in part three of his appeal: clerical celibacy; private masses for the dead; proliferation of holy days; superstitious veneration of relics at pilgrimage sites; self-governing lay fraternities; and unwarranted excommunication. The specific changes proposed in parts two and three of the *Address* outlined a political platform, but not all the complaints and proposals originated with Luther. They overlapped with grievances that for decades had been presented to the emperor by German rulers and to the pope by church councils. Luther was also acquainted with similar criticisms made by humanists such as Hutten and Erasmus. But on the fine points of church law Luther needed assistance from legal experts such as Schurf, who had earned doctorates in both civil and canon law.

When the *Address to the Christian Nobility* was finally published mid-August of 1520, the first printing of 4,000 copies sold out within days. The second edition was also a bestseller but some readers were cautious. John Lang, the Augustinian prior in Erfurt, feared it could become a call to arms and asked that its publication be delayed. Luther admitted that the *Address* was impetuous and lacked restraint; nevertheless, it pleased many readers and, so Luther must have heard, did not displease the elector's court. Lang and Luther had been friends since their days in Erfurt, but the former was surely astonished to read the next sentences in Luther's letter: "We here are convinced that the papacy is the seat of the Antichrist incarnate. To counter his evil and deceit we are allowed to do everything we can for the salvation of souls. For myself, I declare that I owe the pope no more obedience than I owe the true Antichrist."[40] Those words were not only a derogatory statement about the pope but a personal rebuff of papal authority and a signal that Luther had no intention of turning back. Two weeks later Luther received a gift of venison from Elector Frederick's hunting party. Was the venison only a kind gesture or did it signal approval of the *Address*?

For Roman theologians the *Address to the Christian Nobility* was an outrage. In Leipzig Jerome Emser published a German response entitled *Against the Unchristian Book of Martin Luther, Augustinian, Addressed to the German Nobility*. On the title page, below Emser's coat of arms which showed the head of a goat, appeared the warning: "Be careful; the goat will butt you." Emser's book provided earnest and thorough rebuttals to each segment of the *Address*. In order to penetrate Luther's three walls Emser announced he would employ three weapons: a sword, which was holy scripture; a spear, which was church tradition; and daggers, which were statements excerpted from theologians of the early church. Emser was obviously annoyed by Luther's tone, but he refrained from invective and agreed that reform was necessary. Still, he could not resist making fun of Luther's self-portrayal as a fool and chided him for pouring out poison from under his fool's cap. Because he was a priest, Emser repudiated Luther's claim that laity and priests enjoyed the same spiritual status. Although he did not deny that inwardly every baptized person was a priest, Emser named five powers and privileges that ordination bestowed outwardly on those who were accepted into the special order of the priesthood.[41]

Ten days after the *Address to the Christian Nobility* appeared, Luther's Augustinian superior, John Staupitz, resigned his office as vicar-general of the Reformed Congregation. Now that Luther was threatened with excommunication, Staupitz was expected to support the surrender of Luther to Rome. Unwilling to carry out this bitter duty against his former protégé, Staupitz found abdication the only solution. The new vicar-general was Wenzel Linck, Luther's friend and the former prior in Wittenberg, who had accompanied Luther in 1518 to the meeting with Cajetan. The chapter meeting where the transition took place was held at the cloister in Eisleben, where Luther was born. He did not attend, but after the meeting Staupitz and Linck visited Luther in Wittenberg. They asked him to declare in a letter to Leo X that he had never intended to attack the pope in person. Luther consented. It was the last time that Staupitz, who could never bring himself to sever ties with Rome, met Luther face-to-face.

Staupitz finally settled in Salzburg, where the Augustinians had an outpost known to him from earlier visits. He was acquainted with the archbishop of Salzburg, Matthew Lang,[42] a protégé and secretary of Emperor Maximilian. In 1519 Lang was made the archbishop in Salzburg after quick ordination to the priesthood. He worked decisively against the reformation and welcomed Staupitz as a preacher and counselor. Staupitz soon left the Augustinians and joined the Benedictine order at their large and venerable abbey of St. Peter. Lang browbeat the monks at St. Peter to elect Staupitz their abbot, but he served only two years before dying on December 28, 1524. His gravestone is still visible in the Marian chapel of the abbey, where he was buried. For Luther it was a sad ending to a vital friendship. More than a year before Staupitz died, Luther feared he had lost the favor of his mentor but still paid him a gracious tribute: "It is not right for me to forget you or to be ungrateful, for it was through you that the light of the gospel began to shine out of darkness into our hearts."[43]

As Staupitz and Luther were meeting for the last time, two papal nuncios were making their way to Germany with copies of *Exsurge Domine*. One envoy was Jerome Aleander, a scholar who was director of the Vatican Library and otherwise well connected in Rome. The other envoy was John Eck. Armed with 100 copies of the bull, their assignment was to deliver them to Emperor Charles and to the princes, bishops, universities, and major cities in the Holy Roman Empire. The Roman curia intended for the bull to be promulgated throughout the empire and for its provisions, like burning Luther's books, to be implemented. That goal was only partly realized. *Exsurge Domine* was served to only a few princes and perhaps half of the bishops and universities. In Leipzig, where he had debated Luther, Eck was surprised by the lukewarm welcome he received. Duke George, whom Eck had persuaded to turn against Luther, wrote to his agents in Rome that not everything in the *Address to the Christian Nobility* was false and delayed publication of the bull. The bishops of Merseburg and Meissen, however, insisted that *Exsurge Domine* be posted and Luther's writings be thrown onto bonfires where the bishops resided.[44] Their resolve finally prevailed, but apparently only one member of the Leipzig faculty, whose Latin nickname, Vulcan, was perfect for the job, burned a few pamphlets.[45]

It was also Eck's assignment to publish the bull in electoral Saxony. He sent it to the bishop whose jurisdiction extended to Wittenberg, but delivering the bull personally to Elector Frederick and the university was a distasteful prospect. To avoid entering the town, Eck sent one copy by courier to the university, where it eventually reached the rector, who complained it had been delivered in a "thieving and rascally manner."[46] Luther was never formally served with the bull but was able to read it the next day. A copy was made immediately and forwarded to Spalatin, who was already in Worms. Luther provided a cover letter that smacked of buoyant defiance: "I am sending you a copy so that you see the Roman monsters for yourself. If they win, it is all over with faith and the church. With my whole heart I rejoice that the noblest reason I can imagine has brought this evil to my door; I am not worthy of such holy vexation."[47] Eck soon learned that neither Elector Frederick nor his brother, Duke John, was in Wittenberg. Frederick was in Cologne for the crowning of Emperor Charles, and John was at the ducal residence in Coburg, which lay on Eck's route from Leipzig to his home in Ingolstadt. Eck intended to deliver the bull to Duke John in person but, not feeling properly attired to appear at court, he had the bull once more delivered by courier.

Aleander, the other nuncio, caught up with the emperor in Antwerp as he inched toward Aachen and Cologne. After receiving the bull, the emperor quickly warmed Aleander's heart by ordering that Luther's books in Belgium and Holland be destroyed. Proceeding on that authority, Aleander started a campaign that led to successful burnings in Lüttich and Louvain; but after he left the Low Countries and arrived in Cologne with the imperial entourage, he encountered stronger resistance. Aleander concentrated on three archbishops who were present for the coronation. Two of them, Hermann of Cologne and Richard of Trier, gave Aleander no trouble, although Archbishop Hermann, whom Aleander described as meek,[48] left Cologne before the burning, which occurred on November 12, 1520. Aleander realized that Archbishop Richard was a friend of the Saxon court, but Richard did as Aleander expected and allowed the destruction of Luther's writings in Trier. Archbishop Richard had earlier agreed to hear Luther defend himself on German soil and may have harbored doubts about the bull. Very few bishops who executed the provisions of *Exsurge Domine* did it with conviction and enthusiasm. The others were uncertain about what to do and sought advice from the princes in or near their dioceses.[49]

The third prince of the church sought out by Aleander was Archbishop Albert of Mainz. Although he had initiated Luther's case by sending the ninety-five theses to Rome, Albert had done nothing further to promote the judicial inquiry. Aleander claimed that Albert's advisors were, deep down, "radical Lutherans who spoke out against Luther like enemies but treated him like a friend."[50] Aleander's claim contained some truth. One of Albert's advisors was the knight, Ulrich von Hutten, who had offered to protect Luther. Another advisor, Wolfgang Capito, became a reformer in Strasbourg. Rather than strict Lutherans, Albert's advisors were more discrete humanists who, like Erasmus, were critical of papal excess and superstitious piety but cautious about choosing sides. Albert finally promised Aleander to publish the bull and see that Luther's books were burned. Both men were present for the event in Mainz, but it went awry. The official in charge refused to light the fire and instead asked the crowd whether or not the books had been lawfully condemned. When they shouted no, the official jumped down from the pyre and the crowd became rowdy. Aleander was nearly assaulted, but the next day he managed to destroy at least a few of Luther's books.[51]

By then Charles had been crowned emperor and left Cologne to follow the Rhine river south to Worms, where the first imperial diet of his reign was to begin on January 6, 1521. Disregarding the strenuous objections of Aleander, Charles had given in to the urgings of Elector Frederick that Luther be allowed to appear in front of the delegates. For Charles, that was a small concession to Frederick and other German rulers in order to win their sympathy at the diet. Charles' advisors intended to strengthen the emperor's authority and concentrate power in his hands. The German princes, however, wanted the opposite: recognition of their prerogatives and a less centralized government. Luther's case belonged on the sidelines, or so it appeared.

In Wittenberg Luther, outwardly unfazed by the bull, continued his preaching, lecturing, and writing as if, remarked Philip Melanchthon on November 4, 1520, "he was driven by some spirit."[52] Melanchthon was probably more nervous about the future than Luther was. In three weeks he was to marry Katharina Krapp, who belonged to a prominent family in Wittenberg. Her father was a tailor and had served as mayor from 1494 until his death three years before Melanchthon arrived in town. Katharina's brother, Hans, took over his father's business and was also several times elected mayor of Wittenberg. Katharina's mother was alive and well for the wedding and lived another twenty-eight years as Philip's mother-in-law. All of Katharina's family were present at the ceremony, but no member of Melanchthon's family made the trip from their homes far to the south. For that reason Luther invited his parents and sisters to stand in for Melanchthon's family, and they made the much shorter journey from Mansfeld. Present also were friends and colleagues who lived in Wittenberg or came from nearby towns such as Leipzig.[53]

According to Melanchthon, "a friend" urged him to marry because he seemed too mired in his work, but Luther denied that he had anything to do with it.[54] Philip also claimed that he married because his flesh was weak and because he wanted to set a good example for young people. Virtually nothing is known about Katharina and her feelings, but a young, rising star at the university offered a good match. It is possible that Katharina's family pushed her to marry because an unproven rumor suggested she was no longer a virgin. Both Philip and Katharina were twenty-three years old and had been engaged since mid-August. The engagement was the legal foundation of the union and the first stage of the wedding. The second and third stages occurred, according to tradition, over two days. In this case the days were November 26, a Monday, and November 27, a Tuesday, the traditional lucky day of the week, on which most weddings occurred. On Monday the couple probably exchanged vows in the Krapp residence. The vows were followed that evening by the bedding of the couple, which required witnesses. On Tuesday, the day for which Melanchthon had issued invitations, the wedding party and guests processed to the Town Church, where the couple received the traditional admonitions, prayers, and blessings from the priest. That was followed by the wedding feast and merrymaking. Philip and Katharina then went home to Melanchthon's small abode, which was replaced fifteen years later by a stately renaissance-style house.

By the time Philip and Katharina married, the last of Luther's major 1520 books was published and on its way to Rome. It was accompanied by the conciliatory letter to Pope Leo X that Luther had earlier promised to write. The letter was a mixture of fact and fantasy. On the one hand, Luther kept the agreement made with Linck and Staupitz by declaring that he never thought ill of Leo personally and never intended to attack the Roman curia or raise any controversy about it. Instead, Luther argued, Leo had been the victim of his advisors, sitting among those monsters like a lamb among wolves and Daniel in the midst of lions. Eck, claimed Luther, was to blame for everything. He was the pope's enemy, chief among the many flatterers who had pulled the wool over Leo's eyes. On the other hand, Luther lambasted the Roman curia. Not even Leo, he wrote, could deny that the papal court was more corrupt than Babylon or Sodom ever was. The papacy was despicable and all efforts to save it were hopeless. Leo's enemies were those who exaggerated his power and ascribed to him alone the right of interpreting scripture. His predecessors had been led astray by Satan, and Leo should believe none who exalted him but only those who humbled him—presumably as Luther was doing when he told Leo that he was not, and should not want to be, the vicar of Christ:

> Observe the great difference between Christ and his successors, though they all wished to be regarded as his substitutes here on earth. I fear that most of them have viewed themselves as Christ's vicar in all too real a sense! A person is a vicar only when the superior is absent. . . . What is the church under such a vicar other than an assembly of people without Christ? And it follows—what is such a vicar other than an Antichrist and idol? Were not the apostles right to call themselves servants of the present Christ rather than vicars of an absent Christ.[55]

The letter became a preface to *Christian Liberty*, better known as *Freedom of a Christian*, the title of the popular German version prepared by Luther himself. Without dwelling on abstract terms, the book offered a clear explanation of the proper relationship between faith and love. The key to its popularity was the word freedom, which Luther defined in two simple statements: "A Christian is a perfectly free sovereign over all, subject to none; a Christian is a perfectly dutiful servant of all, subject to all."[56] Faith made Christians free from coercion and fear, but it granted no license to ignore and mistreat others. Genuine faith, which brought "complete salvation," issued spontaneously in love that made Christians into servants

of others. That service earned the believer no reward; it was not a meritorious good work. It considered nothing but the need and advantage of others.
That, wrote Luther, is a "truly Christian life" in which faith is active in
love.[57] This template of a flawless Christian was more devotional than
polemical, but there is no evidence that Pope Leo ever received the booklet
or the preface addressed to him.

Through the fall of 1520 Luther's quill had been on fire. In addition to
the major books named so far, he issued two unflinching rebuttals of the
bull *Exsurge Domine*.[58] He also defended in writing a flagrant act of defiance: burning the papal bull. At nine o'clock on the morning of Monday,
December 10, 1520, Luther prepared a bonfire. Alerted by Melanchthon, a
crowd of students and townspeople gathered at the Chapel of the Holy
Cross outside the Elster Gate, the east entrance to Wittenberg. It was the
usual place for burning the rags of people who had died of contagious
diseases. But on that morning the crowd watched as a large batch of books
was cast into the fire: the bull *Exsurge Domine*; the papal decrees known
collectively as the Canon Law of the Roman Church; the standard guide
for priests hearing confessions; some published writings of John Eck and
Jerome Emser; and "certain other books that were added by different
people."[59] By the afternoon students had scoured the town for similar books
and piled them on a cart. They returned to the site of the bonfire, set and
stoked another fire, and heaved the second load of books onto the blaze.[60]
The chapel and the gate are no longer there. Instead, on or near the original
site, diagonally across from the Augustinian monastery where Luther lived,
the event is commemorated by two stone markers set in a small grassy park
containing benches and a large oak tree. The oak now shading the site was
planted in 1830, but the original, so it is said, was planted not long after the
books were burned.

CHAPTER EIGHT

SUBJECT TO HIM ALONE
1521–1522
Wittenberg—Worms—Wartburg

"I am sending you this book, so that you can see by what signs and wonders Christ absolved me of the monastic vow and granted me so much liberty that, although he has made me the servant of all, I am subject to no one but him alone. He is my immediate bishop, abbot, prior, lord, father, and teacher. I accept no other."[1]

On January 3, 1521, less than a month after Luther burned the bull threatening him with excommunication, a second papal edict ousted him from the Roman Church. His time *under* the papacy, as he later called it, was over, and his life *outside* the papacy had begun. Luther was, however, not immediately informed. In Wittenberg he was lecturing on Psalm 22[2] and explaining the sentence: "All those who go down to the dust will bow before God." This verse, he said, testified to the equality of everyone before God. In reality, however, all people might be equal in the eyes of God, but in the eyes of the church they were not. Excommunication was the ultimate sign of inequality; and the gulf between Luther and the church hierarchy was wide: the full force of Roman authority pressing on a single Augustinian friar and professor. As Luther continued the explanation, his words obviously contradicted the reality he faced: "All things belong to God and not to us; we will not envy each other, or puff up ourselves over others. No one is more than another or less than another because all things belong to all."[3] This ideal came easily to Luther because it was the monastic code that governed his daily life. It did not, however, govern the day-to-day operation of the church.

Writing to Staupitz in mid-January 1521, Luther was still unaware of the excommunication, although he sensed the threat was escalating: "Up to this point we have played around, but the matter has now become serious." Animosity on both sides was so strong, he wrote, that the issue could be settled only at the Last Day by God himself.[4] Rome was not waiting, however, and considered the matter concluded. Luther's excommunication was his definitive ejection from the Roman Church, but he was not the only person affected. Anyone who protected him, for example, Elector Frederick, was also a heretic, and any place those protectors lived, such as Electoral Saxony, was deprived of the sacraments. Clergy were encouraged to preach and write against Luther and his followers. The bull would take effect as soon as it was posted on the cathedral door of any archdiocese in Germany. If needed, the emperor's assistance could be sought to enforce the penalties but, strictly speaking, Luther's own case did not have to come before the emperor or the imperial diet. For Electoral Saxony, however, and Elector Frederick, the diet was the court of last resort. While attending the coronation of Emperor Charles V prior to the diet, Frederick met twice with the new emperor and lobbied hard to gain a hearing for Luther. A lobbyist for the Roman side, the papal nuncio, Aleander, defended the Roman position by arguing that Luther was already a declared heretic. No further hearing was necessary and the emperor was not qualified to judge matters of faith. He should order the burning of all Luther's books and prevent new ones from coming onto the market.[5]

When the Diet at Worms opened on January 27, 1521, Charles was still undecided. More than half of the delegates, including some bishops and most secular rulers, had not publicly taken sides for or against Luther. Even the seven electors were not of one mind. When they caucused, Elector Frederick and Elector Joachim of Brandenburg almost came to blows before the archbishop of Salzburg stepped between them. Because the outcome of a vote for or against Luther's appearance was so unpredictable, Aleander tried to prevent it, but failed. His fear was justified. Presented with a proposal to ban Luther's writings without inviting him to the diet, the delegates rejected it on grounds that a popular revolt would erupt if Luther were condemned without a hearing.

Was that a real threat? Yes, but just how real was uncertain. Worms lay on the edge of a region that had recently experienced waves of insurrection. A rebellious network of peasants unleashed a series of revolts, one of which occurred in 1517 only thirty miles (fifty kilometers) south of Worms. In addition, unpredictable knights, such as Sickingen, who had harassed the city of Worms four years earlier, wanted Luther's support for their own military adventures. Even if the threat of violence was exaggerated, impressions gathered locally indicated that popular support for Luther was robust; or so it appeared to Aleander in Worms: "Every day it rains Luther books in both German and Latin; a printshop, unheard of here until now, is thriving. Nothing else sells but the books of Luther, even at the imperial court."[6] Aleander realized the enthusiasm for Luther was more political than religious. Delegates to the diet who wanted to hear Luther out sympathized with his criticism of Rome more than with his theology. For Emperor Charles, a young and untested leader, the political risk of condemning Luther without a hearing was too great.

Imperial diets could last for weeks or months. In March 1521, Emperor Charles finally summoned Luther to the diet—but only for the purpose of recanting his writings. No debate was scheduled. In the meantime, wherever possible, Luther's books were to be collected and burned. Charles was determined to show that he was not soft on heresy and had no intention of departing from the faith of his ancestors. In spite of the narrow terms offered by the emperor, Luther was eager to attend the diet, but the advisors of Elector Frederick were hesitant. A century earlier John Hus went to the stake in Constance despite a safe conduct that the emperor failed to enforce. To arrive at a decision, the chief political officer at the Saxon court, Gregor Brück, jotted down arguments for and against Luther's attendance and sent them to Spalatin. One simple argument seems to have carried the day. If Luther did not go to Worms, his enemies might call him a coward. Even the most famous scholar in Europe, Erasmus of Rotterdam, sent his personal messenger to Worms with a bundle of letters and pondered visiting the diet in person.[7]

Four days after the summons was served to Luther, he climbed into a wagon provided by the Wittenberg town council. The university donated twenty guilders toward travel expenses and Duke John, the Elector's brother, added to the fund. As usual, Luther was not alone. Apart from the imperial herald, who had delivered the summons, Luther's traveling companions included another Augustinian friar, a faculty colleague, a student from the part of Pomerania now in Poland, and possibly another student. The colleague, Nicholas von Amsdorf, and the Pomeranian student, Peter Swawe, had attended the Leipzig disputation in 1519. After transferring to Wittenberg, where he had connections, Swawe had become well acquainted with Luther and his colleagues—well enough at least to accompany him to Worms, a journey of more than 300 miles (500 kilometers). During the trip Luther led a Bible study on the book of Joshua and reportedly entertained the company with his lute. Luther does not mention the lute, but describing the Bible study he said: "I offered interpretations, and the others passed judgment."[8]

The first major stop was Erfurt. Luther was escorted into the city by forty horsemen and Crotus Rubeanus, formerly a fellow student and now rector of the university. To catch a glimpse of Luther, people not only lined the streets but climbed walls and stood on rooftops. The poet Eobanus Hessus praised Luther for performing a feat similar to the sixth labor of Hercules: Luther was cleaning out the church just as Hercules, in only one day, had washed all the dung from the Augean stables. Although it was a Saturday, Luther called his welcome "my Palm Sunday," the day of Jesus' boisterous arrival in Jerusalem prior to his crucifixion. Luther wondered whether Satan was using the pomp to tempt him or to signify that he, too, was heading to his death.[9]

Before leaving Wittenberg, however, Luther had realized not everyone in Erfurt would be glad to see him. When he alerted the Augustinian prior, his friend John Lang, that he would stay overnight in the Erfurt cloister, Luther added "unless it is too dangerous." He had not visited the city since becoming notorious, and Erfurt's absent overlord was still Archbishop Albert of Mainz, who had reported Luther to Rome. On Sunday the university organized a reception, which took place after Luther had preached in the cloister. Although he was not given to nostalgia, preaching as a declared heretic in the very space that molded him into a devout servant of the Roman Church had to give Luther pause. The sermon, however, gave no sign that he felt out of place. His message was direct and by his own declaration "annoying." He pronounced the world "utterly perverted" and blamed it on the absence of faithful preachers. Among perhaps 3,000 preachers, he contended, only four good ones could be found.[10] His words surely insulted some monks and priests who were present; but the same words presumably struck a positive chord in the laity, who resented the privileges enjoyed by their priests and bishops.

The stopover in Erfurt added Justus Jonas to the growing number of Luther's supporters. They became acquainted while Jonas was a law student in Wittenberg, and in 1519 Luther asked Lang to remember him to Jonas, who by then was teaching law in Erfurt.[11] Jonas might have remained in Erfurt, but in early 1521 his former professor in Wittenberg died. Whoever became his successor also became provost of the clergy chapter at the Castle Church in Wittenberg. Jonas was the ideal candidate. Since he had a doctorate in both civil and church law and was studying theology, he was qualified both to teach and to oversee the chapter. Elector Frederick was persuaded by Spalatin, his liaison for university affairs, to offer the position to Jonas, and negotiations were in progress when Luther arrived in Erfurt. By the time Luther left Erfurt on Sunday afternoon, Jonas had decided to join the travelers.

On a route Luther knew well the party rode through Thuringia to Eisenach. That evening Luther became so ill that a doctor was called to bleed him. After drinking schnapps,[12] he fell asleep and the next day was well enough to travel. To Luther the incident was Satan's attempt to disrupt the trip, and he swore that not even the gates of hell would stop him from entering Worms.[13] At Oppenheim the party boarded a ferry to cross the Rhine; they reached Worms on the morning of Tuesday, April 16, 1521. All accounts of the entry agree that it was a spectacle. The wagon was preceded by the imperial herald and a jester who sported a fool's cap and sang: "The one we sought so long has arrived at last; we expected you even when days were at their darkest."[14] When the Hungarian delegation invited Luther to lunch, the door had to be locked against a throng that tried to force its way inside.[15] Afterwards Luther was taken to rooms in the quadrangle occupied by the Knights of St. John, an order devoted to care of the sick. Two Saxon advisers and the imperial marshal were also quartered there because beds were in short supply. Before the diet began in January, Worms counted 7,000 residents; the population more than doubled while the diet was in session.

Luther was not a prisoner, but he was warned against strolling through town by himself. George Spalatin made sure that people who wanted to meet the notorious Wittenberger came to his quarters. Spalatin later claimed that God had given Luther the honor of being the most sought-after person at the diet; he received more visitors and drew more onlookers than the nobility in their finery.[16] One visitor was John Cochlaeus, who became Luther's antagonist and later wrote a hostile biography of the reformer.[17] He was personally incensed by Luther's criticism of the Roman sacraments, but he voiced another complaint that must have caused many people to resist the reformation: the painful loss of his parents' religion that was smeared and dishonored by Luther's arrogant attacks.[18] Another visitor was the sixteen-year-old landgrave, Count Philip, who ruled the strategic territory of Hesse and within a decade became the political and military leader of the Lutheran movement. Shortly before he died, Luther recalled Philip's visit in Worms. Philip, laughing, said: "I hear you teach that a wife can take another man when her husband can no longer perform the marital duty." Luther, also laughing, responded: "No, no, gracious lord, don't say that." When the visit was over, Philip offered his hand and said: "Good doctor, you are right; may God help you."[19] Nineteen years later Philip's support of Luther turned out to be a mixed blessing. In 1540 Philip committed bigamy, which violated the law of the Holy Roman Empire and made him susceptible to prosecution. In hindsight, the question Philip put to Luther was an omen of trouble to come.

On the morning of April 17, 1521, Luther learned that he was to appear before Emperor Charles V at four o'clock that afternoon. He was escorted to the meeting by the imperial marshal, who chose a back way in order to avoid curious onlookers. The meeting was not an official session of the diet but a special hearing held in the bishop's residence, where the emperor and his court were lodged. The room was small, but it was spacious enough for the emperor, the electors, their advisors, and a few delegates.[20] Luther was instructed to answer only those questions put to him by the emperor's spokesman, John Von der Ecken, who had organized the burning of Luther's books in Trier.[21] The first question, asked in Latin and in German, was: Did Luther write the books published under his name? Luther's legal counsel, Jerome Schurf, jumped to his feet and demanded that the titles be read aloud. Von der Ecken then read from a list that presumably corres- ponded to a stack of books and pamphlets on a bench under a window nearby. The list contained the Latin names of twenty-two works: twelve of them under the heading "Books of Martin Luther, German," and ten books designated as "Latin."[22] The second group included the one-volume edition of Luther's lectures on the first thirteen psalms, just published in Basel and ordered by Aleander from the Frankfurt book fair. After scanning the material for anti-papal statements, Aleander added it to the list of books that were presented to Luther on April 17 for his refutation.[23] Like most books on the list, however, the Psalms lectures were not an explicit source of the forty-one propositions damned as heretical by the pope. Hence Luther was being asked to recant a large amount of material that was not specifically condemned in the bull *Exsurge Domine.*[24]

We have two versions of the second question put to Luther by Von der Ecken: 1) Did he stand by the content of those writings? and 2) did he wish to recant anything in them? Either way, after Luther acknowledged the books as his own, he asked for time to think over his answer to the second question. With the emperor's consent, Luther was granted twenty- four hours. That evening he discussed his reply with Spalatin. Given the grave circumstances, it is likely that Schurf and Amsdorf, who worked with Luther on the *Address to the Christian Nobility*, were present to help. The next day, Thursday, April 18, 1521, Luther was again led to the bishop's residence, but the hearing occurred in a larger, torch-lit hall. Two hours passed before Emperor Charles and the princes ended their caucus and were ready for him. When asked for his reply, Luther, dressed in monastic garb, calmly delivered a speech first in German and then in Latin. As required, both were given without notes and each lasted ten to fifteen minutes.

Luther began by explaining why there was no reason for him to recant everything he had written. His books, said Luther, fell into three groups. First were those that explained Christian faith and life so plainly in accord with the gospel that even his critics admitted they were good and useful. The second group contained his censure of the papacy for devastating the entire Christian world. The third group consisted of direct replies to his adversaries. This last group, admitted Luther, contained abrasive language that did not become a monk; but he did not claim to be a saint and his deportment was not at issue. Finally, as requested, he had pondered the strict warning that his writings caused popular unrest and controversy; but, he continued, nothing made him happier than to see zeal and dissension arise on account of God's word. Jesus himself warned that division was inevitable: "I did not come to bring peace but a sword" (Matthew 10:34). The last comment may have sealed Luther's fate because it confirmed the fear of popular uprisings that haunted even his sympathizers. The princes, bishops, and urban envoys were all civil authorities bound to keep order in their domains. Heresy was a religious threat that provoked God's displeasure, but revolution led to anarchy that destroyed lives and the social order. Rulers could stomach a little heresy but not civil unrest. After Von der Ecken demanded a concise answer with no strings attached, Luther made his final statement: "Unless I am convinced otherwise by evidence from scripture or incontestable arguments, I remain bound by the scripture I have put forward. As long as my conscience is captive to the word of God, I neither can nor will recant, since it is neither safe nor right to act against conscience. God help me. Amen."[25]

It was a loaded reply that is still debated. What were "incontestable arguments"? Any argument can be contested. What did conscience mean to Luther in 1521? In particular, what did it mean for conscience to be captive to the word of God when the word of God itself was so complicated? If that word was "the Bible," how did sixteenth-century European Christians draw evidence from a complex written text composed mainly of Jewish traditions? Ever since authors of Christian scripture (the "new" testament) had employed proof texts from Hebrew scripture (the "old" testament), various methods of understanding biblical passages had been tried. Luther himself had admitted that different interpretations of the same text could be valid in different eras. In 1519, when he dedicated the first fascicle of his Psalms lectures to Elector Frederick, Luther confessed that his interpretations were not necessarily more correct than those of Augustine and other expositors who came before him. All interpreters viewed scripture through the lens of their own times and, conceded Luther, his understanding of a psalm would be superseded by the commentators who came after him. Why this humility? Because for Luther human beings were fallible creatures and life was fluid:

> Our life consists of beginning and progressing, not of reaching perfection. The person who has come nearest the Spirit is the better interpreter. If I attain the moon, I will not then assume I am the only one to grasp it nor will I look down on lesser stars. There are degrees of living and doing, why not also degrees of understanding? The apostle [Paul] says that we are transformed from clarity into clarity (2 Corinthians, 3:18).[26]

Although Luther was aware that different interpretations of scripture could be valid, he did not waver. His answer to Von der Ecken was the long version of a blunt statement he had made to Cardinal Cajetan three years earlier: "Divine truth is lord also over the pope, and I do not await human judgment when I have learned the judgment of God."[27] For Luther, the issue at stake in Worms was not *how* to interpret scripture but *who* could interpret scripture and discern the timely truth it contained. His "incontestable arguments" were based on *what* a text said and not on *who* offered the interpretation, that is, not on the pope's interpretation because he was pope. And his "conscience captive to the word of God" was not an internal moral meter that measured right or wrong, but loyalty to the highest authority on which one depended for the truth. For Luther in 1521, that authority was the gospel found in scripture.

Luther was a theology professor at an institution that did not promise freedom of speech. He had sworn allegiance both to the Roman Church and to holy scripture, which he was obligated to teach. Initially he saw no contradiction between them. The indulgence controversy, however, forced him to choose, and he confessed to Cajetan that his loyalty to scripture was higher than his loyalty to the pope. His conscience was now captive to scripture and not to papal interpretations of scripture, no matter how old they were or how divinely inspired they were claimed to be. Luther had just made the same point in defense of the forty-one articles declared heretical by *Exsurge Domine*. The papal bull did not refute any particular article, rather it rejected them *in toto* because they contradicted "Catholic truth" and because the church and its theologians had always taught differently from Luther. Luther did not agree and offered a hypothetical case to explain his reasoning: "If a Turk were to ask us Christians to give reasons for our faith, he would not care how long we have believed a certain thing or how many eminent people have believed it. We would have to ignore those things and direct the Turk to holy scripture as the basis for our faith. . . . Let my opponents now treat me in the same way."[28]

After his final refusal to recant, Luther was dismissed from the gathering and the Saxon delegation waited for Emperor Charles to decide Luther's fate. Because Frederick did not speak with his professor directly,[29] he summoned Spalatin, not Luther, to his quarters and told him that Luther had spoken well but was too audacious.[30] It was neither a compliment nor a rebuke but an expression of anxiety about the emperor's decision. This came quickly and contained no surprises. Because his family had always obeyed the Roman Church, said Emperor Charles, and because Luther would not move a hair's breadth from his errors, "we are not able to depart from the example of our ancestors in defending the ancient faith and giving aid to the Roman See. Therefore, we shall pursue Martin himself and his adherents with excommunication and use other methods available for their liquidation."[31] Despite the unconditional response, Charles allowed a committee of willing delegates to seek Luther's retraction one more time. The committee's convener, Archbishop Richard of Trier, was more than gracious, recalled Luther, but he insisted that his writings be judged by the gospel. That condition was non-negotiable.[32]

After the last attempt at compromise failed, Frederick's advisors told Luther that his safe conduct had been extended and he should leave Worms immediately. Upon learning that the Elector would shelter him, Luther reluctantly agreed. About mid-morning on April 26, 1521, he departed Worms with Jerome Schurf and Amsdorf, but without Justus Jonas, who had traveled with them to Worms.[33] Jonas returned directly to Erfurt in order to prepare his move to Wittenberg. After selling his house, vineyard, and other belongings to his step-brother Bertold, who was a priest in Erfurt,[34] Jonas headed for his new home. Luther's party also left Worms without their official escort, the imperial herald, but at Oppenheim the herald overtook the Wittenbergers before they crossed the Rhine and headed north.

The decision of Emperor Charles was not published until a month later. The official Edict of Worms made Luther and his supporters outlaws and remained in force even after Luther's death. While Luther was alive, however, the edict was a threat rather than a weapon because no attempt was made to enforce it in Luther's home territory. That arrangement was made after Elector Frederick implored Emperor Charles not to harass him with the edict. Charles complied and the edict was never published in Wittenberg or elsewhere in Electoral Saxony.[35] In hindsight the emperor's restraint is puzzling. But in 1521 either course of action—to capture Luther or to ignore him—entailed a political risk for the emperor. Charles owed his crown in part to Frederick's vote and he needed to maintain German political and military support. Moreover, no one at Worms, except perhaps Aleander, anticipated that Luther's resistance would fuel a movement that eventually cost the Roman Church half of its souls in Germany. A few months after the diet ended, an anonymous pamphlet called *The Passion of Doctor Martin Luther* conflated Luther's two weeks at the diet with the last days of Jesus. Pontius Pilate personified Emperor Charles and Pilate's wife the German nation. Using the words of Pilate's wife, the nation said to her husband, the emperor: "Have nothing to do with that innocent man [Luther], because during the night I suffered many things on his account. If he is burned, every bit of German liberty will also suffer because of him."[36] Charles had calculated that it was better to let Luther live in exile than to make him a heroic martyr whose death might convulse the nation.

By the time the Edict of Worms was published, Luther was clandestinely installed in the Wartburg fortress above the town of Eisenach. His journey from Worms to the Wartburg, however, was anything but secret. From Frankfurt he wrote to the painter Lucas Cranach, his friend in Wittenberg, that he would be hidden away in an unknown location, but he hoped that the words of Jesus applied to himself: "For a little while you will not see me, and again a little while you will see me (John 16:16)."[37] When the party reached Hersfeld, only thirty-five miles (fifty-six kilometers) from the Wartburg, Luther was wined and dined in the Benedictine cloister. In awe he reported to Spalatin what happened:

> You would not believe in what friendly fashion the abbot of Hersfeld received us! He sent the chancellor and treasurer a good mile out to meet us; then he himself together with many riders met us at his castle and accompanied us into town. The city council welcomed us inside the gate. The abbot fed us sumptuously in his monastery and made his private

chamber available for my use. On the fifth morning [after leaving Worms] they compelled me to preach. In vain I pled that the monastery might lose its royal privileges if the emperor's officials should interpret my sermon as a breach of the safe conduct, since they had forbidden me to preach while on my way. But I said that I had not consented for the word of God to be bound; and that is true.[38]

After lunch the trip resumed and, as the party approached Eisenach, people came out to escort them into town. It was the evening of May 2, 1521. The next morning the parish priest allowed Luther to deliver a sermon, but the priest played it safe by filing a notarized protest ahead of time.

From Eisenach Jerome Schurf headed north to Wittenberg while Amsdorf and Luther rode twelve miles south to Möhra, where Luther's grandfather had lived and his father had grown up. The next day they headed north through the Thuringian forest in the direction of Wittenberg. Before nightfall, near the Altenstein castle, two horsemen intercepted the party. Luther's Augustinian companion made a quick escape while Amsdorf and Luther, who expected something of the sort, stayed put. The captors were two of Elector Frederick's right-hand men: the castellan of the Wartburg, where Luther was taken, and the resident lord of Altenstein. They were not rogues but reliable noblemen with enough martial training to carry out the assignment without hurting anyone. After trotting fifteen miles (twenty-four kilometers) through the forest, Luther and his escort arrived at the Wartburg near midnight. The protracted journey—from Worms to the Wartburg—was quite different from the secretive mad dash portrayed in popular accounts. The friendly abduction in the forest was the climax of a long trip that, while no victory parade, was public and dignified nonetheless.

Today the Wartburg resembles a fortress, but it was built in the twelfth century as a palace for the counts of Thuringia. Additions and renovations, which demoted the palace to one of several buildings, continued until the late nineteenth century, but most of the fortress was finished by 1521, when Luther arrived. He was not the first noteworthy inhabitant. Princess Elisabeth of Hungary, later St. Elisabeth of Thuringia, was brought to the Wartburg in the early 1200s to prepare for her marriage, at age fourteen, to Count Ludwig IV. As the countess she began to spin wool and make clothes for the poor. At the foot of the Wartburg she built an infirmary and made regular visits to the patients. After her husband died, Elisabeth reclaimed her dowry, vowed not to remarry, and moved to Marburg, where a Gothic church was constructed in her honor after she was made a saint.

Although she left the Wartburg, scenes from her life, both real and legendary, adorn the "ladies' room" in the castle. In 1777 the poet Johann Wolfgang von Goethe spent five weeks at the Wartburg and left behind drawings of its decay. At the castle in 1817, 500 students celebrated the 300th anniversary of the reformation and a reunified Germany. Richard Wagner visited Eisenach and the fortress more than once. It provided the inspiration and location for his opera *Tannhäuser* (1845), which was based on legendary medieval song contests held at the castle.

In 1999 UNESCO designated the Wartburg a world heritage site, but for Luther it was a familiar landmark. Nowhere does he indicate it was a special place. Towering above Eisenach at the northwestern edge of the Thuringian forest, the fortress looked down on the gentle hills and spacious valley enclosing the town that was home to his mother's relatives and himself as a teenaged schoolboy. Luther must have noticed the irony of being secluded above the same landscape where twenty-five years earlier he was free to roam. Instead of earning more freedom through fame he had not sought, Luther was now a notorious outlaw in exile. He was given a spacious room at the end of a narrow passage behind the knights' quarters at the front of the fortress. His window looked out over the valley and presumably contained a bed, a table and chair, and a fireplace or stove. The furniture seen by visitors in the twenty-first century was not there, nor was the spot that allegedly was made by an inkwell Luther threw at the devil. A stairway led down to the chapel and food was delivered to the room during the risky first weeks. Later he was allowed in the courtyard, but outside the castle wall a sheer drop prevented easy access to the countryside.

Luther's custodian was the same captain who had intercepted him in the forest, Hans von Berlepsch; his job was to transform the monk and university professor, Martin Luther, into Junker Jörg, a knight of the lower nobility.[39] For the first time in sixteen years, Luther would not dress as a monk. A doublet replaced his monastic cowl and new hair filled in the monastic tonsure on his head. According to the portrait made by Lucas Cranach, Luther also grew a dark, unruly beard to mark his time as, in Luther's own words, a "strange prisoner, half willing and half unwilling."[40] Throughout the summer of 1521 Luther's whereabouts were a well-kept secret and some opponents never discovered the hiding place. The unflattering biography written in the 1540s by his Roman foe, Cochlaeus, alleged mistakenly that Luther had been held at a castle in the town of Allstedt.[41]

During the second week of his confinement, Luther sent out letters from a place he identified as the "kingdom of the birds" or "his Patmos," the

Greek island on which the evangelist John received visions recorded in the book of Revelation. One letter to Melanchthon was sent from "the land of the birds that sing sweetly in the branches and praise God night and day with all their might."[42] The letters reveal that he suffered from constipation and loneliness, but the ailments did not incapacitate him. Even in exile Luther adopted an enormous agenda. First, he completed a translation of Mary's song, the *Magnificat*, into German with his own commentary on the Lucan text (1:46-55). Since Mary sang the *Magnificat* after the angel's announcement that she would bear Jesus, it belonged to the Advent and Christmas seasons of the church year, for which Luther was also preparing postils. These postils were guides to preaching on the scripture lessons prescribed for each Sunday and festival in the church year. At the request of Elector Frederick, who was fond of devotional literature,[43] Luther had started work before traveling to Worms and he wanted to finish the first two seasons during his forced leisure at the Wartburg. The Christmas and Advent postils were published at the beginning of 1522, and over the years the texts were expanded by Luther and others to cover the entire church year. Owing to their vividness and simplicity, the postils sold well and introduced many readers to Luther's theology and biblical insights.

Heavier theological items were on Luther's plate for May and June; for example, replying to the Catholic theologian Jacob Latomus, a professor at the University of Louvain (Belgium). Born Jacob Masson about 1475, Latomus studied at Paris and joined the faculty at Louvain in 1510, remaining there until his death in 1544. In May 1521, Latomus published a comprehensive defense of the condemnation of Luther's writings issued by the University of Louvain in 1519. Luther also occupied his time with explaining the right use of confession and checking the first printing of his response to another Roman theologian, Ambrose Catharinus.[44] The replies to Latomus and Catharinus, written in Latin, are lucid but seldom-read solutions to crucial issues in Luther's theology. In response to Latomus, Luther defended his assertion that sin remained in believers even after they were baptized—an assertion that required him to give an explicit definition of sin and to explain how it could be present simultaneously with grace in the baptized believer. Luther summarized his position with the formula, "at the same time saint and sinner," which contradicted the medieval view that Christians had to be free of sin to become worthy in God's sight. Some of Luther's supporters misunderstood the formula to mean that Christians need not resist sinful impulses because everything was forgiven. On the contrary, Luther meant that Christian life was a constant struggle against sin, which believers could not avoid but which they could resist.

In response to Catharinus, who emphasized the certainty that believers gained from accepting the infallibility of the pope, Luther responded that the Roman Church was too corrupt to supply certain faith. Instead, believers must rely on the word of God in scripture and the guidance of the Spirit to interpret the Bible appropriately. Since Luther did not consider the Bible a timeless authority on every subject, his criterion was not easy to apply. But it left Christians free to disagree on many things except the gospel, the central message of scripture about God's love and compassion. That gospel, and no human authority, was for Luther the certain and sufficient ground of faith.

At the Wartburg Luther's greatest challenge was how to redefine himself. Elector Frederick, his employer at the university, refused to surrender him to Emperor Charles, but Luther could not assume that Frederick would reinstate a heretic and imperial outlaw in the chair of theology. Luther's teaching career might be over, and yet he told Melanchthon he might return to Wittenberg:

> I have not abandoned the hope of returning to you, only that God must do what is good in his eyes. If the pope will take steps against all who think as I do, then Germany will not be without uproar. The faster the pope undertakes this, the faster he and his followers will perish and I shall return. God is arousing the spirits of many, especially the hearts of the common people. It does not seem likely that this affair can be checked with force; if the pope begins to suppress it, it will become ten times bigger.[45]

Was Luther still a monk? In 1518 Staupitz had released Luther from the vow of obedience to his Augustinian superior. In the Reformed Congregation of strict Augustinians that superior was now his friend Wenzel Linck, but Linck worked out of Nuremberg, not Wittenberg. Would he risk dragging the entire Reformed Congregation into disrepute for Luther's sake alone? What should Luther do about his vows of poverty, chastity, and obedience? Was he obligated to uphold them even though his status as a monk was ambiguous? Where would he go if he survived and was allowed to leave the Wartburg? Back to the cloister in Wittenberg or to a destination outside the Holy Roman Empire, where he would not be pursued? These thoughts were troubling him during July, when an unspecified, week-long illness stopped him from writing and made him consider searching for a remedy in Erfurt or moving there for good.[46]

In mid-August Captain Berlepsch invited Luther to go hunting—perhaps to keep him from brooding. The experience was not uplifting:

> Last Monday I went hunting for two days to see what this bittersweet pleasure of heroes is like. We caught two hares and a few poor partridges—a worthy occupation indeed for men who have nothing to do! I theologized even among the snares and dogs. However great the pleasure of such a thing may be, the mystery of pity and pain mixed into it is equally great. For what else does this picture [of the hunt] signify if not the devil, who hunts innocent little creatures with his ambushes and his dogs—that is, with ungodly teachers, bishops, and theologians?[47]

It is hard to know whether Luther was weighed down more by his ailments or by the poor state of Christianity caused by its "ungodly" leaders. His first letter to Melanchthon combined complaints about physical discomfort with pessimism about the church:

> I sit here the whole day and imagine the state of the church that reminds me of Psalm 89: "Have you, God, created all of humanity in vain?" This abominable kingdom of the Roman Antichrist is a dismal manifestation of God's wrath. I curse the hardness of heart that prevents me from drowning in the tears I should weep for the slain of my poor people![48]

No one else knew the answers to Luther's questions about his future, not Elector Frederick or his advisors, not even Luther's closest friends and colleagues in Wittenberg, whose thoughts were elsewhere. They were busy considering changes to worship and religious life such as allowing priests, monks, and nuns to marry. In June of 1521 Karlstadt proposed a debate on the vow of celibacy, which was required of all clergy. When Luther was informed, he reflected on the issue in a letter to Melanchthon and decided that priestly celibacy was merely a human institution and anyone could dissolve it. But, Luther continued, he had no clear word of God concerning the celibacy of monks and nuns; he needed to examine the matter because he wanted to "help monks and nuns more than anything else," so greatly did he pity "these wretched men, boys, and girls who are vexed with pollutions and burnings."[49] Presumably Luther pitied them because he endured firsthand the frustration of sexual desires that gnawed at the monastic life. On the first day of November, Luther started an extended investigation into the difference between vows that were approved by scripture and pleasing to God and vows that were not. The published result, *A Judgment on Monastic Vows*, was completed by the end of 1521. In the midst of other projects, the 120 pages of Latin in the first printed edition[50] took less than two months to write.

As he wrote, Luther was remembering his own vow and the circumstances under which it was made. He recalled these events in the unusually personal dedication of the *Judgment*, which takes the form of a public letter to his father dated November 21, 1521.[51] Since the letter was written in Latin, his father could not have read it without a translator; it was mainly a reckoning with Martin's past that explained for himself and his peers the new direction his life was taking. Luther's career as an Augustinian friar had begun under the cloud of his father's disappointment; this had left Luther with regret and perhaps guilt over upsetting his father's plans for a good marriage and successful judicial career. The unpleasant meeting between them after his first mass in Erfurt had cut him to the quick, wrote Luther, but now he realized that his father's disappointment was only the expression of care for a son he loved. Moreover, his father had been right: he, Martin, should have complied with the fourth commandment to honor and obey his parents. Fortunately, he continued, God used the unwelcome experience to give Luther a fresh identity and a new purpose. Since his father could not drag him out of the monastery, God stepped in, liberated him, and made out of Luther a new creature, "not of the pope but of Christ."[52]

As a consequence, Luther now believed he was called to lead a movement that would bring to other children the same freedom that he now enjoyed. To his father Luther expressed it this way: "I hope that [Christ] has snatched one son from you in order that through me he might begin to help many of his other children; and I am convinced that you will not only willingly allow this, as you ought, but also rejoice at it with great joy!" To be free, however, Luther had to subject himself to a new authority, one which replaced both his father and the pope to whom his conscience had once been bound. In Luther's own words:

> I am sending you this book, so that you can see by what signs and wonders Christ absolved me of the monastic vow and granted me so much liberty that, although he has made me the servant of all, I am subject to no one but him alone. He is my immediate bishop, abbot, prior, lord, father, and teacher. I accept no other.[53]

From this point on, freedom for Luther meant living bound to Christ, and that freedom made him much more than a protester against indulgences or a critic of the pope. Now he was a man with a larger vision of what religion could be and a mission to realize that vision by making other people free. The decisive turning point in his life was not the ninety-five theses or the Diet of Worms. It happened at the Wartburg, where he adopted a new identity and a new purpose that he believed to have come from God. It was based on a vision of what Christianity could become – a vision he was intent on pursuing. As time went on, however, Luther was surprised to discover that not everybody agreed with his vision or wanted the same freedom that he now enjoyed.

PART TWO

PURSUIT OF A VISION
1522–1546

CHAPTER NINE

MASTER OF A THOUSAND ARTS
1522–1523
Wartburg—Wittenberg

"Woe betide all our teachers that go on their merry way spouting whatever comes into their head. . . . They forget the devil is beside them injecting his fiery darts, that is, the most enticing thoughts adorned with scripture. No warnings or threats will do any good. The devil is the master of a thousand arts."[1]

While Luther was at the Wartburg, a reformation broke out in Wittenberg. It happened not according to a grand plan but in fits and starts. It was marked by disagreements, demonstrations, and defections, by steps forward and steps back. In Wittenberg and most other places, the reformation was not pretty and the result never pleased everyone, not even Luther. For him, the devil, that "master of a thousand arts," was always thinking up ways to undermine his work.

In Wittenberg the leaders of reform were Luther's colleagues, Philip Melanchthon and Andrew Karlstadt.[2] Melanchthon was much younger, but Karlstadt and Luther were impressed by his scholarship and concern for the church. Immediately after arriving at the Wartburg, Luther wrote to Melanchthon, saying they should pray for each other, so that "together they might bear the burden that lay before them."[3] Karlstadt called Melanchthon the "chief leader of the Wittenberg church,"[4] but he and Melanchthon were only two of the many whom Luther named among his Wittenberg supporters: Nicholas Amsdorf and Peter Swawe, who accompanied Luther to Worms; John Agricola, a former student and close friend, who assisted Luther at the Leipzig Disputation;[5] the jurist John Schwertfeger; brothers Jacob Propst, Henry of Zütphen, and Conrad Helt at the Augustinian cloister; the artist Lucas Cranach; the goldsmith Christian Döring; and

Dr. Eschaus, his personal physician.[6] Luther's support was centered at the university but it included prominent townsmen and Augustinian friars.

The above-named were joined by two men who became part of Luther's inner circle: John Bugenhagen from Pomerania, who arrived at the university in 1521, and Justus Jonas, who moved from Erfurt the same year. Jonas' former idol, the humanist Erasmus, was disappointed to learn that Jonas had now become a fan of Luther. Explaining to Jonas why he could not do the same, Erasmus wrote:

> You will ask me, dearest Jonas, why I spin this long complaint to you when it is already too late. For this reason: Although things have gone farther than they ought to have, we should be watchful in case it is possible to still this dreadful storm. We have a pope most merciful by nature, we have an emperor whose spirit is mild and forgiving. . . . If there are things we do not like in the men whose judgment governs human affairs, my view is that we must leave them to their Lord and Master. If their commands are just, it is reasonable to obey; if unjust, it is a good man's duty to endure them, lest worst befall. If our generation cannot endure Christ in his fullness, it is something nonetheless to preach him as far as we may.[7]

Undeterred, in June of 1521, Jonas declared his acceptance of the Wittenberg theology: "The truth of God has sounded forth from Wittenberg and the word of the Lord has appeared in Saxony."[8] Hand in hand with this acceptance went Jonas' refusal to lecture on church law, although, as provost of the All Saints' Chapter, he was obligated to do so. The chapter consisted of priests, called canons, who performed liturgical and pastoral duties at the Castle Church. After negotiating with Spalatin, the course on canon law was assigned to another professor and Jonas was allowed to give lectures in the theology faculty.[9]

Of the sympathizers it was Karlstadt who took the first steps toward religious change. When three priests in the vicinity violated their vows of celibacy and took wives, Karlstadt supported them by declaring that vows taken by priests and monks were null and void. Melanchthon agreed. When Luther was drawn into the debate, he was not fully persuaded by the arguments of either colleague. But he was ready to make an exception for minors whose monastic vows were not truly free: "I am almost ready to decide that those who entered this abyss [monastic life] before or during the age of puberty can leave it with a clear conscience, but about those who have grown old and lingered in this estate, I am not certain."[10] That was in

August of 1521. By November he was certain everyone could leave; and he started an attack on monastic vows in order to "free the young people from that hell of celibacy, totally unclean and condemned as it is through its burning and pollutions; I am writing partly because of my own experiences and partly because I am indignant."[11]

The next issue was reform of the mass. In 1520 Luther rejected the medieval notion that the mass was a refined reenactment of the sacrifice of Jesus. He insisted that biblical accounts of the Last Supper considered it a testament, that is, a promise made by Christ to the disciples before he died. The promise was the forgiveness of sins for all who received the body and blood of Christ in the form of bread and wine. To Karlstadt, the late medieval practice of withholding wine from the laity also contradicted the intention of Jesus, and in July of 1521 he declared it was a sin not to offer all Christians both bread and wine. Luther did not agree that receiving both elements was compulsory: "The Lord's Supper is Christ's institution, to be used in freedom, and it cannot be imprisoned either in whole or in part."[12] Still, he was "very pleased" that Melanchthon and Karlstadt were restoring the reception of both elements to the communion table. Luther declared that never in all eternity would he say another private mass, that is, celebrate mass without communicants present. Private masses violated the intention of Jesus; and the custom of paying priests to say private masses for special occasions made the mass, so argued Luther, a commodity. In November 1521, when he started the attack on monastic vows, he had just finished a book that argued for the abolition of private masses.[13]

Since Luther and his colleagues did not agree on everything, they faced the challenge of making decisions about reform when one or more of them was undecided or thought a specific change might lead to sin. From the Wartburg Luther offered a solution. In words that are frequently quoted but often misunderstood, Luther urged Melanchthon to take action even if undecided:

> If you are a preacher of grace, then preach a true and not a fictitious grace; if grace is true, you must bear a true and not a fictitious sin. God does not save people who are only fictitious sinners. Be a sinner and sin boldly, but believe and rejoice in Christ even more boldly, for he is victorious over sin, death, and the world. As long as we are in this world we have to sin. This life is not the dwelling place of righteousness but, as Peter says, we look for a new heaven and a new earth in which righteousness dwells (2 Peter 3:13). It is enough that by the riches of God's glory we have come to know the

Lamb that takes away the sin of the world (John 1:29). No sin will separate
us from the Lamb, even though we commit fornication and murder a thousand times a day.[14]

Although Luther mentioned fornication and murder, the sin he urged
Melanchthon boldly to accept was not immoral behavior but the imperfect
results of making changes in the mass. If Melanchthon decided to do
nothing, he would sin, and if he decided to take action, he would also sin.
To make the mass conform to what Jesus intended was right even if the
changes were not perfect. In short, "sin boldly" was not a license to unleash
lust, avarice, and hatred, but encouragement to take proper action despite
imperfect results. Without that policy, the reform movement would have
stalled more often than it did.

Melanchthon understood what Luther meant. Although not a priest,
on September 29, the feast of St. Michael, he and several students celebrated the sacrament by receiving both bread and wine. Gabriel Zwilling,
an Augustinian brother whose public sermons earned him the reputation
of a second Luther, also understood.[15] On October 6, Zwilling announced
he would say no more private masses and dissuaded the students and
townspeople from attending public masses where the elements were adored
and wine was reserved for the priest. The new form of mass emphasized
preaching the gospel, offering bread *and* wine to everyone, and speaking in
German the words that Jesus spoke at the Last Supper when he instituted
the sacrament. At the Castle Church, however, most of the priests did not
like the new form, and their resistance forced Elector Frederick, who
wanted no dissension, into action. First, he ordered dissenting priests and
the university professors who approved the changes to resolve their disagreement.[16] Second, he appointed a committee to investigate the influence
of Zwilling at the Augustinian cloister. The committee was not a neutral
body. The members—Melanchthon, Karlstadt, Jonas, Jerome Schurf and
one of Frederick's advisors, Christian Beyer[17]—all favored the reforms. The
committee found that Zwilling's followers in the monastery were mainly
Augustinians from the Netherlands, whose spokesman was Henry of
Zütphen. Henry justified in writing the changes that Zwilling had
announced and proposed that Luther's opinion be solicited prior to a final
decision.[18] Before that could be done, in early November of 1521 thirteen
of the forty Augustinians left the cloister with Zwilling.[19]

At the beginning of December Luther traveled secretly to Wittenberg
in order to see his friends. Nothing indicates that he was unhappy with any

of the reforms, apart from the exit of Augustinian brothers. He did not dispute their right to leave but wished he could be sure they left with clear consciences.[20] To remain out of sight he lodged in Amsdorf's house instead of the cloister and was visited by Melanchthon and the painter Lucas Cranach. Before Luther left Wittenberg, however, anticlerical violence by students and townspeople erupted. On December 3, after barging into the Town Church, they wrenched missals from the priests, chased them from the altars, and pelted them with stones. The next day, the feast of St. Barbara, the tumult moved to the Franciscan cloister. Signs posted at the entrance ridiculed the monks, and a wooden altarpiece was ripped apart by a group that forced its way into the church. Two days later forty rowdy students and citizens marched through town, showing their daggers and threatening to storm the cloister and kill the monks. The city council told Elector Frederick that under such conditions it was not willing to endorse reforms. It looked as if the nascent reformation might last no longer than a few months.

Before returning to the Wartburg Luther gave a positive evaluation of his visit: Except for the fact that Spalatin had withheld three of his manuscripts from publication, "everything else that I hear and see pleases me very much. May the Lord strengthen the spirit of those who want to do right."[21] Luther agreed with the Wittenberg colleagues on the major issues they had discussed: monastic vows, private masses, and offering both bread and wine to the laity. And he promised to deliver a public warning against violent measures. True to his word, on December 14 he sent from the Wartburg another manuscript to Spalatin: *A Sincere Admonition to All Christians to Guard against Insurrection and Rebellion.* Those who have read my writings, claimed Luther, and understand them correctly, cause no sedition. He would always side with those who opposed revolution, because, first, the new order never lived up to expectations and, second, insurrection was incited by the devil in order to discredit reforms made according to the gospel.[22] From now on, the reformation in Luther's eyes became an uphill battle against the wiles of the devil, who tried to suppress it at every turn.

In Wittenberg the devil appeared to be asleep while the reform movement was picking up steam. Its supporters at the university and the Augustinian cloister were joined by townspeople who submitted to the council in December of 1521 their own demands for reform. They asked for: 1) unhindered preaching of God's word; 2) no compulsory public masses; 3) no relics, processions, vigils, lay brotherhoods, or private masses; 4) wine for the laity at the Lord's Supper; 5) shuttering taverns; and 6) closing the houses of prostitution. That was too much reform for Elector Frederick. In mid-December he ordered the citizens to make no further changes in worship and to leave the priests alone.[23]

Despite Frederick's ruling, Karlstadt stepped forward and rekindled the fervor for change. Just before Christmas, he announced that on January 1, 1522, he would preach and preside at an "evangelical mass after the manner instituted by Christ." He promised to distribute bread and wine to the laity, speak only in German the words of Jesus at the Last Supper,[24] and omit the long prayer of thanksgiving and consecration called the canon of the mass. When Karlstadt discovered the Elector's advisors were planning to block his service, he moved it to December 25 and held it in the Castle Church. The night before, Christmas eve, there were more disturbances in both the Town Church and the Castle Church, but Karlstadt's sermon on Christmas day calmed things down. Wearing his academic gown instead of clerical vestments, he explained to the congregants that the evangelical mass was for everyone who had faith in God's promise of forgiveness. Then, to the surprise of many, he celebrated the Lord's Supper in German and distributed both elements by placing the host and the chalice into the hands of each person. Old superstitions persisted, however. After two wafers were dropped during the distribution, no one but Karlstadt dared to pick them up, because wafers had been adored as the sacred body of Christ and were rarely handled by the laity.[25] The service was reportedly attended by more than a thousand people, including the mayor and other town leaders. The number must be exaggerated since a thousand worshipers made up half the population of Wittenberg; but similar numbers were reported in early January for German masses at the Town Church.

A day or two after Christmas visitors from the town of Zwickau arrived in Wittenberg to make contact with Melanchthon and Amsdorf. One visitor, Nicholas Storch, was a weaver. He belonged to a company of cloth workers who gathered around an outspoken Zwickau priest named Thomas Müntzer. Storch was a layman whose spiritual insights into the Bible convinced Müntzer that Storch had more right to preach than the priests. The town council, alerted to this irregularity and fearful of a rumored secret brotherhood, summoned Storch to a hearing that he avoided by fleeing with two companions toward Wittenberg. The companions were Thomas Drechsel and a former student at Wittenberg, Marcus Stübner, and all three lodged temporarily with Karlstadt.[26] Melanchthon, and Amsdorf to a lesser degree, were impressed by their claims to special revelations but not by their rejection of infant baptism. They asked Elector Frederick to recall

Luther who responded only by mail. He felt sure the "Zwickau prophets," as Luther called them,[27] should not be taken seriously. So far they had not done or said anything that Satan could also not do. They should be tested, he told Melanchthon, by inquiring if they had suffered spiritual distress. Scripture described direct encounters with God as marked by terror and consternation. Luther advised Melanchthon not to listen when the "prophets" talked of the glorified Christ unless he had first seen in them the crucified Jesus.[28]

The visit of the "prophets" from Zwickau was not, however, a mere oddity. Their connection to Karlstadt and Müntzer signaled the presence in and around Wittenberg of serious dissent from Luther's view of how reform should proceed. Müntzer himself was in Wittenberg before Luther returned from the Wartburg on March 6, 1521. Around the end of March Müntzer discussed controversial reforms with both Melanchthon and the newly-arrived John Bugenhagen, who was staying in Melanchthon's house.[29] By that time, open conflict had erupted between Karlstadt and Luther over the degree and pace of reform.

In 1522 Karlstadt and Jonas expanded the changes Karlstadt had initiated in Wittenberg. Both were priests at the All Saints' Chapter as well as university professors. Karlstadt preached twice on Fridays and replaced the evening services with a reading from the Bible. Instead of celebrating a Latin mass on weekday mornings, Jonas read a psalm and interpreted it in German for those present. Amsdorf, who also belonged to the All Saints' Chapter, went further. He refused to accept his prebend, which was his portion of the income generated by property that had been donated or bequeathed to the chapter. Amsdorf had no plan to marry and was probably well-off, but to keep him at the university Elector Frederick promised to pay him the amount of the prebend as salary.[30] Karlstadt took a bigger step. On December 26, 1521, the day after the evangelical mass in the Castle Church, he took Melanchthon and Jonas to the village of Seegrehna, across the Elbe from Wittenberg, where they witnessed his engagement to Anna von Mochau. When Karlstadt and Anna married on January 19, 1522, he became the first priest among the Wittenberg reformers to act on their agreement that vows of celibacy were no longer binding. One month later Justus Jonas, who had resided in Wittenberg less than a year, followed Karlstadt's example by marrying a local woman, Katharina Falcke. Until she died twenty years later, Jonas' Katharina was respected and admired by their colleagues. In 1529, the Wittenberg town clerk-to-be reported he was amazed when he saw Melanchthon dancing with Katharina Jonas.[31]

At the Wartburg Luther started 1522 by working on the project for which his exile is best known: a German translation of the New Testament. He mentioned the project to John Lang in December, only three months before the end of his ten-month stay. It was not his own idea, wrote Luther, but a suggestion from "friends." During his visit to Wittenberg he may have heard that Lang, whose specialty was Greek, was also working on a translation.[32] Actually, Lang was translating only the gospel of Matthew while Luther planned to translate all twenty-seven books, a project he miraculously completed before leaving the Wartburg on March 1, 1522. Such speed would be unbelievable without the testimony of Melanchthon, who reported in a letter dated March 6 that Luther arrived in Wittenberg with a German translation of "the entire New Testament."[33] His translation was based on the second edition (1519) of Erasmus' Greek New Testament, which was supplemented by Erasmus' Latin translation and hundreds of annotations. They explained how Erasmus chose the best Greek text using the same method as modern biblical scholars: comparing the texts of very old Greek manuscripts and deciding which word or phrase was likely the oldest and most reliable reading.[34] A close examination of Paul's letter to the Galatians demonstrated that Luther overwhelmingly chose the Greek text to translate instead of the Latin. Of the sixty places where the Greek text of Galatians differed from the Latin translation, Luther chose the Latin version only six times.[35]

Apparently Luther did not expect to finish the translation at the Wartburg. In January of 1522 he wrote to Amsdorf that he might return to Wittenberg after Easter so that he could work on the New Testament translation with colleagues. Admitting he had "shouldered a burden beyond his power," he inquired about staying with Amsdorf; for the translation "is a great and worthy undertaking on which we all should work, since it is a public matter and should be dedicated to the common good."[36] Although Luther returned with a complete text, he asked the best Greek scholar in Germany, his colleague Melanchthon, to check the text and help to prepare it for publication.[37] It was a linguistic match made in heaven: Melanchthon the master of Greek and Luther the wizard of down-to-earth German. May had arrived before the first sheets of the manuscript, which Luther called a "taste of *our* new Bible," were ready for the press.[38] The pronoun is significant. Too often Luther alone is given credit for what he accomplished with the skillful assistance of others. The raw translation was indeed "his," but the German New Testament that was finally published in September of 1522 belonged to Luther, Melanchthon, and perhaps others.

Before Luther returned, however, there was another disturbance in Wittenberg. On January 6, 1522, the Reformed Congregation of Augustinians convened at their cloister in Wittenberg. Staupitz had left the order and the new vicar-general was Wenzel Linck, formerly of Wittenberg, who traveled from Nuremberg to preside at the gathering. Luther stayed at the Wartburg and did not attend, but John Lang, his long-time friend, came from Erfurt. As Luther hoped, the convention adopted articles of reform that permitted brothers to leave the order. A few days later, however, Gabriel Zwilling instigated a destruction of its sacred objects. Wooden altars and fixtures were smashed and set on fire in the yard, along with pictures, statues, banners, and selected altar vessels. Antagonistic characters such as Zwilling, who destroyed objects that were formerly considered sacred channels of divine power, were angry at the deceit perpetrated on them by the pre-reformation church. Convinced that saints had not brought them closer to God, they chopped off their hands, knocked off their heads, and sometimes defaced and burned pictures of them. This kind of destruction, an instance of iconoclasm, was by no means limited to Wittenberg. It was a common feature of Protestant reform, wherever it took place, and figures of saints without arms or hands can still be found in churches and museums. They are reminders of the fierce emotions that also drove the reformation.

After the town of Wittenberg finally adopted reforms on January 24, 1522, Luther decided to return home. His decision was prompted in part by the calamity at the cloister two weeks earlier but also by the new ordinance that would make reforms compulsory before everyone was ready to accept them. Frederick wanted Luther to remain at the Wartburg, but Luther did not comply. Before leaving the Wartburg on March 1, 1522, Luther announced his intention to Frederick by describing himself as a painful relic for the Elector's collection:

> Grace and congratulations from God the father upon your new relic! I have chosen this greeting, my gracious lord, instead of the usual polite address. For many years your princely grace has sought to acquire relics from every possible land, but now God has answered your prayers and without your effort or expense has sent me like an entire cross with nails, spears and whips. Fear not, but stretch out your arms on this cross and allow the nails to sink in; be thankful and joyful.[39]

Frederick was not amused. As soon as he learned his "new relic" was on the road to Wittenberg, he asked Luther to proceed no further. Instead of turning around, Luther sent another letter that expressed his love and concern for the Elector and his own consternation at "the ideas of the devil now unfolding in this drama." As a minister and evangelist who received the gospel directly from heaven, Luther said he was compelled by his conscience to undo what the devil had done during his absence.[40] It was Luther's first opportunity to present himself in the independent pastoral and missionary role acquired at the Wartburg and to take action in that role. As the servant of Christ alone, he was not obligated to obey the Elector; his mission was to gather and guard the people of Christ from the wiles of the devil. He had to return because, in his mind, he alone knew what was best for his flock.

Luther's letter was not a direct answer to the question of why he was returning at a time so inopportune. Frederick needed an explicit statement that he could present to the imperial government and requested Jerome Schurf, Luther's friend and counsel at Worms, to solicit it. After declaring that his return was not meant to flout the authority of any government, Luther gave three reasons: 1) He was "called by the whole congregation at Wittenberg in a letter filled with urgent begging and pleading." Since the letter is not extant, there is no way to verify its content. 2) Satan had intruded into his fold at Wittenberg. The sheep were entrusted to him by Christ, and since some were injured, he must minister to them personally and not simply in writing. 3) He feared a rebellion through which God would punish the German nation. At the Diet of Worms he learned that German princes and magistrates constantly worried about popular uprisings. Exaggerating the danger, therefore, might impress the emperor that his return was wise.

Luther arrived in Wittenberg on Thursday, March 6. Except for the anonymous visit in early December he had been out of town eleven months. The town council welcomed him with a gift of cloth for a new cowl.[41] On Friday or Saturday he gave to Schurf the reasons for his return. Then, on March 9, the first Sunday in Lent, Luther donned his monastic garb and preached in the Town Church. The sermon was the first of eight that together are known as the Invocavit (liturgical name for the first Sunday in Lent), or Wittenberg sermons. Their purpose was to establish new terms for the progress of reform in Wittenberg—terms that distinguished between changes it was necessary to make immediately and changes that were optional but which should become permanent when people were ready. Changes in the mass could not be postponed. There could be no long prayer of consecration that implied the mass reenacted the sacrifice of

Jesus; the words of institution taken straight from the New Testament had to be spoken aloud and clearly in German; no private masses, not even those that were endowed, could be celebrated. Luther preferred that both wine and bread be offered to everyone, but people who were not ready to receive the wine or take the wafer into their hands should be given time to adjust. The mode of receiving the elements, in the hand or on the tongue, did not threaten the forgiveness of sin promised by Jesus: "This is my body given for you; this is my blood shed for you." Not long after the eight sermons he wrote: "Let all Christians store these words in their hearts and meditate upon them when they receive the sacrament. For these words are a thousand times more important than the elements; without them the sacrament is not a sacrament but a mockery before God."[42]

During the eight sermons, Luther named five traditional practices that should remain optional: clerical celibacy, monastic vows, sacred statues and pictures, fasting, and private confession. In every case he followed the policy that he summarized as: "Do not make what is free into a must."[43] Priests and monks should be allowed to marry; all monastic vows could be revoked and both nuns and monks were free to leave their orders; sacred images did not have healing or saving power but need not be destroyed; fasting was optional; private confession was helpful but it was not mandatory and people should not be forced to name every sin they could recall. The reform of images caused the biggest stir, and the sermon Luther preached on this topic was printed separately in eight editions. For receiving the immediate supernatural help that people desired, the cult of saints had long been more important than the mass. For people whose piety centered on praying to saints at altars beneath their statues or pictures, it was hard to grasp how images could serve merely as decoration and inspiration.

Luther's sermons did not mention Karlstadt, the main promoter of reforms in Luther's absence. But the sermons publicly contradicted Karlstadt's views on two points. Karlstadt insisted on offering both bread and wine during communion and argued that pictures and statues had to be removed from the Town Church. There was, however, a more funda-mental disagreement between Karlstadt and Luther. Karlstadt had published a pamphlet which argued that any town that allowed begging and visual images in the churches could not be Christian. The title page proclaimed that Karlstadt now lived in a different town, the "Christian city of Wittenberg." His definition of Christian was based on the Bible, both parts of which, the Old and New Testaments, had for him equal authority. The removal of pictures and statues was based on the prohibition of graven images in the Ten Commandments, and the injunction against begging was based on the fifteenth chapter of Deuteronomy and the twenty-fifth chapter of Matthew. It appeared that Karlstadt's goal was the creation of a Christian society defined by regulations based on specific biblical passages.

Luther had fundamental objections to the way Karlstadt decided what was Christian. In the first place, Luther opposed anything that defined Christians by a set of specific rules and regulations. Living seventeen years in two monasteries where every detail was prescribed or proscribed was enough for Luther. Since 1519, when he first attached the Greek word for "free" to his signature, liberty had grown on him. Choosing to appear in monastic garb for his first sermon back in Wittenberg was itself an act of freedom that he publicly acknowledged: "If the pope or anyone tried to force me to wear only the [monk's] cowl, I would defy that person and refuse. But now, of my own free will, I choose to wear it as long as I want, and when I no longer feel like wearing it, I will lay it aside."[44] At the Wartburg, Luther not only wrote about freedom but also felt it intensely: "What difference does it make," he wrote to his father, "whether I retain or lay aside the cowl and the tonsure? Do they make the monk? Shall I belong to the cowl? Or is it not true that the cowl belongs to me? My conscience has been freed, and that is the greatest liberation we can have."[45]

In the second place, Luther viewed the Bible differently from Karlstadt, and by 1522 both had realized it.[46] Sometimes, like Karlstadt, Luther based his opinions on single verses of scripture. He thought that 1 Timothy 3:2 and 1 Corinthians 14:34 prohibited women from being ordained and that Luke 6:34 precluded the charging of interest.[47] Luther realized, however, that the world was imperfect and that eradicating the charging of interest was unlikely: "Lending money at interest, as it has thus far been practiced, is un-Christian. It is probably not possible that this practice could ever be curbed and turned into a decent system, since all the world is greedy and always looks out for its own interest."[48] Luther did not, therefore, define Christians by strict adherence to those regulations, because for him the Bible was not a law code for Christian conduct. It was a declaration of freedom based on what he called the gospel. For Luther that gospel was "our guide and instructor in the scriptures."[49] It was the good news of God's promise to forgive human sin and redeem a fallen world. The pamphlet *Freedom of a Christian*, which Luther sent to Pope Leo in 1520, described how Christians were able to live by the gospel: "This is authentic Christian living, where faith is truly active through love, that is, it finds expression in works of the freest service, cheerfully and lovingly done, with which we willingly serve one another without hope of reward."[50] Luther made it more explicit in the 1522 pamphlet entitled *Receiving Both Kinds*:

> I have taught in such a way that my teaching would lead first and foremost to a knowledge of Christ, that is, to pure and proper faith and genuine love, and thereby to freedom in all matters of external conduct, such as eating, drinking, clothes, praying, fasting, monasteries, sacrament, and whatever it may be. Such freedom is used in a salutary way only by those who have faith and love, that is, those who are real Christians. On such people we can and should impose no human law—nor permit anyone else to do so—which would bind their conscience.[51]

Applying evangelical freedom to the Lord's Supper, Luther wrote: "We are not Christians because we grasp the bread and chalice with our hands but because we have faith and love."[52]

Luther's return to Wittenberg signaled the end of Karlstadt's leading role in the evangelical movement. It had to do less with Luther than with Elector Frederick, who refused to budge on his order to forgo religious innovations. Luther's sermons slowed down the pace of reform, and Karlstadt was unjustly forbidden to preach or publish. He blamed Luther. Writing to a friend in Nuremberg, Karlstadt reported how Luther, "the good father," insisted on sparing out of love those who were not ready for change and how Luther's soft approach was more attractive than Karlstadt's tougher standard. In Karlstadt's own words: "The honey-lined net was more effective than the unyielding fetter."[53] Upon Luther's return to Wittenberg, the majority of colleagues openly acknowledged him as the movement's leader; and Karlstadt, one of Luther's oldest colleagues and earliest supporters, had to watch from the sideline. He was a casualty of the Elector's need for reforms to be restrained and delayed. It was not, however, the end of his relationship with Luther.

After posing as Knight George in a castle, albeit in exile, returning to a cell in the Wittenberg cloister had to be a letdown for Luther. The monastery was not completely empty, but communal life as it existed before he departed for Worms was severely disrupted. By mid-November of 1522 Luther and the last prior, Eberhard Brisger,[54] were the only brothers in the building. Brisger wanted to leave and if he did, Luther could find no reason to stay behind and "would have to see where God will provide for me." Luther nevertheless had a plan. He asked Elector Frederick to offer him and Brisger a nearby property belonging to the monastery. Instead of a public deed the city council might challenge, Luther wanted the Elector to "look the other way" and give him a private deed to the property. Brisger's inheritance could have paid for the lot, but that proved unnecessary because both men were allowed to stay in the cloister.[55] That lasted three years, until 1525, when the monastery was given to Martin and Katharina as a wedding present.

Before leaving the Wartburg, Luther decided not to continue his lectures on the Psalms, even if he were permitted to teach again in Wittenberg. As a result, he did not lecture again until February of 1523, when he started a course on Deuteronomy that quickly attracted students and auditors. A letter to Elector Frederick dated May 24, 1523, reported that more than one hundred students and other folk were coming from Leipzig to "hear the gospel" from Luther's lips.[56] Besides lecturing Luther had plenty to do: translating, writing, correspondence, preaching, and short trips outside Wittenberg where his arrival might be divulged ahead. Although he was widely known, Luther still considered himself a pastor of Wittenberg Christians: "Satan attempted to wreak so much damage in my flocks," he wrote, "that I could not combat him without causing a great commotion."[57] Luther's local ministry, however, was mainly symbolic. He preached often in the Town Church but he was not the parish pastor; in 1523 the town council elected John Bugenhagen to that office. Since arriving in Wittenberg two years earlier, Bugenhagen had studied theology while teaching classes on the Bible in a private capacity and as adjunct lecturer in the university. Luther asked Spalatin to take money from another professorship and appoint Bugenhagen to the regular faculty because, next to Melanchthon, Bugenhagen was the best professor in town.[58] Instead, and despite opposition from priests at the Castle Church,[59] Bugenhagen became pastor at the Town Church and did not join the university faculty until 1533.

Correspondence took up much of Luther's time. He received local requests in addition to inquiries from afar. In one case he interceded on behalf of a fisherman who was poaching on waters reserved for the Elector and fined 600 pieces of silver. Luther argued that the punishment should not bankrupt the man but only teach him a lesson. Eight days on bread and water was sufficient penalty for a poor man, but the rich "might have to open their purses."[60] Soon after his return, Luther explained to Wenzel Linck why he blamed not only Satan for the public disturbances in Wittenberg, but also Karlstadt and Zwilling. Luther reported, however, that Zwilling had come to his senses and was a "different person." It must have been true, because Zwilling's career turned out to be surprisingly stable.

Most of his remaining years were spent in a prominent pastorate at Torgau, the primary residence of Elector Frederick's brother, Duke John. Luther also told Linck why he had left the Wartburg without permission. The cause of reform had been compromised by Karlstadt and Zwilling, who misled the people and turned Wittenberg into a "theater of Satan." Luther was "forced" to return in order to destroy Satan's work.[61] Behind those words was Luther's conviction that God had given to him, not to Karlstadt or Zwilling, the cause of renewing Christendom and that he, Luther, was subject to no other authority.

In June of 1522 Luther also contacted Staupitz for the first time since before his appearance at the Diet of Worms. Having heard that Staupitz was now the abbot of St. Peter's Benedictine monastery in Salzburg, Luther expressed disapproval and said he could not believe it was God's will. Mainly, however, Luther defended himself against rumors that his own writings caused great offense and were praised only by men who patronized brothels. The truth was, claimed Luther, he was doing nothing but publicizing the pure word of God and could not control how people misused it. Even if great disturbances and monstrosities have arisen, Staupitz should see in them God's counsel and mighty hand. Addressing Staupitz as "my father," he continued:

Remember how from the beginning my cause has always seemed terrible and intolerable to the world and yet has grown stronger day by day? It will also prevail over that which you so deeply fear if you just wait a little while. Satan feels his wound; that is why he rages so and throws everything into confusion. But Christ, who has begun this work, will tread him under foot and all the gates of hell will resist Christ in vain.[62]

Staupitz had set Luther on the path of reform, but Luther did not want him to be disappointed or feel responsible for what Luther did. The cause turned out to be momentous in a way neither could imagine: a cosmic contest between Christ and the devil to be settled on the Last Day. Staupitz chose to withdraw from the battle, but Luther charged on: "I am daily challenging Satan and his armor all the more, in order to hasten the Day of Christ when he will destroy the Antichrist."[63]

Almost two years passed before Staupitz wrote back. His faith in Christ and the gospel had persevered and his love for Luther was unbroken. But no battle with the devil was mentioned, no Antichrist, no Last Day. No criticism of Luther either, only the admission that he did not understand

Luther's attacks on so many external things that did not, in the experience of Staupitz, affect genuine faith or burden consciences. We owe you thanks nevertheless, continued Staupitz, for bringing us back from the husks of the pigsty to the green pastures of life and the words of salvation. But enough writing, Staupitz concluded. "If only we could sit together for just one hour and share the secrets of our hearts."[64]

CHAPTER TEN

A FAMOUS LOVER LIKE ME
1523–1524
Wittenberg

"Do not wonder that a famous lover like me does not marry. It is strange that I, who so frequently write about matrimony and get mixed up with women, have not yet turned into a woman, to say nothing of having married one. . . . But you [Spalatin], who dares not marry even one woman, are a lazy lover."[1]

While Luther was at the Wartburg, his attention was drawn to Archbishop Albert of Mainz, who had forwarded the ninety-five theses to Rome. Albert was also archbishop of Magdeburg, and that domain included the town of Halle, forty-five miles (seventy-three kilometers) southwest of Wittenberg. In Halle Albert usually resided in a fortress-like residence, the Moritzburg, which was built for the archbishops and contained a small chapel. In 1519 Albert desired a larger church that befitted his rank. Pope Leo X authorized him to establish a new chapter of clergy to be modeled on the All Saints' Chapter in Wittenberg and designed to house over fifty priests. Albert also needed room to display his collection of relics, which had swollen to more than double the 9,000 particles possessed by Elector Frederick.[2] The Dominican cloister and its church almost next door to the Moritzburg offered the perfect space. The Dominicans moved elsewhere and their former church, renovated and lavishly appointed, became a cathedral for Albert and the priests in his New Chapter (its informal name). There was yet another connection between Halle and Wittenberg: most of the altar paintings in the Halle cathedral were finished in the Wittenberg workshop of Lucas Cranach.[3]

In early fall of 1521, Luther heard that Albert was offering indulgences to everyone who viewed his relics at Halle. Although not directed at the reformer, the resumption of indulgence sales by the same archbishop whom Luther chastised four years earlier was a slap in the face. He immediately drafted a reprimand against the "idol" at Halle and his "brothel," a reference to the concubines allegedly kept by Albert. Neither Elector Frederick nor Archbishop Albert wanted a public confrontation. To that end Albert sent a friendly delegation to Wittenberg to confer with Frederick's advisors. The result was an extraordinary meeting of reform-minded spokesmen from opposing camps whose common interest was to keep Luther quiet. The head of Albert's delegation, Wolfgang Capito, was a friend of Erasmus and was hoping to reconcile Albert with the Wittenbergers. For their part, Frederick's advisors were determined to keep Luther out of any controversy that might remind Emperor Charles of the Elector's refusal to surrender the monk. At the imperial level, religion and politics always mixed. Albert was not only an archbishop and cardinal but also archchancellor of Germany, the highest political post after Emperor Charles.

Luther was unimpressed by the political scheming and refused to keep quiet. He finished the manuscript, gave it the provocative title, *Against the Idol at Halle*, and sent it from the Wartburg to Spalatin, who presented it to the Elector. When Frederick prohibited its publication, Luther wrote Spalatin that he could not comply with the prohibition and, with more than his usual bravado, he added: "I would rather lose you, the Elector himself, and the whole world [than be quiet]. Why should I yield to the pope's crea-ture [Albert] since I have already resisted his creator? Your worry about disturbing the public peace is charming, and yet you allow the eternal peace of God to be disturbed by the wicked and sacrilegious actions of that son of perdition?"[4] Despite Luther's outburst Elector Frederick stood firm, and *Against the Idol at Halle* never appeared in print, at least not with that title.

In July of 1522, when Luther was back in Wittenberg, the content of the pamphlet was published—but without reference to Albert and with a new title: *Against the Falsely Named Spiritual Estate of the Pope and Bishops*.[5] The "spiritual estate" was the medieval name for the privileged social and political class to which all clerics belonged, but for Luther it was "falsely named." Two years earlier, in his *Address to the Christian Nobility*, Luther had argued that both clergy and laity were spiritual: "All Christians are truly of the spiritual estate . . . for baptism, gospel, and faith alone make us spiritual and a Christian people."[6] Calling himself an "ecclesiastic" by the grace of God,[7] Luther used the pamphlet to give a fierce and satirical tongue-lashing to the "papal bishops." Albert did not respond to Luther's attack, but it was quickly noticed by other opponents. In Leipzig, Jerome

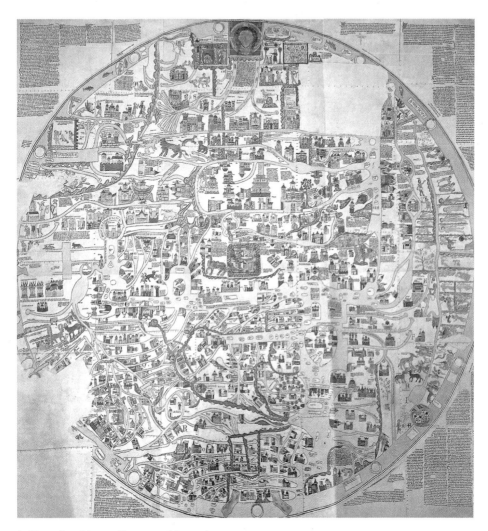

1 Ebstorf world map, Germany, thirteenth century.

2 Hans and Margaret Luder, 1527.

3 Sixteenth-century entrance, Augustinian monastery, Erfurt.

4 Church, Augustinian monastery, Erfurt.

5 Monk's cell, Augustinian
monastery, Erfurt.

6 John Staupitz, ca. 1522.

7 Electors of Saxony – Frederick, John, John Frederick, 1532.

8 Wittenberg skyline looking north across the Elbe River.

9 Augustinian monastery and Luther House, Wittenberg.

10 Luther's study, Luther House, Wittenberg.

11 Castle Church and tower, Wittenberg.

12 Cardinal Albert, archbishop of Mainz, 1526.

13 Emperor Charles V at age sixteen, 1516.

14 Wartburg Castle, entrance arch, 1150.

15 Luther as Knight George, 1521–1522.

16 Upper façade, Town Church,
Wittenberg.

17 Interior, Town Church, Wittenberg.

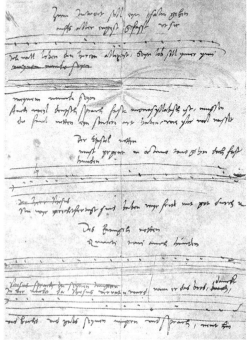

18 Luther's manuscript of the German Mass, 1526.

19 Katharina von Bora, 1528.

20 Katharina's gift portal, Luther House,
Wittenberg, 1540.

Gottes wort
bleibt ewig.

Biblia/ das ist/ die gantze Heilige Schrifft Deudsch.

Mart. Luth.

Wittemberg.

Begnadet mit Kür=
furstlicher zu Sachsen
freiheit.
Gedruckt durch Hans Lufft.

M. D. XXXIIII.

21 Title page, first complete Luther Bible, 1534.

22 Luther preaching, Town Church, Wittenberg.

23 Luther and Melanchthon, 1558.

24 Luther in the midst of other reformers, 1558.

25 Statue of Luther in Wittenberg, nineteenth century.

Emser issued a rebuttal entitled *Against the Falsely Named Ecclesiastic and True Archheretic Martin Luther*.[8] Emser dedicated his booklet to Emperor Charles V and urged him to take further action against the reformer. Both Emser and Luther's Catholic biographer, Cochlaeus, were irritated by Luther's assertion that he deserved the names of churchman and preacher more than the Roman bishops deserved their episcopal titles.[9] Emser's booklet gave twenty reasons why Luther was not a true preacher or prophet and added a scripture reference for each of them.[10]

The papal bishops reproached by Luther were named and ranked according to power and importance. Archbishops such as Albert of Mainz were "spiritual princes" because they ruled lands that belonged to the church, not to a secular prince. If a spiritual prince changed sides and supported Luther, the stakes were higher for him than for secular princes such as Philip of Hesse and Elector Frederick. The secular princes who made their territories Lutheran retained their land and could pass it to their heirs. Archbishops, however, were not supposed to have direct heirs since they could not marry. If an archbishop became Lutheran against the wishes of the clergy who elected him, the pope and clergy could depose him. Before 1555 only the archbishop of Cologne, Hermann von Wied, sided openly with the reformers and tried to make the archdiocese of Cologne evangelical without leaving Rome. His effort came to nothing. After ten years of struggle and uncertainty, Archbishop Hermann was excommunicated by the pope and stripped of his titles and his land by Emperor Charles V.[11]

Just beyond the northeastern edge of the Holy Roman Empire, the grand master of the Teutonic knights, another spiritual prince named Albert,[12] succeeded where Hermann would fail. Albert was not a bishop but became its equivalent once he was elected head of the Teutonic Order and took the vow of celibacy. The large territory over which he presided belonged neither to the empire nor to the Roman Church but to the knights themselves. They chose Albert, a south German count whose mother was a sister of the Polish king, to strengthen their ties to the empire and to Poland. In 1522, while Albert was seeking support in Germany, he was introduced to Luther's writings and one year later sought out the reformer in Wittenberg. When Albert asked Luther for advice about reforming the Teutonic Order, Luther's counsel was to marry and convert the lands of the order into a secular territory belonging to Albert and his heirs. Albert smiled at this recommendation, and Luther published the advice in an open letter to Albert's clerical subjects.[13] Luther also sent two preachers, John Briessmann and Paul Speratus, to prepare the conversion. Two local bishops joined the effort and by the end of 1524 there was sufficient backing for turning Prussia Lutheran. To mollify the Polish king, Albert transferred to him the office of grand master of the Teutonic knights. Then, in 1525, Albert made himself the duke of Prussia and confirmed the Lutheran status of his territory. The next year he followed the rest of Luther's advice and made the duchy of Prussia hereditary by marrying Princess Dorothea of Denmark.[14]

Creating the first Lutheran territory required three years (1522–1525), but in Wittenberg matters moved more slowly. After Luther returned in March of 1522 and slowed down the rate of change, the Wittenbergers handled practical reforms as matters arose. How long should they wait, for example, before making changes to the mass? The Easter service in 1522 was celebrated as before. The tongue was Latin, priests wore traditional vestments, and wine was offered only to worshipers who requested it. By December of 1523, however, Luther's patience with people who wanted minimal change ran out: "We have humored the weak in faith long enough." The result was a new order for celebrating the mass.[15] Luther insisted the order was not binding on churches elsewhere, but at Wittenberg some changes became mandatory. Both bread and wine would be offered to everyone and those who refused to take both would receive nothing. The priest should also refuse communion to people who "could not give a reason for their faith" and answer questions about the Lord's Supper.[16] Luther's hesitation to give communion indiscriminately to all parishioners was partly a reaction to the laity's habit of fulfilling their annual mass obligation by attending church only at Easter.

Thus began the delicate task of creating guidelines that allowed as much freedom as possible to informed and committed believers. Luther's initial goal was to liberate consciences by eliminating compulsory religious rituals that, in his opinion, required little conviction. He tried to counter unthinking piety by holding people accountable for knowing the meaning and benefits of their religious practice. To that end he preached and wrote about the Ten Commandments, the Lord's Prayer, prayer in general, confession, baptism, the Lord's Supper, the Christian creeds, saints, angels, worship, and the Bible. It was a massive campaign of reeducation that lasted the remainder of Luther's life. Luther and his colleagues were asking an entire generation of German believers to abandon the way their ancestors practiced Christianity and to adopt unaccustomed means of expressing their faith. The purpose of religion was no longer to obtain a reward by pleasing God but to allow God to change the heart. For the heart to be changed was to receive the gift of faith, and that faith replaced the meritorious deeds that dominated medieval piety: "I teach that people should trust in nothing other than Jesus Christ, not in their own prayers, merits, or works."[17]

In 1522, Luther published one of his best-selling attempts to reeducate the faithful: the *Personal Prayer Book*.[18] He intended for it to counteract the damage done by medieval prayer manuals, which recommended mnemonic devices such as the rosary and other prayers spoken by rote. Luther's preface minced no words:

> Among the many and harmful books and doctrines which are misleading and deceiving Christians and give rise to countless false beliefs, I regard the personal prayer books as by no means the least objectionable. They drub into the minds of simple people a wretched counting up of sins and going to confession, plus un-Christian tomfoolery about prayers to God and his saints! Moreover, the books are puffed up with promises of indulgences and come out with decorations in red ink and pretty titles. One is called *Garden of the Soul*, another *Paradise of the Soul*, and so on. These books need a basic and thoroughgoing reformation if not total extermination.[19]

Luther then offered his own guide to prayer, insisting that the Lord's Prayer was sufficient on any occasion and that a persistent and heartfelt turning to God was more important than many words. Two years later, he gave specific and surprising advice to an Austrian nobleman about praying for his deceased wife. Luther asked him to stop paying priests for all the vigils and masses they offered daily for his wife's soul. Those actions were "faithless." Instead:

> It is sufficient for your grace earnestly to pray once or twice for her. For God has promised that whatever you ask for, believe that you will receive it and you will certainly have it (Luke 11:9–10). In contrast, when we pray over and over again for the same thing, it is a sign that we do not believe God and with our faithless prayer only make him angrier. True, we should regularly pray, but always in faith and certain that we are being heard. Otherwise, the prayer is in vain.[20]

Prayer was only one activity in which people could be allowed more freedom while learning to be mindful of what they did. Another instance was marriage—both clerical marriage and marriage in general. In both cases Luther relaxed the rules about who could marry, while attempting to instill new respect for marriage as a divine institution. He encouraged not only parish priests but also monks, nuns, and bishops to renounce their vows of celibacy and marry. The prohibition of clerical marriage, he wrote, was not a divine commandment but an injunction of the devil, because it tempted clergy to engage in illicit sex.[21] At the Wartburg, Luther heard that Archbishop Albert of Mainz had arrested two married priests while Albert himself kept several women. Luther warned Albert that if bishops did not stop persecuting married priests, the people would rise up and demand that bishops get rid of their harlots before separating devout wives from their clerical husbands.[22]

By late 1522, clerical marriage was old news in Wittenberg.[23] Karlstadt, Justus Jonas, and Bugenhagen already had wives when Luther's evangelical reconception of marriage appeared in print. The American edition of Luther's works gave it the title, *The Estate of Marriage*, but a better translation is *Married Life*.[24] Part one rejected most of the impediments placed on marriage by the medieval church. For example, the impediment of unbelief prohibited Christians from marrying Muslims, Jews, or heretics. Luther's rejection of that impediment was sweeping:

> Marriage is an outward, bodily thing like any other worldly undertaking. Just as I may eat, drink, sleep, walk, ride with, buy from, speak to, and deal with a heathen, Jew, Turk, or heretic, so I may also marry any of them. Pay no attention to the precepts of those fools who forbid it. You will find plenty of Christians—and indeed the greater part of them—who are worse in their secret unbelief than any Jew, heathen, Turk, or heretic. A heathen is just as much a person—God's good creation—as St. Peter, St. Paul, and St. Lucy, not to speak of slack and spurious Christians.[25]

Although Luther called marriage a worldly thing, he was not divorcing it from God or religion. It was no longer a sacrament, but it was a divine ordinance based on Genesis 1:26–28, which declared that God created human beings male and female and bid them be fruitful and multiply. The institution of marriage applied to everyone except three categories exempted by God: the sexually impotent, men who were castrated, and men and women who were able to resist sexual urges and abstain from sexual intercourse. Members of the last group were "rare, not one in a thousand, for they are a special miracle of God."[26] In all other cases, argued Luther, men and women should marry and fulfill God's created purpose.

In April of 1523, Luther and ten more Wittenbergers—professors and prominent citizens, such as Lucas Cranach—dramatically demonstrated their support of clerical marriage. Lectures had to be canceled while the party, which included several spouses, set off on a two-day journey south to the town of Altenburg. The purpose was to witness the marriage of Wenzel Linck, the successor to Staupitz as vicar-general of the strict Augustinians and former prior of the Wittenberg cloister. Less than a year earlier Linck had resigned his position and left the order to become the evangelical pastor in Altenburg. He soon met Margaret Suicer (or Schweizer), the daughter of a local lawyer, and their nuptials took place on April 14 and 15, 1523. Luther apparently presided at the exchange of vows and honored the couple with a silver cup; and on the way home he praised the event as "Wenzel's marvelous wedding."[27] Linck's marriage had promotional value for the Wittenbergers, but it was only one instance of weddings that followed the flight of monks and nuns from their cloisters. Just one week before Luther left town to attend the wedding of Linck, nine Cistercian nuns, who had escaped from their convent near Leipzig, arrived in Wittenberg and were introduced to Luther. One of them, Katharina von Bora, became his wife.

Katharina was born January 29, 1499, the daughter of Hans von Bora and Katharina Haubitz or Haugwitz. Hans belonged to a scattered line of lower nobility and owned a small estate south of Leipzig, at Lippendorf, near which Katharina was born. She had at least three brothers and one sister. Katharina's mother died before she turned six and her father remarried after placing Katharina in a Benedictine convent to be reared and educated. In 1508 or 1509 she was moved to the Cistercian convent at Nimbschen on the outskirts of Grimma, a town only twenty miles (thirty-two kilometers) from Leipzig and the same distance from Lippendorf. Katharina was not only close to home but found herself in the company of relatives. The abbess of Marienthron was possibly a sister of her mother, and another nun, Magdalena von Bora, was the sister of her father.

Most of the forty-three nuns belonged to the Saxon nobility and passed the time with singing, praying, and handwork such as making beautiful paraments for the church. The convent was wealthy enough to pay more than forty workers to care for animals and crops outside and to cook, clean, and assist the abbess inside. The convent church boasted twelve altars housing 367 relics. The jewels of the collection, which attracted pilgrims, were straw from the manger of Jesus, a thorn from his crown, and a shred of the Virgin Mary's veil. At the age of sixteen Katharina took the customary vows of poverty, chastity, and obedience, and received the ring and veil that symbolized her new status as a bride of Christ. To celebrate his daughter's consecration, Hans von Bora donated a modest sum to the cloister.[28] He was convinced that Katharina was safer, better educated, and guaranteed a more secure future than he could have provided.

In no way could Katharina and eleven other nuns imagine that seven years later, before dawn on Easter Sunday 1523, they would make a prearranged escape from Marienthron in a wholesale grocery wagon. The wagon was driven by its owner, Leonhard Koppe, a prosperous farmer and town councillor in Torgau on the Elbe river, about thirty miles (fifty kilometers) to the northeast. Koppe regularly delivered provisions to the convent, and during the fasting season prior to Easter he brought more barrels of fish than usual. After the escape became legendary, the nuns were said to have hidden in the empty barrels. Three of the nuns went from Torgau directly to their families, but the remaining nine were escorted to Wittenberg by Koppe and Gabriel Zwilling, the fiery Augustinian who was now a pastor in Torgau.

In Wittenberg the nuns received a hearty welcome and were introduced to Luther and to Lucas and Barbara Cranach, who owned the largest house in town. Either then or later, the Cranachs must have taken in Katharina and the Schönfeld sisters, Margaret and Ave. Before long Margaret married a nobleman and Ave married a man who worked in the apothecary owned by Cranach. Thirteen or fourteen years later, long after marrying Katharina, Luther remarked that in 1523 he would have chosen Ave von Schönfeld if he had intended to marry.[29] Ave was probably one of the "three wives" that Luther mentioned jokingly in a letter to Spalatin.[30] It was 1525, two years after the nuns arrived in town, and all of Luther's early colleagues except Amsdorf and Spalatin had married. Egged on by Luther, Spalatin must have told him to speak for himself and explain why he was still single. Luther replied:

> Do not wonder that a famous lover like me does not marry. It is strange that I, who so frequently write about matrimony and get mixed up with women, have not yet turned into a woman, to say nothing of having married one. Yet if you want me to set an example . . . I have had three wives at the same time and loved them so much that I am about to lose two of them to other husbands. The third I can hardly hold on to with my left arm, and she too may soon be snatched away. But you, who dares not marry even one woman, are a lazy lover.[31]

The first two wives were probably the Schönfeld sisters and the third, whom he could barely keep with his left arm (as a concubine) was Katharina, whom Luther did marry two months after teasing Spalatin. The oldest of the Marienthron nuns to reach Wittenberg was Magdalena Staupitz, who had been the cloister's musician and was a sister of John Staupitz. Amsdorf thought Magdalena and Spalatin were right for each other, but the match-making failed and Magdalena Staupitz returned to Grimma as the principal of a new school for girls.

After the nuns reached Wittenberg, Luther wasted no time publicizing the escape. Composed as a public letter to Koppe, Luther's report gave reasons why nuns who left the cloister did so with God's blessing.[32] Hinting that he was partly responsible for the escape, Luther maintained it was in no way shameful and encouraged other families to remove their daughters from the convents. It was a godly action and perfectly safe. The nuns were not robbed or molested, reported Luther, and thus preserved their honor and purity. To critical readers who objected that monastic vows should not be broken, Luther replied that chastity was a gift from God and no person vowing to be chaste was guaranteed to receive the gift.[33] Besides, said Luther, abstinence was neither necessary nor desirable, because God established marriage for satisfying the sexual instinct.

Luther failed to remind his readers that abetting the escape of nuns from their cloisters was a capital crime. In Electoral Saxony neither Luther nor Koppe was in danger of arrest, but in the other Saxony, ruled by Duke George, who remained loyal to Rome, a man was beheaded for this crime one year after Katharina von Bora escaped from Marienthron. The threat of punishment did not, however, stop nuns from leaving. Not long after Katharina escaped, her aunt Magdalena and two other nuns also fled Marienthron. In some cases, nuns stayed in the convent because their families did not want them back. Those families stood to lose big sums if their daughters came home: the money paid to the cloister when their daughters entered the convent, expenses for support of an unmarried daughter living at home and, most of all, a dowry for the daughter who married after leaving the convent. Katharina von Bora's escape from Marienthron was a dangerous undertaking with an uncertain outcome. It was not a frivolous flight into the arms of an eligible Prince Charming.

Katharina lived in Wittenberg two years before she married Martin. Prior to that, she fell in love with a former Wittenberg student, Jerome Baumgartner, who was visiting Philip Melanchthon. Baumgartner was a year older than Katharina and soon returned to his prominent family in Nuremberg. Katharina waited for a proposal but none came, perhaps because Melanchthon warned Jerome to be wary of the marital yoke under which Melanchthon himself suffered.[34] After Katharina had waited over a year, Luther told Baumgartner that Katharina was still in love with him and to act quickly or lose her to another suitor.[35] The other man was a pastor named Caspar Glatz, much older than Katharina, whom she refused to marry even though Luther's ultimatum received no reply from Baumgartner. His parents were presumably unwilling to accept a penniless fugitive from the convent as a proper match for their son. In early 1526 Baumgartner, by then an influential councillor and supporter of the reformation in Nuremberg, married a fifteen-year-old girl with better credentials.[36]

Between 1523 and 1525, the evangelical movement spread rapidly beyond Wittenberg. Luther was busy giving aid and advice, such as recommending evangelical preachers as replacements for priests who opposed reform. Owing to the medieval patronage system, these were not simple transitions. Preachers and pastors were not elected by their parishes but by a patron with the legal right to fill a vacancy. The patron might be a bishop, landlord, university, monastery, or a chapter of clergy such as the All Saints' Chapter in Wittenberg. These patrons collected fees in cash or in kind from the parish and reserved the right of appointment. For example, the Cistercian monastery of Buch, which lay sixty miles (ninety-six kilometers) south of Wittenberg, was the patron of a parish at nearby Leisnig. The town itself had only 1,500 residents, but its parish enclosed more than ten villages, which for decades supplied the Electors of Saxony with beer, butter, cheese, chickens, geese, eggs, and bacon. They also delivered provisions to the monastery of Buch, whose abbot appointed the priest at the parish church.[37]

In 1522 the current priest came out in favor of Luther and was recalled by the abbot. The parish, however, insisted on retaining him as their pastor and rejected the abbot's new appointee. To defend their irregular action and obtain further guidance, the parish elders invited Luther to Leisnig. He set out on September 25, 1522, and spent several days in the parish. Luther quickly grasped the state of affairs and explained how to transform Leisnig into an evangelical parish. If the parishioners called their own pastor, they would have to pay him since the monastery would no longer offer support. The elders had to find a new source of revenue and started work on a plan. In early 1523, two prominent Leisnig citizens arrived in Wittenberg and asked Luther for written support for their intentions.[38] Four days later Luther composed a letter that gave the requested approval and promised to forward directions for adopting evangelical forms of singing, praying, and reading.[39]

Two months later the reformer kept his promise with more than a letter. Luther published the parish's plan[40] for organizing the structure and the finances of an evangelical church in Leisnig. His preface to the plan argued that scripture entitled the parishioners to decide if they were being properly taught and on that basis to "call, appoint, and dismiss" their pastors: "Christ takes the power to judge teaching away from bishops, scholars, and councils and gives that right equally to all Christians."[41] Luther had taken this position in his *Address to the Christian Nobility*, but in 1520 the scenario had been hypothetical. In 1523 a specific parish that desired change was testing the theory by demanding the right to call their own leaders and control their own finances. After the Leisnig church order appeared,[42] Luther wanted it to be a model for other evangelical towns. It remains a useful illustration of how church life had to be reorganized on the ground for every town and territory that adopted the reformation.

The Leisnig ordinance regulated Christian duties assumed by the parish: 1) finding and paying church personnel (pastors, teachers, custodians) and maintaining church property; 2) the "preeminently spiritual undertaking" of providing care for the poor and needy;[43] and 3) establishing procedures for receiving and disbursing funds that supported these duties. The last duty was the most urgent: the creation of a common chest into which all income would be deposited and out of which all expenses would be paid. The chest was not a bank account but an actual trunk containing "interest income, properties, rights, monies, and goods everywhere amassed, collected, donated, vested, and assigned in perpetuity."[44] Income from endowments originally designated for private masses at four side altars in the church was transferred to the common chest. The Roman priests received a stipend until they died, but no more private masses were said for any purpose. Three brotherhoods were also affected. They were semi-private fraternities of laymen and clergy that spent money on celebrations, special masses, charity, and pensions. Before being dissolved by the reformers, brotherhoods were forced to deposit every asset they possessed into the common chest. All other monies previously donated to the church were merged into a reserve fund. If expenses were not covered by all these assets, then "every noble, townsman, and peasant living in the parish" would pay a tax according to what the family could afford.[45]

The common chest was administered by ten trustees or directors: two from the nobility, two from the current town council, three citizens at large, and three from the rural peasantry. They were elected by the parishioners at their annual assembly in January. The chest itself occupied the

safest place in the church. To prevent access by a single director, the chest
was secured by four locks, each of which had its specific key. The four keys
were distributed as follows to each group of directors: one each to the
nobility, the council, the town, and the peasantry. All four directors had to
be present when the chest was opened. The ten directors met every Sunday
at eleven o'clock to transact their business. Every decision was recorded in
the minutes and every receipt and disbursement was entered weekly into a
ledger. The directors appointed two building supervisors to collect alms for
deposit into the chest. At the discretion of the directors, perishables were
distributed daily to the poor and non-perishables were stored in the church
until they were needed. No one was permitted to beg—not monks, students,
or anyone else, man or woman, able to work. The ordinance authorized an
annual salary for three positions: a pastor, a preacher, and a custodian. They
were granted the right to use certain properties for additional support—a
residence, perhaps, and plots in which they could grow vegetables.

The ordinance obligated the directors to hire and pay a schoolmaster
for the boys and an "upright, fully seasoned, irreproachable woman" for
instructing girls under twelve "in true Christian discipline, honor, and virtue."
The common chest also met the financial needs of orphans and children of
impoverished parents. For boys it paid for school or occupational training
and for girls it guaranteed a suitable dowry for marriage. Although Luther
did not compose the ordinance, he thoroughly approved of its content,
including the section on schools. His *Address to the Christian Nobility*,
published three years earlier, advocated not only reform of universities, which
had been accomplished in Wittenberg, but also the establishment of schools
for girls as well as for boys.[46] Luther pursued this agenda after the Leisnig
ordinance was published, but he knew that towns were reluctant to fund
public education. In 1524 he used Psalm 127 to encourage the Baltic town
of Riga to invest in its schools. Every year, he argued, town councils and
inhabitants threw "a thousand guilders down the drain" for personal excess
and religious foolishness and then complained they would starve if required
to pay good preachers and teachers.[47]

In 1524 Luther set his sights even higher. He appealed to all city councils in Germany to "establish and maintain Christian schools."[48] Everywhere,
he asserted, schools "are being left to go to wrack and ruin." Dismantling
education was a stratagem of the devil to undermine the gospel and retain
dominance of the world. If the devil was to be stopped, "it must be done
through young people who have matured in the knowledge of God and
who spread his word." That required Christian determination and money

that Luther was sure could be found: "If we spend such large sums every year on guns, roads, bridges, and dams to insure the peace and prosperity of a city, why should not much more be devoted to the poor, neglected youth—at least enough to engage one or two competent people to teach school?"[49]

Luther's argument was propelled by his sense of urgency. Time was running out. The recovery of biblical languages and the liberal arts by humanist scholars had to be utilized without delay. Now that God's word and grace had granted Germany the most erudite teachers in its history, every town needed a Christian school in which pupils could learn from those teachers. If Germany missed this opportunity, it would slip back into misery and darkness more deeply than it had before. Why? Because in Luther's theology of history, God's word and the gift of unprecedented scholarship would vanish if they were not used:

> God's word and grace are like a passing shower of rain which does not return where it once has been. They were with the Jews but when they left, God's word and grace were gone for good and now they have nothing. Paul brought them to the Greeks, but they left for good and now the Greeks have the Turks. Rome and the Latins had them, but once they were gone they were gone for good, and now Rome and the West have the pope. And you Germans need not think you will have God's word and grace forever, for ingratitude and contempt will for certain drive them way. Seize them now while they are here and hold them fast, for lazy hands are bound to have a lean year.[50]

Luther's address to the town councils in Germany did not stop there. Schools were necessary for training civil servants and teaching biblical languages to clergy. Luther noted a "vast difference between a simple preacher of faith and a person who properly interprets scripture." The simple preacher could get by with German, but Greek and Hebrew were necessary to decipher obscure passages and to combat faulty interpretations.[51] Luther lobbied the councillor for good books and libraries and even proposed a basic curriculum.

Turning parishes overseen by Roman bishops into evangelical parishes without bishops was the main challenge faced by Luther after returning from the Wartburg. It required doing the job of a bishop without being one. Visiting parishes, preaching, recommending pastors, reorganizing finances and poor relief, composing materials for worship, and keeping up with a growing correspondence—all together they represented a fulltime job for which he had no training except his stint as provincial vicar of the Augustinians. Nevertheless, Luther found time for pursuits that were more familiar: interpreting scripture and responding to opponents. Prior to 1522 most of his opponents were Roman theologians, but opposition was forming closer to home. Two defectors from his leadership, Andrew Karlstadt and Thomas Müntzer, became tenacious adversaries. The conflict with Müntzer was short but vehement. The conflict with Karlstadt, drawn out over seven years, had curious twists and turns before it ended their long relationship.

Even though Karlstadt had been displaced as leader of the Wittenberg reformers, he remained dean of the theology faculty until early 1523.[52] He was permitted to lecture but not to publish, and two years passed before his pamphlet against retarding reform appeared in print.[53] By that time Karlstadt was no longer in Wittenberg. In June of 1523, Elector Frederick permitted him to serve temporarily as the pastor in Orlamünde, a village in Thuringia about 100 miles (160 kilometers) southwest of Wittenberg. Karlstadt chose Orlamünde because income from the parish provided his salary for teaching at the university and serving as archdeacon at the Castle Church. Out of that salary Karlstadt had to provide for his family and pay a vicar to substitute for him in Orlamünde. Karlstadt could save money by taking over the parish himself; moreover, he could introduce the reforms that were curbed in Wittenberg: remove images from the church, discourage private confession and fasting, organize poor relief in place of begging, preside in German without vestments at the Lord's Supper; and curtail infant baptism.[54] The parish supported the changes and decided to call Karlstadt, who was gaining supporters in the region, as their permanent pastor. In May of 1524 Elector Frederick denied the parish's request and summoned Karlstadt back to Wittenberg. Instead of returning to his professorship, however, Karlstadt resigned from the university and from his post as archdeacon. He set out to deliver his resignations in person, but the letters had to be dispatched because high water blocked the road north.[55]

Luther and the Saxon court associated Karlstadt with the troublesome priest, and former Wittenberg student, Thomas Müntzer.[56] In 1521 Müntzer was forced to leave his parish and the town of Zwickau because he sharply criticized colleagues and allegedly incited civil unrest. He spent six months in Prague studying early Christianity and medieval mysticism and then moved around until March of 1523, when he was chosen as pastor of St. John's parish in the Thuringian town of Allstedt. There Müntzer married a former nun, Ottilie von Gerson, and, three years before Luther, published the first German order of worship. He was not, however, the same Müntzer as before. In Prague he acquired radical ideas and used them to construct a grandiose mission for himself. Christianity, he decided, had fallen so far from its spotless origin that God, through Müntzer, would restore its apostolic purity before the imminent end of the world. Two things had to be done quickly: Gather the people whom God had elected to live in the purified kingdom of Christ; and destroy the godless remainder who had corrupted Christendom.

In Allstedt Müntzer decided that his followers comprised the elect and bound them into a league committed to the speedy cleansing of a rotten and corrupt Christianity. The rot encompassed not only the pope but also Luther, whose reforms in Wittenberg fell short of the purging that Müntzer believed necessary. In 1524 Luther asked Duke John Frederick of Saxony, the nephew of Elector Frederick, to summon Müntzer to Wittenberg for interrogation. Müntzer refused but agreed to meet the duke elsewhere. The encounter took place in mid-July at the castle in Allstedt. Duke John Frederick was accompanied by his father, Duke John, and in person they heard Müntzer preach a sermon justifying his mission. The fall of Christendom, he said, was caused by mediocre, unholy priests and their bad sermons. Only the elect had the genuine word of God within themselves. The princes should side with the elect and take up the sword against their ungodly enemies.

On July 17, 1524, Müntzer invited Karlstadt, who was still at Orlamünde, fifty-five miles (eighty-five kilometers) south of Allstedt, to join his league of the elect and asked him to convince fifteen other villages to form a similar league. It was obvious to Karlstadt that Müntzer was seeking allies for a popular revolt against the dukes of Saxony. Karlstadt was deeply offended and tore up the letter; but on second thought he picked up the pieces, mounted a horse, and hurried to a colleague who lived nearby. They pieced together the letter so that Karlstadt could prove what Müntzer was asking him to do.[57] Two days later Karlstadt, professing his friendship, sent Müntzer a firm refusal. Such leagues were against God's will, he wrote, and based on a misplaced trust in human might. Müntzer should quit writing letters and organizing leagues. It scares us here at Orlamünde, wrote Karlstadt, when we anticipate the punishment that would be inflicted on us as rebels and criminals.[58] Karlstadt was sincere. In his ninety published pamphlets only one or two sentences can be construed as supporting the use of force.[59]

For Luther and the Saxon rulers, however, both Karlstadt and Müntzer were potential revolutionaries. They publicly criticized Luther for not pushing reforms fast and far enough. In late 1524 Karlstadt finally published his tract on whether or not to proceed slowly with reform. His answer was no, because Jesus said: "He who puts his hand to the plow and looks back is not fit for the kingdom of God (Luke 9:62)." On that basis, common folk had the right to act when Christian magistrates neglected their duties: "Where Christians hold sway, they should not look to the authorities but take action on their own and, without any preaching, upend everything that is against God."[60] Almost simultaneously Müntzer published his attack on Luther. Its title was less genteel: *An Obligatory Defense and Reply to the Spiritless Soft-living Flesh at Wittenberg.*[61] Moreover, both Karlstadt and Müntzer enjoyed a solid following and support for them was spreading, even though Müntzer's followers had burned the chapel at a popular pilgrimage site. In addition to the Bible, both men were influenced by mystical theology and open to the direct influence of the Holy Spirit. For that reason Luther lumped them together as *Schwärmer*, a pejorative term for enthusiasts, romanticizers, and religious fanatics.

Shortly after Karlstadt's refusal to join Müntzer, Luther and two colleagues traveled to Jena near Orlamünde in order to identify preachers showing radical tendencies. According to the pastor in Jena,[62] Karlstadt furtively attended a sermon preached by Luther at seven o'clock in the morning of August 22, 1524. Later that day Luther received from Karlstadt a written request to meet him in person. Luther invited him to the Black Bear inn and the former colleagues, who had known each other twelve years, exchanged barbs as if they were an estranged couple. In the presence of supporters and onlookers, Karlstadt contended that Luther's sermon associated him with Müntzer and protested that he had explicitly refused Müntzer's invitation to join his campaign. Luther insisted that his sermon did not mention Karlstadt by name and admitted that Karlstadt had never advocated violence. The conversation might have ended there, but Karlstadt announced he would prove that Luther did not preach the gospel correctly and offered to debate him. Luther challenged Karlstadt instead to write against him publicly and, to show he meant what he said, Luther gave Karlstadt a gold coin. Karlstadt held it up to the bystanders as proof of Luther's challenge and put the coin in his purse. Then he offered his hand to Luther and they drank to the agreement.[63] Afterward, however, Luther reported to Spalatin that Karlstadt still adhered to Müntzer's murderous notions and, given the opportunity, might yet make trouble.[64] That report contradicted what Luther had said to Karlstadt at Jena, and it resulted in Karlstadt's banishment from Saxony.

Karlstadt kept to the agreement and wrote against Luther. Without invitation, Müntzer did the same, but Luther fired the first volley in his *Letter to the Princes of Saxony Concerning the Rebellious Spirit.*[65] Directed solely against Müntzer, the published letter was the first open challenge to defectors from his own ranks. According to Luther, Müntzer was prepared to unleash a revolt against the Saxon rulers, and he immediately alerted Elector Frederick and his brother, Duke John, insisting that God had entrusted the sword to rulers and tolerated no hesitation. If the Saxon princes did not act, God would demand an explanation. Luther also worried the princes might fall for Müntzer's claim that he was guided directly by the Holy Spirit. To undermine that claim, Luther cited Müntzer's refusal to submit his views to impartial judges and reminded the princes that Müntzer's followers had burned down a chapel. Moreover, claimed Luther, Müntzer was full of bravado, bragging about his spiritual gift and his mission to annihilate the godless. Luther, by contrast, when he had taken on the pope, started humbly and trembled with fear. Yet, added Luther, he was not afraid to defend his views in a public debate at Leipzig and to reassert them at Worms in the emperor's presence.[66] For the sake of those ideas, Luther maintained, he suffered excommunication and was now a fugitive.

Conversely, argued Luther, Müntzer and his disciples had suffered very little and had sacrificed almost nothing. Even worse, they were capitalizing on the risks Luther accepted: "They use and enjoy our victory, take wives, and ignore the laws of the pope. But they did not fight or risk their lives for any of those things, whereas I had to put both life and limb on the line. Now I have to boast of myself just as St. Paul did of his sufferings. It is silly, and I would rather not do it if I could rebut the lying spirits in another way."[67] Luther did not hesitate, however, to recount the positive results of his trials. Although he and his followers had only "the first fruits of the Spirit", he claimed that "we know at least what faith, love, and the cross are, and there is nothing on earth more important to know than faith and love. On that basis we can recognize and decide which teaching is correct or incorrect, which agrees with faith or not, in the same way that we recognize and judge this lying spirit."[68] Müntzer was not only a threat to the princes but also a threat to Luther and his vision. Müntzer had his own vision of what Christianity should be, but the vision could become reality only if those Christians who were God's elect destroyed all the others. Luther realized that some Christians were more earnest and devoted than the rest, but the rest were not to be treated like heretics or heathen and should certainly not be executed.

By the end of 1524 Luther was no longer wearing monastic garb. Instead of a monk, he was now a teacher and reformer. At the university he was lecturing on selected books from the Old Testament and serving on a team that was translating all thirty-nine books from Hebrew into German. Most of his time was occupied with those jobs, for which he received no salary. Luther's teaching was considered compensation to Elector Frederick for building the Augustinian monastery in which Luther still resided. By contrast, his colleague Melanchthon, who was neither a priest nor a monk, received an annual salary of one hundred gulden while protesting that he had no desire to profit from theology.[69] Absent a salary to negotiate, Luther requested help with his teaching load so that he could participate fully in the work of translation. He asked Elector Frederick to pay Melanchthon to lecture on the Bible instead of teaching Greek, which Luther said was a waste of Melanchthon's time and should be turned over to a younger person. Although Melanchthon was only twenty-seven, Elector Frederick granted the request.[70]

Unlike Luther's academic responsibilities, the unofficial and unpaid job of reformer was not neatly defined—least of all by Luther, who did not call himself a reformer. In correspondence he used the word only once, and in that case the "reformer" was the Turk, meaning the Ottoman Turks threatening Vienna.[71] Between 1517 and 1522 Luther's primary reforming task was to criticize Catholic practices and respond to Catholic theologians as the occasion arose. That task continued to the end of his life. In 1523, however, the government of the Holy Roman Empire ordered Luther to stop publishing new books and admonished Elector Frederick to enforce the order. After Luther was notified, he responded to Frederick with a summary of his reforming work, which was both general and benign:

> My sole purpose from beginning to end has been and still is to write, teach, preach, perform, and endorse nothing but that which serves and strengthens the word and honor of God and, in addition, promotes the true and holy faith and love of neighbor—all of this for the well-being of Christendom.[72]

However, he did not stop there. Claiming that he wanted to refrain from harsh polemics, he stated why this was not possible. In both Latin and German his opponents were slandering him, God, and the gospel. That slander forced him to issue rebuttals, not to protect his own innocence but to defend the truth of the gospel.[73]

In fact, Luther freely criticized Catholic practice without being attacked first. In 1524, a ceremony that honored the medieval saint, Bishop Benno of Meissen, raised his hackles. After intense lobbying from

Duke George, whose Catholic part of Saxony included Meissen, Benno had been canonized in 1523. On June 16, 1524, his bones were to be transferred in gold and silver receptacles from the original grave to an elaborate marble sepulcher in the Meissen cathedral. The surrounding nobility, including Elector Frederick, were invited to attend this celebration. Luther was furious and set to work on a pamphlet entitled *Against the New Idol and the Old Devil about To Be Elevated at Meissen*. It was published in Wittenberg and reprinted at least eight times. Luther's antagonist in Leipzig, Jerome Emser, received a copy prior to the event and issued one of several Catholic replies. As usual, Luther minced no words. He assumed the devil was behind a pompous carnival like the transfer of bones. If Benno were a genuine saint, he would not wish to be honored in this way. Instead, Benno was a papal saint, not a Christian holy man, because the upshot of Benno's elevation to sainthood was to turn people away from trust in Christ and lead them to rely on the merits, relics, and prayers of the saints.[74] We can respect true saints, said Luther, without relying on them: "I believe St. Elisabeth at Marburg was holy, and St. Augustine, Jerome, Ambrose, Bernard, and Francis, but I will not stake my life on them. I want my faith to be certain and to have a firm basis in scripture."[75]

Overall, however, Luther was spending less time on polemics and more time encouraging and overseeing the spread of reform. That required staying connected with preachers who were establishing evangelical churches—some of them far from Wittenberg. On September 1, 1524, he wrote to Henry of Zütphen, the evangelical pastor in Bremen, for "no other reason than finally to greet you with my own hand."[76] Henry had studied in Wittenberg from 1520 to 1522 and lived with Luther in the monastery before leaving to become prior of the Augustinian house in Antwerp. Luther's ideas had infiltrated the Low Countries (Belgium and Netherlands), but they belonged to the Habsburg family and Emperor Charles V suppressed Lutheran sympathizers. In 1522 Henry was arrested, but friends helped him to escape. On his way back to Wittenberg he passed through Bremen and was persuaded to remain as the preacher at a local chapel. Luther's letter, which reached him there in the fall of 1524, contained a string of good news. Nicholas von Amsdorf and four others were to become preachers in Magdeburg. John Bugenhagen was invited to become the pastor at a church in Hamburg. And delegates from seventy-two towns meeting at Speyer agreed to abide by the word of God regardless of the cost.[77]

In Hesse Count Philip was requiring the "pure" gospel to be taught in all the parishes. Although he had conversed with Luther at Worms, Philip offered his support only after he met Philip Melanchthon near Frankfurt in April of 1524. Returning from a visit to his mother in southwestern Germany, Melanchthon and his friend, Camerarius, who later reported the incident,[78] were on their way north when they were met by Philip of Hesse and his retinue, who were heading south to Heidelberg. Assured by Count Philip that he need have no fear, Melanchthon replied he was an unimportant person and not afraid. After joking that he might turn over Melanchthon to the papal legate in Germany, Philip of Hesse inquired about Luther's teaching and the reforms in Wittenberg. In addition to his answers, Melanchthon promised to send Count Philip more details in writing.[79] In September of 1524 Melanchthon kept his promise by forwarding to Philip a concise summary of evangelical theology as taught in Wittenberg.[80] Two years later Count Philip made Hesse an evangelical territory and sealed the action with a church order that preceded by two years a similar document in Electoral Saxony.

Reform was also under way in Zurich. In January of 1523 Luther was informed of a debate between Ulrich Zwingli, the leading preacher, and a representative of the bishop of Constance. It was the first public signal that Switzerland might also have a reformation, but Luther advised waiting to see what happened.[81] He did not suspect that Zwingli would become his chief evangelical opponent or that their disagreement about the Lord's Supper would severely hamper the Protestant movement. More encouraging news came from Strasbourg, and he congratulated Katharina Schütz Zell, wife of the evangelical preacher Matthew Zell, on their marriage and their shared efforts on behalf of reform.[82] Closer to home, Spalatin wanted to leave the court of Elector Frederick because fewer people were listening to his advice and he wanted to marry. Luther argued that Spalatin's experience was too valuable and besides, if he deserted the Elector during his final illness, Spalatin would regret it for the rest of his life.[83] Spalatin must have agreed. Three months after Frederick died, Spalatin left Wittenberg and only three months later the friend Luther had called a "lazy lover" was also married.

CHAPTER ELEVEN

REBELLION IS INTOLERABLE
1525
Wittenberg—Thuringia

*"If anyone thinks this is too harsh, remember that rebellion is intolerable
and that the destruction of the world is to be expected every hour."*[1]

The reformation in Wittenberg was not made by Luther alone, or by
Luther with his colleagues, but by Luther, his colleagues, the town council,
and the courts of Elector Frederick and his successor, Elector John. The
relationship between the court and the theological faculty was close because
most of Frederick's advisors openly supported the reforms that changed
religious life. Many of them belonged to noble families: Friedrich von
Thun, Hans von Dolzig, Philip and Fabian von Feilitzsch, Gregor von
Brück, Hugo von Einsiedel, John von Taubenheim, Hans von der Planitz,
and Hans von Löser, who held the post of hereditary marshal.[2] As 1524
ended, Luther was presiding at Löser's wedding in the village of Pretzsch
on the Elbe river about twenty miles (thirty-two kilometers) southeast of
Wittenberg. Löser was a friend and later became the godfather of Paul
Luther, the third son of Martin and Katharina.[3] In 1523 Luther dedicated
to Löser a commentary on the seventh chapter of 1 Corinthians. It rejected
the requirement of clerical celibacy and argued that marriage was intended
for all but a few.[4] The tract was meant as a wedding present, but the gift
was at least a year premature. When Löser's wedding finally took place, the
theological faculty was represented not only by Luther but also by Philip
Melanchthon, Nicholas Amsdorf, and Justus Jonas.

The ceremony was a festive introduction to a series of turning points for
Luther and the reformation. Until 1525 the reformation was a small but
expanding evangelical movement that used the Bible and Augustine to
modify medieval piety and to challenge the authority of popes and bishops.

Desire for reform led to the rejection of specific practices: in Electoral Saxony it was the selling of indulgences, in Zurich compulsory fasting during Lent, and in Strasbourg the requirement of clerical celibacy. Soon reformers elsewhere rejected those practices and others: private masses, withholding wine from the laity, praying to saints, venerating their relics and visiting their shrines, and monastic vows. Before 1525, however, dissent was emerging inside the ranks of reform. Karlstadt and Müntzer began to move away from Luther because he was not radical enough; and in Zurich, extremists demanded deeper and faster changes than Ulrich Zwingli was negotiating with the city council. In Zurich and in sizable areas of Germany, however, the evangelical movement remained intact.

During 1525 the movement was strained by social upheaval and theological controversy. Both threatened Martin Luther's vision of a bona fide Christian Germany and tarnished his own reputation. The social upheaval was caused by the Peasants' War. It started on a small scale in southwest Germany when peasants, who were bound to the estates on which they worked, rebelled against their landowners. The scattered rebellions caught fire and coalesced into a massive uprising of townspeople and villagers. Their leaders compiled lists of grievances, raised regional armies, and drafted constitutions for an egalitarian society. The medieval social order was under attack by the "common man," a German term for all villagers and townsmen who were not princes, counts, dukes, knights, bishops, abbots, or urban aristocrats. A few militant nobles joined the revolt as commanders, but the rebels lost most of the pitched battles.

They were, however, more successful with guerilla-like raids. For example, on Easter Sunday of 1525 the peasants caught the count of Helfenstein and his soldiers outside their garrison above Weinsberg, a town ninety-five miles (150 kilometers) southeast of Frankfurt. When the count tried to bargain with the attackers, they stabbed him to death and forced twenty-four nobles and their servants to run a gauntlet of lances before leaving their naked corpses lying in a field.[5] The widely publicized atrocity caused alarm, but the end of the war was near. One month after Weinsberg, Thomas Müntzer rallied a collection of six thousand poorly armed recruits to face a professional army at least twice its size. It was commanded by the Catholic Duke George of Saxony, and his brother-in-law, the Protestant Count Philip of Hesse. The result was predictable. On May 15, 1525, outside Frankenhausen in Thuringia, five thousand peasants were slaughtered. It was the last major battle of a conflict that claimed perhaps 80,000 lives, about twice the estimated number that died in the American Revolution.

Soon after the war ended, a close observer inscribed a summary of the tragedy on the title page of Luther's earlier tract entitled *Admonition to Peace*:

> In the year 1525 a horrible spilling of blood was caused by a widespread peasants' war. Almost every region of Germany rebelled against the authorities with the result that about two hundred thousand peasants were woefully slain. It reached Alsace, Franconia, the Rhineland, the Black Forest, the Nördlingen crater,[6] Thuringia, Meissen, Swabia, and elsewhere. In the rebellious towns and countryside more than three hundred thousand people were killed by the sword and other weapons. O God, please forgive us and have mercy on us![7]

The estimate of casualties was much too high and the rebellion was more extensive than described, but the author's anguish captured both the savagery and futility of the revolution. Near Electoral Saxony, Frankenhausen was not the only case of savagery. Instead of committing his forces to that battle, Elector John led them on reprisal raids through parts of Thuringia that supported Müntzer. The towns were subjected to heavy penalties, and in one of the last actions of the war, the soldiers of Elector John defended the count of Henneberg against the rebels.[8]

In *Admonition to Peace*, written before the battle at Frankenhausen, Luther condemned the lords who oppressed their subjects and commended the willingness of the peasants to accept correction and instruction. But he also condemned the rebellion because it would finally result in the utter destruction of Germany.[9] To make his point, Luther issued another tract against the rebellious peasants because they conscripted "many good people" to join them unwillingly. Although he admonished rulers to have mercy on the peasants who were forced to fight with the rebels, he condoned the killing of the rebels themselves:

> Therefore, dear lords, here is a place where you can release, rescue, help. Have mercy on these poor [conscripted] people. Let whoever can, stab, smite, and slay. If you die in doing it, good for you! A more blessed death can never be yours, for you die while obeying the divine commandment in Romans 13[:1-2] and in loving service of your neighbor, whom you are rescuing from the bonds of hell and the devil.... If anyone thinks this is too harsh, remember that rebellion is intolerable and that the destruction of the world is to be expected every hour.[10]

The rulers did not need Luther's permission to justify the carnage. But the words did irreparable damage to Luther's reputation, especially after Thomas Müntzer and his adjutant were beheaded and their heads exhibited as a warning to their sympathizers who survived. Luther's words are still quoted out of context in order to convict Luther of uncritically siding with all authorities and condoning their use of lethal force. Luther was immediately called a lackey of the princes and, in 1525, both supporters and opponents urged him to retract his words or at least to explain them.

Luther finally published *An Open Letter on the Harsh Book against the Peasants*, but it was scarcely a retraction. God's word, he said, declared both divine wrath and divine mercy. No one cared about mercy when the peasants were raging, robbing, burning, and plundering; but after their defeat, all the talk was suddenly about mercy. Luther claimed he had written more about mercy than anyone for a thousand years,[11] but harsh words were necessary in order to stymie the devil, who was planning to lay waste to Germany.[12] Inciting rebellion was the best way for Satan to suppress the gospel, because rebellion had more devastating consequences than theft and murder. They hurt only individuals or small groups, but insurrection destroyed entire societies and would cripple all of Germany. The battle was cosmic, God versus the devil, and rebellion that led to anarchy and devastation smothered the gospel and the hope it offered for a renewed Christian society.[13]

Thomas Müntzer had also believed in a cosmic conflict between God and Satan, but, unlike Luther, he concocted out of scripture a scenario that required him not only to preach a purified Christendom but also to cleanse it by annihilating the godless, false Christians who were corrupting the church. Müntzer called that purified Christendom the "new apostolic church," but it was far more than a religious institution. It was the thousand-year reign of Christ prophesied in Revelation 20 that would issue from the peasant uprisings. The peasants who followed Müntzer were the "elect people of God," who would take the sword away from princes and wield it to kill the godless and bring in the egalitarian society over which the elect would rule. With utter certainty about that scenario and his own righteous mission within it, Müntzer marched his poorly armed and poorly trained legion of "true Christians" to defeat and death at Frankenhausen.[14]

The manipulation of historical material made it possible for Müntzer to become the hero and Luther the villain in this story. Socialist historians in

Russia and East Germany turned Müntzer into the poster boy of their proletariat revolution by ignoring the religious motivation behind Müntzer's actions and his call for annihilation of the godless. At the same time they condemned Luther because he defended the social order and did not believe that God would use murderous insurrection to further the cause of the gospel. Luther can be criticized for what he wrote, but he did not advocate killing his adversaries or the people he judged not to be earnest Christians.

Theological controversies were not as lethal as war, but they were pernicious enough to splinter the evangelical movement. The most divisive issue was the presence of Christ in the Lord's Supper. Before 1524 Luther simply endorsed the presence of Christ's body and blood in the bread and wine of communion, although he rejected the medieval philosophical explanation of how that happened. The first serious challenge to his view came from Karlstadt in a tract entitled *A Dialogue or Conversation concerning the Abominable and Idolatrous Misuse of the Most Honorable Sacrament of Jesus Christ.*[15] It was published in early November of 1524. Karlstadt had left Saxony and arrived in Strasbourg, where he lobbied the leaders of reform to adopt his rejection of Christ's presence in the sacrament. The Strasbourg reformers were already wavering between Luther's theology and the teachings of Ulrich Zwingli, the chief reformer in Zurich, whose views were similar to those of Karlstadt. To help them make a decision, the Strasbourg reformers requested Luther to clarify his stance on the Lord's Supper. By mid-December of 1524, both the request from Strasbourg and Karlstadt's *Dialogue* had arrived in Wittenberg, and Luther was pondering his replies to both.[16] The easier task was to honor the request from Strasbourg, and he completed it with *A Letter to the Christians at Strassburg in Opposition to the Fanatic Spirit.* The fanatic spirit was Karlstadt, whom Luther blamed for exacerbating the uncertainty in the city.[17]

Luther explained his insistence on the presence of Christ in the sacrament and identified the cause of disagreement among reformers. First, he admitted that he, too, had been on the verge of denying that the body and blood of Christ were in the sacrament; but he was compelled by the words of Jesus in biblical accounts of the Last Supper—that the bread was his body and the cup of wine the new testament in his blood. That text, said Luther, "is too powerfully present and will not allow itself to be torn from its meaning by mere verbiage."[18] Second, Luther fingered the devil as the cause of dissension. Satan was distracting the reformers from the gospel by embroiling them in arguments among themselves. Instead of falling into that trap, the reformers should realize that agreement among them was not mandatory. If you do not destroy images, as Karlstadt would like you to, said Luther, you are not guilty of sin. If you do not receive the sacrament, he continued, you can yet be saved through the word and faith. In this perilous night, the devil's chief aim was to turn us away from the true lamp [Christ] and "draw us into the darkness with a shower of the devil's own sparks."[19] Luther's counsel fell on deaf ears, his own included. The Lord's Supper controversy turned fierce and defied every attempt to resolve it—at the cost of Protestant unity.

As the controversy flared, Luther responded directly to Karlstadt with a long, two-part pamphlet.[20] The issue was: how did the forgiveness that Christ obtained for humanity through his death on the cross reach sinners during their lifetimes? According to medieval doctrine forgiveness was transmitted through the sacraments. In the Lord's Supper it happened through the miracle of transubstantiation when a priest changed the essence of the bread into the body of Christ and the wine into the blood of Christ. Luther rejected that explanation; but he was unable to renounce Christ's presence because he insisted on taking the words of institution literally.

Karlstadt found another way to explain the words of Jesus. If those words were taken literally, then the forgiveness of sins they promised came through the sacrament. In that case, concluded Karlstadt, the death of Christ on the cross was superfluous. Christ need not have died; instituting the sacrament was sufficient. If, however, the words of Christ were taken figuratively, "this is my body" referred not to the bread at the last meal but to Jesus' physical body that died on the cross. And "this cup is the new testament in my blood" referred not to the wine in the sacrament but to the very blood of Christ shed on the cross.[21] Christ did not say to eat and drink in remembrance of the sacrament but in remembrance of him, that is, in remembrance of Christ's death on the cross. Forgiveness of sin came through meditating on the cross and encouraging that meditation was the purpose of the sacrament.

For Luther the Lord's Supper served a different purpose. It was the means through which forgiveness was conveyed, and it gave recipients the comfort and certainty of knowing that forgiveness obtained by Christ on the cross applied specifically to them. That comfort and certainty came to each person through the words spoken to them—the body and blood of Jesus in the bread and wine was "given for you for the forgiveness of sins." Prior to 1524 Luther had maintained that the words of institution were more important than the elements (bread and wine), because the words announced the purpose of the sacrament and declared the reality of what was happening. But taken literally the words also said that the bread was the body of Christ and the cup of wine contained his blood. For Luther, those words had to be just as true as the words that assured recipients of forgiveness. Either all the words of Jesus were true or none of them were trustworthy. Luther's concern was not, however, biblical literalism but the effect of Jesus' words. All who received the sacrament could be certain they were forgiven:

> Even if Christ were given for us and crucified a thousand times, it would all be in vain if the word of God were absent and it was not distributed to me with the bidding: this is for you, take what is yours.[22]

Although Luther's insistence on the immediate personal benefits of the sacrament is understandable, it is impossible to know how much a theological interpretation mattered to ordinary sixteenth-century believers. In all likelihood they brought to the sacrament a significance of their own that was more experiential than intellectual. But to theologians who agreed with Luther's "curious doctrine of the Eucharist,"[23] as one historian called it, and to others who agreed with Karlstadt and Zwingli, it mattered enough to split the Protestant movement. To Karlstadt and Zwingli, believing that the body and blood of Christ were physically or really present in the Lord's supper smacked of the magic and superstition they were determined to abolish from Christianity. To Luther and those who agreed with him, it was neither magic nor superstition but a divine guarantee that the Lord's Supper was not only a memorial but the actual delivery of forgiveness. Late 1524 marked merely the beginning of the Lord's Supper controversy. It persisted for the rest of Luther's life, and he resisted every effort at compromise, in spite of the political advantage offered by a united Protestant movement.

Preoccupied with Karlstadt and the Lord's Supper, Luther delayed answering another challenge published in late 1524. This challenge was delivered by the Dutch humanist Erasmus in a Latin treatise on the freedom of the will or, more precisely, free choice. Erasmus and Luther never met in person, but by 1524 they had exchanged letters and voiced their criticism of each other to third parties. From a distance each scholar kept a wary eye on the other, but not until Erasmus finally gave in to pressure and attacked Luther directly did they become literary adversaries. On

November 17, 1524, Luther assured his friend Nicholas Hausmann that he would answer Erasmus; nevertheless, Luther felt that Karlstadt's challenge demanded more urgent attention than Erasmus' defense of free choice.[24] On January 11, 1525, Luther said he would answer Erasmus when he had time, and on January 23 he told Amsdorf he would start on the reply as soon as he finished *Against the Heavenly Prophets*,[25] which appeared in print on February 2. Seven months passed, however, before Luther could be found diligently at work on *Bondage of the Will*,[26] the common but inexact English title of his rejoinder, which is better rendered as *Bound Choice*.[27] It was not published until the end of 1525, sixteen months after Erasmus' book appeared.

Why did it take so long? Luther could have offered many plausible excuses for the uncharacteristic delay. In early 1525 his teaching schedule required regular lectures on the minor prophets of the Old Testament. On February 1, he concluded a course on Obadiah, and in March and April he lectured on Jonah and Micah. Moreover, he was completing a verse-by-verse commentary on Deuteronomy. The commentary was based on lectures that began in early 1523 after the Wittenberg team translated Deuteronomy from Hebrew into German. The lectures were delivered in the Augustinian cloister to a small gathering that included George Rörer, the recorder of his lectures and sermons, and John Bugenhagen.[28]

In February of 1525 Luther reported that he was also committed to finishing the commentary on Deuteronomy and completing the postils he started in 1521 at the Wartburg fortress.[29] His obligation to Elector Frederick was part of the commitment, because the Elector had suggested the first set of postils, which were published in 1522.[30] The postils were not sermons ready for delivery but guides to the epistle and gospel readings prescribed for worship during the church year. The first set, covering Advent and Christmas, was so popular it sold out. Two years later he resumed work on the postil for the season of Epiphany, which began after Christmas. By mid-March of 1524[31] he had completed material for the fifth Sunday after Epiphany and sent that manuscript to the printshop behind Cranach's apothecary. Before the type had been set, however, the manuscript was stolen and printed elsewhere.[32] Despite that setback Luther kept working. He rewrote the stolen section, made his comments shorter, and consulted his earlier sermons on the same biblical passages. The completed collection, known as the Lenten postil, ended with the Sunday before Easter. It was published by November of 1525, when a buyer of the postil mentioned that he purchased a copy for six groschen.[33]

On April 4, 1525, Philip Melanchthon reported that Luther had finally started work on *Bound Choice*,[34] but one distraction followed another. On Easter Sunday, Luther embarked on a tour that started with the dedication of a school in his birthplace of Eisleben.[35] The town was located on the southern edge of Thuringia, which was vulnerable to the peasant uprisings moving northward. Luther had received a list of grievances from peasant leaders in the south, and while in Eisleben he started the response entitled *Admonition to Peace*.[36] From Eisleben Luther traveled west by wagon to the picturesque town of Stolberg, which was known for minting coins. It was also the birthplace of Thomas Müntzer, who elsewhere in Thuringia was stirring up the common people and recruiting allies for a revolution. Luther was not in Stolberg because of Müntzer, but to visit a prominent friend of the Wittenbergers. Local supporters of Müntzer might have protested his visit, but no record of trouble exists. On the contrary, the town council honored his visit with gifts of wine and Einbeck beer.[37]

As the journey continued, however, Luther realized he was in unfriendly territory. When he preached at Nordhausen, some parishioners rang small bells to interrupt his sermon. Luther was urging them to imitate the patience of Christ on the cross,[38] but the protesters seemed eager for the peasants camped nearby to take their town and make it a Christian commune of the sort Müntzer proposed.[39] Although Luther seemed unfazed by the rebuffs, he later claimed that he had risked life and limb by being there.[40] This was possibly true. When the routes taken during the last half of his journey are matched to documented instances of pillaging by peasant bands, it appears Luther could have witnessed enough mayhem to make him afraid for his life and fearful that the social order was collapsing.[41] Still, his attitude was mostly defiant. On the way home he wrote to a relative, John Rühel, advisor to the counts of Mansfeld, that the devil was unquestionably behind Müntzer and the rebelling peasants. If the uprising continued and Luther could manage it before he died, he promised to marry his Kate to spite the devil.[42] Luther's swagger was a far cry from the anxiety of John Eck, his persistent adversary since the Leipzig debate. In 1525, after most of the fighting had ceased, Eck refused to leave Ingolstadt in Bavaria because he was afraid of falling into peasant hands.[43]

Luther returned to Wittenberg on May 6, 1525, only nine days before the rout of Müntzer and the peasants at Frankenhausen. On May 3, he stopped in Weimar to consult with Duke John, the brother of Elector Frederick. Luther impressed upon John that swift action by the princes was necessary to halt the peasants before it was too late. Duke John assured him that both nobles and townsmen had been summoned to Weimar and ordered to be armed and ready for battle. Both men knew that John's brother, Elector Frederick, was close to death and that Duke John would soon succeed him. Frederick died two days later, on May 5, 1525, and Luther headed for home.

Once in Wittenberg both Luther and Melanchthon were asked by Spalatin to evaluate the traditional protocol for the funeral of a prince. They approved most of the ritual but insisted that no masses be held, no black vestments or altar cloths be used, and no offerings brought in procession to the altar. Luther returned their answers to Spalatin with the comment: "Death is oh so bitter—not so much to the dying as to the living whom the dead leave behind."[44]

Frederick died at his hunting lodge in Lochau fifty miles (eighty kilometers) south of Wittenberg. The body was placed on a bier and drawn through towns and villages as bells rang and people gathered to pay their respects. Church bells also signaled the cortège's approach to Wittenberg. Eight members of the nobility carried the bier in procession, while other dignitaries and residents escorted the corpse into town. At the entrance to the Castle Church coins were distributed to the poor by Lucas Cranach and Christian Goldschmidt. The bier, accompanied by twenty men carrying torches and coats of arms, was placed in the middle of the nave. After hymns and psalms were sung by pupils and priests from the All Saints' Chapter, Philip Melanchthon delivered a Latin address and Martin Luther preached a sermon in German. The corpse, with sentinels present but without hymns or chants, remained in the church overnight.

Before sunrise the next day, Thursday, May 11, 1525, a grave was dug near the altar. Between six and seven o'clock the office of matins was sung and bells rung to assemble the people. After Luther preached a second sermon, the body was buried while the choir sang the Nicene Creed and a chant based on Job 2:10: "Shall we receive good at the hand of God and not receive ill?"[45] With Luther and Melanchthon watching, the prince who enabled Luther and the early reformation to survive, was lowered into his grave without having met in person the leader he protected.[46] According to a later chronicle cold weather made the funeral and the days following quite dreary. Spring in Germany could be pleasant, but in mid-May frost was so common that the period was called the "ice saints" (Eisheiligen) after the saints assigned to those days. In 1525 the "ice saints" were true to their name: a heavy frost ruined the grapes and nuts froze on the trees.[47] The return of the body to Wittenberg, its burial in the Castle Church, and the frigid weather all foreshadowed Martin Luther's own funeral, which took place at the Castle Church in late February of 1546.

Although Luther had promised John Rühel that he would wed Katharina if the peasant uprising continued, a month passed before he again mentioned marriage—but without naming Katharina.[48] It is certain, however, that by June 10 the couple had agreed to marry soon. Writing that day to Spalatin, without reference to his own plans, Luther argued passionately from scripture and human experience that marriages should not be delayed. That was the sole cause, he insisted, that so many marriages failed.[49] The warning may have been intended for others, but Luther had himself in mind; three days later, on the evening of June 13, 1525, he and Katharina were married at the Augustinian cloister where Luther resided. Martin and Katharina had known each other for two years, but the quiet ceremony caught most Wittenbergers by surprise. Besides Pastor Bugenhagen, who presided, only four guests were present: Justus Jonas (who could not help crying); John Apel, professor of law and rector of the university (who had served three months in prison for abetting the escape of a nun and marrying her), and Lucas and Barbara Cranach.[50]

Not everyone was happy about the marriage. To celebrate a wedding only one month after the slaughter at Frankenhausen appeared to be in bad taste. Jerome Schurf, the law professor who defended Luther at Worms, frowned on the marriage of a former monk to a former nun. He predicted the world and the devil would laugh at the reformer and destroy all he had accomplished.[51] From Basel, Erasmus reported to a friend that Luther married a pretty nun who was twenty-six years old but without any means. It is curious that Erasmus should have mentioned Katharina's age, but without that report, if it was accurate, the year of her birth would be unknown. Erasmus also wrote that a few days after the wedding Katharina bore a child, but in 1526 he learned that the rumor was false and retracted his claim.[52]

Melanchthon was peeved because he was neither notified beforehand nor invited; but he was careful to express his irritation only in Greek and only to his friend Camerarius:

> You might be amazed at this unfortunate time, when good and excellent people everywhere are in distress, that Luther not only does not sympathize with them but, as it seems, rather waxes wanton and diminishes his reputation just when Germany has special need of his judgment and authority. These things have occurred, I think, somewhat as follows. The man is

certainly pliable, and the nuns have used their arts against him most successfully. Contact with the nuns has probably softened or even inflamed this noble and high-spirited man. In this way he seems to have fallen into this untimely change of life. The rumor, however, that he had previously dishonored Katharina is manifestly a lie. Now that the deed is done, we must not take it too hard or reproach him, for I think that he was compelled by nature to marry. This mode of life, while indeed humble, is nevertheless holy and more pleasing to God than celibacy.[53]

Melanchthon's remarks may indicate a slight strain in their relationship. Whether or not that was true, Melanchthon's frank descriptions of the reformer are valuable and show, if nothing else, how a milder personality perceived him at close range. The letter to Camerarius continued:

I have unmistakable evidence of Luther's godliness, so that for me to condemn him is impossible. I pray that he should be humbled rather than exalted, as this is perilous not only for the priesthood but also for everyone. ...I have hope that this state of life [marriage] may calm him down, so that he will discard the low buffoonery which we have often censured. As the proverb goes: "A new state of life, a new mode of living."[54]

Between the exchange of vows and the traditional wedding banquet two weeks later, Luther disclosed to Amsdorf, who never married, why he finally succumbed:

The rumor is true that I was suddenly married to Katharina in order to forestall the unrestrained gossip that commonly swirls around me.... Nor did I want to pass up this fresh opportunity to comply with my father's wish for progeny. At the same time, I wanted to confirm what I have taught by practicing it; for I find that many people are still timid despite such great light shed by the gospel. God has willed this thing and made it happen. I feel neither passionate love nor burning for my spouse, but I cherish her.[55]

The banquet was a reunion of relatives, friends, and former colleagues. Luther's parents attended, together with friends from Mansfeld such as John Rühel. Also invited were Amsdorf and Wenzel Linck, who were no longer in Wittenberg. It was Linck's wedding three years earlier in Altenburg that drew the theological faculty away from Wittenberg.

Leonhard Koppe, who in 1523 helped Katharina and the other nuns escape, was also invited. The university, which Luther made famous, sent the couple an embossed silver goblet; the town of Wittenberg provided beer and wine; and the electoral court made sure that Luther received the venison he requested.[56] Elector John himself, who had just succeeded his brother, donated 100 florins to the couple and allowed them to set up housekeeping in the monastery. If Katharina was living in the stately home of the Cranachs, it must have been a shock to move into bachelor quarters that were untidy and cluttered. Since 1519 a man named Wolfgang Sieberger had served as Luther's personal attendant. In 1525, he was mainly the housekeeper for Luther and his colleague Brisger, who soon married and moved out of the cloister. Sieberger stayed on with Martin and Katharina until Luther's death, but despite his loyalty Sieberger was lazy and never became fond of order and cleanliness.[57]

The newly-weds took almost nothing into the cloister except the 100 florins from Elector John and the unexpected gift of twenty florins from Archbishop Albert of Mainz.[58] Katharina had no dowry and Luther's salary would have been small, if he was earning anything at all. After the turmoil of the Peasants' War the university had no money and only one-fourth the enrollment of four years earlier. Luther and Melanchthon pleaded with Spalatin and Elector John to replenish its coffers, and late in 1525 faculty salaries were increased. Luther and Melanchthon were to receive 200 guilders per year. Professors of law and medicine were paid less, but they supplemented their salaries with consulting fees from outside the university. In 1539 printers offered Luther 400 florins a year for the rights to all his books, but he turned them down. His reason: God and the electors of Saxony had given to him all that he needed, so much in fact that he never demanded royalties for his books or charged students to attend his lectures.[59]

Katharina proved to be more realistic than her husband about the budget required to run a large household. She kept track of income and expenses and saw to it that repairs were made to the cloister and new paint and plaster applied to the rundown interior. She also had a fountain installed and resurrected the cloister garden. At her direction Luther was soon ordering seeds for vegetables from Wenzel Linck in Nuremberg and John Lang in Erfurt. The new home also received two clocks from Nuremberg, one from Linck and the other from Frederick Pistorius, former abbot of a Benedictine monastery. After forty-three years of keeping time by church bells and the sun, Luther for the first time owned a clock and surmised he needed mathematicians to teach him how it worked. [60]

Martin and Katharina had barely occupied the cloister when an unlikely guest arrived. It was Andrew Karlstadt. With his wife and child, Karlstadt had been caught in the turmoil of the Peasants' War and detained in Frankfurt. Shortly before the wedding banquet Luther received a letter from Karlstadt begging him to intercede with Elector John so that Karlstadt and his family could return to Saxony.[61] Luther responded with sympathy but demanded that Karlstadt forswear in writing that he had ever supported Müntzer or insurrection of any kind. Karlstadt complied, and Luther published his statement with a preface that defended his own decision to relieve the plight of Karlstadt and his family.[62] Karlstadt's wife and child returned to Saxony at the end of June and lodged with her parents in Seegrehna, across the Elbe from Wittenberg. Soon after his wife's return, Karlstadt secretly entered Saxony and found refuge with the Luthers. For eight weeks he stayed with them under cover. In mid-September, Elector John decided that Karlstadt could remain in Saxony but must reside within three miles of Wittenberg.[63] That allowed Karlstadt to join his wife and son in Segrehna; and in February of 1526 their son Andrew was baptized in the presence of the Luthers, Jonas, and Melanchthon. Katharina became the child's godmother. Luther reported to Amsdorf that one year earlier nobody could have predicted such a turnaround.

Despite the distractions caused by the peasant rebellion and his marriage, Luther delivered regular lectures. When the summer of 1525 ended, however, Luther stopped his lectures and did not resume them until the end of December. That window of three months finally gave Luther time to answer Erasmus' defense of free will, a task he had put off for a year. On September 28, 1525, he told Spalatin that he was totally occupied with Erasmus and free choice: "I will make every effort," he continued, "to show that Erasmus said nothing correctly, since in truth nothing he said was correct."[64] Luther did, however, compliment Erasmus for making the unfree will the subject of his challenge: "Indeed, as you should know, this is the cardinal issue between us, the point on which everything in this controversy turns."[65] Actually, the topic of the free or unfree will was not solely Erasmus' choice. It was suggested to him either directly or indirectly by the English king, Henry VIII. In 1523 Henry was told by the Catholic Duke George of Saxony that predestination and the unfree will were to blame for all of Luther's errors.[66] Erasmus mentioned that letter when he sent to Duke George a copy of *Freedom of the Will*, or *Free Choice*, as soon as it was published in 1524:

I am sending Your Highness a book on free choice, about which I read in your very learned epistle. The most serene King of England and Pope Clement VII spurred me on with their letters; but I was goaded far more fervently by the deceitfulness of those raving maniacs [Protestant reformers] who, if not restrained, will topple both the gospel and good scholarship. I wanted the tyranny of those Pharisees [Catholic authorities] abolished, not merely replaced by others. But if we have to live under tyrants, I prefer popes and bishops to those sordid oppressors, who are more intolerable than all the others.[67]

Erasmus need not have worried that Protestant reformers would destroy good scholarship. All the leading reformers were trained in the classics and most had earned advanced degrees. They had no intention of abolishing the study of Greek, Hebrew, and Latin, since the knowledge of those languages helped to make the reformation possible. Writing to a familiar supporter in 1523 Luther emphasized that point:

Do not worry that we Germans are becoming more barbarous than ever before or that our theology causes a decline of learning. Certain people are often afraid when there is nothing to fear. I am convinced that without humanist studies untainted theology cannot exist, and that has proven true. When humanist studies declined and lay prostrate, theology was also neglected and lay in ruin. There has never been a great revelation of God's word unless God has first prepared the way by the rise and flourishing of languages and learning, as if these were the forerunners of theology as John the Baptist was for Christ.[68]

Erasmus agreed in theory with many changes made by the reformers and could have joined forces with Melanchthon and Luther. In late 1520 Luther wrote that, God willing, he and Erasmus would remain one.[69] Instead, in 1524 and 1525, with Erasmus under intense pressure to prove he did not support Luther, the debate over free choice widened the distance between them. The issue was more important for Luther than for Erasmus. Erasmus declared it was not necessary for Christians to form an opinion about free choice, but Luther insisted that a correct opinion on the matter was essential. The forty-one statements that served as grounds for Luther's excommunication included a denial of free will, which Luther explained as follows: "It is a profound and blind error to teach that the will is by nature free and can, without grace, turn to the Spirit, seek grace, and desire it."[70]

That statement contradicted a tenet of scholastic theology that attributed to the human will, even in a state of sin, enough natural power to seek God's grace. It was the medieval theological version of "God helps those who help themselves," or "Every person is free to decide for or against God." For Luther, the reality that made it false was the power of sin. Instead of leaving the will some natural freedom, sin bound the will so that it could not seek God's grace until God's grace released the will from the chains of sin. Once liberated from the power of sin, the will was indeed able to respond to God's grace with faith and gratitude, but salvation was still solely the work of God. If the free will could choose God on its own, then salvation was not solely God's work. It was a joint venture of the human and the divine for which believers could always claim partial credit.

In *Free Choice* Erasmus chose Bible passages to support the joint venture. He also maintained that some matters in scripture were ambiguous and that even some clear passages should not be taught to everyone. In addition, he claimed that Luther's denial of free will supported the notion that everything happened out of necessity. For Erasmus that kind of determinism led to complacency and depravity since human striving to be good could never alter a predetermined outcome. Luther's reply was a response to the points made by Erasmus. He argued that scripture was not ambiguous but absolutely clear on the power of sin, the bound will, and the initiative of God's grace. Luther also upheld the necessity of all that happens. Nothing could be more comforting, he insisted, especially to those who suffer, than to know that God's will was in control of everything, the bad as well as the good. God did not force people to act against their will, however, and certainly not when they received the Spirit and grace of God:

> If God works in us, the will is changed, and being gently breathed upon by the Spirit of God, it again wills and acts from pure willingness and its own inclination. It does not act from compulsion, and therefore it cannot be ... overcome or compelled even by the gates of hell. Rather it goes on willing and delighting in and loving the good, just as before it willed and delighted in and loved evil. . . . Here there is no free choice or freedom to turn oneself in another direction or to will something different, so long as the Spirit and grace of God remain in us.[71]

It might have been wise for Luther to stop at that point. Instead, he argued that we were always captive—either to the god of this world, that is, to Satan and the power of sin, or captive to the "true God," who overcomes Satan and breaks the power of sin. Captivity to the true God, however, was for Luther a "royal freedom," which enabled us readily to will and to do what God wills. To exemplify these two captivities, Luther called up an illustration that was used by theologians before him:

> The human will is placed between God and Satan like a beast of burden. If God rides the beast, it wills and goes where God wills.... If Satan rides it, it wills and goes where Satan wills.... The beast cannot choose to run to the other rider or seek him out, but the riders themselves contend for the possession and control of it.[72]

It was one thing to say the human will could not freely choose God's grace, but it was another to say, as this illustration did, that the human will could not freely turn away from that grace. In his reply to Luther published in 1526, Erasmus said he agreed that we cannot choose to receive grace but he disagreed that we cannot freely turn our back on the grace we have once been given. That, he said, is like saying that people who stand in the sunshine cannot close their eyes.[73]

Bound Choice appeared in print on or just before December 31, 1525. Luther called the book a refutation of Erasmus written in a hurry.[74] It was not a bestseller nor could it have been. Like *Free Choice* it was a Latin tome written for scholars; nevertheless, both books were translated into German. Erasmus was hurt by the accusations in Luther's book and told him so: "The whole world knows your nature; truly you have so guided your pen that you have written against no one more rabidly and, what is more detestable, more maliciously than against me.... I would wish you a better disposition were you not so marvelously satisfied with the one you have."[75] In 1533 Luther reportedly uttered a slur that Erasmus never heard: "If I were to cut open Erasmus' heart, I would find there nothing but ridicule about the Trinity, about the sacrament, etc. Everything is a laughing matter for him."[76]

The subject of the Luther-Erasmus debate was theologically important to both men, but the controversy had little impact on their lives or on the reformation. It was too little too late. Luther did not need *Bound Choice* to secure his leadership or to convince Elector John of Saxony to intensify his support of the reformation. As for Erasmus, *Free Choice* was published too late to dispel the suspicion that he sympathized with Luther. And although *Free Choice* confirmed Duke George's stand against the reformation and pleased King Henry, ten years later Henry severed the English Church from Rome and executed the friends of Erasmus. Nor did *Free Choice* prevent Pope Paul IV from including the writings of Erasmus alongside those of Luther in the first Roman *Index of Prohibited Books* (1559). There at last both men rested on common ground.

CHAPTER TWELVE

A COARSE AND UNRULY PEOPLE
1526–1527
Wittenberg–Torgau

"We Germans are a wild, coarse, and unruly people. It is hard to start anything new with them unless dire circumstances force them to it."[1]

In 1525 the profile of the German Reformation began to change. According to historians, before 1525 momentum for the reform movement came from the bottom up, that is, from the laity and clergy who read the compelling pamphlets written by Luther and many others. After 1525 the momentum came from the top down as reforms were established by princes and magistrates in the territories and towns they governed. The early evangelical movement was a populist endeavor, a wildfire that no one controlled, but beginning in 1526 the civil authorities brought the conflagration under control. The support of civil authority was necessary for the evangelical movement to survive the attacks of its enemies: the Catholic emperor and princes in Germany and the Catholic cantons in Switzerland. Moreover, there was no separation of church and government in pre-reformation Europe, no tradition of legitimate free churches. Despite the tension between secular rulers and Roman bishops, parishes and monasteries were subject to one or both of these overlords. However, once princes and town councils were convinced by the evangelical message, they disregarded the bishops, challenged the emperor, and decided by themselves to approve or reject changes in religious policies proposed by the Protestant reformers.

As a rule, historians have lamented the shift from populist movement to government-authorized reforms, but for the most part Luther did not. Elector John was a stronger supporter of the reformation than his deceased brother, the former Elector Frederick, ever was. Frederick had grudgingly allowed a few reforms but Elector John threw his full weight behind the proposals submitted by Luther and his colleagues. By 1526 the religious profile of Wittenberg was undergoing conspicuous alterations. No monks were left at the Franciscan cloister and the Augustinian house was now occupied by Martin, Katharina, and their housekeeper. The All Saints' Chapter was on its last legs. Few, if any, former priests and friars were seen on the streets. German was used in worship at the Town Church near the square. Latin was still used for the Sunday mass in the Castle Church, but when it was time for the sacrament, German words of institution replaced the Latin prayer of consecration and both bread and wine were offered to communicants. Elector John attended worship in the Castle Church when he was in town. It remained the university chapel and continued to be used for academic celebrations, disputations, and funerals. Both Luther and Melanchthon would later rest there.

The German order of service that became standard for Sunday worship at the Town Church was adopted soon after Christmas of 1525. Long promised and finally completed by Luther, the *German Mass* reached a wide audience, not only because Luther wrote in German but also because he insisted that it was adaptable: "Do not make it a rigid law to bind or entangle anyone's conscience, but use it in Christian liberty as long, when, where, and how you find it to be practical and useful."[2] The *German Mass* was necessary, wrote Luther, owing to the confusion caused by the German services already in circulation. Before the Peasants' War, Thomas Müntzer had created a German liturgy for his parish in Allstedt, and towns such as Nuremberg and Strasbourg had adopted their own German orders. In Luther's view, however, they were not German enough. Nicholas Hausmann, his friend and pastor in Zwickau, sent Luther a sample of German orders to peruse. Luther returned them with the comment: "I do not object to the mass sung in this manner. But I hate to see Latin notes set over German words. I told the publisher about the German manner of singing, and that is what I want here."[3]

When Luther asked for assistance to find the style and rhythm he desired, Elector John sent two musicians from the court in Torgau: the cantor Conrad Rupsch and John Walter, who one year earlier had edited the first Lutheran hymnal.[4] In November of 1525 they worked with Luther on finding proper tones for chanting the German liturgy. According to Walter, Luther himself composed the chant for the words of institution at the Lord's Supper and for the traditional biblical readings: the epistle and the gospel.[5] The other compositions for public worship were left to professional musicians.

The preface to the *German Mass* revealed a disappointment infrequently mentioned by Luther. It appeared in the section that distinguished among three forms of worship for Wittenberg. First was a Latin service that altered the traditional mass to fit Luther's theology of the Lord's Supper. Second was a German service mainly for local worshipers, among whom, lamented Luther, were many who did not believe and were not yet Christians. Most of them came to church out of curiosity, "hoping to see something new, just as if we were holding a service among the Turks or the heathen in a public square or out in a field."[6] Third and most desirable, he declared, was an informal service intended for people who earnestly desired to be Christian and "professed the gospel with hand and mouth." They would meet in a house to pray, read, baptize, share the Lord's Supper, and do "other Christian works."[7] Elaborate singing would not be necessary and only a few directions would be needed for conducting baptisms and the Lord's Supper. The worship would be "centered on God's word, prayer, and love."[8] Unfortunately, it was not yet possible:

If I had people who wanted to be Christians in earnest, the rules and regulations would soon be ready, but as yet I neither can nor desire to start such an assembly or to make rules for it. For I do not yet have the persons for it, nor do I see many who want it. But if I should be requested to do it and could not with good conscience refuse, I should gladly do my part and help as best I can. . . . However, if I tried to organize it only because I wanted it, it might turn into a sect. . . . We Germans are a wild, coarse, and unruly people. It is hard to start anything new with them unless dire circumstances force them to it.[9]

Why the disappointment? Because, like most reformers, Luther was an idealist. His dream of a reformed Christianity went far beyond tweaking the traditional structure of Christendom: formal worship in sacred buildings according to a ritual that was governed by rubrics and approved by the clerical hierarchy. Evangelical or Lutheran worship, as Luther imagined it, would be informal and spontaneous, and whatever guidelines were needed would arise from the communal experience itself and not be imposed from above. If love, prayer, and God's word guided evangelical services, religion would not be confined to churchgoing but would spill over into daily life. Separating the secular from the religious was more difficult. Criticizing the tradition of referring to celibate priests, nuns, and monks as "the religious," Luther insisted that marriage was the most religious state of all because "nothing should be called religious except that inner life of faith in the heart where the Spirit rules."[10] By the same token, the good works of Christians were neither meritorious nor limited to religious activities. Seeking justice and demonstrating love in daily life were just as religious as prayer, reading the Bible, delivering or hearing homilies, or receiving the sacraments. If all of that resembles the ideal monastic life of common prayer and work—although stripped of celibacy and the demand for perfection, and adapted for all "earnest Christians" outside the cloister—it is no coincidence. Luther never completely abandoned the monastic ideal. The man left the monastery, but the monastery never left the man.

Again like most reformers, Luther had to settle for less than he envisioned. Because support for his informal worship was lacking, he had to work within the religious structure that he knew: a network of parishes, each with a sacred building and clergy who presided over communal worship that stuck to traditional patterns. Consequently, Luther focused on improving the parish system and supplying two essential resources: the *German Mass* and the catechisms. By pressing Elector John to accept these resources, Luther was, for the first time, officially requesting approval for new forms of parish life. Before 1526, he was reacting against the authority of Roman bishops and recommending gradual changes. The ninety-five theses (1517) were mainly a statement of protest and the initial reforms in Wittenberg were not authorized by Elector Frederick before he died (1525). In 1526, however, Elector John appeared ready to endorse the proposal mailed to him on October 31, 1525, eight years to the day after Luther sent the ninety-five theses to Archbishop Albert of Mainz. It had taken that long to move from the protest against indulgences to a true reformation.

Luther's proposal was an agenda with several items, the first of which was to secure the future of the university. Money was the top priority and George Spalatin had a plan: expropriate the endowment funds donated to the All Saints' Chapter and transfer those funds to the budget of the university. Since private masses were no longer performed, a chapter of priests living off the income from those endowments was no longer needed. Luther wanted the All Saints' Chapter dissolved while Elector Frederick was alive, but the relic collection, which was managed by priests in the chapter, was too dear to Frederick's heart. Elector John adopted Spalatin's plan and sent two counselors to Wittenberg to arrange transfer of the funds. Two-thirds of the money was to be used for the university and one-third set aside for the Castle Church, but the Town Church, where

Bugenhagen was pastor and services were held in German, became the center of reformation worship.[11] Frederick's relic collection was brought secretly to the residence of Elector John in Torgau. A goldsmith stripped the sacred objects of their valuable parts and separated them into piles of gold, silver, precious stones, and pearls. The gold and gems were made into jewelry and utensils. The silver was sold in Nuremberg for 25,000 guilders and the cash used to pay expenses at the Torgau court.[12]

The second item on the agenda sent to Elector John concerned the new German service. It had already been introduced at the Town Church by the deacon, George Rörer, who chanted the liturgy.[13] The third item, however, required the Elector's intervention:

> The parishes everywhere are in such miserable condition. No one makes donations or payments of any kind; private masses no longer generate income. The people pay so little respect to the pastors that in a short time there will not be a functioning parsonage, school, or pulpit. God's word and worship will perish unless Your Grace passes strict laws and carefully regulates the maintenance of parishes and pulpits.[14]

The first challenge was to estimate how much regulation was needed, and Luther asked Elector John to authorize an inspection of the parishes to determine their condition. The impetus came from the Elector's son, John Frederick, who wanted Luther to mimic the apostle Paul by visiting town after town in order to remove from office those priests who sympathized with fanatics such as Müntzer. The inspection would resemble a visitation—the term used for a bishop's annual tour of the parishes in his diocese. In 1525 the territory ruled by Elector John was divided among several dioceses, but none of the bishops supported the reformation. In the absence of bishops, Luther thought it natural for the Elector to initiate the visitation.

On this point, however, Elector John dragged his feet, and with good reason. According to the 1521 Edict of Worms, Luther, John himself, and all supporters of the reformation were still imperial outlaws; and a new diet of the empire, opening in June of 1526 at Speyer, was ready to force compliance with the edict. Just as pressing was the diet's second purpose: to raise money and troops to defend Hungary and Austria from the Ottoman Turks. Fortunately for the Lutherans, the two purposes were incompatible and offered them unanticipated leverage: If the emperor wanted troops and money from the Lutherans, he must accept their religious reforms. The

Lutheran advantage was recognized by Archduke Ferdinand, the emperor's younger brother, who presided over the diet, and for him money and soldiers were more important than religious unity. For the time being, despite the Edict of Worms, Lutheran cities and territories were allowed to maintain their religious status without fear of reprisal. This decision in the summer of 1526 cleared the way for Elector John to authorize the visitation in Electoral Saxony.

That summer life in the Luther household changed forever. The former monk became a father and the former nun a mother. On June 7, 1526, the first child of Martin and Katharina was born in Wittenberg. It was a boy. The parents named him Johannes after his godfather, John Bugenhagen, and like the boy's grandfather young Johannes would be called Hans or Hänschen (little Hans). Two hours after the birth Hänschen was baptized by George Rörer, deacon at the Town Church. Present were Bugenhagen, Justus Jonas, and Lucas Cranach. The next day Luther announced the birth to his relative in Eisleben, John Rühel, and asked him to relay the news to John Agricola, principal of the Latin school in the same town. Agricola had been a favorite student and colleague before leaving Wittenberg with his wife Elsa. Luther called him "Master Eisleben":

> Please tell Master Eisleben on my behalf that at 2:00 pm yesterday my dear Kate, by God's great grace, gave to me a little Hans Luther. Tell Master Eisleben not to be surprised that I approach him with such news, for he should bear in mind what it is to have sun [i.e. a son] at this time of year.[15] Please greet your dear sun-bearer [wife] and Eisleben's Elsa. I commend you herewith to God. Amen. As I write this, my weakened wife is asking for me.[16]

No birth announcement to his parents is extant, but Luther sent personal notes to Hausmann and Linck, and someone notified Spalatin, who sent congratulations less than a week after the birth. Calling himself a happy father, Luther thanked Spalatin and told him about the garden he had planted and fountain he had built. "Come see us," he beckoned, "and you will be crowned with lilies and roses."[17] Shortly after the birth, Luther preached at the Castle Church in the presence of Elector John, his son, Prince John Frederick, and Duke Francis of Lüneburg, a large territory that was about to adopt the reformation.[18] Two weeks later, Elector John sent Luther and his expanding family a haunch of venison.[19]

Spalatin's congratulatory note and Luther's invitation to visit reflected the warm relationship they sustained after Spalatin moved to Altenburg.

He married a local woman, also named Katharina, and invited Luther and Melanchthon to the wedding. Although they and others had made the same trip three years earlier to the wedding of Wenzel Linck, few, if any of Spalatin's former colleagues attended. Melanchthon waited five months before sending congratulations, and Luther sent regrets—but only at the last minute. His Katharina was crying while begging him not to go and, besides, undertaking the trip in mid-November with only one companion was dangerous for a heretic who was also an outlaw. Three weeks after the wedding, however, Luther sent a second letter, promising Spalatin to be present with him in a very unusual way:

> When you have embraced your Katharina in bed with the sweetest kisses, think also to yourself: "My Christ has given me this person, this very best creature of my God; to him be praise and glory." I will predict the day on which you receive this letter, and that night in the same way I will love my Katharina in memory of you.[20]

In late August of 1526, Luther sent Wenzel Linck, now a Lutheran pastor in Nuremberg, the latest news from Wittenberg.[21] The letter was written one day after the Diet of Speyer decided to allow each city or territory to retain its current religious status until a national council was held. Luther knew the diet was in session but the good news had not reached him. Wrongly, therefore, he told Linck that nothing would be accomplished at the diet except the usual drinking and carousing. Prior to the diet, added Luther, Elector John ordered new ramparts for Wittenberg in case the Edict of Worms was enforced and the town was attacked. Wittenberg was fortified to such an extent that Linck would no longer recognize it. Luther also admitted to lecturing unwillingly on the book of Ecclesiastes because the Hebrew was so difficult. In September he apparently stopped lecturing before reaching the end, although Luther, or George Rörer who was taking notes, or someone else added enough material for the lectures to be published in 1532. Luther objected to the pessimism of Ecclesiastes but was unable to avoid expressing his own:

> Regardless of what the state of the world has been, it has always seemed intolerable. . . . The world cannot be content with the present; it is always tormented by the future. So it is that Germany is always looking for something new. When the gospel began, everyone ran to it eagerly, but now that the gospel has prevailed, we are bored and forget its great blessings.[22]

In the lectures on Ecclesiastes, Luther mentioned adversaries whom he called "sacramentarians." The word applied to reformers such as Andrew Karlstadt who rejected the real presence of Christ in the Lord's Supper. Beginning in 1526, Ulrich Zwingli became the foremost critic of Luther's assertion of the real presence, and Luther started using the word for him and his supporters. The word "sacrament" originally meant sign or symbol; in Luther's mind Zwingli was a sacramentarian because he reduced the Lord's Supper to a symbol instead of the real miracle that took place. Both Zwingli and Luther, however, blamed the same source for the abuses they sought to remove from the sacrament. That source was the Roman mass, the heart of which was the Lord's Supper. In 1522 Luther had pointed out how the exclusive power of priests to change bread and wine into the body and blood of Christ created a clericalism on which Rome built its wealth and authority:

> If we take away the mass, then we are rid of everything. The mass is the crux and the basis of the papacy and all its clergy. On that foundation they have built their endowed institutions, cloisters, and churches; supported their bellies, bodies, livings, and status, not to mention their wealth, glory, and pomp. That will all collapse even if we do not assail it.[23]

Some form of the Lord's Supper had to replace the mass, but Luther and Zwingli could not agree on what happened in the sacrament or how it should be conducted. Luther's habit was to tar similar adversaries with the same brush; hence Zwinglians were not the only sacramentarians. In one letter he identified five or six such groups and named their leaders.[24] One of them was Caspar von Schwenckfeld, a nobleman of Silesia, a region that lies mostly in southwestern Poland but in the 1500s was heavily German. After studying in Germany, Schwenckfeld became the chief counselor of Duke Frederick of Liegnitz (now Legnica). He read Luther and the Bible so avidly that in 1521, the year Luther was excommunicated and outlawed, Schwenckfeld was able to convince Duke Frederick of the need for religious reform. In 1523 loss of hearing forced Schwenckfeld to retire to the family's estate close to Liegnitz. Further study and a spiritual revelation led him to reject the real presence of Christ in the Lord's Supper. Together with his friend, the teacher Valentin Crautwald, Schwenckfeld rearranged the words of institution and concluded that sacramental bread was only spiritual food, not the real body of Christ in the way Luther insisted.

After sending his proposal to Luther and receiving no reply, Schwenckfeld and Crautwald decided to visit Luther in person. By horse and wagon it was a three-day trip if the weather in late November of 1525 was favorable. They made it by December 1 and met with Luther, Bugenhagen, and Justus Jonas. According to Schwenckfeld's account, the only one extant, the discussions were friendly, although Crautwald had expected Luther to be obstinate.[25] After observing church life in Wittenberg, Schwenckfeld complained that he expected to find more devout and virtuous believers in Wittenberg and asked Luther to bar misbehaving and lukewarm churchgoers from the Lord's Supper. The lack of zeal was disappointing, admitted Luther, and he planned to hold special worship services for the few who lived full Christian lives. As of now, though, he could not find even one true Christian.[26] Luther's reply to Schwenckfeld was echoed one month later in his preface to the *German Mass*, in which he described a form of worship for earnest Christians even though he could find none. On the words of institution, the visit of Schwenckfeld and Crautwald to Wittenberg produced no agreement. Jonas was so dismayed that he promised 100 gold coins to anyone who could resolve the dispute.[27] In 1529 Schwenckfeld was forced out of Silesia, but his followers survived, and in 1734, 500 of them emigrated to Pennsylvania, where they established a Schwenckfelder church. Schwenckfeld himself spent most of his later life in southern Germany around Ulm where he died.

1527 started out badly for Luther. On January 1, he unloaded his frustration on Wenzel Linck in Nuremberg:

> Persuaded by the king of Denmark, I wrote a humble and suppliant letter
> to the king of England [Henry VIII]; I had high hopes and wrote with a
> guileless and candid heart. He has answered me with such hostility that he
> sounds ... as if he rejoiced in the opportunity for revenge. These tyrants
> have weak, unmanly, and thoroughly sordid characters that make them
> unworthy of serving any but the rabble. ... I disdain them and their god
> Satan.[28]

It was not the first time that Luther linked his theological critics to Satan, but the king of England was not just any theologian. The controversy between Henry and Luther had ignited in 1520 after Luther published the *Babylonian Captivity of the Church*. It redefined the Catholic sacraments and reduced their number from seven to two. A year later Henry responded with a defense of the seven sacraments. On May 12, 1521, as Luther's books were burned outside St. Paul's Cathedral in London, the lord chancellor, Cardinal Wolsey, held a copy of Henry's manuscript. Pope Leo X rewarded the king with the title "Defender of the Faith" and the readers of Henry's book with an indulgence. After Henry adopted the reformation, an English prior remarked that the "Defender of the Faith" should be told he was now the "Destroyer of the Faith."[29]

The name-calling started with Henry, who labeled Luther a poisonous serpent and infernal wolf. Luther did not respond until Henry's Latin text was translated into German and published in 1522. His reply, *Against Henry the King of England*, charged that Henry's book was full of lies and Henry himself was the king of liars. The king's raging and railing made him worse than a livid whore on the street.[30] On that rancorous note the exchange might have ended if it were not for King Christian II of Denmark. Christian told Luther that Henry VIII was ready to make England Protestant on the condition that Luther apologized for insulting Henry three years earlier. If Christian was right, England could provide needed backup for Lutheran territories in Germany against a Catholic alliance organized by Duke George of Saxony. This Catholic league brought together four strong Catholic rulers who were dedicated to wiping out the "damned Lutheran sect."[31] On September 1, 1525, Luther sent his apology to Henry and offered to recant the insults but not the content of the *Babylonian Captivity*.

Luther's letter was out of character and pointless. In 1525 Henry VIII had no intention of swinging his support to Luther, and the church in England was nine years away from breaking with Rome. German merchants were smuggling Luther's pamphlets into London, where they found eager readers, but the agents of Chancellor Wolsey were constantly on their trail. Thomas Cromwell, the architect of the English Reformation, was still a young lawyer. Henry did, however, take note of Luther's letter and must have smiled at the naïve groveling. He responded to Luther promptly but not personally. The reply, printed in Latin, was sent to Luther by Duke George, who forwarded it, no doubt with glee. Henry blamed Luther for sending 70,000 people to death during the Peasants' War and for defiling a nun by marrying Katharina. Again, Luther did not respond. However, when a German version of Henry's tract implied that Luther had recanted all his teachings, he replied with his *Against the Blasphemous Book of the King of England*. This text was bitingly unapologetic, but he was irritated at himself for having believed the report of King Christian. Nevertheless, Luther expressed no regret about sending the book. It was done for the sake of the gospel; and anything done for that reason was bound to reap slander and scorn. Instead of flinching, Luther paraphrased Psalm 138:7: "The wrath of my enemies is my gladness and delight."[32]

On April 22, 1527, the Monday after Easter when Luther was preaching, vertigo prevented him from completing the sermon.[33] It was an early sign of what was to come. On June 16, when his uncle, Heinz Luder, came for a visit, Luther seemed well. Uncle Heinz was followed by Elsa, the ailing wife of John Agricola of Eisleben. Although Katharina Luther was pregnant and nauseous, Luther invited Elsa to convalesce in Wittenberg. After she arrived, Luther thought she appeared sicker in spirit than in body and prescribed reliance on scripture rather than taking medicine from the apothecary or applying ancient poultices.[34] On July 6, Luther himself suffered a fainting fit so sudden and severe that he expected to die in front of his wife and friends.[35] He reported the incident to Spalatin, who also was ill and warned Luther that the plague had reached Wittenberg. The rumor was absolutely untrue, replied Luther, but a month later he was proven wrong. He alerted Melanchthon, who was out of town, and reported that everyone hoped the plague would be mild, but he confessed that Hans Lufft, the printer, had been ill for nine days and seemed delirious.[36]

How sick was Luther in July? The cause of his dizziness and fainting might have been poor circulation, or Ménière's disease, a disorder of the inner ear that causes severe vertigo, ringing, and hearing loss. A report on the July 6 incident by Justus Jonas suggests it was Ménière's disease. Jonas and his wife were invited to supper at the cloister when Luther complained of a loud, maddening noise in his left ear and took to his bed. Jonas followed and saw him about to faint, when Luther said: "Doctor Jonas, I am very nauseated; bring me some water or I will throw up." Jonas was so alarmed that he started to shake and spilled water on Luther's face and back. After seeing that a doctor was called, Katharina arrived in the room and found Luther in fervent prayer. Luther asked to see his one-year-old Hänschen and commended him and Katharina to God as if he were certain of dying.

Luther did not die, and the next day he assured Jonas that the spiritual attack was twice as agonizing as the physical pain.[37] Luther's name for these spiritual attacks was *Anfechtungen*, often translated as "temptations," but better understood as assaults of doubt and despair, which he blamed on the devil. These bouts of melancholy would today be diagnosed as depression and treated with medication. Like depression, the *Anfechtungen* temporarily kept Luther from working, but the volume of pages he produced, the lively *Table Talk*, two thousand letters, regular lecturing, and his frequent trips all demonstrate that depression did not disable him. While Luther was ill in 1527, Bugenhagen reported that he rarely missed a lecture or failed to preach on Sundays.[38]

On August 10, 1527, Elector John asked Luther and his family to follow the university to the town of Jena in order to avoid the plague.[39] Luther ignored the request. Five days later, however, Bugenhagen and his family moved into the cloister and one early victim of the plague died, almost in Luther's arms.[40] On August 20, George Rörer tried to quash a rumor that in Wittenberg the plague was spreading rapidly. Only seven or eight people, he claimed, had been infected and during the prior ten days no one had become ill.[41] The respite was deceiving. In September and October the number of victims climbed, and the Luthers took in two patients: the wife of a local physician and a sister-in-law of Karlstadt. Luther worried about his son, who became ill, and about Katharina. She appeared more vulnerable after the death of Hanna Rörer, a sister of Bugenhagen who was also the pregnant wife of George Rörer.[42] Bugenhagen himself took ill, but he stayed in town with Luther and the deacons Rörer and John Mantel in order to hold services and provide pastoral care.

Luther advised other clergy to do the same in a booklet that answered a question sent to him by the Lutheran pastors in Breslau (now Wroclaw, Poland). They wanted to know whether or not people should flee when the plague struck their area. The obligation to remain, wrote Luther, applied to city officials, pastors, deacons, doctors, nurses, and caretakers. Other citizens were free to leave, but those who stayed should take advantage of the available medicines and treatments.[43] Although Luther gave people a kind of permission to leave, he did not expect the exodus to be so large:

> The panic and hasty flight are astounding. I did not anticipate that Satan, monster that he is, terrified people so or, what is worse, rejoices that he strikes such fear into hearts that he is able to chase away and humiliate our distinguished university. He despises our school above everything else and, it appears, not in vain.[44]

What kind of plague was it? Probably a milder cousin of the bubonic plague known as the Black Death, which had decimated Western Europe around 1350. Bubonic was one of three infections traceable to *Y. pestis*, the bacterium that caused periodic but smaller epidemics in the following centuries. If *Y. pestis* did strike Wittenberg, it was much less virulent than the Black Death or the smallpox epidemics in the Americas that killed millions of natives in the 1500s.[45] Luther was apparently not infected by *Y. pestis*, but he did suffer weak spells through the rest of 1527.

Despite his weakness, Luther kept preaching and lecturing. In addition, Luther and Bugenhagen were called on to review guidelines for the visitation of parishes that was about to start in earnest. The review required not only reading at home but traveling to Torgau to discuss the guidelines with Spalatin and with Melanchthon, who had prepared the draft. The meetings were held at the end of September and the end of November. The second meeting was attended by John Agricola, who strongly disagreed with Melanchthon and Luther on one point. Neither Luther nor Melanchthon wanted a public dispute with Agricola, and for the time being they were able to smooth his ruffled feathers because, according to Luther, the conflict "did not amount to anything."[46] Later that turned out not to be true, but in Torgau Luther and Melanchthon had other things on their minds.

On November 25, 1527, just as Melanchthon arrived in Torgau, his wife Katharina gave birth to their third child, a son named George. Melanchthon did not know about the birth until he returned to Jena, where the university was waiting out the plague. He announced the birth to Spalatin with the comment: "God's kindness makes our domestic matters easy to bear; if only our public affairs could be so tranquil!"[47] Then, on December 10 in Wittenberg, Katharina Luther gave birth to a daughter named Elisabeth. By then the father was home and received the news upon returning from a lecture. Later that day Luther reported to Jonas that everyone was improving except the pigs:

> The mother in childbed is well but weak, and our little son Hans is also well and happy again. The wife of Dr. Augustine is well, too, and against all expectations Margaret von Mochau [Karlstadt's sister-in-law] has escaped death. Instead of these people we have lost five pigs. May Christ, our comfort, allow the plague to rest content with this tribute and cease. My own condition is what it has been, as the apostle [Paul] says: "As dead, and behold I live."[48]

The visitation guidelines edited and approved at Torgau became the *Instruction of the Visitors for the Parish Pastors in Electoral Saxony.* Melanchthon and Luther have been called the primary authors of the final version, but early drafts passed through the hands of so many people that it is more accurate to view it as a joint project.[49] Ten years after the ninety-five theses, Luther's conflict with Rome and the gradual coalescence of a Lutheran movement finally resulted in the first officially approved and organized Lutheran church in Saxony. Commonly called a church order, the *Instruction* was similar to a modern constitution. It contained both a theoretical and a practical section. The theoretical section stated the theological principles, or doctrine, on which the Lutheran church was founded. Pastors were expected to endorse those principles and teach them to their parishioners. The theological section was kept simple and was organized like the catechisms for children and laypeople already in circulation. The practical section dealt with parish organization, the order of worship, preaching on current issues, and parish schools. Several paragraphs attempted to correct the distortions of Christian freedom heard by the visitors: Christian freedom did not mean that people needed no government or were exempt from paying taxes. It did not mean that parishioners could shirk their duty if civil authorities were to ask them to take up arms against the Turks. And Christian freedom did not mean that spouses could treat marriage as a human agreement that was easily dissolved by divorce or desertion. At the root of these misunderstandings was a false notion of free will. Hearts and behavior, according to the *Instruction*, could not be changed by willpower alone. To attain true faith, sincere love, personal restraint, patience, forgiveness, and generosity, God's help was indispensable.

Waiting ten, five, or even three years for the official approval of reforms and a new church order was exactly what Karlstadt, Müntzer, and the radical followers of Zwingli were not willing to do. In a letter sent from Torgau, Luther wrote that Karlstadt was stubbornly defending his old interpretation of the Lord's Supper.[50] How he knew this, Luther did not say, but eight months later he called Karlstadt a "viper in our bosom" and wished he would join the radical types in Strasbourg.[51] Karlstadt never rebaptized anyone, but the dissenters who did rebaptize caught Luther's attention in 1527. After his fainting episode on July 6, Luther said in the presence of Bugenhagen and Jonas, that before the incident he was planning to write about "the sacred baptism of Christ against Zwingli and corrupters of the sacraments."[52]

The so-called corrupters were the early Anabaptists in Zurich, who broke with Zwingli in 1525. After the Zurich council was persuaded to adopt the reformation, a group of Zwingli's followers objected that the reforms did not go far enough. They focused on the routine baptism of infants because it made every citizen a church member and by default handed religious authority to the magistrates. The dissenters argued that infant baptism was absent from the New Testament and that adult or believers' baptism would force citizens to take their faith seriously. They tried to convince Zwingli and the magistrates that only mature believers who publicly declared their faith should be baptized. At the time, they did not intend to form a separate church; rather, they wanted to transform church members in Zurich into more earnest Christians. One dissenter, Conrad Grebel, who had aggressively supported Zwingli, refused to allow his newborn daughter to be baptized, and some priests stopped baptizing infants born in their parishes.

In early January of 1525, the dissenters decided to wait no longer on a decision by the council and introduced believer's baptism among themselves. On January 21, they gathered at the home of the mother of Felix Mantz, a priest who studied under Zwingli. A man called George Blaurock asked Conrad Grebel to baptize him, and then Blaurock baptized Mantz and others who were present. Because most people prior to the reformation were baptized as infants, Zwingli and other critics called the dissenters rebaptizers, or its equivalent with a Greek prefix: Anabaptists. They called themselves brothers and sisters, or brethren, but as the movement spread northward different names became common. In Holland and northern Germany most of them were Mennonites. In Moravia they became Hutterites. When similar groups emerged in England a century later, they were called simply Baptists. The pejorative term Anabaptist is still used by historians for the earliest advocates of believer's baptism; but they belonged to a larger group of European reformers who refused to cooperate with governments and advocated free churches.

In 1526, Zurich made rebaptism punishable by death. Felix Mantz was the first Anabaptist to be executed, but not before he escaped from jail twice—the second time by descending from an unlocked window on a rope with Grebel and Blaurock. Grebel fled to the Swiss countryside but took sick and died in 1526. Blaurock was caught and banished, but beforehand he was forced to watch the drowning of Mantz. In 1529 Blaurock was arrested in the Tyrolean region of Austria and burned at the stake. On Easter 1525, the popular pastor at Waldshut (southwestern Germany), Balthasar Hubmaier, underwent a second baptism and "rebaptized" three hundred of his Waldshut parishioners. When the peasants in his vicinity revolted, Hubmaier organized resistance to the Austrian troops that were sent to crush it. Hubmaier then fled Waldshut and ended up in Moravia, where he published tracts and quarreled with another Anabaptist apostle, Hans Hut, who preached the radical ideas of Thomas Müntzer. Hubmaier's books came to the attention of the Austrian authorities and in March of 1528 he was burned at the stake.

In 1527 Martin Luther was aware of separatists in Zurich and knew of Hubmaier by name, but otherwise Luther's knowledge of Anabaptists was limited.[53] Although well informed of their presence in Strasbourg,[54] no one kept him abreast of the Augsburg Anabaptists, who lived clandestinely alongside Catholics, Zwinglians, and Lutherans. In March of 1527, Luther claimed that Augsburg was divided into six sects but did not mention Anabaptists.[55] By then, however, four itinerant leaders (called apostles) of the Anabaptists had stayed for short periods in the city. One of them was Hubmaier, who reputedly baptized another apostle, Hans Denck, who then baptized yet another, Hans Hut. By autumn Luther had learned of Anabaptist activity in Silesia and in Thuringia. He was also told that similar groups were evading capture in Catholic Bavaria: "They cannot be confined or repressed by fire or sword; they abandon spouses, children, families, and everything they have."[56] Since Anabaptists were called other disparaging names, it is impossible to know in every case to whom Luther and his correspondents referred. Luther was more interested in defending infant baptism than acquiring precise knowledge of who the "rebaptizers" were, how they lived, and what they taught. For Melanchthon in Jena, who was better informed, the Anabaptists posed a grave threat; in November of 1527 he postponed work on a catechism in order to write against them.[57]

Luther did not plan his letter challenging the Anabaptists until late December. It was addressed to the two pastors who contacted him from the Catholic Saxony of Duke George. The letter, which turned into a booklet, came off the press in February of 1528, just before *Instruction of the Visitors*. Its title, *Concerning Rebaptism to Two Pastors*, is deceivingly matter-of-fact, because the text itself demonstrated unusual tolerance and made astonishing statements about faith that still contradict popular Christian notions.

First, Luther realized that his strongest argument for infant and child baptism was historical. Although not explicitly mentioned in the New Testament, child baptism had been practiced by Roman and Orthodox churches since the early centuries of Christianity. That fact led Luther to write a surprising addendum: Much that is Christian and good existed "under the papacy," including the true holy scriptures and true baptism. Since both Lutherans and Anabaptists inherited those treasures alongside others, why then a reformation? Because, argued Luther, the popes, influenced by the devil, corroded the treasures with greed and superstition. Although God had preserved the treasures, the reformers still needed to wipe away the corrosion. Instead of merely cleaning the treasures, however, Luther charged the Anabaptists with destroying them. By refusing to baptize infants and children, they were throwing out the baby with the holy water of a good tradition.[58]

Second, Luther contradicted the notions that 1) certainty of faith is required before baptism; and 2) the more faith the better. His earlier experience with confession convinced him that, no matter how hard he tried, he could never be certain of confessing all his sins. He recalled that he and others like him sought one absolution after another, one father confessor after another, because "we sought to rely on our confession just as those to be baptized now want to rely on their faith." What then? "Baptizing without end would result. . . . Neither the baptizer nor the baptized can base baptism on a certain faith." Why not?

> Because it happens in this matter of faith that often people who claim to believe do not believe at all, while people who think they do not believe and despair, have the greatest faith. . . . Even if I were never again certain of my faith, I still am certain of the divine command that God has bidden to baptize. . . . In this I cannot err, for God's command cannot deceive.[59]

Anabaptists were not swayed by Luther's arguments for infant baptism, but the arguments were consistent with his theology. The divine commands and promises on which faith relied were more powerful and trustworthy than the faith itself. To make salvation dependent on the quality or the quantity of faith based salvation on human effort and fickleness rather than on God.

The last months of 1527 were busy and difficult. Luther had resumed lecturing in mid-August as the university moved to Jena. The audience, therefore, was restricted to a remnant of students who stayed in Wittenberg. Despite illness and plague, Luther persisted. For two months he lectured on 1 John, a book with only five chapters, and on Titus and Philemon from mid-November to mid-December. On Christmas Eve he promised the city council of nearby Zerbst that he would send John Pfeffinger to be their pastor, but not without reminding the magistrates that good pastors were scarce and should be better paid. The council should ask itself why now, in this "time of the gospel," they were hard-pressed to pay 100 guilders when the year before they paid 300 to 400 guilders to a priest who did not preach the gospel.[60] Paying new Lutheran preachers well was a priority for Luther, but he did not have the final say. He could only recommend candidates and advocate for a good salary. In the end, Pfeffinger decided to stay with the parish he was serving.

Luther was cheered, of course, by the uncomplicated birth of Elisabeth, the stamina of Katharina, and the recovery of Hänschen. Later he recalled:

"During the plague what a precious thing it was to stay alive."[61] The Bugenhagens were still with the Luthers, and they rejoiced at the birth of a son, John Jr., on the last day of the year. But most of Luther's friends and close colleagues were absent and he missed them. Between December 28 and 31 he sent letters to Spalatin in Altenburg, Linck in Nuremberg, Amsdorf in Magdeburg, Hausmann in Zwickau, and Jacob Propst in Bremen. Justus Jonas, who was still in Nordhausen, received two letters. On December 29 Luther wondered why Jonas had not returned to Wittenberg since the plague was "dead and buried." Most of the residents who fled had returned and Melanchthon reported from Jena that the university would soon do likewise. Luther described himself as healthy in body and spirit to the extent that Christ aided him against Satan.[62] The next day, however, Luther's tone was wistful:

> Would that you all were here again! We prayed for the Lord to stop the plague, and it seems that we were heard. There is no sign of it anywhere, not even where the fishermen live. Moreover, the air is clean and healthy. Satan and his legion rejoice that we are so far from one another. Greet all our friends, especially your Katharina. Pommer [Bugenhagen] and my Katharina send their very best.[63]

CHAPTER THIRTEEN

A NEW SONG
1528–1529
Wittenberg—Torgau—Marburg

"We lift up a new song to praise and honor God's name for what he has done. At Brussels in the Netherlands God made known his wonders through two young men whom he richly adorned with divine gifts. . . . They have died for his word and now they are martyrs."[1]

From the Wartburg in 1521, Luther had challenged his colleagues in Wittenberg not to wait on his return but to expand the movement that sprang from his protest against indulgences. Urging Melanchthon and his colleagues to get started, Luther addressed them as if they were early Christian missionaries:

You lecture, Amsdorf lectures, Jonas will lecture. For goodness' sake, do you want the kingdom of God to be proclaimed only in your town? Do not others also need the gospel? Will your Antioch not release a Silas or a Paul or a Barnabas for some other work of the Spirit?[2]

Gradually, Luther's plea was heard. By the beginning of 1528, few of the early colleagues at the cloister or the university remained in Wittenberg. Besides Melanchthon, only Bugenhagen and Jonas, both of whom moved to Wittenberg in 1521, had stayed. Nicholas von Amsdorf was in Magdeburg; Spalatin and Eberhard Brisger, the last Augustinian to leave the cloister, were in Altenburg. Wenzel Linck had been in Altenburg but moved to Nuremberg. John Lang returned to the Augustinian cloister in Erfurt, married, and embarked on a frustrating campaign to make the town evangelical. John Agricola was in Eisleben, Jacob Propst in Bremen, and both John Briessmann and Paul Speratus, who spent only brief periods in

Wittenberg, were sent to Prussia after Duke Albert adopted the reformation. In 1528, despite persistent conflict, one of Luther's oldest friends, Nicholas Hausmann, was still in Zwickau; and Caspar Cruciger, who had studied with Melanchthon and Luther, was about to return to Wittenberg as a colleague of his former teachers.[3]

Within seven years (1521–1528), Luther's goal of spreading his message throughout Germany appeared partially successful. Evangelical movements elsewhere in Germany were started by Lutheran reformers, but only one, John Frosch in Augsburg, had lived and studied in Wittenberg. Martin Bucer and Wolfgang Capito, who were vacillating between Zwingli and Luther, became leaders of reform in Strasbourg. In Hesse where Count Philip ruled, the chief reformer was Adam Krafft, who met Luther and Melanchthon in 1519 at the Leipzig disputation. Andrew Osiander, preacher at the Church of St. Lawrence, made the imperial free city of Nuremberg a Lutheran stronghold; Frosch, Stephen Agricola, and Urban Rhegius fought for evangelical reform in the metropolis of Augsburg; and John Brenz was in Schwäbisch Hall, another free city in the south. Only a few had seen Luther in person. Bucer and Brenz attended the Heidelberg disputation in 1518, but neither Osiander nor Rhegius had met the reformer.

Luther still faced strong opposition from Catholic rulers and theologians; but stopping his campaign or negotiating a religious settlement was out of the question. By 1528 several of Luther's disciples had been executed and exalted by him as martyrs. For centuries martyrdom had convinced believers their cause was just and true, and it was no different during the sixteenth century. Religious conflicts in Europe produced an estimated 5,000 victims who were judicially executed because of their beliefs and regarded as martyrs by their contemporaries.[4] Not all executions were recorded. In 1523, for example, the Hungarian parliament passed a proposed anti-Lutheran edict authored by the same Cardinal Cajetan who had earlier interrogated Luther. It stated that "all Lutherans and those favoring them shall have their property confiscated and themselves be punished as heretics and foes of the most holy Virgin Mary."[5] The Hungarian edict may have resulted in no martyrs at all; but for Luther, to compromise with Rome was to imply that all Lutheran martyrs had died in vain.

Luther's opponents had their own martyrs, and the smaller the religious group the more important their martyrdoms became.[6] The smallest (Anabaptists) had the highest percentage of martyrs, while the largest establishment (the Roman Church) had the lowest number. The percentage of martyrs claimed by evangelical-Lutherans, evangelical-reformed (the disciples of Zwingli and later of John Calvin), and English Protestants lay in the middle. Some martyrs were prominent. In 1531 Ulrich Zwingli was killed on the battlefield during a devastating defeat of Swiss Protestants by the Catholic cantons. The next day his slayers held a mock trial over Zwingli's body and decided it should be quartered and the pieces burned.[7] The English Catholics Thomas More and John Fisher were executed under Henry VIII and the Protestant Thomas Cranmer under Henry's Catholic daughter, Bloody Mary. Most martyrs, however, were ordinary folk who were memorialized in writing and in music. The Anabaptists, who were persecuted by Catholics and Protestants alike, assembled the richest collections of songs and stories, which they published in *The Sacrifice of the Lord* and the *Martyrs' Mirror.* Anabaptist collections featured significant numbers of women (twenty to thirty percent) among the martyrs. The earliest was Weynken Claes, who was burned at the stake in The Hague on November 20, 1527.[8]

After the Diet of Worms in 1521, the papal legate to Germany, Jerome Aleander, had suggested a perfect way to diminish Luther's appeal: burn a half-dozen Lutherans and seize their possessions.[9] Luther himself escaped capture, but by 1528 others were dying for the evangelical cause. Since 1523 six supporters had been tried and executed; the details of their last days were available to the public in nineteen pamphlets.[10] Luther himself wrote three of the pamphlets, including *The Burning of Brother Henry*, which commemorated the martyrdom of Henry of Zütphen, which took place twenty miles (thirty-two kilometers) north of Bremen. Henry was an Augustinian friar from Antwerp, the main commercial center of Belgium, which was also a Catholic stronghold. After studying in Wittenberg Henry returned to Antwerp and, together with Jacob Propst, another Augustinian who studied in Wittenberg, exposed the Antwerp friars to Luther's writings. When the brothers publicized Luther's ideas outside the cloister, they were arrested and all but three of them recanted after being sentenced to death. On July 1, 1523, two of the friars who did not recant, Hendrik Voes and Jan van der Esschen, were burned at the stake in Brussels. Soon after he was informed, Luther published a hymn in their honor. Like the accounts of early Christian martyrs, Luther's lyrics told a triumphal story that praised their faith and steadfastness as death drew near. The music was adapted from medieval folk ballads and printed with the lyrics on a broadsheet before it appeared with the title, *A New Song*, in the earliest Wittenberg hymnals. It was the first of thirty-six pieces of sacred music attributed to the reformer.

Both Henry of Zütphen and Jacob Propst escaped from Belgium and headed to northern Germany, where they became evangelical preachers in Bremen. Propst remained there until his death in 1562, but Henry was soon lured outside the city, where he was corralled and beaten by a mob before they set him ablaze. Luther was notified of Henry's death by Propst, who, like Luther, published an account of the martyrdom.[11] For a time it seems that Propst and martyrdom were linked in Luther's mind. In a letter to Propst at the end of 1527, Luther mentioned early martyrdoms among the growing sect of Anabaptists. To that point only two or three Anabaptist executions could have reached Luther's ears, but it was enough for him to remark on the courage they demonstrated prior to dying "by fire and drowning."[12]

Martyrdom was not the only bond between Propst and Luther. Their friendship began in early 1521 while Propst was studying in Wittenberg and living in the cloister with Luther. One recollection from that period indicates that Propst could be as blunt as Luther. At mealtime in the cloister on Palm Sunday, Luther said that "many papists" objected that he preached against the necessity of fasting but himself continued to fast. If Luther was sincere, they argued, he should not fast but eat meat during Lent. Jacob Propst was at the table and set a chicken before Luther, saying: "So if we teach meat is allowed, why don't we eat it?"[13] Like Jonas, Propst was a friend with whom Luther could share both good and bad times. In 1534 he invited Propst to be a godfather to his youngest child, Margaret. It was a happy occasion; but six years earlier, in 1528, Luther admitted to Propst how troubled he was by the plague's devastation and by his own physical and spiritual frailty. It was true, wrote Luther, that his family and the Bugenhagens had survived the plague and greeted newborns: the Luthers a daughter and the Bugenhagens a son. But even those gifts, however precious, did not soothe the grieving reformer.

Martyrdom was not the only reason that Luther refused to negotiate with opponents. A compromise in 1528 would undermine the establishment of Lutheran churches, which had started in earnest two years earlier after the Diet of Speyer had cleared the way. The inspection of parishes in Electoral Saxony, called the visitations, was to proceed as soon as the *Instruction of the Visitors* was published in late March. Luther himself prepared a preface for the *Instruction* and planned to join a team of visitors in order to witness the conditions. They were certain to be miserable, wrote Luther, because the Roman bishops had shirked their duties.[14] Luther hoped that "all devout and peaceable pastors" would subject themselves in a spirit of love to the Saxon visitation and willingly accept the visitors until "the Holy Spirit brings to pass something that is better."[15] Luther made it sound as if the *Instruction* were provisional; but neither he nor Elector John foresaw a return to the old order of papal bishops and parishes, celibate clergy, and the medieval mass. Compromise was out of the question.

As the visitation in Electoral Saxony began, John Bugenhagen was invited to the cities of Braunschweig and Hamburg to assist with the official adoption of the reformation. Bugenhagen's absence meant extra work for Luther. He took over as preacher in the Town Church, and in 1528 alone he delivered 180 sermons and homilies. Before Bugenhagen returned, Martin and Katharina were visited by unexpected sorrow. After only eight months, Elisabeth Luther died on Monday, August 3, 1528. In a letter to Hausmann Luther described his grief: "My little daughter, Elisabeth, has expired. I marvel that my soul is so sick. . . . I never imagined that parents could love their children so much!"[16] Some relief was delivered by the birth of a new daughter on May 4, 1529. Luther asked Amsdorf to serve as her godfather and to shepherd the "poor heathen" through baptism into Christendom.[17] The baby girl was named Magdalena after Katharina's aunt, Magdalena von Bora, who lived with the Luthers and was called "Muhme Lene" by the children. In February of 1530, Luther closed a letter to his ailing father with the promise of intercession from family members Käthe (Katharina), Hänschen (John), Lenchen (Magdalena), Muhme Lene, and "the whole house."[18]

Luther's active participation in the visitation was confined to short tours in late 1528 and January of 1529. In February a lingering illness forced him to forgo the next excursion; and in March, along with the bailiff in Wittenberg, Hans Metzsch, Luther was released from further participation. Metzsch reported another reason Luther was kept at home. Since the visitation had drawn Luther and Melanchthon out of town, over 100 students had left the university.[19]

The respite from travel gave Luther more time to work on his catechisms. Prior to the printing press, catechesis or instruction in the Christian faith was delivered mainly through sermons. Luther's preface to the *German Mass* (1526) proposed that a German lesson or sermon on the catechism be held on Monday and Tuesday mornings. He mentioned five parts: the Ten Commandments, Apostles' Creed, Lord's Prayer, baptism, and the Lord's supper.[20] For Sunday afternoons, when servants and young people attended church, the *Instruction of the Visitors* recommended sermons that explained word for word the Commandments, the Creed, and the Lord's Prayer.[21] Luther's short explanations of the five parts were first printed on large charts. Writing from Wittenberg on January 20, 1529, the deacon George Rörer mentioned that affixed to one wall of his "heated room" were placards containing the shortest form of Luther's catechism. "I am sending for another set immediately," Rörer continued, "so that the same messenger can deliver the charts to you with this letter."[22]

Luther was preparing two catechisms at one time: the short or *Small Catechism* for "simple folk and pastors" and the German or *Large Catechism*, mainly but not exclusively for clergy. He had assumed the task after John Agricola, who was originally chosen to work on the project, moved to Eisleben. By the summer of 1529, Luther's catechisms appeared in print, but they were not the first instructional booklets produced in Wittenberg. Between 1522 and 1529, sixty-two printings of thirteen such booklets had appeared.[23] Luther based his catechisms not on those booklets but on the expanded edition of his own *Little Prayer Book* first published in 1522. The catechisms were also influenced by the sermons Luther preached in 1528 and by the controversy between Agricola and Melanchthon. The subject of the dispute was when and how frequently evangelical believers should repent for their sins. Agricola's answer was "not too often," because confessing and repenting for every sin was a mainstay of medieval religion that Luther had abolished. Too much repenting made people uncertain of forgiveness, argued Agricola, and fearful of the Ten Commandments because these were used to remind people of their sins. Agricola thought he was being true to Luther by minimizing the role that confession, repentance, and the Ten Commandments played in Christian instruction. Evangelical believers should first absorb the good news of God's unconditional forgiveness before they were reminded to repent of their sins and to improve their lives.

Melanchthon was concerned that too much emphasis on forgiveness before repentance would prevent people from feeling contrite about their sins and striving to amend their lives. If sins were forgiven unconditionally, why bother to repent or refrain from sinning at all? According to Melanchthon, "this would be a sin greater than all the errors hitherto prevailing."[24] When Agricola and Melanchthon met face-to-face at Torgau in November of 1527, Luther had mediated the personal dispute, and his catechisms also offered a middle way. They presented the Ten Commandments as both prohibitions of sinful behavior and encouragements of the opposite: the correct way to honor God and treat others. The *Small Catechism* started the explanation of each commandment with the phrase, "we are to fear and love God," and followed it by a prohibition and a positive instruction. For the seventh commandment, "do not steal," the explanation read: "We are to fear and love God, so that we neither take our neighbor's money or property, nor acquire them by offering shoddy merchandise or crooked deals, but instead help them to improve and protect their property and income."[25] According to Luther's preface, the visitation showed that pastors and laity needed this straightforward instruction and needed it quickly:

Dear God, what misery I beheld. The ordinary person, especially in the villages, knows absolutely nothing about the Christian faith, and unfortunately many pastors are completely unskilled and incompetent teachers. Supposedly they all bear the name Christian, are baptized, and receive the holy sacrament, even though they do not know the Lord's Prayer, the Creed, or the Ten Commandments. As a result, they live like simple cattle or irrational pigs and, in spite of the gospel's return, have mastered the fine art of misusing their freedom.[26]

In addition to the *Small Catechism*, which soon dominated the market, Luther had already realized that a better way to instill the evangelical version of Christianity into hearts and minds was through music. After the song praising the martyrs in Brussels (1523), Luther wrote twenty-seven more hymns before 1530, most of them in 1523 and 1524, and eight more before he died. Four Luther hymns appeared in the oldest Wittenberg hymnal, the *Achtliederbuch* (*Book of Eight Hymns*) along with three hymns by Paul Speratus, who converted early to the evangelical cause. While serving as cathedral preacher in Würzburg, Speratus ignored the vow of celibacy and married a woman named Anna Fuchs. Forced out of Germany and Austria and imprisoned briefly in Moravia, Speratus and his wife finally sought refuge in Wittenberg. The year was 1523, and they arrived in time for the best-known hymn of Speratus, "Salvation unto Us Has Come," to be included in the *Achtliederbuch*. The original chorale recapitulated early Lutheran theology in fourteen verses,[27] and Lutheran hymnals still offer a translation of the original chorale—but wisely with fewer verses. Speratus also translated three books of Luther from Latin into German before accepting the invitation of Duke Albert to assist with the reformation in Prussia.

John Walter's *Spiritual Songbooklet*, which was published in the summer of 1524, laid the foundation of Lutheran choral hymnody. It contained twenty-four chorales by Luther, but Walter's arrangements for several voices made it ground-breaking. The *Songbooklet* did not, however, contain "A Mighty Fortress Is Our God," Luther's best-known hymn, which became a Lutheran anthem. Composed in all likelihood between 1527 and 1529, "A Mighty Fortress" was included in two collections whose first editions are no longer extant. It does appear, however, in a 1533 hymnal edited by Luther himself and printed in Wittenberg. The chorale was a resounding affirmation of divine power on which believers could rely after the devil had done his worst. That theme spoke to all the devils concurrently gnawing at the reformer: Luther's illnesses and spiritual attacks, the plague, the death of his daughter Elisabeth, the building of fortifications around Wittenberg, the reappearance of the Turks and their siege of Vienna in 1529, ongoing conflict with Catholics and Zwinglians, and a decision by the second Diet of Speyer in 1529 to rescind its 1526 decision permitting Lutherans to proceed with reforms. The chorale also resonated with the *Large Catechism* at the point where Luther explained the sixth petition of the Lord's Prayer:

> This is what "lead us not into temptation" means: when God gives us power and strength to resist, even though the attack is not removed or ended. For no one can escape temptations and allurements as long as we live in the flesh and have the devil prowling around us. We cannot help but suffer attacks and even be mired in them, but we pray here that we may not fall into them and then drown.[28]

Among God's most precious gifts, Luther ranked music second only to theology. Analyzing and debating the faith was mainly for theologians, while for laypeople music was the most effective means of transmitting the gospel. In 1620, a Jesuit critic paid Luther's hymns a backhanded compliment by claiming they exterminated more souls than all the reformer's sermons and writings.[29] By the time Luther died, the number of laypeople who sang Luther's hymns far exceeded the number who heard his sermons or read his pamphlets. In north Germany evangelical hymns in the Low German dialect were already published in 1523, the same year that Luther's musical tribute to the early martyrs appeared in Wittenberg. By the end of that year, broadsheet versions of Luther's earliest hymns were circulated and sold by itinerant craftsmen and peddlers. In Magdeburg one enterprising cloth-maker stationed himself beneath the statue of Emperor Otto I, sang aloud two of Luther's early hymns, and then sold copies to the crowd he attracted. For being a public nuisance or hawking without a license, the cloth-maker was arrested and jailed until 200 citizens demanded his release. On May 22, 1524, the townspeople petitioned the magistrates to allow evangelical sermons, and in late June Luther visited Magdeburg for the first time since 1506. After Luther's visit the city council allowed not only evangelical sermons and hymns but also the reception of both bread and wine in the Lord's Supper. In late September Luther sent Nicholas Amsdorf to supervise reform in Magdeburg, which became the first officially evangelical-Lutheran city in northern Germany.[30]

The importance of hymns to the growth of the reformation cannot be overstated. A conservative estimate sets the number of hymns, songsheets, and hymn-related materials printed during the sixteenth century at two million copies.[31] Luther and Speratus were not the only early reformers who wrote and relied on music. In 1524, the same year she married the future reformer Caspar Cruciger in Wittenberg, Elisabeth Meseritz wrote a Christmas hymn, "The Only Son from Heaven." And thirty years later in Prussia, the Lutheran Duke Albert, sixty-four years old, penned a popular hymn of comfort: "Let My God's Will Prevail Always."[32] Philip Melanchthon valued music as highly as Luther did.[33] In addition to three hymns for church festivals, ten of the more than 600 Latin poems by Melanchthon were set to music. Better known was the praise of music that appeared in his prefaces to sheet music published in the Wittenberg print-shop opened by George Rhau in 1524. Melanchthon emphasized the special impact of music on the emotions because the lyrics entered the ears more quickly and stuck more stubbornly in the brain if those words were accompanied by music. Music also relieved suffering when "sweet melodies of God's mercy" were heard. Melanchthon experienced in person the effects of music on his struggle with melancholy. In order to cheer him up, students gathered at his house for nightly serenades accompanied by strings. Six days before he died, Melanchthon dreamed of the melody to which, as a boy chorister, he sang the words of Jesus at the Last Supper: "I have eagerly desired to eat this Passover with you before I suffer."[34]

By themselves, however, catechisms, hymns, and visitations were not able to guarantee a stable reorganization of church life. Constitutions, or church orders, had to transform the plans of reformers and the wishes of laity into guidelines that were acceptable to all parties: citizens, local magistrates, and princes. Lutheran church orders were necessary for Electoral Saxony and for all the cities and territories in which John Bugenhagen was consolidating churches. On May 16, 1528, Bugenhagen headed for Braunschweig in response to a call from the city council for "a person who had the required

prestige, authority, and charisma for the enormous undertaking of trans-
forming the entire character and constitution of the church."[35] It was the
first installation of Lutheranism by Bugenhagen, and it was soon followed
by missions to Hamburg, Schleswig-Holstein, and Lübeck. Bugenhagen
also composed Lutheran church orders while on lengthy visits to his native
Pomerania and to Denmark, where in 1537 he crowned King Christian III
and Queen Dorothea. Altogether Bugenhagen was absent from Wittenberg
longer than any of Luther's colleagues who lived permanently in the town.
On most journeys Bugenhagen was accompanied by his wife, Walburga, and
their children. However, as they left for Braunschweig in May of 1528,
the only child in the wagon was a daughter named Sara. The two sons
who should have been on-board had died the month before: Michael, the
older, on April 26, 1528, and John earlier in April, a little more than three
months after his birth in the Luther residence.[36]

When the Bugenhagens arrived in Braunschweig, the process of reform
was under way, but not without a conflict that no one seemed able to
resolve. In Bugenhagen, however, Braunschweig found an outside mediator
who commanded respect and reconciled enough differences for a majority
of Braunschweig's magistrates to accept an evangelical-Lutheran church
order. Bugenhagen accomplished the feat within four months by using his
native tongue—the Low German dialect that he learned in Pomerania and
that prevailed in Braunschweig, Hamburg, Lübeck, and across the north
German coastal plain. Theologically, Bugenhagen was true to Luther, but
personally he was quite different: even-tempered, attentive to practical
details, and able to apply his pastoral experience in Wittenberg to a new
setting. For laity the new order mandated changes to worship, to schools,
and to the financial structure of the town. The council of Braunschweig
softened the shock by allowing their citizens to express their own wishes.
For example, the bakers' guild insisted that children from poor families
receive the same education as children of the wealthy.[37] How many requests
were honored by Bugenhagen is unknown, but the new constitution was
approved by early fall of 1528.

After that, in October, the Bugenhagens headed for Hamburg, Elector
John having extended their leave of absence from Wittenberg. Bugenhagen
needed two more extensions before a new church order for Hamburg was
approved on May 15, 1529, and ceremonially announced from all the
pulpits.[38] The project turned out to be much harder than Bugenhagen
expected. Luther and the Hamburg magistrates had expected Bugenhagen to
use the Braunschweig order as a template for Hamburg, but it was not that

simple. When the job was complete, Bugenhagen wrote to Luther, Jonas, and Melanchthon that it "cost him much sweat but, thanks be to God, it was not in vain."[39] Bugenhagen was not sitting at a desk for the five months. For almost a month he was out of town chairing a debate about the Lord's Supper, in which a former Wittenberg colleague, Andrew Karlstadt, participated. While in town Bugenhagen gave lectures on Paul's epistle to the Romans and preached around the city. Apparently his sermons were better received in Hamburg than in Wittenberg, where he was teased by Luther and others about his long-windedness. Luther told the story of a housewife in Wittenberg who always had Sunday dinner ready when her husband returned from church. One Sunday, her husband returned as she was starting preparations. Explaining why dinner was late, the wife said she assumed Pastor Bugenhagen was preaching that morning.[40] In Hamburg Bugenhagen also showed parishioners how to adapt the interior of their churches to Lutheran worship; and he reassured couples who were uncertain about the meaning of marriage that Lutherans no longer considered it a sacrament.

As the interim minister in Wittenberg during Bugenhagen's absence, Luther dealt with two delicate cases. The first case involved an unfaithful wife and a noble refugee. The main character in the second case was a renegade nun. Both cases illustrated how the mix of religion and politics affected Luther's judgment. The first case started in 1525 as a scandal at the court of Joachim I, the Catholic Elector of Brandenburg, which was adjacent to Electoral Saxony. The daughter of a prominent Berlin family, Katharina Blankenfeld, met Elector Joachim and agreed to become his mistress, even though she was married to a man named Wolf Hornung. During an angry argument with his wife, the cuckolded Hornung wounded Katharina with a knife. In retaliation Elector Joachim forced Hornung to renounce all rights to his wife and leave Brandenburg. Hornung was living in Saxony when, two years later, Katharina indirectly contacted Luther about a reconciliation and asked the reformer to intervene with Hornung. Luther invited Hornung to a conversation in Wittenberg, but the aggrieved husband refused any rapprochement. Luther turned his frustration on Elector Joachim—not only for pastoral but also for political reasons.

Until his death in 1535, Elector Joachim was a more stalwart defender of the Roman Church than his brother, the cardinal archbishop of Mainz. Joachim refused to allow evangelical preachers to enter Brandenburg even though he was surrounded by rulers who adopted the reformation. When Joachim discovered that his wife, Elisabeth, had received both bread and wine from a clandestine evangelical preacher, he threatened to execute her.

In 1528 Elisabeth fled Brandenburg and found refuge in Saxony at the residence of Elector John. Elisabeth's banishment fueled Luther's anger against Elector Joachim and led the reformer, over the next two years, to expose Joachim's infidelity with Katharina and other lovers. In letters to Joachim, which were made public, Luther both chastised and belittled the Elector. Professing also to be Hornung's advocate and counselor, Luther eventually delivered an ultimatum to Katharina Blankenfeld. Unless within eight weeks God led her to repent and regain her right mind, he would declare her husband divorced from a public adulterer. Katharina responded by declaring the divorce herself and retaking her maiden name. It was a sorry performance by all sides, not least by the pastoral counselor Luther, who published Katharina's declaration with his own spiteful remarks.[41]

Instead of adultery, death threats, and divorce, the second case involved abandonment—not of a spouse but of a convent. In 1528 a Saxon noblewoman escaped from the cloister in which she was placed as an orphaned child. At the time, about 1500, she was between five and ten years old and already recognized as Duchess Ursula of Münsterberg. In spite of her noble status Ursula was frail and poor during her twenty-eight years in the order of Magdalen women. The convent was located about eighty miles (130 kilometers) southeast of Wittenberg, not in Electoral Saxony but in the Catholic territory of Duke George. On the evening of October 6, 1528, Ursula and two sister nuns escaped the convent by walking out the garden gate and making their way, almost certainly prearranged, to nearby Leisnig. Nothing proves that Luther was involved with this escape, but he had previously been contacted by a nun who hoped to leave the same convent if she could find protection in Electoral Saxony.[42] From Leisnig, Ursula and her companions, Dorothy and Margaret, headed for Wittenberg and on October 16, 1528, were taken in by Martin and Katharina. Four days later Luther informed Spalatin of the nuns' arrival and their destitution. Ursula had not a penny to her name.[43] The burden of making the nuns comfortable fell on Katharina because one week later Luther left to participate in the visitation of parishes near Wittenberg.

By 1528 many monks and nuns had left their cloisters and some houses, like the one in which Ursula and her companions were now lodging, were emptied. Their escape was less remarkable than it would have been in 1524, when the Cistercian nun Florentina von Oberweimar fled her convent in Eisleben. Florentina defended her action with a pamphlet that recounted the mistreatment she endured after deciding that remaining a nun would lead her straight to hell. Her defense was published in Wittenberg with an open letter from Luther to the counts of Mansfeld. He implored them to allow monks and nuns to leave their cloisters and to stop their superiors from recruiting new members. Florentina's escape, he said, "was a miraculous sign from God."[44]

Ursula's escape was not miraculous, but it was scandalous, both because she was a duchess and because it was sharply protested by Luther's tenacious enemy Duke George. In 1523 George had suffered humiliation when Luther and Leonard Koppe arranged the escape of Katharina von Bora and her companions from their convent barely twenty miles (thirty-two kilometers) from the duke's residence in Leipzig. Ursula's convent at Freiberg[45] was over fifty miles (eighty kilometers) from Leipzig, but Duke George was angry nonetheless and demanded, without success, that Elector John send Ursula, Dorothy, and Margaret back to Freiberg. Duke George also tried to block the publication of Ursula's defense, which soon appeared in Wittenberg with an afterword by Luther. Like Florentina's tract, it was a piece of Protestant propaganda against monasticism, but at the end of 1528 it was hardly necessary. The wave of escapes had passed its peak. In 1532, Luther claimed that monks and nuns were disappearing "like snow melting in the sun."[46] And he took the credit: "God rewards me for destroying monasticism; nuns and monks run to me so that I might feed them."[47] Luther overestimated his influence. Monasteries needed monks and nuns, true, but they also needed income. Late medieval cloisters benefited from the rents, endowments, and donations that Protestant towns and territories were now confiscating and depositing into their own treasuries. As for Ursula of Münsterberg, after boarding two months with the Luthers, she relied mainly on the Lutheran dukes of Prussia and Silesia for shelter and support. The last sign of life was a letter dated February 2, 1534, in which Ursula bequeathed whatever she had accumulated to her sister fugitive, the ex-nun Dorothy.[48]

By mid-May of 1529, John Bugenhagen had been absent from Wittenberg for exactly a year and Luther was feeling overwhelmed by the extra work. He had been unusually good about replying to mail, but now he fell behind in his correspondence. On June 20 Luther gave Linck in Nuremberg a testy reason for not answering his questions more promptly:

Every day I am overwhelmed with so many letters that they lie in piles on tables, chairs, stools, sills, desks, and in boxes. Every available surface is filled with letters, inquiries, cases, disputes, and petitions. Matters of church and state have all fallen on me. In Nuremberg you can repose and play at leisure in paradise because you have a government that does its job efficiently while you enjoy idleness and security. We however are plagued with business of the court, little of which has to do with church matters.[49]

To complicate Luther's life, three more nuns from Ursula's convent knocked at his door on June 4. They escaped with the help of their parents and, reported Luther, Duke George was again raging.[50] Luther was relieved, therefore, to hear that Elector John was ordering Bugenhagen back to Wittenberg.[51] He started counting the days. On June 5 he told Jonas, who was out of town inspecting parishes, that Bugenhagen should be on the way home.[52] One week later Bugenhagen wrote to say he would soon arrive, and Luther relayed that news to Jonas. With Bugenhagen resuming his duties as pastor, Luther thought he would have time to assist Jonas with the visitation.[53]

Luther's hope went unfulfilled. On June 23, 1529, the Bugenhagens finally arrived home. That same day, despite strong misgivings, Luther provisionally accepted the invitation of Philip of Hesse to attend a colloquy with Zwingli in early autumn at Philip's castle in Marburg.[54] The urgency of Philip's invitation resulted from decisions taken at the second Diet of Speyer, which had ended in April. Like all the diets since Worms in 1521, the Diet of Speyer was held in the absence of Emperor Charles V and that left Archduke Ferdinand in charge. In 1529 he was no longer in a conciliatory mood. He blamed the evangelical princes for the Turkish victory in Hungary that resulted in the death of his brother-in-law, King Louis, and allowed Suleyman to threaten Vienna. The evangelical towns and territories, which in 1526 were allowed to proceed with reforms, were now accused of violating the Edict of Worms against Luther and his supporters. No more "innovations" were permitted and Protestants were ordered to tolerate the Roman mass in its pre-reformation form. The evangelical side entered a written protest, but it was rejected. A proposed compromise also failed and the diet ended in a stand-off.[55]

The protest of 1529 gave rise to the word Protestant, but the Protestants were not unified. Significant cities of southwest Germany sympathized more with Zwingli than with Luther. Among those cities Strasbourg was prominent, but its chief delegate at Speyer, Jacob Sturm, signed a mutual defense pact with Elector John of Saxony, Count Philip of Hesse, and the Lutheran cities of Nuremberg and Ulm. That action split the German Protestants into evangelical-Lutheran and evangelical-Reformed or Zwinglian cities and made all of them weaker.[56] Protestant vulnerability to a military attack by Emperor Charles and the Catholic rulers was immediately recognized by Philip of Hesse. Before leaving Speyer he lobbied for a meeting of Lutherans and Zwinglians in order to resolve their differences on the Lord's Supper. An agreement would clear the way for creating a strong and united Protestant front. Philip insisted that the meeting be held in his castle at Marburg, the residence of the counts of Hesse. Known, therefore, as the Marburg colloquy, the meeting took place on October 1–4, 1529, only five months after the second Diet of Speyer had ended.

At first, both Zwingli and Luther refused Philip's invitation to attend. When Zwingli pled that the journey from Zurich was too long (270 miles or 440 kilometers) and the roads unsafe, Philip sent him a map and promised him safe conduct once his party crossed the Hessian border. Zwingli and three companions traveled overland from Zurich to Basel, where a boat was waiting to take them and the theologian John Oecolampadius thirteen hours down the Rhine to Strasbourg. On September 18, 1529, the Swiss contingent and the Strasbourg delegation—composed of Jacob Sturm, Martin Bucer, and Caspar Hedio—departed for Marburg. After ten days they arrived at the residence of Count Philip, who greeted the party personally before escorting them to quarters inside the castle.

The Lutherans had not yet arrived. Although Luther was not supposed to leave Electoral Saxony and did not attend the Diet of Speyer, he could travel safely to Marburg because Hesse was adjacent to Saxony and Philip was on his side. Neither Luther nor Melanchthon, however, wanted to attend. Melanchthon, said Luther, was worrying himself sick about a grand Protestant alliance and feared that a partial agreement with the Swiss would kill the chance of negotiating with Catholic theologians in Germany.[57] Luther had already decided that nothing was to be gained from meeting Oecolampadius and Zwingli, because both sides had put every thought in writing and showed no sign of budging. Nevertheless, Elector John convinced Luther to give Philip of Hesse a positive answer; Luther agreed to attend, but he told Philip outright: "I know I cannot give an inch and, after reading their arguments, I remain certain they are wrong."[58]

On July 8, 1529, both Melanchthon and Luther formally accepted the invitation. Elector John now asked Luther to draft a theological agreement for the Lutheran alliance that had formed as a result of the Diet of Speyer. Paragraph 10 of the document, henceforth called the *Schwabach Articles*, declared the "true body and blood of Christ" to be present in "the bread and the wine" of the Lord's Supper.[59] The statement contradicted the convictions of both Zwingli and Oecolampadius, but the Lutheran theologians were glad to have official backing. The prospect of success at Marburg was therefore gloomy: the Wittenbergers were opposed both to a theological compromise and to military resistance against Emperor Charles V. However, making resistance by a united Protestant force achievable was Philip's chief reason for hosting the colloquy.[60]

On September 15 or 16, a large Lutheran party left Wittenberg. It included Luther, Melanchthon, Justus Jonas, their younger colleague Caspar Cruciger, the deacon George Rörer, and perhaps Veit Dietrich, who was Luther's assistant. Their journey to Marburg lasted two weeks. It was a route Luther knew so well that prior to entering Hesse it resembled a travelogue of his life. The Wittenbergers stopped first in Torgau to confer with Elector John. Then, except for Mansfeld and Eisleben, the journey took them through locales in which Luther had lived, studied, or conferred: Erfurt, Jena, Weimar, and Grimma. In Altenburg Spalatin greeted the party, and the Lutheran ministers of both Gotha and Eisenach, Myconius and Justus Menius, joined the travelers. In Eisenach, as ordered by Elector John, the captain of the Wartburg fortress began to trot alongside the wagons.[61]

Escorted by forty Hessian horsemen, the large wagons crossed the Lahn river and entered Marburg on the morning of September 30. The town rises almost vertically from the river and requires climbing or switchbacking on narrow streets in order to reach Count Philip's imposing castle perched on top. The wagons therefore took the bypass, as it were, a road that struggled upward around the edge of town and into the courtyards of the castle, where the Lutherans were heartily received and royally treated by Count Philip. On October 2, 1529, Lutheran theologians from south Germany arrived: Andrew Osiander from Nuremberg, John Brenz from Schwäbisch Hall, and Stephen Agricola from Augsburg. At least five Hessian theologians attended the event, as did Duke Ulrich of Württemberg, who was living in exile at Philip's castle. Little more than eight years had passed since the Diet of Worms condemned Luther and all his supporters, yet Marburg was hosting the largest and most diverse group of Protestant theologians so far assembled.

The colloquy itself lasted only three days. On Friday, October 1, 1529, separate preliminary discussions were held between Luther and Oecolampadius and between Melanchthon and Zwingli. According to most of the seven accounts of the proceedings, these four theologians were the main speakers throughout the colloquy, but they offered no new arguments. Zwingli and Oecolampadius saw no advantage in a "bodily eating" of Christ in the sacrament and sought to explain Jesus' words "this is my body" as a spiritual feeding through faith. The words needed explaining, Zwingli insisted, because "it was not true that God places many incomprehensible matters before us."[62] Besides, explained Zwingli further, a body was finite and could be present only in one place. The resurrected body of Christ was in heaven, and the sacramental bread could only signify it, not contain it. Luther repeated that the words of Jesus were "a clear and powerful text"[63] and resorted to showmanship to make his point. On Saturday morning he took chalk and wrote "This is my body" on the table and covered it with a velvet cloth.[64] When Zwingli demanded proof that Jesus could be present in the bread of the Lord's Supper, Luther removed the cloth and pointed to the text. In his most recent book, however, Luther had explained his position at length. Since Christ was both divine and human, his resurrected body was united with God and could be anywhere that God was present, and God was everywhere. No physical space of whatever size could exclude God:

> Nothing is so small but God is still smaller, nothing so large but God is still larger; nothing is so short but God is still shorter, nothing so long but God is still longer; nothing is so broad but God is still broader, nothing so narrow but God is still narrower. God is an inexpressible being above and beyond all that can be described or imagined.[65]

If it was true of God, then the resurrected body of Christ was also in the smallest things, such as the bread and wine of the sacrament.

It is tempting to see Oecolampadius and Zwingli as modern theologians using logic and comparing scripture passages to comprehend a statement of Jesus, which by itself seems preposterous; and to regard Luther and Melanchthon as less sophisticated thinkers, who simply assumed God was everywhere and that Jesus meant his words literally. But conceptions of the cosmos change. Zwingli's static view of heaven as a detached space to which the body of Christ was confined may now appear less probable than Luther's conviction that the resurrected body of Christ—portrayed in the Bible's Easter stories as penetrating doors and materializing out of nowhere—was diffused throughout a dynamic cosmos composed of dancing particles and multiple universes. In their sixteenth-century world, however, the theological goal was more modest: determining how best to avoid magical abuses of the mass while simultaneously finding meaning in the words of Jesus that his body and blood were present in the sacrament. The misfortune of Marburg was not that theologians disagreed, rather that they did not agree to disagree while accepting that they stood on common evangelical ground.

Before the colloquy concluded, Luther was asked to draft a document that could be signed by the ten principal theologians.[66] It contained fifteen paragraphs, collectively called the Marburg Articles. Only the fifteenth dealt with the Lord's Supper, and within that article they agreed on all but the crucial point: whether or not "the true body and blood of Christ are bodily present in the bread and wine." Nonetheless, they added that "each side should show Christian love to the other side insofar as conscience will permit, and both sides should diligently pray to almighty God that through his Spirit he might confirm us in the right understanding."[67] That was harder for Luther to do than for Zwingli. At one point, when each man asked the other's pardon for his sharp remarks, Zwingli declared that he deeply desired Luther's friendship. Then, "almost weeping," Zwingli added that he was looking forward to meeting Luther more than anyone else in France or Germany. Luther responded coolly: "Pray God that you may come to a right understanding of this matter." Oecolampadius quickly chided Luther to pray the same for himself.[68] When Martin Bucer asked what Luther did not like about the Swiss position, he replied:

> Our spirit is different from yours; it is clear that we do not possess the same spirit, for it cannot be the same spirit when in one place the words of Christ are simply believed and in another place the same faith is censured, resisted, regarded as false, and attacked with all kinds of malicious and blasphemous words. Therefore, as I have previously said, we commend you to the judgment of God.[69]

Luther had indeed said it earlier, but now Zwingli shed tears.

Philip of Hesse, who was present at the entire colloquy and expected it to last a week, adjourned it early because of an epidemic called the English sweating sickness. Unlike the plague, it was probably a viral pulmonary disease that erupted in England five times between 1485 and 1551.[70] The 1529 epidemic spread to Hamburg and then southward further into Germany. Count Philip himself left Marburg on the morning of October 5, the Lutherans left in the afternoon, and the delegations from Zurich, Basel, and Strasbourg left that day or the next. Count Philip left the castle confident that the colloquy was a success. For him, if not for Luther and Zwingli, the Marburg Articles showed enough agreement and good will upon which to base a broad Protestant alliance.

On the way home from Marburg, the Wittenbergers received frightening news: The Turks were attacking Vienna "with all their might."[71] This

Turkish army of 75,000 soldiers was larger than the force that defeated the Hungarians in 1526, and it was still led by Suleyman the Magnificent, who threatened to extend the rule of Islam to the Rhine river. Archduke Ferdinand took the threat seriously, and before the Turks headed for Vienna in September of 1529 he was frantically recruiting troops. No help from his brother the emperor was in sight, but he did receive one-third of the 16,000 troops promised him by the second Diet of Speyer—the same diet that caused Philip of Hesse to seek a Protestant alliance and hold the Marburg colloquy. On September 28, two days before Luther arrived in Marburg, the Turks reached the gates of Vienna in heavy rain. Ferdinand was depending on fewer than 20,000 soldiers to defend the city, and it should have taken at most a few days of bombardment to bring Vienna to its knees. Heavy rains, however, had already bedeviled the Turkish army in Hungary and the mud had forced them to abandon their heavy artillery. The projectiles from their light cannons bounced off Vienna's walls like tennis balls, and digging mines or trenches under the walls was foiled by rain and mud. After a fourth assault failed in mid-October, the Turks folded their tents and left the field.[72] By the time news of the siege reached the Wittenbergers, it was over; but in the spring of 1530 the Turkish threat and the Protestant protest alarmed Emperor Charles sufficiently to draw him back to Germany for the first time since 1521.

CHAPTER FOURTEEN

DEAD TO THE WORLD
1530
Wittenberg—Coburg

"If princes as princes are permitted to resist the emperor, let it be a matter of their judgment and their conscience. Such resistance is certainly not permitted to a Christian, who has died to the world."[1]

In the spring of 1529 Luther's father, Hans Luder, visited Martin, Katharina, and his grandson Hänschen in Wittenberg. Hans was accompanied by Martin's brother, Jacob Luder, Jacob's wife, and their brother-in-law, George Kaufmann. Ten months later, Jacob wrote that Hans was gravely ill in Mansfeld, and on February 15, 1530, Martin wrote a letter of consolation to his ailing father. The letter was taken to Mansfeld by Kaufmann's son, Cyriac,[2] whom Luther asked to determine whether his parents were in a fit state to be transported to Wittenberg, where Katharina wanted to care for them.[3] Luther's letter was written to comfort himself as well as his father. This "cursed life" on earth, wrote Martin, was nothing but a vale of tears; the longer we lived, the more malice, fear, and misfortune we suffered, and there was no escape until the dirt was shoveled over our bodies. Consolation came from faith in God's promises. For Luther, one of those promises was a speedy reunion of loved ones in heaven. Should his father not recover, assured Luther, "our faith is certain and we do not doubt that with Christ we will see each other again soon." The exit from this life was much shorter than the time it took to travel from Mansfeld to Wittenberg. "Only a little while and everything will be different."[4] Cyriac Kaufmann returned to Wittenberg with the news that Hans Luder could not be moved. He died in June without seeing his son again.

Hans Luder's last illness coincided with the slow return of Emperor Charles V to Germany in order to end the religious schism caused by Hans' elder son. A new diet was set to begin on April 8, 1530, in the city of Augsburg, and Emperor Charles was headed north fresh from his coronation in Italy by Pope Clement VII. The inhabitants of Rome, where the emperor should have been crowned, had not forgotten the sack of their city by Charles' soldiers two years earlier, and thus Bologna was chosen to host the celebration. At first the people of Bologna were honored, but after their city was disfigured in order to resemble Rome and the coronation was delayed until three months after Charles arrived, enthusiasm waned. Finally, on February 22, 1530, the pageantry began. After Charles had sworn on the gospels to be a faithful champion of the Roman Church, Pope Clement placed the imperial crown on his head. The coronation made Charles V, at the age of twenty-nine, the twentieth sovereign of the Holy Roman Empire. He feared becoming the last if he failed to prevent a Turkish invasion and the dismemberment of his empire by a Protestant schism.

Since the diet was set to begin in April, the Saxon Elector and his chief political advisor, Gregor Brück, started to plan for it in March of 1530. The official announcement of the diet was sent from Torgau to the Wittenberg theologians along with preliminary travel plans. Pastoral duties kept Bugenhagen at home, but Jonas, Melanchthon, and Luther were to travel with the Elector's party from Torgau, would be joined in Thuringia by Spalatin and Agricola, and would then proceed to the town of Coburg. The Saxon party paused there for a week before covering the last 150 miles to Augsburg. They were tracking the slow progress of Emperor Charles from Italy to Germany and knew there was time to stop and rest. Since 1920 Coburg has belonged to Bavaria, but in 1530 it was the southernmost residence of the Saxon Electors.

The announcement of the diet implied that both Protestants and Catholics were to be treated equally, but it was still too dangerous for Luther to attend in person. The ideal refuge was the Lutheran city of Nuremberg, halfway between Coburg and Augsburg, but Nuremberg depended on the emperor for its independence and commercial success and did not want to harbor an imperial outlaw when Charles was so close. Coburg was the second choice and, as planned, Luther remained behind on April 24 when Elector John and his entourage left for Augsburg. Before daybreak Luther and his assistant Veit Dietrich moved into the Coburg fortress.

That afternoon Luther described for Melanchthon the new surroundings. He was assigned to a house inside the fortifications and given keys to all the rooms. Thirty people worked in the fortress; among them were twelve night watchmen and two lookouts with bugles guarding the towers.

Why bother with such details? Because, admitted Luther, there was nothing else to write about and without his friend Philip the fortress was a sad place.[5] Sad perhaps, but not too sad to call on his sense of humor. The small crows circling the fortress inspired him to sign off from "the kingdom of the birds" and, in a subsequent letter to Spalatin, to envision the squawking flock as his own diet:

> Here you might see magnanimous kings, dukes, and other nobles of the kingdom, who seriously care for their belongings and offspring, and with untiring voice proclaim their decisions and dogmas through the air.... This suffices as a joke, but a serious and necessary joke to chase away the thoughts seizing me.[6]

Luther's "papers" had not yet arrived, but what papers did he intend to consult on such an unpredictable journey? Material for preparing future classes? Perhaps. Before leaving Wittenberg, Luther was lecturing on the Song of Songs in the presence of both George Rörer, who took notes, and Veit Dietrich, who would later edit the notes and have them published.[7] In April of 1530, Luther did not suspect six months would pass before he resumed the lectures in November. Did he bring ideas and notes for sermons? Probably not. Before leaving Wittenberg, Luther had declared he would never again preach publicly,[8] but his resolve did not last and he may have delivered as many as ten sermons while away from Wittenberg.[9] The first sermon was given on April 16, one day after the party arrived in Coburg. It was the Saturday before Easter, but it was also the day after Good Friday, and Luther chose to preach on suffering and the cross—not the suffering of Jesus, but the crosses that all believers had to bear. To make his point, Luther chose the legend of St. Christopher, who carried a child across a raging stream. The load became heavier and heavier until the child made itself known as the creator and redeemer of the world. Luther's point: At first the evangelical message seemed a pleasant, childlike teaching, and everyone wanted it. "No oven was as hot as people were then!" But, like Christopher carrying the child, the new converts did not notice the weight of the gospel until they reached the deep water; that is, "until the waves rolled out and pope, bishops, princes, and the crazy rabble set themselves against it." In like fashion, said Luther, unknown crosses and suffering awaited the Saxon party in Augsburg, but bearing crosses belonged to believing and their "beloved child," the gospel, must be carried to the other shore or be drowned.[10]

The day before his colleagues left Coburg, Luther alerted a friend in Nuremberg that four living and very eloquent "letters" were coming his way—Jonas, Melanchthon, Spalatin, and Agricola—and that he, Luther, would gladly be the fifth. Instead, five days later at Coburg, Luther was hard at work on an exhortation to all the clergy attending the diet. The pamphlet took aim at the bishops, making them responsible for corrupting the church and refusing to join the evangelical movement. He exploited old antagonisms between bishops and the monastic orders that were exempt from episcopal authority: "I heard no weeping from bishop or parish priest when I attacked the monastic life and the monks became fewer. I know that no greater service was ever done for bishops and priests than freeing them from the monks." He dragged out "old skeletons," as he put it, so that the clergy could see what conditions would be like "if our gospel had not come."[11] The first skeleton was the indulgence scam, and it was followed by the medieval practices and rituals rejected by the reformers. Finally, Luther came to the underlying issue:

> You allege that nothing should be changed or modernized without the consent of the church. Who is the church? Are you? Then show the seals and credentials or prove it another way with actions and fruits. Why are we not also the church, since we are baptized as well as you, teach, preach, have the sacraments, believe, pray, love, hope, and suffer more than you? . . . Do not keep chanting "church, church, church" at us. Better for you to make certain that you are the church.[12]

Luther's written exhortation to the clergy at Augsburg was very different from his speech to the Diet of Worms. In 1521 Luther had defended his books and criticized papal tyranny but the speech did not go into detail. The exhortation of 1530 was much sharper and packed with specifics. First, Luther addressed the skeletons, that is, the practical reforms that Lutherans had made and why they were necessary. Then he listed thirty-two more topics that should concern the "true Christian church." Except for the last five—respecting authority, establishing schools, visiting the sick, providing for the poor, and ministering to the dying—the list covered what should be taught to laypeople: the meaning of religious concepts such as the gospel, grace, faith, hope, love, and Christian liberty; definitions of sacraments, church, bishop, deacon, the preaching office, prayer, and good works; and finally the catechism and how to read and interpret scripture.[13]

Those topics taught by a "true church" were contrasted with ninety-four practices and customs observed in the "pretended" church. The majority of them identified feast and fasting days that were celebrated during the church year with special masses, abstentions, elaborate processions, and ornate vestments.[14] Luther conceded that some of those customs could be tolerated if they were meant for children, but he added: "That we old fools march around in bishops' hats and clerical pageantry and take it seriously, yes not only seriously but as articles of faith, so that it must be called a sin and torment the conscience of anyone who does not venerate such child's play—that is the devil himself."[15] If that were not sharp enough, he delivered to the bishops an ultimatum comprising two demands they must have found unacceptable. In summary: he asked them to resign and let Luther and his supporters exercise the office of bishop; or stay in office, allow Lutherans to proclaim the gospel, and Luther would teach them how to be proper bishops.[16]

If the goal of the Lutherans was to convince Emperor Charles to accept them as legitimate Christians within the empire, it was a wise decision not to allow Luther to address the diet. In contrast to his *Exhortation* to the bishops, the Lutheran description of beliefs and practices submitted to the emperor was benign. Composed and edited mainly by Melanchthon, the description later known as the *Augsburg Confession* became the litmus test of Lutheranism. Melanchthon started writing it after arriving in Augsburg and receiving a copy of 404 theological statements that John Eck had excerpted from writings by various reformers and stamped as heresy. Eck's strategy was to put all non-Catholics into one heretical basket by arguing that the beliefs of Anabaptists, whom both Lutherans and Catholics opposed, originated with Luther. After Eck sent an elegant hand-written copy of the 404 statements to Emperor Charles V, Elector John and the Lutheran theologians feared that Charles might prejudge the Lutherans as no better than Anabaptists. In the *Confession*, therefore, Melanchthon made a sharp distinction between Lutheran beliefs and the unorthodox views held by Anabaptists but went easy on his Catholic opponents.

After nine days Melanchthon and his colleagues had finished a first draft and forwarded it by mounted messenger to Coburg for Luther's response. After reading the draft, Luther endorsed it with enthusiasm: "It pleases me very much; I know nothing to improve or change in it." Then Luther added words that after his death became controversial among Lutherans themselves: "Nor would this be appropriate, since I cannot tread so softly and quietly."[17] Luther partisans ever since have accused

Melanchthon of trying to appease the emperor by watering down Luther's religious convictions. They failed, however, to realize that Melanchthon and the Lutheran princes were not addressing a toothless Roman clergy from afar but staring into the face of a young Catholic emperor who wielded real power that could punish the Lutherans and reverse their reforms. Moreover, Luther did not intend his words to be taken as criticism. He was simply acknowledging what his colleagues already knew from experience: the temperaments of Luther and Melanchthon were poles apart. One year earlier the contrast was colorfully illustrated by Luther himself:

> For this I was born: to fight and take the field against mobs and devils. Therefore many of my books are stormy and war-like. I must pull out the stumps and roots, hack away at thorns and thistles, drain the swamps. I am the coarse woodsman who must blaze a new trail. But Master Philip comes neatly and quietly behind me, cultivates and plants, sows and waters with joy, according to the gifts that God has richly given him.[18]

Between Luther's positive response, dated May 15, 1530, and June 25 when the *Confession* was submitted, Melanchthon and his colleagues worked daily to prepare a final draft and to convince Count Philip of Hesse to sign it. For the Saxon and Nuremberg Lutherans the *Confession* properly sought to obtain recognition from the emperor, not to antagonize him. Philip of Hesse, however, toyed with a different strategy. Philip was not eager to settle for recognition from the emperor, and the procession of his entourage into Augsburg was a show of Lutheran bravado marked by the display of five letters, VDMIE, which stood for the Latin phrase, "the word of God stands forever." Melanchthon asked Luther to assist in bringing the impulsive count to heel, but Philip finally agreed to sign the *Confession* before Luther's letter from Coburg could reach him.

At Coburg in May Luther suffered an attack that resembled his *Anfechtungen*. He was unable to read and Elector John ordered his personal physician to send Luther medicine. Feeling better in early June, Luther had two visitors. One was Hans Reinicke, who had accompanied him to school in Magdeburg, and another was Argula von Grumbach, a widow and the author of early reformation pamphlets, whose son studied in Wittenberg. Six years earlier Argula had advised Luther to marry, and during this visit in 1530 she gave Luther advice about how best Katharina could wean their one-year-old daughter, Magdalena. On June 5, Luther passed on the advice in his reply to a letter and package sent by Katharina. She had enclosed a picture of Magdalena, probably drawn with charcoal or ink, that was so dark Martin could hardly make out her features. According to Veit Dietrich, Luther attached the picture to a wall opposite the table on which they ate. The package also contained reading glasses that Martin, now forty-five, tried out. We do not know how many pairs Luther had already tested, but his response was typically blunt: these were the worst of all. He also complained of too many visitors. The Coburg fortress, he wrote, had become a pilgrimage destination and he needed a quieter place to hide.[19]

Truly bad news, however, was on its way. Later that day or on the next, Luther learned from Hans Reinicke that his father had died. Since Reinicke was at Coburg only three days earlier, he must have received the news while traveling home to Mansfeld and hurriedly forwarded it back to Coburg. The same night, at the end of a letter to Melanchthon, Luther reflected on his father and his death:

> Even though it comforts me that my father, strong in faith in Christ, fell gently asleep, yet sadness of heart and the memory of the most loving dealings with him have shaken me in the innermost parts of my being, so that seldom if ever have I despised death as much as I do now. . . . Since I am now too sad, I am writing no more, for it is right and God-pleasing for me as a son to mourn such a father, from whom the Father of mercies has brought me forth and through whose sweat [the Creator] has fed and raised me to whatever I am. I rejoice that he has lived until now so that he could see the light of truth.[20]

Two weeks later, Veit Dietrich described Luther's mourning to Katharina: "After two days he had recovered although it was very hard. While reading the letter [from Reinicke], he said to me: 'So my father is also dead.' Then he promptly clutched his Psalter, went into his room, and wept so profusely that the next day his head hurt. Since then he has betrayed no further emotion."[21]

It was not a coincidence that two weeks after the death of his father Martin wrote a letter to his own son, Hänschen Luther, who had just turned four. Luther received a positive report from the boy's tutor, who was studying at the university and living with the Luther family. To encourage his son to keep up the good work, Luther conjured up a children's paradise for Hänschen and his playmates, the sons of Melanchthon and Jonas:

I know of a pretty, beautiful, and cheerful garden where there are many children wearing little golden coats. They pick up fine apples, pears, cherries, and yellow and blue plums under the trees; they sing, jump, and are merry. They also have nice ponies with golden reins and saddles. I asked the owner of the garden whose children they were. He replied: "These are children who like to pray, study, and be good." Then I said: "Dear sir, I also have a son, whose name is Hänschen Luther. Might he also be permitted to enter the garden, so that he too could eat such fine apples and pears, and ride on these pretty ponies, and play with these children?" Then the man answered: "If he likes to pray, study, and be good, he too may enter the garden along with Lippus and Jost."[22]

This paradise was open only to children who earned it, in contrast to the heavenly paradise for which, according to Luther's theology, no good conduct reports were necessary.

At last, on June 15, 1530, Emperor Charles V and his elaborate train of courtiers and clergy halted before the gates of Augsburg. The entourage was guarded by a thousand infantry, an outsized bodyguard, and in the rear cooks, apothecaries, falconers, and two hundred Spanish dogs. Ready to welcome him was the archchancellor of the Holy Roman Empire, Archbishop Albert of Mainz, and the German princes with their retinues, decked out in bright colors as if they were prepared for a tournament. Behind them were delegates of sixty-one free imperial cities and the mayors of Augsburg at the head of an enormous militia and two hundred armored horse.[23] After the welcome ceremonies, Emperor Charles was escorted to his quarters in the bishop's palace.

Charles wasted no time getting to the business at hand. The festival of Corpus Christi was to be celebrated the next day with a high mass and a grand procession featuring the consecrated host carried high in an ornate monstrance. Because the Lutheran princes considered Corpus Christi an indecorous display of the sacramental bread, they had decided not to participate, but Emperor Charles insisted and after supper summoned the princes to the palace. They discussed both the Lutheran refusal to participate and the emperor's previous order that no Lutheran preaching be allowed during the diet. The next morning Charles agreed to a compromise on the preaching matter: neither Catholics nor Lutherans were allowed to preach publicly during the diet. The Lutherans did not budge on the Corpus Christi festivities and the celebration took place without them.[24]

While this drama unfolded in Augsburg, Melanchthon was suffering from anxious exhaustion and Luther was sulking. At Worms he had been the center of attention, but in Augsburg Melanchthon wore the mantle of leadership. On June 5 Luther felt rejected after three messengers from Augsburg came and went without mail for him. On June 7 hurt feelings prevailed and he threatened to send no more letters to his Augsburg colleagues.[25] Such behavior was out of character, and Luther tried to make up for it after Jonas requested a letter of consolation for the struggling Melanchthon. Luther sent Melanchthon three letters in four days, and by the end of June the *Augsburg Confession* had been signed and presented to the emperor. On June 23 Lutheran theologians and princes gathered for a final reading and signatures. Since the *Confession* was a political document presented to the emperor, the signers were not theologians but officials of Lutheran cities and territories willing to defend it: Nuremberg, Reutlingen (an imperial free city in southwest Germany), Electoral Saxony, Hesse, Lüneburg, Brandenburg-Ansbach, and Anhalt, a small territory adjacent to Electoral Saxony.

In the afternoon of June 25, 1530, the German version of the *Confession* was read by the Saxon chancellor, Christian Beyer, before Emperor Charles and as many of the princes who could fit into a small chapel in the bishop's palace. The reading lasted two hours, and one source reported that Emperor Charles napped. Another source, however, claimed that Beyer read so loudly and distinctly that he could be heard in the courtyard below.[26] Both reports could be true. Emperor Charles understood German poorly, and so to him Beyer's reading was probably a droning in the background. Four letters were posted to Luther that day—one each by Melanchthon and Elector John, and two by Jonas. The next day Melanchthon sent Luther a copy of the finished *Confession* and described the hostility it had aroused. Then, anticipating possible negotiations, he sought Luther's advice about the concessions Lutherans might offer.[27] Three days later Luther penned a reply that sounded like a criticism of Melanchthon: "For me personally, more than enough has been conceded. If the papists reject it, I see nothing more to concede." Those words, however, merely answered Melanchthon's question. The criticism came later in the letter. Luther bristled at Melanchthon's statement that he was subject to Luther's authority: "If this is not simultaneously and in the same way your cause, then I do not want it to be called mine and imposed upon you. If it is my cause alone then I will handle it by myself."[28]

The reading of the *Confession* did not settle the issue of what to do about the Lutherans or the German Protestants who had not signed the confession. The latter were unofficially led by Jacob Sturm, who represented Strasbourg. A clever politician, he realized the non-Lutheran evangelical cities that did not sign would be isolated unless they reached a détente with the Lutherans. Toward that end, Sturm convinced three other cities to join Strasbourg and submit their own confession in order to prove that their view of the Lord's Supper was closer to that of Luther than to the view of Zwingli. Sturm summoned Capito and Bucer from Strasbourg and sequestered them until the confession of four cities was finished. He spent the rest of the diet courting the Lutherans so that, when the diet was over and the Lutheran *Confession* was rejected, he and Philip of Hesse could invite the Lutherans to join a defensive alliance against Emperor Charles.

First, however, the Lutherans awaited a Catholic response. Its preparation was assigned to the Catholic theologians in attendance at Augsburg, who numbered about twenty. After their first draft was rejected as too polemical, the theologians produced a milder refutation of the *Confession*. Known as the *Confutation*, it was read to the diet on August 3, 1530.[29] The Lutherans asked for a copy and Emperor Charles offered it, but only with conditions the Lutherans could not accept.

By this time, July had come and gone and Luther was still waiting at the Coburg fortress. His letters to colleagues in Augsburg had three themes: He was very pleased with the *Confession* as far as it went; Melanchthon should stop worrying and let God determine the outcome; nothing will come of any negotiations and you should go home. Luther regarded the *Confession* as Melanchthon's composition and praised the final draft as he had the first. At the same time, Luther lamented the *Confession*'s failure to reject completely the papacy and its authority.[30] Going that far would have made it impossible for Emperor Charles to accept Lutheranism as a legitimate religion in his empire, and that acceptance was the happy ending for which Melanchthon hoped. Luther did not agree and considered acceptance by the emperor a Lutheran fantasy that Melanchthon and his colleagues should abandon. Luther was the bushwhacker willing to reject and condemn everything contrary to the gospel and let God take care of the consequences. Melanchthon was the gardener willing to cultivate an agreement between opposing sides so long as it did not silence the gospel. He knew the odds of success were small, but he pursued a settlement in order to avoid the probable aftermath of failure: Emperor Charles reversing the Lutheran reforms and forcing all German Protestants back under the pope.

Was Luther courageous or foolhardy for opposing a détente with Charles and the German Catholics? The answer depends on who gives it, and Luther delivered his unambiguous answer in a commentary on Psalm 118, his favorite, written at Coburg in mid-June. In Latin, the first word of Psalm 118 is *confitemini* and it means to confess in the sense of declare or confess one's faith.[31] Luther called the psalm "the beautiful *confitemini*," and his commentary was published under that title. He dedicated the book to Frederick Pistorius, the abbot of St. Giles, a Benedictine monastery in Nuremberg, which was turned over to the city after Pistorius joined the reformation. In the dedication to Pistorius, dated July 1, 1530, Luther describes why he abhorred compromise:

> This is my own beloved psalm. Although the entire psalter and all of holy scripture are dear to me as my only comfort and source of life, I fell in love especially with this psalm. Therefore I call it my own. When emperors and kings, the wise and learned, and even saints could not aid me, this psalm proved a friend and helped me out of many great troubles. As a result, it is dearer to me than all the wealth, honor, and power of the pope, the Turk, and the emperor. I am most unwilling to trade this psalm for all of it.[32]

Psalm 118 was also the source of his personal motto, verse 17: "I shall not die, but I shall live and recount the deeds of the Lord." Luther called this verse a masterpiece and the source of great comfort in the midst of death:

> Here you see how the right hand of God mightily lifts the heart and comforts it in the midst of death, so that the heart can say: "Though I die, I die not. Though I suffer, I suffer not. Though I fall, I am not down. Though I am disgraced, I am not dishonored.". . . Furthermore, the psalmist says: "I shall live." Is this not astounding? The dying live; the suffering rejoice; the fallen rise; the disgraced are honored.[33]

Having recently lost his father, Luther might have pondered verse 17 for himself as well as for his readers. According to a later report, he wrote out the verse with plainsong notes on a wall in his quarters at Coburg.[34]

During July and August Luther made the most of his free time: writing pamphlets and letters, dictating a short psalms commentary, translating the Hebrew prophets, and receiving visitors, which included his brother Jacob from Mansfeld and the brother of Hänschen's tutor from Wittenberg. Melanchthon's closest friend, the Greek scholar Camerarius, rode up from Nuremberg to see Luther, and the Augsburg Lutheran reformer, Urban Rhegius, stopped by on his way north to a new challenge in the duchy of

Lüneburg. On occasion, Luther was bothered by headaches, dizziness, weakness, and congestion, but he rarely missed a full day at the desk and was hoping to return home soon. On July 15, he was expecting his Lutheran colleagues to leave Augsburg and to pick him up at Coburg.[35] One month later, August 14, 1530, still at Coburg, he informed Katharina of a rumor that the Catholic *Confutation* of the Lutheran *Confession* had been publicly read but not handed over to the Lutherans for rebuttal. The rumor was true, and Luther again expected his colleagues to leave Augsburg because their Catholic opponents "had shied away from the light."[36] At that point no one realized that the Lutherans would not leave Augsburg until October 4.

Throughout August a series of negotiations between various constellations of Catholics and Lutherans tried to reach agreement. The first round stalled, but new teams of theologians made some progress on doctrines. The Catholic team included scholars who had written against Luther and some who had met him in person: John Eck, John Cochlaeus, and his old Erfurt teacher, Arnoldi von Usingen. For a while Melanchthon's hopes were high. The *Confession* had claimed that Lutheran doctrines were so well grounded in scripture that even the Roman Church could not disagree with them. Melanchthon had added: "For the dissension and quarrel are chiefly over some traditions and abuses."[37]

Melanchthon was right about where the stickier conflicts were, but awareness of them was not enough. Although the negotiations on doctrines did bring the two sides closer, they broke down over the "abuses" described in the *Augsburg Confession* as "corrected."[38] The list is familiar: receiving bread and wine in the Lord's Supper; allowing priests to marry; abolishing private masses; allowing only voluntary fasting; abolishing monastic vows; limiting the authority of bishops. Neither Luther nor the Roman theologians were willing to give ground on the "corrected" abuses. Doctrines were discussable because they were concepts that mattered mainly to theologians; but religious practices were not negotiable because they gave access to the presence and power of the divine, and that access was the reason religion existed.

Soon after the Catholic *Confutation* was read to the diet, Melanchthon started work on a rebuttal without having to rely on his memory. Before the Lutherans were denied a copy of the *Confutation*, they decided to create their own copy from the oral presentation. Melanchthon's friend from Nuremberg, Camerarius, wrote down as much of the text as possible while it was being read and notes were made by others present. By collating the stenograph of Camerarius with the notes, the Lutherans recreated a text of the *Confutation* which captured "in substance all the main points" of the document as read.[39] On September 19, Melanchthon reported that his defense of the *Confession* against the Catholic *Confutation* was almost finished, adding with satisfaction: "I have written accurately and vehemently."[40]

Three days later, on September 22, Emperor Charles V invited the delegates to the bishop's palace for his verdict on the diet. He announced that the Catholic *Confutation* had refuted the *Augsburg Confession* and gave all the evangelical rulers until April 15, 1531, to inform him whether or not they would return to Rome. Elector John's former chancellor and political advisor, Gregor Brück, officially rejected the emperor's verdict and tried to submit Melanchthon's defense, which was called the *Apology*, a synonym for defense derived from Greek and Latin. The emperor reportedly reached for the *Apology*, but his hand was pulled back, perhaps by his brother, Archduke Ferdinand, and a warning whispered into his ear. The emperor's verdict thus became the Imperial Edict of Augsburg. The Lutherans were given one more chance to accept the edict, but they refused.

At Coburg Luther welcomed reports that the diet was over. During the negotiations he had accurately predicted their failure and expected Emperor Charles to refer the religious standoff to a council of the church. Luther called the emperor an "excellent man" who was hoping to restore unity and peace but who was besieged by so many "demonic monsters" that success was unlikely.[41] In letter after letter he had assured Katharina of his imminent homecoming, and on September 23 and 24 he told her again he "hoped" to be back with the family in two weeks.[42] He was wrong about the arrival but he was right that the Saxon party would soon leave Augsburg. While he waited for them at Coburg, Luther preached in the fortress chapel on September 29, the festival of Michael and All Angels. Most of the sermon dealt not with good angels but with the fallen angel, the devil, whose wiles were on display in Augsburg: "The devil tried to tear us away from our faith. If he had succeeded, the consequence would have been murder all around."[43] But, said Luther in a second sermon on October 2, two gods were present in Augsburg: our true God and the world's god, the devil. The devil looked powerful while Christ appeared weak, but grace and mercy were on our side and we should give God thanks and praise that the divine word remained firm and that we stood by it.[44]

Elector John and Luther's colleagues arrived at Coburg on October 1 and they all left for home on October 4. Before leaving, Luther's mind turned to music and he sent a personal request to a prominent composer in Munich, Ludwig Senfl. After declaring that his love for music was abundant and often liberated him from great vexations, he asked Senfl to send him the music for Psalm 4:8: "I will both lie down and sleep in peace; for you, O Lord, make me lie down in safety." The tenor melody (*cantus firmus*) had delighted Luther in his youth—as a boy chorister he had presumably sung the text in Latin—but now he wanted an arrangement for more voices and hoped Senfl had one at hand. Luther then indicated the reason for his request:

> Indeed I hope that the end of my life is at hand; the world hates me and cannot bear me, and I in turn loathe and detest the world. Therefore may the best and most faithful shepherd take my soul to him. And so I have started to sing this antiphon[45] and am eager to hear it arranged. In case you do not have the plainsong, I am enclosing it with the tenor notes.[46]

Happier thoughts seem more appropriate for a man who after six months was about to return home; but the emperor's edict caused Luther to anticipate an attack that would end in his death. On October 1 he started a *Warning to His Dear German People* about the likelihood of war and pondered the consequences for himself. If war came and God did not see fit to rescue Luther, he would thank and praise God nevertheless:

> I have lived long enough, I have certainly earned death, and I have begun for my Lord Jesus to take revenge on the papacy. Only after my death will they begin to take Luther seriously. Even now, if I were to be murdered in a papal or clerical uprising, I would take a throng of bishops, priests, and monks with me, so that people will say that Dr. Martin was escorted to his grave in a grand procession.[47]

Before the Wittenbergers arrived home, on October 13, 1530,[48] Luther's attention was drawn to more than his own death. Philip of Hesse, supported by Jacob Sturm from Strasbourg, proposed an alliance of evangelical princes and cities to defend Protestants against a Catholic attack. The alliance would only be stable if the Strasbourg and Wittenberg theologians could agree on the mode of Christ's presence in the Lord's Supper. Before the diet had ended, Melanchthon and Martin Bucer from Strasbourg discussed the issue, and Melanchthon reportedly said Bucer's views were more acceptable than he expected and comparable even to Luther's view.[49] After that, Bucer was sent to meet with Luther at Coburg. That conversation also ended on a positive note. It was no surprise when Luther learned from his own prince, Elector John, that Philip of Hesse had proposed the alliance.

For Luther, however, the Lord's Supper was not the only issue. Since returning to Wittenberg in 1522 he had consistently opposed military resistance of any kind to the emperor. The advisors of Elector John were arguing, however, that resistance was legal. To hammer out a consensus, Elector John called the theologians to Torgau. At the conference, which convened in late October, Luther found a way to support resistance to the emperor while at the same time maintaining that, strictly speaking, it was not permissible to Christians.[50] The cleanest expression of this paradox appears the following January in a letter to Linck: "If princes as princes are permitted to resist the emperor, let it be a matter of their judgment and their conscience. Such resistance is certainly not permitted to a Christian, who has died to the world."[51]

With that hurdle overcome, Elector John was able to accept the offer of Philip, and the strongest Protestant alliance of the reformation was about to be born. It was formed by written agreement on the last day of 1530 at Smalcald (Schmalkalden), a town twice as big as Wittenberg and the second largest town in Hesse. It was also the site of Count Philip's second residence. Smalcald was geographically the most convenient location for the count of Hesse and the Elector of Saxony to meet. It was so close to Thuringia, to which it now belongs, that Smalcald felt like home to both rulers. On December 31, the league was created as "a Christian association for defense and protection against violent assault," and it decided immediately to petition Emperor Charles to soften the Edict of Augsburg. The official charter of the league was signed on February 27, 1531. Besides Electoral Saxony and Hesse, its members included four additional subscribers to the *Augsburg Confession*, plus the north German cities of Magdeburg, Bremen, and Lübeck, and seven south German cities with Strasbourg at the head.

The strongest Lutheran city in the south, Nuremberg, did not join, although it had signed the *Augsburg Confession*. It refused to endorse the right of subjects to fight against the emperor and cited as support Luther's long opposition to resistance. After Electoral Saxony responded that the reformer now supported resistance, Luther's early advocate and senior statesman in the Nuremberg government, Lazarus Spengler, asked Luther to clarify his position. Luther offered a weak excuse for changing his mind and appearing to endorse resistance. The Saxon theologians, he said, postponed a decision on the matter until they were shown legal arguments that justified resistance. In reality, Luther was caught where he never wanted to be: watching his theology used as evidence by both sides in a political quarrel.[52] By saying Christians were dead to the world but princes could act as princes, he was attempting to keep theology from being compromised by politics. It was a noble purpose but, as it turned out, a hopeless endeavor.

CHAPTER FIFTEEN

TRUE RELIGION
1531–1534
Wittenberg—Torgau

"True religion demands the heart and the soul, not deeds and other externals, although these follow if you have the right heart. For where the heart is, everything else is also there."[1]

After returning from Coburg, Luther complained regularly of weak spells and headaches. On December 18, 1530, he was too dizzy to complete his sermon,[2] and the complaints continued into 1531. He blamed one headache on old wine he drank at Coburg, but by then Luther had been home over three months.[3] Five days later he sensed weakness in the head: "I am kept from writing, reading, or talking very much; I live like a sick man."[4] A week later, Luther divulged more of the strain under which he suffered. He told the pastor in Eisenach that he was unable to answer a letter from his own uncle: "I am swamped by letters from every direction. They all presume that only Luther can expedite their affairs. Hardly any messengers are able to wait [for a reply]. They have no place to stay and other things to do. They want the replies to be ready soon after the messages are delivered! ... By myself I will not immediately tend to everyone's business."[5] When frustrated and feeling poorly, Luther could be peevish, but he kept working.

He resumed giving lectures on the Song of Songs after returning to Wittenberg in mid-October of 1530, but he stopped on December 6, and did not start again until May of 1531. Most of Luther's time was occupied with letters, sermons, and the Psalms. At Coburg Luther had dictated to Dietrich a short explanation of each psalm and by late September they had reached Psalm 24. The work was interrupted by his return to Wittenberg and halted in January of 1531. A related project was pressing: revising the entire German Psalter, which had first appeared in 1524.[6] The team that was translating the Old Testament from Hebrew into German was reassembled and met at the cloister fifteen times from mid-January to March 15, 1531. In addition to the revision itself Luther planned to explain the psalms in short summaries, like those he dictated at Coburg, and to introduce the revision with a defense of the team's method. In 1533 all three items appeared in print together: the revised German Psalter, the defense, and the summaries.[7]

The defense demonstrated how the Wittenberg team chose German words to render awkward or difficult Hebrew passages. Sometimes, explained Luther, the team refrained from a literal translation of the Hebrew: "We departed rather freely from the letter of the original and at times followed an interpretation that differed from what the Jewish rabbis and grammarians taught."[8] Why? Because "whoever would speak German must not use Hebrew style. Once they understand the Hebrew author, they must concentrate on the sense of the text and ask themselves: 'What do Germans say in such a situation?' Once they have the German, let them drop the Hebrew words and express the meaning freely in the best German they know."[9] At other times, however, the team translated the Hebrew literally "because everything turned on those very few words." As an example, Luther chose verse 18 of Psalm 68: "You have ascended on high; you have led captivity captive."

> It would have been good German to say "you have set the captives free." But this is too weak and does not convey the fine, rich meaning of the Hebrew, which says literally "you have led captivity captive." The Hebrew words imply not only that Christ freed the captives but also that he captured and led away captivity itself, so that never again could it take us captive. Thus [Christ accomplished] an eternal redemption.[10]

Obviously Luther was not a literalist in the mode of Christian fundamentalists who believe the infallible original text of the Bible can be determined and for whom its every word is sacred. But neither was Luther a modern textual critic for whom the Old Testament was primarily or exclusively Hebrew scripture. Instead, Luther treated Hebrew scripture as the "Old Testament," the first part of the Christian Bible. In that regard, Luther was like the authors of New Testament books, who cited or alluded to more than 300 "Old Testament" passages to illustrate or prove their points.

By putting a readable Bible into the hands of a large number of Christians who had never held or seen one, Luther and other reformers made Christianity a religion of the book to a degree unprecedented. To Luther it seemed like a good idea, but the consequences went beyond anything he and other translators imagined. On one hand, Luther anticipated correctly that a readable Bible in the hands of Protestant laity would give them a source of authority greater than the pope and convince them the reformers were right. It was in Luther's interest, therefore, to revise the German Old and New Testaments until the texts were as comprehensible as possible. During Luther's lifetime, the September 1522 German New Testament was revised six times before the first complete German Bible appeared in 1534. The German Bible in its entirety was revised three times before Luther died.

On the other hand, Luther did not anticipate how many Protestants would ignore his claim that the ultimate importance of reading the Bible was to encounter the gospel. In 1537, he listed the following means by which the gospel provided guidance and help: preaching, baptism, the Lord's Supper, confessing sin and receiving forgiveness, and the mutual consolation of believers.[11] Strikingly absent was reading the Bible, even though the gospel was embedded in the Bible. Luther had no way of foreseeing that once people could read the Bible, going to church to hear the gospel in its various forms might seem superfluous. Or that people reading the Bible on their own would use parts they liked to support bizarre beliefs and prejudices. Or that Christians would equate Christianity with the Bible and disregard their predecessors, who over centuries preserved the Bible for them to read. Or that Christians and non-Christians would extract familiar passages such as the Ten Commandments and wield them as political weapons. Instead of finding freedom through the good news contained in the Bible, some readers would end up enslaving themselves verse by verse to a paper pope.

As he became older and the students appeared younger, Luther worried about losing the gospel contained in the Bible. In the 1530s he warned readers and students how bad it had been "under the pope," before the gospel was brought to light, and how that darkness might return to Germany if the emperor forced them back to Rome. If German Protestants allowed the emperor to reverse the reformation, wrote Luther after the Augsburg Diet, they would be guilty of exterminating everything good that had been established by the gospel.[12] What would be lost? Evangelical preaching, baptism, the Lord's Supper, and more:

You will abet the burning of all the German books, New Testaments, Psalters, prayer books, hymnals, and all the things we wrote and which they [Catholics] themselves admit are good. You will help to keep everyone ignorant of the Ten Commandments, Lord's Prayer, and the Creed; for this is the way it used to be. You will have to prohibit anyone from knowing Christian freedom. You will keep people from placing their trust in Christ and deriving all their comfort from him. For none of that existed before; all of it is something new. ... You will have to help with destroying Christ's word and his whole kingdom and with rebuilding the kingdom of the devil.[13]

That *Warning to His Dear German People* was about to be published when April 1, 1531, arrived. It was the deadline for Lutherans to tell the emperor whether or not they would return to Rome. The next day was the beginning of holy week, and Luther preached on the prescribed text without mentioning the ultimatum.[14] There was no need. It was not to be enforced because two Catholic electors, one of them Archbishop Albert of Mainz, asked Emperor Charles to consider further negotiations with the Protestants. Once again imperial politics favored the Lutherans. In order to have their votes for his brother, Archduke Ferdinand, to become king of Germany and to receive Protestant money and soldiers to fend off the Turks, Charles agreed that talks could begin. Lutherans, at least, could expect the Imperial High Court to postpone the charges against them for not obeying the Edict of Augsburg.[15] When Luther was notified that conversations with Catholic theologians would resume, he agreed to cooperate for the sake of peace and to gain breathing room.[16]

By the end of 1531 only two of Luther's closest colleagues, Jonas and Melanchthon, were left in Wittenberg. One week after Luther returned from Coburg, John Bugenhagen left for Lübeck, a prosperous city east of Hamburg that was struggling to establish the reformation and invited Bugenhagen to write its Lutheran constitution. Upon arrival on October 28, 1530, Bugenhagen was greeted by a demon-possessed young woman who complained: "Were there not enough preachers in Lübeck already? Why summon another from Wittenberg?"[17] Elector John and Luther were asking themselves the same question because neither wanted Bugenhagen to leave Saxony for another indefinite period. His absence meant that Luther preached more frequently in the Town Church, especially during the Easter season of 1531. When the summer semester started, Luther also resumed lecturing. After finishing the Song of Songs in June, he immediately started on Paul's epistle to the Galatians. Beginning on July 3, Luther lectured almost every week, hardly pausing for semester breaks, and covered all six chapters of Galatians by mid-December. After the lectures were published in 1535, they earned a reputation as his paramount theological book.

During 1531, while he was lecturing on Galatians, distractions were plentiful. On April 30 Luther comforted the sister of Jerome Weller, the tutor of his children, who anguished over predestination. Luther gave her the same advice he had received from Staupitz: keep the heart fixed on God's love in Christ.[18] On May 4 Elector John summoned Luther to Torgau to meet Duke Henry of Saxony, the brother of Catholic Duke George. Henry wanted to hear Luther preach. That night Luther rose at 2:00 am and traveled to Torgau to comply with the Elector's order.[19] The unreasonable request evoked no complaint from Luther—at least none that was recorded. On May 20 Luther sent a long letter of consolation to his gravely ill mother. She died soon afterward, one year after Luther's father.[20] On June 16 Luther complained to Elector John that the Wittenberg bailiff, Hans Metzsch, had not heeded a warning to stay away from prostitutes. After Metzsch insisted he could not live without women, Luther denied him the sacrament.[21] Besides feeding the gossipmongers, the standoff caused a rift that Elector John referred to the Wittenberg town council. On June 26 Luther told Linck in Nuremberg that he suffered blows from Satan so heavy that he feared Satan might kill him. In the same letter, Luther complained that trivial matters were also slowing him down.[22] We are left to wonder which was worse: Satan or too many trifles. On July 3, the day on which Luther delivered the first lecture on Galatians, he was visited by Magdalena Staupitz, the sister of his mentor. She was now headmistress of a school for girls and resided in a house that belonged to a convent. The officials of Elector John were confiscating convent property and intended to take possession of her house. Luther implored the Elector on her behalf and Magdalena Staupitz retained her home.[23]

A few months later, on November 9, Katharina Luther delivered her fourth child, Martin Jr. Ten days earlier Luther had invited John Rühel, his relative and friend in Eisleben, to be the godfather,[24] and the baptism presumably took place in Wittenberg on November 10, 1531, Luther's own forty-seventh birthday. For his birthday the next year, the princes of nearby Anhalt sent Luther a boar. Through his friend Nicholas Hausmann, for whom Luther had found a new position in Anhalt, he assured the princes that the boar would be relished by him and four colleagues at a birthday party for Martin the saint (November 11), Martin the father (November 10), and Martin the son (November 9).[25]

To be Martin Luther Jr. must have felt heavy, even in childhood. When he was almost seven, Luther called Martin a little rascal and started to worry.[26] At age fourteen Martin was present at his father's deathbed and he was the only son to study theology; yet no records indicate that Martin Jr. ever worked as a pastor. When Katharina died in 1552, he was the oldest child left at home, and in 1560, when he married a daughter of Wittenberg's mayor, Martin Jr. was the only child living in the cloister. By that time he might have been addicted to alcohol. In 1563 two young princes of Pomerania were sent to study in Wittenberg and were given quarters in the cloister still occupied by Martin Jr. and his wife. Preparations for the princes' arrival had not been made. The cloister was filthy, almost bare, and the second floor was occupied by seven rowdy students who came and went at all hours. Martin Jr. himself appeared to have no money and spent his time boozing with buddies whom the custodian of the princes called good-for-nothings. When Martin Jr. refused to remedy the conditions, the custodian complained and the Pomeranian princes received better quarters.[27] Two years later Martin Jr. was dead at the age of thirty-four.

Martin Jr. was born while his father was lecturing on Galatians, a New Testament letter sent by Paul to churches in central Asia Minor (Turkey) he had previously organized. Like most early churches the Galatian Christians included both Jewish and gentile converts. After Paul left, some of the Jewish converts insisted that gentile converts had to be circumcised and observe Jewish laws. Paul was incensed and accused the Jewish Christians of turning to a gospel that was different from what he preached to them. According to Paul, both Jews and non-Jews who believed in Christ were free from all laws and rituals. Why, asked Paul, do you want to be enslaved to them again? If you do, he continued, "I am afraid that my work for you may have been wasted" (Galatians 4:11).

Luther was asking the same question of Protestants. In principle, they had been freed by the reformation from all the binding laws and rituals of medieval Catholicism. If now, under pressure from the emperor, Protestants failed to resist and returned to the slavery of their former religion, the mission Luther had embraced at the Wartburg was dead. There was no turning back, he cautioned, if they wanted to enjoy Christian freedom. Although Luther had lectured on Galatians prior to the ninety-five theses, now was the perfect time for a new course:

We have taken it upon ourselves to lecture on Paul's epistle to the Galatians once more—not because we want to teach something new . . . but because, as I often warn you, we face the utmost danger that the devil may take from us the pure teaching of faith and substitute the teaching of works and human traditions. . . . Therefore, the subject of faith can never be discussed and taught enough. If it is lost forever, the knowledge of truth is lost forever. But if this teaching flourishes, everything good flourishes—religion, true worship, the glory of God, and the accurate perception of how things are.[28]

After defending his decision, Luther summarized the purpose of Paul's letter. It was the same purpose that had driven Luther since the indulgence controversy: "To establish the teaching of faith, grace, remission of sins, and Christian goodness so that we can perfectly distinguish between Christian goodness and all other kinds of goodness." Christian or heavenly goodness, continued Luther, is given to us by God without our work or merit. It does not come from our good deeds or from our obedience to the law. Daily life does require us to obey the law, and that obedience may deliver legal or moral goodness, but it is not the same as Christian goodness:

Our theology teaches a precise distinction between these two kinds of goodness or justice . . . so that morality and faith, works and grace, secular society and religion may not be confused. In each pair both things are necessary, but both must be kept within their limits. Christian goodness applies to the new person, and the goodness of the law to the old person born of flesh and blood.[29]

The tactic pursued by Luther in his lectures was to demonstrate how Paul made the same distinctions for the Jewish Christians in Galatia who misunderstood freedom from the law. For Paul, himself a converted Jewish scholar, the law was the Torah, the first five books of the Old Testament, which included the Ten Commandments, ceremonial regulations, and moral injunctions. Paul argued that all Christian converts, Jews and non-Jews, were free from those laws through their baptism. With that baptism came the Holy Spirit, who was the source of all the goodness and morality that converts needed. Christians no longer lived under the law but in and through the Spirit.

Luther's lectures brought the same argument up to date. For him Paul's Jewish Christians were the Catholics of medieval Christianity. Their religion was based on laws and regulations—some biblical, some not—that believers had to obey in order to appear good in God's sight. Luther aligned Catholics with the Pharisees, the Jewish legal experts whose laws and human regulations Jesus rejected. But that was not all. Luther added to Catholics, whom he called papists, others who resisted his vision of true religion: Anabaptists, Zwinglians, Muslims, and the Jewish people of his own time. All of them, Christian or not, argued Luther, contradicted his definition of Christian goodness: It was a heavenly gift freely given and received and not earned by human merit based on obedience to the law. Luther's stereotyping of his adversaries was simplistic and unfair, but that was his way of transposing the Pauline message to sixteenth-century Christianity.

It was all clear to Luther, but it proved hard for religious people to grasp. For them religion and morality were one and the same. They were taught that obeying customs and laws and doing good deeds pleased God and earned them the rewards promised by their religion. Throughout his career Luther fought the identification of religion with morality, but it was a hard sell. To many listeners of early Lutheran sermons, becoming good and pleasing in God's sight by faith alone and not by works sounded as if they were exempted from moral rectitude and generous behavior. Luther's 1520 German treatises on good works and Christian freedom argued vigorously against that misperception. On the basis of Galatians, chapter five, he emphasized again that genuinely good works were the fruit of faith and the Spirit. Obedience to just laws and morally good behavior followed spontaneously from faith because, like faith, good works were gifts of the Spirit. In 1531, lecturing on Galatians to an academic audience, he again drew the line between faith and morality by redefining the term "doing":

> In theology we have to rise higher [than in philosophy] with the word "doing," so that it becomes altogether new. . . . In theology doing is always understood as doing with faith, so that doing with faith is a separate sphere, a new realm so to speak, one that is different from moral doing. When we theologians speak about doing, it is necessary that we speak about doing with faith. In theology we have no right reason and good will except through faith . . . because "without faith it is impossible to please God" (Hebrews 11:6).[30]

Separating religion from moralism was Luther's revolutionary innovation and simultaneously the reason why he was often misunderstood and rejected. It defied the age-old purpose of religion: to gain access to the divine and then to please the gods in order to obtain their blessing and reward. The exercise of religion required designating holy ground or building temples where sacrifice to the gods could be made; consecrating holy people like priests with power to mediate between believers and the gods; creating sacred rituals and ceremonies to assure the presence of the gods; telling stories about the gods and the world, how it began and how it would end; and devising a moral code that taught believers how to behave in order to gain eternal rewards. Christianity had mostly fit that template, and Luther's attempt to alter it was bound to meet enormous resistance, even though he was able to sum up his view in one sentence: "True religion demands the heart and the soul, not deeds and other externals, although these follow if you have the right heart. For where the heart is, everything else is also there."[31]

After the lectures on Galatians concluded on December 12, 1531, Luther reported the political news to Amsdorf. The new negotiations between Catholics and Protestants that Luther had endorsed were moving ahead because the Turkish army, estimated at 300,000 soldiers, was again threatening Hungary and Emperor Charles needed Protestant support. Agreement had not yet been reached, but it was expected at a conference that was to start on Easter Monday 1532, and run concurrently with a new imperial diet opening further south in Regensburg. Emperor Charles stipulated that Catholic negotiators at the conference, to be held not far from Coburg in the town of Schweinfurt, deal only with those Protestant delegates that signed the *Augsburg Confession*. That stipulation excluded the important city of Strasbourg, which had joined the Protestant Smalcald League but had not signed the *Confession*.[32] Strasbourg's chief theologian, Martin Bucer, did not fully agree with Luther's view of the Lord's Supper; but the Turkish threat and the prospect of making peace with the emperor pushed Strasbourg to sign the *Confession* and to participate in the conference.[33] In June the Schweinfurt talks moved to Nuremberg, which was closer to the diet, and Emperor Charles finally agreed not to enforce the Edict of Augsburg if his terms were met. Luther, who was not present at the conference, advised Elector John to accept the emperor's terms, and both sides signed a formal truce called the Peace of Nuremberg (1532). Officially the truce was temporary, but it was an unexpected boon to the German Reformation. Emperor Charles would not attempt to enforce the Edict of Augsburg against Protestants for another decade.

Electoral Saxony was represented at Schweinfurt and Nuremberg by Duke John Frederick because his father, Elector John, was recovering slowly from the gangrene that cost him one of his toes. From Torgau Luther reported the Elector's plight to Katharina and asked for her prayers because the devil had bitten the Elector and punctured his foot.[34] The only Lutheran theologian present in Schweinfurt was George Spalatin, who arrived in time to preach on Easter morning in a church set aside for the Protestants. Spalatin was to preach again on Easter Monday, but so many townspeople tried to enter the church that the service was moved outside and Spalatin was forced to deliver an open-air sermon.[35] Luther, together with Bugenhagen, who had returned from Lübeck, congratulated Spalatin on the success of his sermons and conveyed greetings from Melanchthon and Katharina Luther to Spalatin, his wife Katharina, and their daughter Hanna, who was only three months old.[36]

Before the Diet of Regensburg adjourned in late summer of 1532, it appropriated money and troops to defend the empire against the Turks. Duke Joachim of Brandenburg was chosen to command the army's division in the region that included Wittenberg. Duke Joachim was the son of Elector Joachim, who remained Catholic and had been harshly criticized by Luther for taking as his concubine the wife of Wolf Hornung. Nevertheless the son, Duke Joachim, informed both Luther and Melanchthon of his military assignment and turned to them for Christian counsel. Luther gracefully assured the duke of his prayers and then described the right attitude that Christians going to war should adopt. First, they should rely on God's power and not on their own; second, Christians should not assume they alone were righteous and the enemy utterly unrighteous; third, Christians should by no means seek honor, land, and booty but only the glory of God and the defense of those for whom they fight.[37] Those instructions reflected earlier thoughts Luther had put down in a book titled *Whether Soldiers, Too, Can Be Saved.*[38] Both that book and the letter to Duke Joachim vividly exhibited Luther's idealism. If Duke Joachim inculcated the right attitudes in his soldiers, assured Luther, the war would undoubtedly be conducted on a high plane.[39]

On August 15, 1532, Elector John suffered a stroke at his hunting castle in Schweinitz, twenty miles (thirty-one kilometers) east-southeast of Wittenberg. Melanchthon and Luther hurried to his bedside in time to console him and witness his death the next morning. The body was rushed to Wittenberg because no balsam for embalming the corpse was available around Schweinitz.[40] Since the Elector was the university's patron, the funeral was held with modest fanfare on August 18 in the Castle Church. A constant tolling of bells was the only pomp. Behind a wooden cross, clergy, faculty, and students processed ahead of the bier, which was escorted to the church by the Elector's counselors followed by the mourners. At the entrance they stopped to sing Luther's arrangement of "Out of the Depths," and inside the church students and choir boys chanted in German: "Now let your servant depart in peace" and "My soul magnifies the Lord."[41] Luther refused to deliver a eulogy: "I will not now praise the Elector for his great virtues but let him remain a sinner like the rest of us." His sermon emphasized the suffering and "real death" of Elector John that occurred two years earlier at the Diet of Augsburg. Signing and standing behind the *Augsburg Confession* was a far more bitter death and took more courage than his physical demise. The academic tradition also called for a Latin oration, which was written and delivered by Melanchthon at the interment. Because Duke John Frederick could not reach Wittenberg in time for the funeral of his father, he requested a memorial service in the Castle Church later that week. It was held on the Thursday following the funeral and Luther preached again on the same text.[42]

Shortly before his death, Elector John had issued instructions for a new visitation of parishes in Electoral Saxony. It was one of many topics discussed by the Wittenberg theologians with the new Elector, John Frederick, who succeeded his father at the age of twenty-nine. John Frederick was well prepared to become the third and last Elector of Saxony during Luther's lifetime. He was still a teenager when Luther thanked him for supporting reforms and dedicated to him a German commentary on the *Magnificat*.[43] At first, however, Luther did not expect much from John Frederick as a ruler; he was too worldly and listened to other nobles rather than to his scholarly advisors. Luther was wrong. The transition from father to son went smoothly and Elector John Frederick proved himself early. In 1533, after revising his father's instructions, John Frederick went ahead with the second visitation and joined Philip of Hesse as co-leader of the Smalcald League.

Elector John Frederick was soon tested by Duke George, ruler of the Catholic part of Saxony. A protest by Luther sympathizers near Leipzig led Duke George to demand the formal identification of his subjects who did not confess or commune in the prescribed Roman manner. Easter was approaching and Luther's followers had to decide if they should pretend to be Catholic and accept only bread at communion. They wrote to Luther for advice. Under no circumstances, he replied, should they participate in the Lord's Supper if they could not receive both bread and wine. Duke George had no right to force them to act against their conscience.[44] When Duke

George learned of the letter, he complained to Elector John Frederick and demanded action against the reformer. In the past when Duke George complained about Luther, Electors Frederick and John sent George a polite answer and half-heartedly asked their advisors to calm Luther down. Elector John Frederick, however, told Duke George that Luther had the right to give advice and comfort to evangelical believers everywhere and reminded Duke George, who was over sixty, that he should stop harassing Lutheran sympathizers and make peace with God before it was too late.[45] John Frederick's unvarnished reaction was a foretaste of the Elector's uncompromising pro-Lutheran policies, which in some cases overrode Luther's own advice.

From 1532 until 1546, Luther sent 172 letters and formal opinions to Elector John Frederick. Sixty of them were written and submitted by Luther together with his closest theological colleagues. In the absence of a Lutheran bishop, they formed a team or panel of authorities that exercised supervision of the evangelical churches in Electoral Saxony and advised the Elector on religious matters whether John Frederick requested the advice or not. A similar team of theologians had existed informally since Elector John took office in 1525 and consisted of Luther, Melanchthon, Bugenhagen, and Jonas. That nucleus remained in place until 1534, when young Caspar Cruciger, who joined the theological faculty at the age of thirty, also became part of the team and a favorite of Luther. When he died in 1548 at the age of forty-four, the colleagues who informed Melanchthon called Cruciger not only Luther's disciple but also his much beloved son.[46]

As Lutheran churches both inside and outside Electoral Saxony became better organized and pastors became available, Luther's team in Wittenberg faced many problems that can be assigned to four categories: theology, politics, church organization, and marital matters. Two-thirds of the formal opinions submitted by the Wittenberg panel dealt with matters in the first two categories, while one-third concerned cases belonging to the last two. Statistics, however, do not express the variety of disputes and pleas that absorbed so much of Luther's energy during his last fourteen years. Already in 1533 Melanchthon estimated that he had written over 600 briefs for marital disputes.[47] As for Martin Luther the provocative professor and reformer—he became Luther the controversial judge, counselor, and administrator. His short term as provincial vicar of the strict Augustinians had given him some experience with management and personnel, but only some. Moreover, Luther's new roles were mundane in comparison to his dramatic clashes with pope and emperor. He realized, however, that helping evangelical pastors and parishes to flourish was also essential to his larger mission of restoring true religion to Germany.

Luther's expanding family also required more attention than previously. When Elector John died in August of 1532, Katharina was pregnant with the Luthers' fifth child. Paul Luther, named after the apostle, was born on January 29, 1533, one hour after midnight, and was baptized the same evening in the Castle Church. His godfathers were Jonas, Melanchthon, the Electoral marshal, Hans Löser, and Prince John Ernest, the young son of the deceased Elector John and the half-brother of Elector John Frederick. In 1524 Luther had presided at Löser's wedding; and in 1531 Luther dedicated to Löser a brief commentary on Psalm 147 in appreciation for taking him on a hunting trip. Löser went after real game while Luther sat in the carriage and did spiritual hunting: "I bagged Psalm 147 together with its exposition, and this was my happiest hunt and the grandest game [I caught]. Now that I have brought it home and carved it, I want to tell you about it, lest I have a bad conscience for having concealed a prize won on your [Löser's] estate and be found ungrateful."[48]

Paul Luther's godmother was Margaret Lindemann. She and her husband, Casper, a professor of medicine, had lived in Wittenberg less than a year. Luther already knew Casper as a relative of his own mother, also named Margaret, and the former personal physician of Electors Frederick and John. Margaret and Casper were quickly accepted into the circle of the reformer's academic friends; Jonas, his wife, and John Bugenhagen were charter members of that circle, and on September 10, 1532, they were dinner guests of the Luthers, along with Felicitas von Selmenitz, a Thuringian noblewoman and widow who lived in Wittenberg while her son studied at the university. Felicitas made contact with the reformers and asked for copies of their writings. She studied them avidly and underlined them freely. Luther also gave her a copy of the 1534 German Bible, which still exists and contains a notation of the gift in his own hand.[49]

Katharina Jonas and Margaret Lindemann were good friends of Katharina Luther, and Elizabeth Cruciger may have joined them. A month before Paul's birth, Elizabeth brought Katharina a gift made of gold. Luther sent thanks to her husband, and reported that Katharina was sending Elizabeth a gift that was not equivalent except in the good will and warmth that accompanied it.[50] At times, it was apparently not easy to be a friend of Katharina Luther. Behind her back Wittenbergers talked about Katharina's lordly manner and acquisitive habits. In 1533, one woman complained that Katharina stirred up quarrels instead of settling them, as was her duty.[51] She and Katharina Melanchthon were not close, although charges of envy and hostility made against Melanchthon's wife are based on poor evidence.[52] Melanchthon himself got along well with Katharina Luther and was exceptionally helpful to her and the children after Luther died.[53] Even before his death, when Luther and Jonas were out of town, Melanchthon would check on their families and include a report in his letters.

Despite their occupation with local matters, neither Luther nor Melanchthon was forgotten as the reformation advanced outside Germany. Nowhere were the stakes higher for the Roman Church than in England, where King Henry VIII asked the pope to annul his marriage to Catherine of Aragon, the aunt of Emperor Charles V. Henry VIII wanted a male heir, and the marriage with Catherine had produced only a daughter, Mary, the future Catholic queen of England known as Bloody Mary. When no annulment came forth from Pope Clement VII, Henry decided to divorce Catherine and marry Anne Boleyn. To support Henry's intention, the new lord chancellor, Thomas Cromwell, a canny Protestant sympathizer, suggested that theologians on the continent be asked for their opinions. In 1531 a Basel scholar named Simon Grynaeus was selected to sound out the German and Swiss reformers. Grynaeus, who had known Melanchthon personally since at least 1524, asked for his friend's judgment. Melanchthon responded by undermining the main argument of Henry VIII: that his marriage to Catherine, who was briefly married to Henry's older deceased brother, violated the law in Leviticus 18:16: "You shall not uncover the nakedness of your brother's wife." According to Melanchthon Henry had indeed transgressed that law, but the laws of Moses had nothing to do with the salvation of Christians and Henry could stay married to Catherine with a good conscience.[54]

In 1531 Luther was contacted about the same matter by Robert Barnes, an English Augustinian friar, who had been imprisoned for his Protestant views but in 1529 had escaped to the continent. Barnes had already met Bugenhagen and published a strong defense of royal supremacy that induced King Henry to grant him a safe conduct back to England. Before leaving Germany, Barnes asked Luther for his opinion of a potential divorce, but the feud of the previous decade between King Henry and Luther made it unlikely that Henry expected Luther's support. Upon his return to England, Barnes presented Luther's judgment to Cromwell and Henry, but it was no more favorable than the opinion of Melanchthon. According to Luther, to divorce Catharine now was a greater sin than having married her: "For how many marriages are there in the world which have been made through sinning? Yet they ought not and may not be put asunder." For Luther, Henry's desire for a male heir was an inadequate ground for divorce. Queen Catherine might still give birth to a boy or, if that did not happen, the next queen might not give Henry a son. Luther concluded: "Before I would approve of such a divorce I would rather permit the king to marry still another woman and to have, like the [Old Testament] patriarchs and kings, two women or queens at the same time."[55] That was not the only time that Luther showed he could tolerate bigamy.

The first complete German Bible was finally published in September of 1534 by Hans Lufft in Wittenberg.[56] Luther made no mention of it, but only three letters written by him in September are extant. Earlier in the year, however, he implied that completing the translation was a high priority: "I have enough to do with our own folk—teaching, encouraging, correcting, and supervising them. By itself the task of translating the Bible is enough to keep all of us busy. Satan tries his best to make me desert my valuable work and chase after matters of no substance."[57] In October the unbound German Bible was available to purchase for two gulden and eight groschen, five times more expensive than Luther's German New Testament of 1522[58] and one percent of Professor Luther's annual salary. Buyers who could afford it, however, received their money's worth. The 1534 Bible contained over 100 woodcuts, some of them gilded, plus Luther's prefaces to each testament and selected books, the Apocrypha, and hundreds of marginal notes by Luther himself. Hans Lufft had already printed some of Luther's small books, but the 1534 Bible and its successors made Lufft and local booksellers wealthy. After Luther died, Lufft remained a preferred printer of Lutheran books. His family occupied a large house behind the town hall, and he served as both alderman and mayor. Lufft outlived Luther by almost forty years and must have been the oldest, or nearly the oldest, person in Wittenberg when he died in 1584 at the age of eighty-nine.

CHAPTER SIXTEEN

TO BETTER ACCOUNT
1535–1538
Wittenberg—Torgau—Smalcald

"In every life, it happens that many things we plan, say, and do have harmful consequences. But God uses these failings to humble his saints and turns our misdeeds to better account. Perhaps God would not bother if we did not have this defect."[1]

On December 17, 1534, two months after the full German Bible had appeared, the sixth child and third daughter of Katharina and Martin was born. The next day, before a small gathering of witnesses, she was baptized and named Margaret after Luther's mother. The godfathers were Jacob Propst in distant Bremen[2] and Prince Joachim in nearby Anhalt. Neither man was able to attend, but Joachim was represented by Luther's friend Nicholas Hausmann.[3] The godmother was Anna Göritz, who accompanied her husband to Wittenberg after he was banned from Catholic Saxony by Duke George.[4] The Luthers now had five living children. When Margaret was born, Hans was eight, Magdalena five, Martin three, and Paul almost two. Luther was fifty-one and Katharina thirty-five. Born during the plague of 1527, their first daughter, Elisabeth, had died in 1528 before turning one. Another epidemic struck Wittenberg in August of 1535 when Margaret was eight months old. She survived, but Luther accidentally put her at risk. One day he came home and without thinking touched the mouth of Margaret before washing his hands. When Luther realized what he had done, he was aghast because it not only endangered his daughter but also "put God to the test."[5]

In addition to the family, a few nephews and nieces lived with the Luthers, some of them while studying at the university. The house's occupants also included a housekeeper, one or more tutors, and sundry guests.

The cloister resembled a large boarding house more than a family home. Owing to Katharina's business acumen the Luthers also acquired nearby land that made them by 1542 the principal property-owning citizens in Wittenberg.[6] The largest field, purchased in 1531 and located beyond the town's east gate, had a barn and a "little house." Because cattle and pigs were sold nearby, Luther once called Katharina the "lady of the pig market,"[7] but he appreciated Katharina's hard work on the land and was grateful for it. In October of 1535 he reported to Jonas: "My lord Katie sends greetings. She drives the wagon, takes care of the gardens, buys and puts cattle out to pasture, brews, etc. In between she has started to read the Bible, and I have promised her fifty guilders if she finishes before Easter. She is very serious about it and is now starting the book of Deuteronomy."[8] The previous year when he was away from home, Luther drank a beer that disagreed with him and reported it to Katharina: "I said to myself what good wine and beer I have at home and what a pretty lady or (should I say) lord. You would do well to ship the whole cellar full of my wine and a bottle of your beer. Otherwise the [bad] beer here will keep me from traveling home."[9]

In the Holy Roman Empire, the Peace of Nuremberg was still in effect and the Protestant Smalcald League faced no threats from Turkish armies or Emperor Charles V. Both adversaries had turned their backs on Europe. The Turkish leader, Suleyman, had given up on western expansion and decided to make Persia the next target for extending Islam, but in early 1535 the Turks were in Baghdad after barely penetrating Persia. Emboldened by Suleyman's withdrawal from Europe, Emperor Charles V mobilized a naval crusade to challenge Muslims on the Barbary coast of Africa. The armada reached Tunis in June of 1535 and Charles, at the head of his troops for the first time, conducted a successful siege of the city. It surrendered after the pirate chief Barbarossa fled to Algiers. Back home Emperor Charles was hailed as a conqueror of the Turks, but the glory was short-lived. Five years later Barbarossa and his pirates again controlled the Mediterranean.

The threat that unnerved both Catholics and Protestants in Germany was the siege of a city in their own backyard: Münster in the northwestern county of Westphalia. Radical Anabaptists from the Netherlands took control of the town in early 1534 after the Catholic bishop, Franz of Waldeck, allowed the temporary adoption of a Protestant constitution.[10] Its author was the persuasive preacher, Bernhard Rothmann, who started as a Lutheran reformer but was converted by followers of the Anabaptist apostle, Jan Matthijs. Using the prophecies of a radical lay preacher named

Melchior Hofmann, Matthijs predicted the world would end at Easter of 1534 and invited true believers to Münster, now the new Jerusalem, in order to survive the Last Judgment. Over a thousand Münsterites were rebaptized and hundreds more from outside hurried to the city. Frightened by the concentration of radicals in his diocese, Bishop Franz conferred with Philip of Hesse and decided to besiege the city. The Anabaptist response was to expel from Münster 2,000 of its residents who had refused to be rebaptized.

After the world failed to end at Easter, Matthijs joined a sortie outside the walls of Münster and was killed in the resulting skirmish. His place was taken by the fanatical John of Leiden, who declared the new Jerusalem to be an Anabaptist kingdom modeled on the throne of the Israelite king, David. He appointed a council of twelve elders to govern the city, and over the protest of the town's women, introduced polygamy. In September of 1534, John of Leiden was crowned the new King David, who would deliver the Anabaptist kingdom to Christ upon his return. While waiting, John of Leiden decided to send out twenty-seven missionaries to four towns in the region. Each team was given a gold coin to leave behind as a token of God's wrath if the town refused to join the Münsterite kingdom. The town of Soest, which received eight missionaries, was not intimidated. After the council condemned them to death, the missionaries were bundled into a wagon and taken away to be executed by the sword.[11]

By 1535 German printers and booksellers had stirred up fears of a Münster-like takeover that was scarier than a Turkish invasion.[12] The anxiety was so widespread that each region of the empire was required to share the cost of suppressing the revolt. The siege of Münster continued until Bishop Franz, supported by Philip of Hesse and the Catholic Habsburgs in Brussels, retook the city on June 25, 1535. After John of Leiden and two prominent followers were sentenced to death, they were bound and their bodies maimed with white-hot tongs. Their remains were taken to the cemetery of St. Lambert Church and suspended in three cages attached to the church's tower. The cages, which still hang there, and the tongs, which were displayed in front of the city hall, served as flagrant warnings against future attempts to turn Münster into the kingdom of God.[13]

Luther's reaction to the fall of the Anabaptist kingdom was "I told you so." In 1532 both he and Melanchthon had warned the preacher Rothmann against Zwinglians and fanatics.[14] In early 1535 Luther also wrote prefaces for two pamphlets that attacked the Münster Anabaptists. The longer pamphlet was written by the Lutheran reformer Urban Rhegius and

addressed to the city of Osnabrück, only thirty-two miles (fifty-one kilometers) from Münster. Rhegius argued methodically against the beliefs of
the Münsterites and claimed they were condemned because they had revived
two heresies from early Christianity.[15] Luther's preface commended Rhegius,
but most of it defended Luther himself against the charge that all the
fanatics sprang from him and his writings. Luther's tactic was disarming: he
cheerfully pled guilty. Like Judas the traitor, who was a disciple of Jesus, all
heretics were Christians whom the devil led astray; but as Jesus was not the
devil because Judas was his disciple, neither was Luther the devil because
fanatics such as Rothmann were early sympathizers. Nor was the Bible a
heretical book because the fanatics twisted its content to support their
outlandish claims.[16]

Luther's defense was persuasive, but even when a preface might not
benefit himself, he usually agreed to provide it. A preface by a well-known
colleague was the sixteenth-century version of a book blurb: who wrote it
mattered more than what it said. Accordingly, Rhegius sent his manuscript
to Luther, who added his preface and gave it to Lucas Cranach, who
selected a woodcut for the title page and printed the pamphlet in his shop.[17]
Having Luther and Cranach adorn your book was great publicity, and it
must have worked for Rhegius. Original prints of his 1535 warning against
the Münster Anabaptists (including Luther's preface) are held by libraries
from Oxford to Leningrad, from Sweden to Switzerland, and in Chicago.

In the 1530s critics and adversaries on three sides were perturbing
Luther and the newly-planted Lutheran churches: Anabaptists, most of
them less radical than in Münster; followers of Zwingli in Germany as well
as Switzerland; and Roman Catholics, the only legally recognized religion
in the Holy Roman Empire. For Lutherans, the prospect of mutual toleration between themselves and Catholics seemed brighter than between
Lutherans and either Zwinglians or Anabaptists. The status of Zwinglians
within Germany was little better than the status of Anabaptists, whom
Lutherans, Catholics, and Zwinglians all condemned. In addition, the
new pope was more willing than his predecessor, Clement VII, to call a
general council of the church at which Lutherans could make their case for
legitimacy.

In 1534 Alessandro Farnese, the scion of a noble Tuscan family, was
elected Pope Paul III at the age of sixty-six. Paul's solid humanist education,
early transgressions, and love of art were typical of renaissance popes, but
Paul distinguished himself as a cardinal who favored reform. Soon after his
elevation, Paul III created new cardinals whom he appointed to a commis-

sion that openly identified abuses in the Roman Church and recommended ways to remove them. The commission's report was presented to Pope Paul in March of 1537. Within a year Luther possessed a copy of the document and dismissed it as the "monstrosities of Roman cardinals."[18] Contrary to Luther's opinion, the report was an earnest proposal by leading cardinals who wanted to see their church refined. The report appeared, however, at a bad time—two months before a council, to which Pope Paul had invited both Catholics and Protestants, was to convene in Italy. Most Protestants were refusing to attend any council that did not meet in Germany, where they expected to receive a fairer hearing. Luther had long been pessimistic about the Roman Church reforming itself, and the hostile political atmosphere added fuel to his dismissal of the cardinals' call for reform.

Pope Paul III was nevertheless serious about a council that would make reforms and restore a unified church. In 1535 he sent envoys to other European heads of state in order to gain their support. One envoy was Peter Paul Vergerio, an ambitious Italian lawyer who was serving as papal nuncio at the court of Archduke Ferdinand in Vienna. Vergerio's job was to persuade German rulers to accept the Italian location (Mantua) for a new council. On August 5, 1535, Elector John Frederick of Saxony was informed that Vergerio would pay him a visit, but the Elector was embarking soon on a long journey to Austria. That presented Vergerio with the irresistible opportunity to meet Martin Luther himself. If he persuaded Luther to attend the council in Mantua, his mission to Germany would be judged a phenomenal success. Vergerio arrived in Wittenberg on November 6, 1535. At their meeting the next day, Luther assured Vergerio that a council was necessary, but not for the Lutherans who already had the pure word of God. Vergerio chided Luther for thinking he was wiser and holier than the church councils and learned theologians that preceded him.[19] For almost twenty years Luther had listened to that rebuke and was, as always, unmoved. His report to Jonas disclosed more about the meeting:

> Out of the blue the legate of the Roman pope showed up in town. . . . This man seems to fly rather than to ride horseback. How I wished that you had been here! The legate invited me and Pommer [Bugenhagen] to breakfast, since I had refused a meal the previous evening because of a bath. So I ate breakfast with him in the castle, but I am not permitted to write to anyone about what I said. During the meal I acted as myself, but I also played the Englishman [Robert Barnes], whom the papal legate had also invited, as a disagreeable person.[20]

It is understandable that Luther wished to take a bath before meeting the first papal envoy in fourteen years to lay eyes on the heretical outlaw. Luther wanted to look as good as he could and prepared himself appropriately. According to anonymous observers and the *Table Talk*, the next morning Luther summoned his barber for a shave and haircut before leaving for breakfast with the nuncio. Instead of walking to the castle at the other end of town, Luther and Bugenhagen rode the short distance in a carriage. It all paid off. Vergerio's report to the pope's private secretary described Luther as looking young and healthy (he was about to turn fifty-two).[21] Less likely but possible was Vergerio's report that Luther dressed up as a renaissance dandy to meet him.[22] Since he had recently been elected dean of the theological faculty, Luther might, as reported, have worn a gold medallion around his neck; but even Luther, who had a playful side, scarcely acted the buffoon in the presence of a papal legate and the solemn Bugenhagen. Then again, he had nothing to lose.

Luther's letter to Jonas revealed that in late 1535 the English envoy Robert Barnes had stopped over in Wittenberg. The Protestant Reformation in England was still fresh; it had arrived on the back of a small but gory political revolution, aided by coincidence and an opportunistic chancellor, Thomas Cromwell. Since the pope would not grant an annulment of his marriage to Catherine of Aragon, King Henry VIII cut ties with Rome and in 1534 declared himself supreme head of the English Church. His former chancellor Thomas More, who had written against Luther and refused to acknowledge the king's supremacy, was beheaded in July of 1535. Henry's first wife, Catherine of Aragon, conveniently died in January of 1536 and the second wife, Anne Boleyn, who failed to give Henry a son, lost her head in May of the same year. By then Henry's actions had made enemies of powerful Catholic sovereigns: Emperor Charles V, Archduke Ferdinand of Austria, and King Francis I of France. Hence Cromwell thought it advisable to seek Protestant allies, the strongest of whom were Lutherans in northern Germany. In spite of Cromwell's earlier failure to obtain support for his king, Robert Barnes was sent back to Saxony to invite Philip Melanchthon to visit England[23] and to investigate what it would take for England to join the Protestant Smalcald League.[24]

In December of 1535 an English delegation headed to Germany to support Barnes. The leaders, Bishop Edward Foxe and the archdeacon of Canterbury, arrived in time to attend a meeting of the league in Smalcald. Joining the league, however, required prior theological agreement, and that necessitated discussions, which were held in Wittenberg. The English delegates wanted Melanchthon to be involved in those talks, and Luther asked Elector John Frederick to summon him from Jena, where the Wittenberg faculty was escaping another epidemic.[25] The talks started in January and dragged on until the English delegation departed on April 10, 1536. Luther said the debates were nothing but wrangling and complained about the cost to the Elector of keeping the Englanders in town. In earlier debates with Karlstadt and Zwingli, admitted Luther, he learned to dislike such useless talks and now he was sick and tired of them.[26] Nevertheless, the Wittenbergers and the English delegates were able to hammer out a set of Latin statements on which they agreed.[27] The statements are known as the *Wittenberg Articles*, but they were published neither in Germany nor England and almost disappeared completely until they were rediscovered in Germany in 1905.[28]

Despite their elusiveness, some historians believe the *Wittenberg Articles* influenced the *Ten Articles* adopted later in 1536 by the Convocation of English Clergy.[29] The *Ten Articles* were a mix of Protestant and Catholic viewpoints that reflected the English bishops, who were variously uncertain whether at heart their king was Protestant or Catholic. Like mutinous seamen, the bishops had agreed to throw their old captain (the pope) overboard but could not agree on what kind of ship remained or how to steer it, since their new captain (King Henry) could not make up his mind. Suddenly, in 1537, after receiving notice that the Smalcald League had refused Pope Paul's invitation to a council in Italy, Henry VIII approached Elector John Frederick about renewing discussions. A year passed, however, before Henry invited a Lutheran team to talks in England. The delay was caused in part by the birth of Prince Edward, the king's only male heir, and the death twelve days later of his mother, Queen Jane (Seymour). It was out of the question for Luther to travel to England, and Elector John Frederick was unwilling for Melanchthon to leave. Still, in 1538 the moment was pregnant with the possibility that England would turn Lutheran. Luther tingled with anticipation as he wrote to Edward Foxe: "When these [Lutheran] envoys return, we hope to hear truly good news about your English church."[30]

Good news was expected in part because the head of the English team was Thomas Cranmer, archbishop of Canterbury. He was a good friend of the Nuremberg Lutheran reformer, Andrew Osiander, and in 1532 Cranmer had married a niece of Osiander's wife.[31] Cranmer's Protestant theology was closer to that of Zwingli than of Luther, but none of the Germans knew that or, if they realized it, thought it would make any difference. Nor did it. It was not Cranmer who caused the talks to fail but conservative members of the English team who insisted that private confession to a priest was necessary and not merely advisable. The frustrated Lutherans finally asked King Henry himself to tell them where he stood on compulsory private confession and other Catholic practices. Traveling in the south of England with only a conservative bishop in tow, Henry failed to take the Lutheran side and that, together with political bickering, sank the negotiations. By October 1, 1538, the Germans had left England with nothing to show for their efforts.[32] Two years later, after losing favor with Henry, both Thomas Cromwell and Robert Barnes were executed. Before his death, Barnes submitted a confession, which was sent to Luther with a request that it be published. In his preface Luther hailed Barnes as a martyr and described Henry as an opportunist who deprived the Roman pope of England and its money but kept the power of a pope for himself. Barnes had warned Luther: "My king is not the guardian of religion; he *is* the religion."[33]

In Germany, the Smalcald League was prospering without England. By 1536 the league had adopted a constitution just in time to receive a host of new cities and the duchies of Pomerania and Württemberg. Located in southwest Germany, Württemberg was closer to Switzerland and the south German cities than to Lutheran strongholds in the north. A Protestant compromise set up a Zwinglian superintendent for churches in the south of Württemberg and a Lutheran superintendent in the north. In faraway Wittenberg Luther was appalled and, abandoning his non-cooperative stance, asked Philip of Hesse to propose to Martin Bucer a new attempt to find Protestant agreement on the Lord's Supper.[34] Bucer and Jacob Sturm, still the chief political strategist in Strasbourg, jumped at the proposal, and Philip arranged a meeting between Melanchthon and Bucer. The two theologians forged a common statement and returned home with positive reports. Bucer was elated because a solid Protestant agreement had never seemed closer. Luther gave his qualified approval but wanted to slow down the process by gathering opinions from preachers on both sides.[35] Count Philip had little choice but to wait a year while Bucer, sometimes in person, canvassed the south German preachers in search of their support.

In early 1536 Luther proposed that Lutheran and south German theologians meet face-to-face in Eisenach (Thuringia) on May 14. Bucer, Capito, and their party set out from Strasbourg on April 17 and arrived in Eisenach at the appointed time, but Luther was nowhere to be found. Four days passed without word from Luther, so Bucer decided to press on. At last they encountered a messenger on his way to tell them that Luther was too weak to travel and requested a week's delay. Bucer decided to lead his party straight to Wittenberg, and the meeting finally opened there on May 21, 1536. Was Luther really ill or was he forcing Bucer's party to meet him on home ground? Until Easter Sunday, by his account, Luther had suffered a prolonged weak spell that was so serious he expected to die.[36] But in 1536 Easter Sunday was April 16, one month before the meeting in Eisenach was to begin. Moreover, at the end of April Luther traveled thirty-three miles (fifty-five kilometers) south to Eilenburg in order to preside at the second marriage of his colleague Caspar Cruciger.[37] Although Eisenach was much farther from Wittenberg, Luther's inability to attend a meeting there one month after he recovered is questionable.

From Eisenach north, Bucer's south-German party of twelve, except for Capito, who had visited Luther once in Wittenberg, found themselves in unaccustomed territory. Luther's homeland was nothing like theirs. They came from Melanchthon's world, the denser urban environments of Baden, Swabia and the Rhineland. In May the rolling expanse of central Thuringia sported wildflowers and fields of ripening grains. But the closer to Wittenberg, the flatter and bleaker the landscape became, the stranger also the names of villages. The towns were primitive in contrast to the south. Wittenberg was a minor exception: it had the Electoral castle and its church, the university, and the stately houses of Cranach and now Melanchthon, for whom the Elector had just built a small renaissance-style mansion to keep other universities from luring him away.[38]

The south Germans and two Lutheran pastors who joined their party at Eisenach and Gotha arrived on Sunday afternoon, May 21, and were taken by Melanchthon and Cruciger to meet Luther. Early the next day Luther received Bucer and Capito in order to set an agenda. Capito, six years older than Luther, had not seen the younger reformer for over a decade, but Bucer had discussed the Lord's Supper with him five years earlier at Coburg. After a midday break, Capito and Bucer returned to Luther's house to find not only Luther and Melanchthon, but also five of their colleagues: Bugenhagen, Jonas, Cruciger, Menius, and Myconius. Luther declared he was not yet convinced of the sincerity of the south Germans and set down two conditions: Bucer and his colleagues had to recant their previous teaching that only bread and wine were received at communion and they must accept Luther's view that the actual body and blood of Christ were received by every communicant, both believers and unbelievers. Bucer was rattled, and he pointed out that neither he nor the others had ever written that only bread and wine were received in the Lord's Supper.

The next day Bucer repeated the position of the south Germans, and the Lutherans called a recess to discuss their response. To the surprise of Bucer and his colleagues the Lutherans accepted their position and received them as dear brethren in the Lord—precisely what Luther refused to call the Swiss seven years earlier in Marburg. The south Germans even submitted themselves to the *Augsburg Confession* and the *Apology*, as Elector John Frederick desired. Then Melanchthon formulated a common statement for them all to study, and on Monday, May 29, 1536, both sides signed the *Wittenberg Concord*.[39] What happened on the preceding Thursday was probably more important than the paper agreement. The participants had marked the festival of Christ's Ascension by celebrating together the Lord's Supper. They repeated the joint communion on Sunday before their departure. At times Luther may have acted high-handedly, but he was serious about the agreement. One year later, while Bucer was still selling it to the south Germans, he wrote to Capito about their task: "I was thinking to myself how this effort will put all of you into a sweat; but at the same time I was praying that Christ would not allow you to labor in vain. . . . I am convinced that both you and Bucer are acting sincerely and candidly; and I rejoice that everyone who writes or speaks to me about you feels the same."[40]

The *Wittenberg Concord* of 1536 was intended to unite the German Protestants before they decided whether or not to attend the papal council in 1537. That decision would officially be made at a convention of the Smalcald League early in the same year. Beforehand, however, Elector John Frederick declared that he would refuse the pope's invitation and preferred instead a "free, Christian council" called by the league itself. For that purpose the Elector requested from Luther a list of theological topics that should be on the council's agenda. The Elector eventually gave up the idea of a Lutheran council, but he still wanted Luther's list and to have it discussed by Lutheran colleagues.[41]

Luther started work almost immediately. On December 15 he invited the out-of-town theologians—Agricola, Amsdorf, and Spalatin—to meet at Torgau on December 28 and 29 to discuss his first draft. On December 18 and 19, however, severe heart pains interrupted his writing and he dictated the remainder of the document.[42] Known as the *Smalcald Articles*, Luther's draft followed the Elector's instructions but not to the letter. The topics were divided into three parts: Parts I and II, concerning the Trinity and the redemptive work of Jesus Christ, were not debatable. The articles in part III, wrote Luther, could be discussed with "learned, reasonable people or among ourselves," but he stopped short of including the Catholic theologians in that discussion. Luther gave the papal side absolutely no benefit of the doubt. "The pope and his kingdom do not value these things [the contents of part III] very much; the conscience means nothing to them; money, honor, and power mean everything."[43]

For Luther there was no middle ground and Elector John Frederick, who liked it that way, indirectly permitted Luther to attack the papacy as forcefully as he wished. Part II of the *Articles* gave him the perfect opportunity. After emphasizing that faith was the only means of benefitting from the redemptive work of Christ, Luther lambasted the Catholic mass as the "most terrible abomination." His broadside was aimed mainly at the private mass, which was held without communicants, because it did not require or strengthen the faith of believers. Its performance was a "cultic act," endowed by people for the sake of others who were not present and often dead. All such cultic acts, wrote Luther, were abominations,[44] and therefore defenders of the private mass and Lutherans would remain eternally opposed to each other. Besides giving Luther free rein, however, Elector John Frederick may have ordered the *Smalcald Articles* because he needed a personal declaration of Luther's theology in case disputes arose among his colleagues after Luther died. That could happen soon, realized the Elector. He remembered Luther's illness in April of 1536 and, at the wedding of the Elector's son two months earlier, Luther had suffered a dizzy spell that prevented him from completing the ceremony.

At Torgau, between December 28, 1536, and January 3, 1537, Luther's articles were reviewed and signed by seven additional theologians: Jonas, Bugenhagen, Cruciger, and Melanchthon from Wittenberg; Amsdorf from Magdeburg; Spalatin from Altenburg; and Agricola from Eisleben. Before signing they inserted one clause against praying to saints.[45] And Melanchthon, while accepting the articles as true and Christian, added to his signature the following condition: "Concerning the pope I maintain that if he would allow the gospel, we too may (for the sake of peace and general unity among those Christians who are now under him and might be in the future) grant to him superiority over the bishops that he has by human right."[46] Melanchthon and Luther agreed that the pope was only the bishop of Rome and had no divine authority over other bishops; but Melanchthon was holding out for reconciliation with the Roman Church if it agreed that the pope's authority was a human arrangement and that practices such as the private mass and praying to saints should be abolished.

Spalatin prepared the final clean copy of the articles and took it, along with a cover letter from Luther, to Elector John Frederick. The Elector read it twice and replied with a congratulatory letter that expressed his deep satisfaction and appreciation.[47]

The convention of the Smalcald League was set to open on February 7, 1537, in its hometown. Smalcald numbered 4,500 inhabitants, but it had to feed and house the retinues of sixteen princes, six counts, twenty-eight urban delegations, forty-two theologians, and the observers sent by Emperor Charles, the pope, and the kings of France and Denmark. It was an economic bonanza for the merchants and the town, which provided the guests with 1,000 liters of wine from public cellars. It was high tide for the league, but it had to make a decision that critically affected its future: whether or not to attend the papal council in Italy that would open in May. Either way, thought Luther before it began, the outcome would be a brawl.[48] On January 30, Luther, Melanchthon, and Bugenhagen left Torgau with the Electoral party and arrived one week later, on February 7, in Smalcald.[49] Luther was quartered in the house of a Hessian financial officer whom he may have known from Erfurt. He unpacked in a large, unheated room on the second floor and there he remained for most of his nineteen days in Smalcald.

After the first night he passed a small stone with bloody urine but it was not painful. On February 9 he felt well enough to preach an early sermon in the town church, a late Gothic structure with acoustics so poor that Luther surmised he sounded no better than a shrew.[50] The convention opened the next day in the auditorium of the courthouse and wasted no time deciding that it would send no delegates to the papal council in Mantua. Against the wishes of Luther and Elector John Frederick, Melanchthon advised Count Philip and others not to bring up Luther's *Smalcald Articles* for discussion in the plenary sessions. They were too polemical and would stir up old disagreements between the north German Lutherans and the south German cities. Hence the *Articles* were handed over to a committee of theologians and were not endorsed by the league's members as their doctrinal basis. In his quarters on February 11 Luther delivered a pastoral homily on the Apostles' Creed to a modest gathering— but the next day he was stricken with sharp pains in the kidneys and bladder before passing another stone. Luther felt useless but still raved about dinners with the nobles and patricians who offered superb bread, pastries, wine, meat, and fish.[51]

The political drama was over but Luther's personal struggle escalated. Beginning on February 19 the urinary discomfort intensified and caused nausea, severe pain, diarrhea, and weakness. After praying and surrendering himself into divine hands, Luther declared he had bothered God enough: "If God chooses to listen, he can now do whatever he thinks is best."[52] Doctors brought no relief and his condition deteriorated. Luther did not want to die in Hesse, so arrangements were made for him to travel home. The departure was held up by special preparations to keep Luther comfortable and by the zealous astrologer Melanchthon, who insisted the phase of the moon was unfavorable for travel.[53] Finally, on February 26, 1537, Luther's party headed home in a coach provided by Elector John Frederick; it was followed by a wagon with medicines and a copper pan holding heated briquets for warming up covers that protected Luther from the cold. The road was rough and the party traveled only ten miles (sixteen kilometers) before stopping for the night at the village of Tambach. The jostling of the coach and the red wine Luther drank before bed must have loosened the blockage because it gave way around one thirty in the morning. The same night Luther wrote Katharina that God had opened his urinary tract and he felt as if "born again."[54]

Luther was not out of danger. The next day on the way to Gotha the pains returned, and in the coach Luther made his confession and received absolution from Bugenhagen. The party stayed five days in Gotha, and Luther decided to dictate a last will and testament to Bugenhagen. It was the first of two wills, the second of which was made in 1542 and concerned family and property. The main theme of the first testament was the church: first, that he had opposed the papacy with a clear conscience; and second, that Elector John Frederick and Count Philip of Hesse, with God's help, must persist in pure teaching and thank God for having saved them from the Antichrist.[55] The rest of the journey was quiet. They stayed an extra day in Altenburg, where Luther was cared for in Spalatin's home. Katharina had made it as far as Altenburg after Elector John Frederick advised her to hurry to Smalcald. Before Luther's party arrived in Altenburg, however, she received word of Luther's improvement and left for home.[56] On March 14, 1537, Luther finally reached Wittenberg in better shape than when he left Smalcald.

By early April Luther had regained his strength and was preaching and writing, but administrative duties for the university and the church needed his attention. Since the summer semester of 1535 Luther was serving as dean of the theological faculty. Part of his job was to arrange academic disputations at which candidates for the Doctor of Theology degree defended in the Castle Church a set of theses written by Luther himself or, in a few cases, by Melanchthon. Twenty-eight sets of theses written between 1535 and 1545 are extant, and thirteen of them were defended in formal disputations by doctoral candidates. Three months after Luther returned from Smalcald, he presided at a disputation during which two candidates successfully defended theses on faith and good works. As dean of the faculty it was also Luther's job to keep a record of the doctoral degrees awarded by the faculty.[57]

Luther and his colleagues also presided at the ordination of candidates for the ministry. Before 1535, pastors of parishes that became Lutheran were not reordained; most of the early Lutheran pastors, like Luther himself, had already been ordained to the Roman priesthood. The Wittenberg theologians had rejected the medieval sacrament of ordination and accepted in its place the installation of a pastor in the parish he was formally called to serve. The inspection of parishes under Elector John Frederick had shown, however, that persons unfit for parish ministry were being accepted without having their competence evaluated. To obtain qualified pastors, on May 12, 1535, the Elector officially charged the theological faculty in Wittenberg to examine new candidates and to ordain those who passed. The first ordination recorded in the faculty register was presided over by Luther on June 24, 1537. It was the first of 740 ordinations conducted by the faculty before Luther's death in 1546.[58]

Writing to Bugenhagen, who was in Copenhagen for a royal wedding, Luther reported on July 5, 1537, that he had returned to his primary job: lecturing on books of the Bible.[59] Two years earlier he started a lecture course on the forty-nine chapters of Genesis, but time and again illness and political obligations, such as the journey to Smalcald, interrupted his progress. It had been eight months since his last lecture,[60] but during the next two years Luther made impressive headway. Arriving at chapter twenty, in which Abraham and Sarah lie to King Abimelech, Luther suggested how God worked in the lives of believers. Yes, he admitted, even saints such as Sarah and Abraham lied, but God used our weaknesses to humble us and then to bestow on us richer blessings. God had frequently altered Luther's own foolish plans and granted him a far better outcome than Luther had expected. "In every life," he continued, "it happens that many things we plan, say, and do have harmful consequences. But God uses these failings to humble his saints and turns our misdeeds to better account. Perhaps God would not do that if we did not have this defect."[61]

Imagine the students in that lecture hall trying to comprehend the essence of Luther's teaching.[62] Their famous professor was a former monk, who tried to live a perfect, godly life, but now he was telling them that God did not reward perfection but instead repaid their imperfections with richer blessings. It was like telling a child it did not have to be perfect to enjoy its parents' love. And it was a powerful statement of good news not only because of what was said but because of who said it. The words of the teacher captivated many of Luther's readers, but surely best of all was to hear the words from his own mouth.

CHAPTER SEVENTEEN

INDEBTED TO MY PAPISTS
1539–1541

Wittenberg—Weimar—Eisenach—Leipzig

"I myself . . . am deeply indebted to my papists that through the devil's raging they have beaten, oppressed, and distressed me so much. That is to say: they have made a fairly good theologian of me, which I otherwise would not have become."[1]

In September of 1538, Luther explained to his friend in Bremen, Jacob Propst, why his followers had so many adversaries:

> Were there no other proof that we are chosen for the kingdom of God and have the true word of God, this would suffice: we are constantly attacked by so many sects that branch out in new forms, some of them originating with us, not to mention the papists, my usual struggles with Satan, and contempt for the word of God in our own ranks. In that way we are no better off than the apostles, the prophets, or even our Lord himself.[2]

The explanation was prompted by the recurrence of an old controversy between two of his colleagues: John Agricola ("Master Eisleben") and Philip Melanchthon. In 1526 Melanchthon named Agricola one of his best friends.[3] Then, one year later, Agricola took umbrage at what Melanchthon had written about the importance of the law—especially the Ten Commandments—in the Christian life. At that point Luther was able to smooth over the disagreement, but ten years later it flared up after Agricola returned to Wittenberg, expecting to be offered a university position. This time, in 1537, Luther took the side of Melanchthon against Agricola, and the Antinomian controversy, as it is called, was in full swing. The designation Antinomians meant "opponents of the law" and referred at first specifically to Agricola and his sympathizers. They argued that the law should not be preached or taught—either for reminding believers to repent of their sins or for teaching them moral behavior. Preaching the Ten Commandments implied, insisted Agricola, that salvation required doing good works that satisfied the law. Faith alone would be insufficient.

For his part, Melanchthon feared that ignoring the law would cause believers to disregard the Ten Commandments and continue in their sinful ways. The complaints of Lutheran preachers confirmed his fear, and in 1539 Luther also defended preaching the law. The gist of his reasoning was: In the early stage of the reformation (the 1520s) evangelical preachers stressed the good news of salvation by faith alone, because the Roman clergy threatened people with damnation if they did not obey the commandments and papal decrees. Teaching the law to such people would have exacerbated their anxiety and despair. In the 1530s, however, people who were no longer under the pope were taking salvation for granted and either ignoring the Ten Commandments or breaking them with abandon. And "our sweet-talking Antinomians make these people, who are already overconfident, so secure that they fall away from grace."[4] Even in the early period, insisted Luther, he never neglected the Ten Commandments and cited as evidence his sermons and catechisms. And now, he claimed, "I myself, as old and as learned as I am, recite the commandments daily word for word like a child."[5]

After three academic debates in 1537 and 1538 brought no resolution to their conflict, Agricola offered to sign a recantation. Luther responded with criticism so unkind that reconciliation became impossible. According to the *Table Talk*, Luther invited university colleagues to a meal at which he put Agricola on the spot. A glass was marked with lines at three levels: the top line represented the Ten Commandments; the second line marked the creed; and the third line the Lord's Prayer. Luther filled the glass with wine and gulped it down. After the glass was refilled, Luther handed it to Agricola, who managed to drink only enough to lower the level to the first line—the Ten Commandments. Luther boasted to the gathering: 'I knew it beforehand! Master Eisleben can put away the Ten Commandments, but he has to leave the creed and the Lord's Prayer in peace.'"[6]

Nothing good emerged from the Antinomian controversy. After Elector John Frederick agreed to investigate his grievances, Agricola was forbidden to leave Wittenberg until the dispute was settled. Instead of waiting, Agricola fled to the duchy of Brandenburg where the new Elector, Joachim II, was introducing the reformation and invited Agricola to become his court preacher. Agricola eventually regained his good standing in Electoral

Saxony, but Luther never softened. The permanent rupture of their close relationship was a tragedy caused less by theology than by longstanding personal loyalties. Before 1517 Agricola had arrived in Wittenberg with his conscience racked by guilt and despair. Luther's lectures rescued Agricola by convincing him that the gospel and faith, not satisfying the law, brought the certainty of God's forgiveness and therefore relief to his conscience.[7] It was understandable that Agricola reacted as he did to Melanchthon's insistence on preaching the law, repentance, and good works. Agricola was convinced by experience and Luther's early writings that only the gospel, unsullied by the law, was the heart of his mentor's theology.

In addition, the two men developed a close personal relationship—so close that, looking back in 1540, Luther admitted his love of Agricola was exceeded only by his love for Melanchthon.[8] Luther took Agricola under his wing, monitored his studies, and in 1519 took Agricola as his recorder to the Leipzig debate. Agricola finished his degrees and started to offer lectures in Wittenberg. After moving back to Eisleben in 1525, he was chosen as the preacher for Saxon delegations at the Diets of Speyer and Augsburg.[9] In December of 1536 he was part of the theological team that originally signed Luther's Smalcald articles; ironically, in light of the Antinomian controversy that was heating up for the second time, his signature appeared directly below that of Melanchthon.[10]

What about Luther? Was his spurning of Agricola best explained by the platitude that love can quickly turn to hate? Or was Luther unable to tolerate disagreement even from those he loved? Perhaps both. Being Luther's close colleague or friend could be a precarious asset. His rejection of Karlstadt, with whom he was never so close as he was with Agricola, suggests that Luther tied collegial friendships to like-mindedness and deference. Since 1521, Luther believed he was subject only to the Lord himself, who had shown him the genuine gospel and entrusted him with its propagation. Feeling the weight of that divine sanction, Luther would do almost anything to ensure that the reformation prospered, and that included adapting the evangelical message to a shifting audience. Agricola could not accept the adaptation, and Luther's heartless behavior drove Agricola away.

By late 1539, Pope Paul III had thrice postponed the council originally set to open in 1537, and Emperor Charles V was seeking other means of restoring religious unity to Germany. Unity was still desirable owing to a new Turkish advance in southern Europe and the threat of war with France. After resisting proposals for public religious discussions between Protestant and Catholic theologians, Emperor Charles finally agreed. On June 12,

1540, the first meeting opened in Hagenau, which is north of Strasbourg but still 400 miles (650 kilometers) from Wittenberg. As Melanchthon started his journey south, he reportedly told well-wishers that he had lived in meetings and in meetings he would die. He almost did. Soon after Melanchthon reached Weimar he fell severely ill. Elector John Frederick sent his own physician and summoned both Luther and Caspar Cruciger to Weimar. They found Melanchthon nearly unconscious and unable to take any food or drink. When Melanchthon woke up, he begged Luther to let him die, but Luther declined and told his colleague he had to serve God a little longer. After Melanchthon still refused to eat, Luther threatened: "Either you eat or I will excommunicate you!"[11] On July 2, 1540, Luther wrote to Katharina: "I gorge myself like a Bohemian and swill like a German; thanks be to God. Amen. The reason is that Master Philip was truly dead but now like Lazarus has risen from death."[12] Risen perhaps, but still in no condition to continue his journey to Hagenau. Instead, Luther took Melanchthon to Eisenach, where they met Amsdorf, who was summoned from Magdeburg in order to discuss a matter that deeply upset Melanchthon: the bigamy of the Protestant leader, Philip of Hesse.

In March of 1540 Philip married Margaret von der Sale, the teenaged daughter of his sister's lady-in-waiting. Philip already had a wife and children and therefore entered a state of bigamy or double matrimony. Margaret's mother refused to allow her daughter to become Philip's concubine, so he decided on marriage after ascertaining that Old Testament patriarchs such as Jacob had more than one wife. Civil statutes threatened bigamists with severe punishment, but Philip tried to turn that in his favor by pointing out an incongruity that put him on God's side: What God permits (bigamy) the law forbids, and what God forbids (whoring) is winked at by the law. His wife, claimed Philip, was unable to satisfy his sexual urges and instead of prostitutes he wanted a more suitable partner in a proper Christian marriage. He promised not to abandon his current family and to obtain from his first wife written consent to his second marriage.

Philip also consulted the Strasbourg reformer, Martin Bucer, who agreed to seek the approval of Luther and Melanchthon. If they refused to agree, said Philip, he would turn to Emperor Charles for authorization. That was a clumsy threat but it caught the reformers' attention.[13] They strongly recommended that the marriage be kept secret and their own counsel considered confidential as if it had been given in the confessional. Soon however—not least because Philip told his sister—the secret was out and the bigamy caused a public scandal. The damage had just been done when Luther and Melanchthon arrived in Eisenach to discuss the matter with Martin Bucer and Philip's advisors. In December of 1539 Bucer, Luther, and Melanchthon had signed a letter that Philip interpreted as their grudging green light to marry a second time.[14] Even more embarrassing was the presence of Bucer and Melanchthon at the wedding. Philip and his advisors now felt compelled to admit publicly that he had married Margaret and to publish the reformers' advice. Luther was dead set against publication. He stood by the confidential intent of their counsel and told Elector John Frederick that he would offer the same advice again unless he were informed of Philip's habit of giving free rein to his lust.[15] Although Luther had been deceived, he regarded the counsel as fitting, and God would not mind if a lie were told out of necessity to protect the confessional.[16] What happened there had to stay between God and the sinner, even if the sinner were insincere.

Melanchthon suffered abysmal regret and Bucer damaged his reputation in Strasbourg, but Luther kept a low profile and has thus received more criticism from historians than from his contemporaries. Count Philip himself acknowledged that Luther's intentions were good and called him a most distinguished theologian.[17] Other leaders of the Smalcald League were angry at Philip, but he lost nothing more serious than influence. Philip was secretly pursuing a policy of peaceful cooperation with Emperor Charles,[18] and before long Charles quietly pardoned him. The bigamy did aggravate the distrust between Philip and his bitter opponent, Duke Henry of Wolfenbüttel, the only Catholic lay prince remaining near the Lutheran heartland.

Despite the bigamy, the religious colloquies in 1540 and 1541 gave some participants hope that a peaceful solution to the standoff between Catholics and Protestants could be achieved. The first meeting in Hagenau led to a second meeting in Worms at which the emperor's chancellor set the agenda. Melanchthon made the long journey and met in person for the only time a young Frenchman named John Calvin, who would soon become famous as the reformer of Geneva. Theologians and diplomats from both sides attended the colloquy and each party was given eleven votes. The Protestants were more united than the eleven Catholic princes because three of the latter, Joachim II of Brandenburg included, were either neutral or inclined toward the reformation.

In 1539 the Catholics had lost Luther's brusque and zealous enemy, Duke George of Saxony. He was succeeded by his brother Henry, who favored the reformation and walked out of the funeral mass for Duke

George in order to listen to a homily by his own Lutheran chaplain. As Duke Henry rode through town after town to receive the homage of his subjects, the first approved Lutheran communions were celebrated in the formerly Catholic duchy. For the weekend of Pentecost (May 24–25, 1539) Duke Henry invited Elector John Frederick and the Wittenberg theologians to Leipzig, where twenty years earlier Luther had debated Eck under the eyes of Duke George. This time Luther traveled to Leipzig with Melanchthon, Justus Jonas, and Caspar Cruciger; local students escorted the Wittenbergers into the city as they had in 1519.[19]

On Saturday afternoon before Pentecost Luther preached in the castle where the debate had been held, and on Sunday in the Church of St. Thomas. Only the Saturday sermon has been preserved—perhaps by Cruciger. Not feeling well, Luther decided to spare his listeners a triumphal summary of reformation teachings and delivered instead a shorter homily on the nature of the true church. It was inspired by a saying of Jesus: "Those who love me will keep my word, and my Father will love them, and we will come to them and make our home with them" (John 14:23). That saying, said Luther, described the true church because it ruled out the possibility that Jesus meant to establish an earthly kingdom or the Roman institution governed by popes, cardinals, and bishops. The true church, therefore, must consist of evangelical communities:

> The church exists as a dwelling so that God may be loved and heard—not by wood and stones or by dumb animals, but by people who know, love, and praise God. So that you may be able to trust God with certainty in all things, including cross and suffering, you should know that it is the true church, even though it be made up of scarcely two believing persons. That is why Christ says: He who loves me keeps my word; there I will dwell, there you have my church.[20]

For believers to keep God's word, however, it had to be proclaimed to them. Therefore, said Luther, the words of Jesus also meant: "My church is where my word is preached purely and is unadulterated and kept."[21] That required preachers who knew the pure word, as Luther defined it, and a place for people to gather if more than two or three wanted to listen. Those places were available in the brick and stone churches already present in locations that adopted the reformation, and together they became the organized Lutheran Church. Luther obviously preferred it over the Roman Church, but organized religious institutions were for him never identical with true religion or the reformed Christendom he was still seeking. True Christendom, like true religion, consisted only of people who conveyed to one another the word of God, believed it, and kept it with all the freedom, charity, crosses, and shortfalls that it brought. Religious institutions served only as facilitators of that true religion.

Luther was nevertheless pleased when Elector John Frederick and Duke Henry resolved to make Ducal Saxony a Lutheran territory. Less than two months after Luther's sermon, Duke Henry commissioned five "visitors" to inspect the churches in the district of Meissen and stop the Catholic practices that had prevailed. Two of the visitors, Jonas and Spalatin, ensured that Electoral Saxony served as the model for a Lutheran Ducal Saxony. A middle-of-the-road arrangement was offered by the Catholic bishop of Meissen with the help of two old enemies of Luther: John Cochlaeus, chaplain of the deceased Duke George, and Jerome Aleander, who in 1539 was the papal legate to Prague. The Wittenbergers rejected the bishop's plan, and Luther urged a follow-up visitation in Ducal Saxony because the first inspection had left the majority of Catholic priests in their positions. He reported "it was snowing letters" asking for Lutheran replacements and he wanted to fill the requests, but Electoral Saxony had no pastors to spare.[22]

While the eyes of Luther and Elector John Frederick were fixed on Ducal Saxony, the religious discussions at Worms were postponed until April of 1541 and moved to Regensburg in Bavaria. At Regensburg it looked as if Protestants and Catholics might be able to agree on two topics: justification by faith and the presence of Christ in the Lord's Supper. In the end, no agreement was reached, owing to resistance from theologians on both sides. Neither group, Catholic or Protestant, was willing to budge on the same practical issues that had divided them since the ninety-five theses of 1517: indulgences, celibacy of priests, enumerating sins at private confession, private masses, and so forth. The imperial diet meeting at the same time in Regensburg referred the matter to a church council or the next diet. It was a canny move that proved to be the kiss of death for religious unity in Germany.

While Melanchthon represented Electoral Saxony at Worms and Regensburg, Luther remained in Wittenberg giving lectures, preaching, ordaining new pastors and, beginning in July of 1539, revising the German Bible that had been published only five years earlier. Luther reassembled the core of his translation team—Melanchthon, Bugenhagen, Jonas, and the Hebraist Aurogallus—and added Cruciger and Rörer, who kept a record of their progress. The team met around seventy times between mid-July 1540 and early February 1541.[23] During that period John Mathesius was a regular guest at Luther's table and one of the people whose transcripts of what they heard were to form the *Table Talk*. Since the revision team met in Luther's home before the evening meal, Mathesius observed them at work and in all likelihood gathered more details from Rörer. From those sources Mathesius reconstructed a typical session:

> Doctor Luther entered the room with his old Latin and new German Bible plus the Hebrew text he always carried. Philip [Melanchthon] brought the Greek text, and Cruciger had the Hebrew and the Aramaic versions. At hand were also commentaries by Jewish rabbis, and Doctor Pommer [Bugenhagen] came with his familiar Latin version. Every participant had studied the text to be translated that day, had reviewed the Greek, Latin, and rabbinic commentators, and was prepared to make suggestions. The deliberation started as the presider asked each person in turn for comments about the German wording he presented or what they had found in the old commentaries. The responses were reportedly so wonderful and instructive that George Rörer wrote down a few and turned them into small glosses that were printed in the margins of the Bible.[24]

The printing started before a complete manuscript of the revised Bible was available. By early April of 1541 the printers had already passed the prophet Ezekiel, but Luther was still composing an additional explanation of the new temple described in the last chapters of that book. The printers urged him to finish but Luther complained of "weakness of the brain."[25] The addition was later inserted at the end of Luther's preface to Ezekiel and the revised complete German Bible finally appeared in September.[26]

Before 1541 Luther had a long history of headaches, weakness, dizziness, depression and kidney stones, but he described the most recent condition differently—as flux of the head. It sounded like the last stage of a severe cold or influenza. He could not understand how his old, overworked head could hold so much mucus and finally told the Lord: "Either it stops or I stop."[27] Reports of Luther's infirmities abound, but his extant correspondence does not specifically mention the close call suffered by Katharina in January of 1540. According to Melanchthon and Jonas, she failed to recover after a miscarriage and became deathly ill.[28] On February 26, Luther reported that he was well and that Katharina was regaining her appetite and able with support to walk through the house.[29]

Luther's deteriorating health during the late 1530s might have exacerbated the scoldings he delivered to adversaries, but that remains a conjecture.

The only active adversaries were Catholic rulers and theologians, but for Luther the "adversary" was any person or group who would not cooperate with his mission to restore a purified Christianity to Germany. By that definition one obvious target was the Jewish people who, unlike Jews in other countries, had not been expelled at large from the Holy Roman Empire. However, on August 6, 1536, Elector John Frederick decreed that Jews could not reside, do business in, or travel through Electoral Saxony. Ten months later Luther responded to a request from Rabbi Josel von Rosheim, one of the Jewish spokesmen in the empire. Josel wanted to travel through Electoral Saxony and asked Luther to help him obtain permission from the Elector. Luther refused under the pretext of having lost influence with the princes because Jews had misused "his service" in such matters. Nevertheless, alleged Luther, the Jews should be treated kindly but not "strengthened in their error and become even more bothersome." In addition, Luther revealed his intention to write a pamphlet in order to win "some from your venerable people . . . and bring them to your promised Messiah."[30]

In 1523 Luther had already expressed hope that some Jews would accept Jesus as the true Messiah if Christians dealt gently with them. Christians should be guided by the law of love, "receive them cordially, and permit them to trade and work among us," so that they might "hear Christian teaching and witness our Christian life." If some of them refused, what of it? "After all," admitted Luther, "we ourselves are not all good Christians either."[31] Those words brought accusations that Luther was too friendly toward the Jews, and his good will toward them did not last. In 1537, the same year he refused to help Josel of Rosheim, Luther said the following while lecturing on the twelfth chapter of Genesis:

> Let the unfortunate Jews confess they are not the true seed of Abraham. They are in error and under God's wrath because they oppose true religion. Or if they do not admit it, we ourselves will force them to the blasphemous declaration that God is a liar. For what middle ground can there be?[32]

Had Luther's attitude toward Judaism changed that much in fourteen years? Probably not. Luther had always been ambivalent about their status in God's eyes. In his early lectures Luther had accused those Jews who did not become Christian of presuming that good works would save them; and he put the Jewish people in a category with heretics and others whom he called arrogant and self-righteous.[33] However, during the 1520s hopes were high among reformers that the message of a merciful God who accepted

Jews and non-Jews on the basis of faith would attract many converts. Luther expressed the same hope to a baptized Jew named Bernard, whom he knew in Wittenberg.[34] In 1525, however, explaining why Jews were permitted to lend at interest, Luther pronounced the permission no longer valid "since the Jews have ceased to be the people of God."[35]

None of the above was exceptional, not even the content of Luther's 1537 treatise *Against the Sabbatarians*. It was addressed to a "good friend," who reported that Jews "at various places" were persuading Christians to become like them: circumcised, keeping the sabbath, and denying that Jesus of Nazareth was the Messiah. The "good friend" was identified later, but no evidence pointed to Jewish recruitment of Christians in his region of eastern Saxony.[36] Whatever impelled Luther to write *Against the Sabbatarians*, the treatise itself had nothing to do with Christians being forced into Judaism. Instead, it challenged the argument made by Jewish rabbis that the sins of Israel prevented God from sending the Messiah. According to Luther, the Old Testament named no such sin and therefore Jesus of Nazareth must be the promised Messiah because God always kept his promises. Luther's argument, like most of his later writing about the Jews, was based on what Luther knew best, the Old Testament, but only as a Christian book. The issue he cared about was not the status of contemporary Jews in Germany but his "true" understanding of their scripture, namely, that it was a book of promises and lessons for Christians who had replaced Jews as God's people. Jewish scholars disliked Luther for the same reason they disliked all Christian reformers and theologians: they took Hebrew scripture away from the Jews and called them liars because they refused to admit that the Messiah predicted in their scripture was Jesus of Nazareth.

Luther was only one of many Protestants who defended the validity of the Old Testament as a Christian book. In 1537 Urban Rhegius used the Easter story of Jesus on the road to Emmaus for the same purpose. In one of the oddest books published in Luther's lifetime, Rhegius attempted to recapture the "things" Jesus said to the disciples so they would believe he was the crucified and risen Messiah: "Was it not necessary that the Messiah should suffer these things and then enter into his glory? Then beginning with Moses and the prophets, Jesus interpreted to them the things about himself in all the scriptures."[37] Rhegius titled the book *A Dialogue concerning the Beautiful Sermon from Moses and the Prophets That Christ Delivered according to Luke 24 between Jerusalem and Emmaus to the Two Disciples on Easter Day*.[38] His 500 pages of proof-texts from the Old Testament were cast as a dialogue with his wife Anna, who was said to know Hebrew. The purpose of the book was not explicitly anti-Jewish, but the effect was the same. By arguing that Old Testament promises to the patriarchs and prophets intentionally pointed to Christ, Rhegius had to deny that the promises applied to Jews who refused to convert.

Rhegius' book was first published in Wittenberg in 1537, less than a year before *Against the Sabbatarians*; but, unlike Luther's book, the *Dialogue* by Rhegius was often reprinted throughout the sixteenth century and translated into Low German, Dutch, Danish, English, and Czech. Even if the book was more popular with printers than with readers, it suggested that some people, perhaps especially theologians, needed reassurance of the Christian intent of Old Testament promises. Except in towns with large Jewish quarters, ordinary folk who were Christian probably had little contact with Jews. Although Luther reported a visit in the mid-1520s by two or three rabbis,[39] he had little contact other than through books and hearsay. Jews had formerly lived in Wittenberg, presumably in the Jüdenstrasse that still exists, but no unconverted Jews of record resided in Wittenberg during Luther's lifetime.[40] Whenever residents walked by the Town Church, they might have looked up and seen the vulgar *Judensau* (Jewish sow) relief on the exterior wall. It dates to around 1300 and can still be found on more than twenty-five medieval churches in Germany.[41] Luther was also acquainted with rumors of Jews poisoning wells and ritually murdering Christian children. He repeated the allegations and once said, whether or not they were true, the Jews were fully capable of doing such things secretly or in the open.[42] Not all Lutheran reformers agreed. In Nuremberg, Andrew Osiander convincingly refuted the veracity of ritual murder stories and by doing so elicited from the Catholic theologian John Eck an angry defense of their authenticity.[43]

In the preface to his collected German writings, which appeared in September of 1539, Luther paid a rare compliment to his Catholic opponents:

> I myself ... am deeply indebted to my papists that through the devil's raging they have beaten, oppressed, and distressed me so much. That is to say: they have made a fairly good theologian of me, which I otherwise would not have become. And I heartily grant them what they have gained in return—honor, victory, and triumph—for they wanted it that way.[44]

The compliment was obviously insincere, and in the mid-1530s Luther's attacks on his Catholic opponents became more severe. It began with

Cardinal Albert of Mainz, who had demonstrated ambivalent feelings toward the reformation despite having sent the ninety-five theses to Rome. In 1534, to hide his own misappropriation of tax revenue, Albert blamed his financial secretary and ordered his execution. Luther was drawn into the matter by the victim's brother and by Elector John Frederick. Because Albert's nephew, Joachim II of Brandenburg, was leaning toward the reformation, Luther was urged not to attack Albert, but to no avail. In early 1539 Luther's diatribe was published with the mild title *Against the Bishop of Magdeburg, Cardinal Albert*.[45] For Luther, the pamphlet was a matter of conscience, but Elector John Frederick realized that his polemical skills could be politically useful.[46]

Luther was still under attack himself. During the conflict with Cardinal Albert, the talented poet Simon Lemnius, whom Melanchthon encouraged to study in Wittenberg, published in 1538 a slender volume of epigrams that both flattered Albert and indirectly ridiculed important Wittenbergers. After Lemnius was placed under house arrest and the printer of the epigrams jailed, Luther issued a harsh admonition and the poet fled to the safety of Albert's territory. From there Lemnius took revenge on the Wittenbergers by publishing an obscene attack on the married lives of Luther, Jonas, Spalatin, and their spouses.[47] After Melanchthon's son-in-law was exposed as having conspired with the poet, Melanchthon himself, who was rector of the university, was suspected of going easy on Lemnius. Although Melanchthon submitted to the Elector a written declaration of his innocence, he considered leaving the university but finally decided against it.[48] The Lemnius affair apparently caused no friction between him and Luther. During the affair, Melanchthon gave thanks for Luther's recovery from a two-week illness because the church needed his authority to rein in the fanatics and heretics.[49]

In 1541, the enmity between Elector John Frederick and the Catholic Duke Henry of Braunschweig-Wolfenbüttel led Luther to another politically motivated attack.[50] Count Philip of Hesse also became involved after insults were exchanged between him and Duke Henry. Owing to Philip's bigamy, it was easier for Henry to slander him than Elector John Frederick. Duke Henry, however, was also vulnerable. His mistress, Eva von Trott, bore Henry three children before she was driven away and died. Her death, however, was a hoax. Henry hid her in a castle and she bore him seven more children. Although the controversy eventually produced close to one hundred pamphlets, Luther's contribution, *Against Hanswurst*, was provoked not by an attack on Luther himself but by insults aimed at Elector John

Frederick. Duke Henry had called Frederick a "fat, malicious, lying drunkard" and accused him of obstinate heresy and apostasy from the true Catholic Church. Luther made fun of Henry by naming him after a well-known clown figure ("Hanswurst"), who wore sausages around his neck. In most of the pamphlet, however, Luther refuted the charge that he started the reformation and contested Henry's assumption that Rome was the true church.

The last issue, who was the true church, dominated Luther's thinking during his last years. He answered the question by adopting a distinction made by St. Augustine that Luther was using in his lectures on Genesis: Both a false and a true church had existed since Cain and Abel.[51] Before the time of Jesus, the true church already consisted of faithful Israelites who trusted God's promise of a Messiah; and Protestants, who now believed that promise was fulfilled in Jesus, inherited membership in the true church after Catholics forfeited their place by restricting the church to the Roman bishop and all those loyal to him. This argument seemed preposterous to Catholic theologians because they held the reverse: Catholics were the true church and the Protestants broke off from them.

Luther supported his position by listing the specific marks of each church that made it either true or false.[52] Beyond that comparison, which was polemical and obviously favored the Lutherans, Luther reviewed the beginning of the reformation in order to argue that his purpose had never been to start a new church. His original intention was to use an academic debate to call attention to the abuse of indulgences. The perpetrators of a division were indulgence preachers like Tetzel together with Albert of Mainz and Pope Leo, who profited from indulgences and refused to listen to well-meaning critics like Luther.[53] Behind Luther's defense was a view of the reformation that differs completely from the conventional modern perspective. The reformation was not a denominational split in which Protestant churches left the same Roman Catholic Church that had existed from the beginning of Christianity. Instead, Protestants (mainly Lutherans in Luther's view) preserved true Christianity and the true church that had always existed even though the Roman hierarchy, popes and bishops, betrayed it and defected, as it were, to a false church of heretics and the devil. After he had listed marks of the false church, which Luther called "novelties"—indulgences, pilgrimages, private masses, purgatory, monasteries, and popes—he gave the reason why there could be no reconciliation for him:

> If such novelties under the papacy were or could be simple novelties, for the sake of peace they could to some extent be tolerated in the same way that

one puts up with a new coat. But if these novelties must be observed as laws of the church and be called sacred worship, proper living, and being spiritual, then they are nothing but satanic poison and hellish murder. . . . We are forced to believe that if we observe these laws, we earn mercy and life, but if we do not observe them, we earn wrath and death. That coercion makes truth out of lies, God out of the devil, and hell out of heaven.[54]

History is always a reconstruction of the past that reflects the bias and the unavoidable short-sightedness of those who write it. And when religion is the subject, there is no way to verify what was true or false. One person's true religion was the other person's heresy or fanaticism. Religious colloquies did not succeed in reconciling Catholics and Lutherans—not to mention other Protestants, Muslims, and Jews—because hidden beneath the differences about what was true and what was false were the stakes identified by Luther: mercy and life, or wrath and death. Tradition, customs, injustices, and ethnic loyalties also played their parts, as they still do in the choice and exercise of religion. In sixteenth-century Europe, however, religious conflicts were so bitter and conciliation so rare because, for most people involved, including Martin Luther, everything was at stake.

CHAPTER EIGHTEEN

A PRODIGIOUS SINNER
1542–1546
Naumburg—Wittenberg—Leipzig—Halle—Eisleben

"Now join with us prodigious and hardened sinners lest you diminish Christ for us. . . . You can be a bogus sinner and have Christ for a fictitious savior. Instead, get used to the fact that Christ is a genuine savior and that you are a real sinner."[1]

On January 20, 1542, Martin Luther consecrated the first German Lutheran bishop who was not already a bishop under the pope. It happened in the cathedral at Naumburg, seventy-five miles (120 kilometers) southwest of Wittenberg. One year earlier the Catholic bishop of Naumburg had died, and Elector John Frederick decided to select the next bishop even though it was not his prerogative. Bishops were elected by the priests who belonged to the chapter of clergy at the cathedral, but in Naumburg the chapter had not adopted the reformation. Adhering to custom, they elected a moderate and learned Catholic bishop, Julius von Pflug. The Elector was not deterred. While Pflug was pondering his acceptance, John Frederick, with the half-hearted consent of Wittenberg theologians, selected Nicholas von Amsdorf to become the new bishop. Other than being Lutheran, Amsdorf fit the usual criteria: a celibate priest from a noble family. On January 17, 1542, the clergy chapter proclaimed Julius von Pflug the new bishop as Elector John Frederick, accompanied by Luther, Melanchthon, Amsdorf and Spalatin,[2] arrived in Naumburg. Two days later, Luther consecrated Amsdorf the new bishop of Naumburg.[3]

The evening before, Luther met with secular authorities (mayors, counts, etc.) within the diocese and convinced them to support a Lutheran bishop. Luther's argument was simple: A Catholic bishop would *ipso facto* prohibit the gospel from being preached. If the clergy chapter refused to cooperate with the Elector, the secular authorities were absolved of their loyalty to the chapter and were free to support the Elector's choice. The argument rested on weak legal evidence, but the secular officials agreed and the next morning they attended the consecration of Amsdorf. Despite the secular support, Amsdorf lasted only four years in the office of bishop. The Naumburg clergy chapter never accepted him and Amsdorf received minimal backing from Elector John Frederick. It was not the first time that Luther and his colleagues had been pushed by the Elector to bow to his will against their better judgment.

During Holy Week of 1541 Justus Jonas left Wittenberg to serve temporarily as the Lutheran preacher in the town of Halle. Archbishop Albert, whose favorite residence was in Halle, had left the city earlier that year after a conflict over taxes and the town's sympathy for the evangelical movement. Halle was part of Albert's archdiocese of Magdeburg, but the town council ignored that fact and allowed the evangelical backers to call a Lutheran preacher from Wittenberg. They settled on Justus Jonas and invited him for a trial period of two months. Extension after extension followed until December of 1544, when Jonas was officially installed as pastor at the Market Church of Our Lady.

Jonas' departure from Wittenberg was difficult for him and Luther. For twenty years they had comforted each other during personal trials, participated in joint family events, and, together with Melanchthon and Bugenhagen, steadily turned Electoral Saxony into a Lutheran territory. Now the best Luther could do was to keep Jonas abreast of the news. In February of 1542 the news was bad. The Turks were in Hungary seeking permission to cross Poland in order to invade Germany. In Basel Karlstadt had died and a rowdy ghost, throwing rocks and gravel, was haunting Karlstadt's house and grave. In Strasbourg, Martin Bucer's wife and son and all their daughters had died in the plague that also brought grief to other theologians. Wolfgang Capito, who had lost a son, daughter, and stepson, had himself died three months earlier. Caspar Hedio, who had accompanied Bucer to Marburg, lost five children, and one victim, named Wilhelm Zwingli, was the son of Ulrich, the Zurich reformer.[4]

On August 26, 1542, Luther notified the headmaster of the Latin school in Torgau that, as agreed, he was sending his son John (Hänschen), now sixteen, to study grammar and music there. The headmaster, Marcus Crodel, was to keep an eye on John and on Florian von Bora, Katharina's nephew, who accompanied John. To this point, the boys had been privately tutored in the Luther home, but Luther decided that John and Florian needed the example set by a crowd of many boys because "it seemed to accomplish more than individual, private education."[5] Within a day or two, Luther discovered that Florian had stolen a knife from John's younger brother Paul, lied about it, and taken it to Torgau. Luther instructed Crodel to give the scoundrel a severe thrashing three days in a row, or send him back to Wittenberg.[6]

Two weeks later, Luther had to write Crodel about a more serious matter. John's sister, Magdalena (Lenchen), was on her deathbed and wanted to see her brother. Luther was sending a carriage so that John could rush home.[7] As Magdalena lay dying, Luther reportedly said:

> The spirit is willing but the flesh is weak. I love her very much. . . . In the last thousand years God has given to no bishop such great gifts as God has given me (for one should boast of God's gifts). I am angry with myself that I am unable to rejoice from my heart and be thankful to God, though I do at times sing a little song and give thanks. Whether we live or die, we belong to God.[8]

Magdalena died in the arms of her father around nine o'clock in the morning of September 20, 1542.[9] Also present were Katharina, Melanchthon, George Rörer, and perhaps young Hans. The rector of the university announced the death and asked faculty and students to assemble at four o'clock for the funeral.[10] As the coffin was escorted from the home, Luther turned to the mourners and said: "Do not be sorrowful; I have sent a saint to heaven." And, remembering Elisabeth, who had died fourteen years earlier, he added: "In fact, I have now sent two of them."[11]

On the way home from Smalcald in 1537 Luther himself had expected to die and drew up a will in the presence of Bugenhagen. Three years later he saw no reason for a testament and informally appointed Katharina his "universal heiress" and the natural guardian of their children.[12] After the illnesses of 1541, however, he decided to draw up a second testament. It circumvented the provision of Saxon law that prohibited a spouse from inheriting any property other than her dowry and personal belongings. In the will, which resembled a living gift of deed, Luther transferred into Katharina's name all their property. This testament was executed on January 6, 1542, and was witnessed by Melanchthon, Cruciger, and Bugenhagen.[13] Luther gave three reasons for the gift: because Katharina was a faithful and pious wife, who at all times held him dear and gave birth to and reared their children; she would be able to pay off the debts that were left after Martin died; and most of all, so that Katharina would not have to depend financially on the children but instead be honored and respected by them as God commanded. A mother was the best guardian for children, added Luther, and he was confident that, if she remarried, Katharina would still share everything with them. Luther named Elector John Frederick the protector and administrator of the gift, and the Elector formally confirmed the will two months after Luther's death.

In the remainder of the testament Luther made revealing comments about their net worth. Since Luther never demanded royalties, he had received no income except his salary and the gifts he listed on a household inventory recorded in 1542.[14] Yet he and Katharina had accumulated substantial property and run a big and burdensome household. It was astounding, Luther remarked, that they were able to manage it all. "The miracle," he added, "is not the lack of ready cash [we have] but the modest size of the debt."[15] Luther did not say it, but the cloister was a money pit. Much of their reserves went toward remodeling the house from cellar to roof and installing a new bathroom with a tub. The brewhouse, stalls for hogs, horses, and cows, and the gardens also required maintenance. As a gift for her husband in 1540, Katharina ordered a new entrance to be constructed of prime Elbe sandstone. On each side of the door were niches for seats under small baldachins, one of which displayed a relief of Luther's face and the other his seal, the Luther rose.[16] For the construction and maintenance undertaken between 1532 and 1541, the Luthers purchased piles of building material that contributed to their debt. In 1542, when the house had to be appraised, Luther called it impossible but nonetheless set the value at 6,000 guilders.[17] Since Luther's testament was not notarized, Luther concluded it with the request that everybody acknowledge him to be the person who in truth he was, "namely, a public figure known both in heaven and on earth, as well as in hell, having respect and authority that one can trust more than any notary . . . especially since this is my very well-known handwriting."[18] Very well known to contemporaries, perhaps, but also tiny and hard for future generations to read.

The purpose of the appraisal required in 1542 was a reassessment called the Turkish tax. It became necessary because the Ottoman Turks had returned to Central Europe. In 1541 the army of Suleyman the Magnificent crushed the German forces of Archduke Ferdinand and placed much of Hungary under Turkish control.[19] It was left to the Imperial Diet of Speyer, in 1542, to authorize the special tax in order to field a massive army that would defend Germany against the Turks. Although Luther was exempted from the tax, he decided to pay his share.[20]

In the late 1520s, when the Turks first menaced Germany, Luther considered their threat to be a sign that God's final judgment upon the world was near.[21] When the Turks returned in 1541, Luther was convinced that time was running out for the German people to amend their wicked ways and recover their trust in God. The reformer was happy to comply with the Elector's request that he urge pastors to pray for deliverance.[22] The appeal that Luther issued, however, was much stronger than a request for prayer. It was a harsh reprimand of his fellow Germans for ignoring the word of God preached to them for the past twenty years. Instead of behaving in accord with faith and love, they had filled every corner of the country with thieving and greed. Germany was no better than the sinful generation of Noah, which had been exterminated by the flood. It was no wonder that God was now sending the Turks to bring Germany to its senses.[23] To avoid disaster, urged Luther, the German people should at last begin to take God seriously and trust in his mercy. If they did, then the Turks, acting as God's instrument, would have taught the Germans finally to pray and fear God as they ought. Otherwise, the German people would either be overrun by the Turks or would rot in sin and complacency.[24]

In 1545 Luther went a step further by calling the Turks part of Satan's army and labeling the papacy a creation of the devil. Luther suspected that the reformation, by restoring Christ to the center of Christianity, had provoked the devil to initiate the final battle against God. The reformation was, therefore, not just another medieval reform movement that future historians could study; for Luther, it was the prelude to the Last Day and to the arrival of God's eternal kingdom. Luther also imagined the devil was behind all his adversaries: Anabaptists, sacramentarians, even Müntzer, whom he called "Satan's prelude and introduction."[25] None of them, however, appeared to Luther as devil-driven as the Turks, the papists—and the Jews.

Two months after Magdalena's death, Luther was working on his best-known and most reviled anti-Jewish publication, *The Jews and Their Lies*. In the first paragraph Luther claimed he did not believe a Christian could be duped into becoming Jewish. But, he alleged, "the devil is the god of the world, and wherever God's word is absent the devil has an easy task, not only with the weak but also with the strong."[26] Later in the book Luther warned Christians against the Jews, since "wherever they have their synagogues, nothing is found but a den of devils."[27] Papists and Jews seemed similar to Luther not only because the devil was behind them but also because all religions that did not accept the gospel of faith and love believed: "If I do this, God will be pleased." In other words, they opposed true religion: instead of seeking to change their hearts, they tried first to alter their actions so that God would reward them. According to the *Table Talk*, Luther made that comment while he and others were discussing a book called *The Entire Jewish Faith* by a Jewish convert named Antonius Margaritha.[28]

Margaritha, the son of a Jewish rabbi, had converted to Christianity in 1521 and earned money by teaching Hebrew in Augsburg. *The Entire Jewish Faith* was published a few months before he lost a debate with Josel of Rosheim, the learned spokesman for German Jews, at the Diet of Augsburg in 1530. The purpose of Margaritha's book was to show Christians who might think well of Jews that every aspect of Jewish religion—the Talmud, prayers, worship, rituals during their holy days—was motivated by their hatred of Christians.[29] After Augsburg, Margaritha taught Hebrew in Leipzig, where a second edition of *The Entire Jewish Faith* was published. Luther was not the only user of this book. It was reprinted at least four times after it first appeared in 1530.[30]

Luther's book, *The Jews and Their Lies*, was an indirect reply to another book, *Messiahs of the Christians and Jews*, which was published in 1539 and came from the pen of the Hebrew professor at Basel, Sebastian Münster.[31] Münster hoped that learning Hebrew and reading Hebrew books would lead to the mutual toleration of Christians and Jews. His book, *Messiahs*, was a dialogue between a Christian and a Jew that ended in a standoff. Neither participant was able to convince the other that his interpretation of the Old Testament was correct and "his Messiah" the only true candidate.[32] That happy ending did not please Luther at all. His academic career was based on the conviction that only a Christian interpretation of the Old Testament was correct and that challenges by Jewish scholars threatened not only his view but Christianity itself. Their insistence that the promises and prophecies of the Old Testament applied only to the Jewish people were to Luther nothing but lies. In *Against the Sabbatarians* (1538) Luther had summed up the putative lie that undergirded the others he was trying to refute in 1543: Either Jesus of Nazareth, who came 1,500 years ago, was the Messiah or God had lied and not kept his promises.[33]

Modern readers, especially after the Holocaust, have found Luther's bitter rejection of Judaism repulsive, mainly because of its recommendations of what to do about Jews in Germany. These recommendations took up a small portion of *The Jews and Their Lies*, but in part Luther included them because of the changed political situation in the 1530s. By then, Jews were thought to pose a political and religious threat to the newly Protestant cities and territories.[34] In Hesse, Count Philip had officially tolerated and protected Jews since 1532, but in 1538 the policy was up for renewal and it faced strong opposition from the clergy. Count Philip decided against expulsion but, on the advice of Martin Bucer, he required Jewish subjects to comply with fourteen restrictions if they were to remain in Hesse.[35]

Elector John Frederick had already prohibited Jews from living in, working in, or traveling through Electoral Saxony, so none of Luther's advice was relevant for his own prince. Luther did not, therefore, bother with conditions for a permanent residence in Saxony. The measures he suggested went further and aimed at expulsion. For example, Philip of Hesse prohibited Jews from building new synagogues, while Luther advised that synagogues should be set afire.[36] Luther's recommendations were based on false information from Margaritha and others, but he was also infected with the anti-Jewish virus that had afflicted Christianity ever since its beginning and had permeated late medieval Europe. Relying on the biblical prospect that a Jewish remnant would come to believe that Jesus was the Messiah, Luther called his advice a "sharp mercy" that might "save at least a few."[37] And he never advocated exterminating the Jews or physically harming them. Preachers, he wrote, should teach their parishioners to be on guard against Jews and avoid them but "not to curse them or harm their persons."[38] He also suggested that European Jews return to their land at Jerusalem "and leave us our government, our country, our life, our property, and our faith."[39] Luther's recommendations can hardly be called mercy of any stripe, but neither were they roundups leading to wholesale murder like the Holocaust.

The harsh and contemptible polemics of Luther's last years reinforced the obvious all too well: Luther was a prisoner of his age and its prejudices. The sixteenth century produced a few voices in favor of limited political and religious toleration, but even Erasmus of Rotterdam, a paragon of humanism, betrayed a dislike of Jews.[40] After Luther's death, his late writings against Turks, Jews, and the papacy never became bestsellers nor did they dominate later historical perceptions of Luther.[41] In his own day, however, Luther's crude language did not pass unnoticed. In 1543, the Zurich reformer Henry Bullinger recoiled from the insults used by Luther to demean both the Swiss reformers and the Jews. After sampling the gratuitous vulgarity in one book, Bullinger admitted that Luther skillfully offered useful arguments against Jewish claims but said he simultaneously discredited his good points with scurrilous language.[42] Two years later Bullinger pilloried the same book: "If it had been written by a swineherd and not by a famous pastor, it might have been judged excusable but just barely."[43] Bullinger was no saint, however. He also made disparaging remarks about the Jews and rejected their claims to be God's people on grounds similar to those used by Luther.[44]

Luther's anti-Jewish writings were not widely known until the twentieth century, when they fell into the lap of the Nazi propaganda machine. Since the Holocaust most historians have not made Luther responsible for the murderous anti-Semitism of the Nazis. The identification of Luther with the Holocaust has been suggested mainly by post-World War II Anglo-American books such as *The Rise and Fall of the Third Reich*, *Hitler's Willing Executioners*,[45] and perhaps implicitly by the *History of God*, whose author alleged that Luther was "a rabid anti-Semite, a misogynist, was convulsed with a loathing and horror of sexuality, and believed that all rebellious peasants should be killed."[46] None of that was true. Luther's repugnant anti-Semitism was not foaming at the mouth; his motives and arguments can be identified and explained even though they are indefensible. Luther spoke highly of women, defended marriage, and criticized the widespread misogynist literature of his era.[47] Instead of loathing sexuality he turned his back on the celibate life and embraced sexual intercourse in a proper marriage, which he recommended for everyone except those who had the gift of abstinence. He rejected both tyranny and rebellion, and blamed both princes and peasants for the 1525 Peasants' War. During battle, acknowledged Luther, it was impossible to distinguish between ringleaders and half-hearted rebels, but mercy should be shown to captives and those who surrendered. For Luther rebellion was not a noble cause. It was nothing but war, "which brings with it a land filled with murder and bloodshed; it makes widows and orphans and turns everything upside down, like the worst disaster."[48]

It is fair, however, to ponder how it was possible for the person who counseled an Augustinian brother with merciful sentences such as "God dwells only in sinners" also to advocate the burning of synagogues. The person to whom Luther wrote those words in 1516, George Spenlein, was still alive in 1544 and serving as a Lutheran pastor near Erfurt. Soon after Spenlein assumed office, a bitter quarrel broke out between Spenlein's deacon and the town's schoolmaster. Luther was aware of the conflict and knew that both the deacon and the schoolmaster were seeking redress for the injustices they claimed to have suffered. Before Spenlein could settle the quarrel, he was advised by Luther to convince both men to drop their demands because "when the pursuit of justice cuts too close to the quick there will never be peace." Luther continued: "Whoever wills to be a Christian must in such a case give up his fine notion of justice and for the sake of peace allow God to render judgment and make room not only for grace but also for peace."[49]

Unfortunately, Luther did not take his own advice: he passed harsh judgment on his adversaries without waiting for God to render it. His battles, so he thought, had much more at stake than a local quarrel such as Spenlein faced. The Last Day was edging closer and true religion was under attack from the devil. Luther's lifework, to bring true religion to Germany, was faltering, and desperate measures were necessary. Twenty-two years earlier, when Luther's strident language was already puzzling readers, Luther gave the following explanation:

> You say you do not understand why I attack and scold the big shots and bishops so harshly and call them fools and asses since Christ everywhere taught forbearance. My answer is: I have demonstrated patience and humility long enough. I have begged and pleaded; three times I have agreed to meet them where they were; and I have always shown myself to be subservient. The entire world knows this.[50]

The time for pleasantness and politeness had passed and would never return: "For God's word is almighty; therefore, faith and the Spirit are busy and never resting and must always be active and engaged in combat."[51]

For Luther's earliest biographers, who did not fully approve of his polemics, they served God's purpose nonetheless. Mathesius commented: "The Lord himself, who aroused such burning zeal in his chosen instrument, will certainly also pardon his servant."[52] And, at the interment of Luther in the Castle Church, Melanchthon said: "A few people who should not be despised have complained that Luther was sharper than we could bear. I will not quarrel with them or with Luther's defenders. I respond rather with that which Erasmus often said: 'Because the maladies were so severe, God has given our age an abrasive physician.'"[53] Luther's early disgust at the damage to souls and wallets for which he held the Roman hierarchy responsible did not weaken, rather it intensified over his lifetime.[54] The pope and other adversaries were undermining the heart of true Christianity that he believed God called him to recover: the free gifts of faith and the love and the desire for justice that flowed from faith. In his world, that was worth fighting for—with words and, when unavoidable, with weapons.

On October 4, 1544, Luther and Bugenhagen traveled to Torgau to dedicate a large hall reputed to be the first space intentionally reconstructed for Lutheran worship.[55] The two-story chapel was built into the north wing of the Hartenfels castle, the Torgau residence of Elector John Frederick, who entrusted the project to his chief engineer. The original design has not been altered. On the north side, mounted on the wall below the balcony, is the imposing pulpit to which eyes are drawn before they search for an altar. In fact, there is no altar, only a stone table at the west end of the chapel, and it stands on a platform away from the wall so that a minister can face the worshipers. In contrast to an altar, which implied the Lord's Supper was a sacrifice, the table from which bread and wine were served demonstrated instead that the sacrament was a sacred meal. A balcony slightly behind and above the table was occupied by the organ, installed soon after construction, with room on both sides for a choir. The workshop of Lucas Cranach supplied original paintings for the chapel, but Cranach did not design the three reliefs that still decorate the pulpit. The central relief shows the twelve-year-old Jesus teaching in the temple and alludes to the interpretation of scripture as the core of preaching. To the left of that relief is a depiction of Jesus forgiving the adulteress and represents the proclamation of grace and forgiveness. The third relief displays Jesus casting hawkers and money-changers from the temple as a warning that unsound preaching defiled God's house.

Luther's homily at the dedication was based on a gospel story that had two parts. In the first half Jesus defended himself from the accusation that he had violated the sabbath by healing a man.[56] The lesson Luther drew from the text was simple: Christian worship was not restricted to a specific time or place but could occur wherever believers were assembled. If they did not wish to gather in a church building, such as the chapel being dedicated, "one could just as well preach outside by the fountain or somewhere else." The second half of the text told the story of a marriage feast at which a guest was advised not to sit at the head table but to take the lowest place. The story's punch line seemed benign: Those who exalt themselves will be humbled and those who humble themselves will be exalted. Instead of extolling humility as a virtue, however, Luther gave the story a sharper social edge: All worshipers who would gather in this chapel were equal, regardless of their social status:

> Do not think that you alone must sit at the head of the table or that you must not give way to anybody. For the God who made you a lord, a regent, a doctor, or a teacher, is just as much the God of the poor beggar at your door. And God's eyes look just as straight at him as they look at the greatest lords or princes on earth. In short, whether you are at the top or the middle or at the bottom, all are made equal by faith.[57]

The sermon said nothing about the design of the chapel or its sacred character, but that is not surprising. For Luther the church was always first and foremost the believers themselves. The church became visible when and where the faithful assembled and not in permanent structures. Once Luther realized the gospel would take root in only a few earnest believers, he emphasized the hiddenness of the church and insisted it was an object of faith, like everything else in the Christian creeds:

> This article, "I believe in the holy Christian church," is as much an article of faith as the rest. Natural reason cannot recognize it even if it puts on all its glasses. The devil can cover it over with scandals and divisions such that you cannot avoid being offended. God, too, can conceal it behind faults and shortcomings of every kind, so that you too are fooled and pass false judgment on it. The church will not be known by sight but by faith.[58]

Nevertheless, the older Luther apparently needed visible evidence for himself. Writing to Linck in 1543, Luther complained bitterly about too much work and the stone that was causing him much pain. There was no time to read and pray in private, and Linck should ask the Lord to take Luther's soul in peace. "I've had enough; I am worn out; I am nothing any longer." Then, as if consoling himself, Luther wrote: "I do not leave our churches looking badly; they flourish in pure and sound teaching; and they grow day by day through many excellent and sincere pastors."[59]

Although he lived three more years, Luther died before most of the close friends and colleagues whom he had known in Erfurt and Wittenberg. Lang, Linck, Amsdorf, Cranach, Jonas, Bugenhagen, Propst, Dietrich, Cruciger, Rörer, Melanchthon, and the old Saxon chancellor Brück all outlived the reformer. The exceptions were Hausmann and Spalatin. In 1538, when Hausmann was installed as the new pastor in his hometown, he suffered a stroke and died the same evening. Katharina, Jonas, and Melanchthon broke the news gently, but Luther took it hard and spent the day in tears.[60] Spalatin died at home in Altenburg in January of 1545 after two years of deep depression. Amsdorf, Melanchthon, Luther, and Elector John Frederick had all tried to console him but Spalatin never recovered. Luther's letter to Jonas contained a sentiment learned from Staupitz and once used on Melanchthon. After telling Spalatin, who brooded over his mistakes, that he was a feeble sinner, Luther urged:

Now join with us prodigious and hardened sinners lest you diminish Christ for us. He is not a savior of fictitious or petty sinners but of genuine ones, not only the lowly but also the big and powerful ones; indeed he is the savior of all sinners. My Staupitz consoled me this way when I was down-hearted. You can be a *bogus* sinner and have Christ for a *fictitious* savior. Instead, get used to the fact that Christ is a genuine savior and that you are a real sinner.[61]

In April of 1544 death skirted the Luther home. Wittenberg was beset by an epidemic of measles and the virus flared up in all four children. According to Luther, after Margaret's apparent recovery she struggled ten weeks with a high fever. "I would not be angry with the Lord," he wrote, "if he took her out of this Satanic age." He wished the same for himself and the entire family and looked forward to the end of Satan's fury. Luther reported the illnesses to Jacob Propst, saying again that it was time for him to die. "I have lived long enough, if one may call it living."[62] On January 17, 1546, one month before Luther died, he expressed the same feelings to Propst, adding to the old complaints a new one—that he had only one good eye:

Old, decrepit, lethargic, worn out, cold, and now one-eyed as well, I am writing to you my Jacob. I was hoping that I had merited the rest that, it seems to me, is rightfully mine, but I am so overwhelmed with things to be written, said, and done that it seems as if I had never before written, said, or accomplished anything.[63]

The loss of sight in one eye is worth noting, because people who saw the younger Luther in person commented on his remarkable eyes. The oldest statement came from Cardinal Cajetan, who met Luther in 1518. Cajetan called him a "beast" with "very deep eyes" and "fantastic ideas in his head."[64] His Latin word for deep was *profundus*, which can also mean bottomless, unfathomable, penetrating, or mysterious. According to Swiss onlookers who saw him in 1524 at the Black Bear Inn in Jena, Luther's eyes were a deep black and twinkled like a star. Melanchthon described them as bright and joyful like the eyes of a lion, and two observers said Luther had the eyes of a falcon. Opponents were not so kind: Luther's eyes were demonic, or they glistened like the eyes of one possessed. The papal nuncio Vergerio agreed: Luther's eyes were frenzied as if he were possessed by the devil.[65] The eyes must have been penetrating indeed if observers who both admired and hated him saw reflected in Luther's eyes their own conflicting judgments.

Luther wrote more than once that he was tired of living in general, but he was also tired of living in Wittenberg. Away from home in 1545, he wrote Katharina that he would like to have matters arranged so that he did not have to return to Wittenberg. Katharina should sell everything except the cloister, which should be returned to Elector John Frederick, and move to Zöllsdorf. It was better for them to leave Wittenberg now than for her and the children to leave after his death. Luther himself would rather eat the bread of a beggar than ruin his final days with "the filth at Wittenberg," which was destroying his hard and faithful work.[66] Luther had earlier considered leaving, and at times his sermons scolded the Wittenbergers for laxity, laziness, and flouting the Ten Commandments: cheating and stealing in every way possible, immodesty and whoring, usury, greed, drunkenness, and superstitious behavior.[67] But Luther never remained away for good. In 1545, he reluctantly made his way home by way of Leipzig and Torgau. Melanchthon suspected that differences between him and Luther had led to the escapade, but more than likely it was Luther the idealist confronting the reality he must have suspected for years: Wittenberg was home to no more true Christians than any other place.

Near the end of his life Luther's chief adversary was still the papacy. His last written blast, *Against the Roman Papacy Instituted by the Devil* (1545), was aimed at the pope. One historian called it the "most intentionally violent and vulgar writing to come from Luther's pen,"[68] but it was not as passionate as some earlier books because this tome was not his idea. Elector John Frederick and Chancellor Brück asked Luther for a book after Pope Paul III chastised Emperor Charles V for making concessions to Protestants. At the same time Pope Paul was convening the long-expected church assembly that became the historic Council of Trent. It rejected the reformation and began changing the remainder of medieval Christianity that stayed loyal to Rome into the future Roman Catholic Church. The Council of Trent was to open on March 25, 1545, the day on which Luther's *Against the Roman Papacy* appeared in print. It was the harbinger of a new religious epoch in Europe: A variety of Christian churches was about to replace the old order of medieval Western Christianity that had been subject alone to the pope.

Against the Roman Papacy turned out to be milder than Brück envisioned when he told the Elector that Luther should "hew away with the axe, for which by God's grace he has a greater talent than other men."[69] The case Luther presented against papal primacy and authority was not new, and his arguments were identical to those he used against John Eck in 1519 at the Leipzig Disputation. Luther's charge that the pope was a creature of the devil was not that old, but it was already part of Luther's scenario for the last days of the world. The vulgarity was limited mainly to a set of eight cartoons supplied by Cranach and annotated with verses by Luther himself.[70] But his case against the papacy was sober and to the point: There was no help for Rome and all its churches unless the papacy was replaced by a proper bishop who would preach the gospel purely and guarantee that other clergy did as well. This bishop of Rome was one among equals and should not attempt to subject the bishops or any secular governor to the authority of Rome.[71] Twenty-five years had passed since 1520, when Luther had made the same proposals.

On January 17, 1546, Luther told Propst he had started another anti-Catholic book: a refutation of theses issued by the theological faculty at Louvain in Belgium, the same faculty that had condemned him many years earlier. He was much angrier now, admitted Luther, than an old theologian ought to be, but "the monsters of Satan must be resisted even if we must blow at them with our last breath."[72] Luther was not able to finish the manuscript before, five days later, he left Wittenberg for Eisleben by way of Halle.

In the last year he was alive Luther passed through the town of Halle several times and preached three sermons in the same church, the Market Church of Our Lady. The last two were delivered in January of 1546, when Luther stopped in Halle on his last mission to reconcile the counts of Mansfeld. On January 25, Luther left Halle and headed for Eisleben, but that evening flooding and ice floes forced him to turn back. The next day he preached the second sermon while waiting for the water to subside. Part of the sermon was devoted to criticizing Archbishop Albert and the exhibition of his relics in Halle. Although the town itself had accepted the reformation, Luther still thought of it as the favorite residence of Albert, who had died in September of 1545, just four months before Luther's sermon. On Luther's last journey, he was still thinking of the person who, almost thirty years earlier, had sent the ninety-five theses to Rome and turned his academic protest against indulgences into a hard-nosed and unresolved conflict with the papacy.

Finally, on January 28, the counts of Mansfeld sent a troop of horsemen to escort Luther, his two sons, his assistant John Aurifaber, and Justus Jonas to Eisleben. On the way Luther suffered a dizzy spell, but the journey continued. The negotiations with the counts took place every second or third day, but Luther limited his participation to one or two hours. At St. Andrew's Church in Eisleben Luther preached four times and on February 14, the date of his last letter to Katharina, he ordained two pastors.[73] On February 16 and 17 partial agreements were reached by the counts, but on the seventeenth weakness prevented Luther from participating. According to the reliable eyewitness account written by Jonas and Coelius, the court preacher at Mansfeld,[74] Luther ate supper and discussed with his companions whether or not they would recognize one another in the life to come. After retiring to his room at about eight o'clock, he suffered pains and tightness in his chest. For an hour he napped on a day bed before moving to his bedchamber and sleeping until one o'clock in the morning of February 18, 1546. Jonas, Luther's sons Martin and Paul, and a servant, Ambrosius, stayed by him. But the pain and weakness had not subsided and Luther acknowledged he might have to remain in Eisleben, where he was born and baptized.[75]

After walking a few steps Luther again lay down on the day bed and was covered with warm towels. By this time Coelius and Aurifaber had returned with two doctors and both Count Albert and his wife Anna. After hearing Luther say he was dying and observing his stillness, Countess Anna and the doctors rubbed his pulse with a strong concoction, perhaps a common mixture of rose water and aqua vitae, which Katharina had given to her husband. When Luther remained still, Jonas and Coelius asked him loudly if he was ready to die trusting in Christ and standing by what he had taught. A distinct "yes" emerged from his mouth before Luther turned on his right side and went to sleep. Around a quarter to three in the morning Luther suddenly turned pale, his nose and feet went cold, and he took a deep, soft breath, expelling his spirit without moving a muscle or showing any signs of pain or distress.[76] Dying without agony was the sign of a good death, which demonstrated that the person was right with God. At Luther's deathbed, ordained ministers were present but there was no priest, no confession of sins, and no anointing with oil.

On its journey back to Wittenberg Luther's body spent the night in Halle, the same town where flooding held up his last trip to Eisleben. Wax impressions of Luther's face and hands reputedly were made that evening. But the earliest plausible date for the creation of the "death mask" was early in the 1600s when, enhanced with ears and a throat, the mask and face were part of a life-sized effigy of the reformer that still existed in the 1930s. In all likelihood neither a death mask displayed formerly in Eisleben or any other casting was made directly from Luther's corpse.[77]

Luther's funeral in Wittenberg was similar to the rites for Elector Frederick in 1525. On February 22, 1546, a long procession of notables and family escorted the body into Wittenberg through the gate and past the cloister, the university, and the houses of Melanchthon and Cranach to the west end of town, where it entered the Castle Church. No one living in Wittenberg had ever seen so many bystanders outside the gate or mourners filling the side streets and market square along the one-mile stretch.[78] A crowd of one thousand reportedly filled the Castle Church after the coffin was brought in and set down in front of the pulpit. Then proper chants and hymns were sung before Bugenhagen preached the sermon and Melanchthon delivered the customary Latin oration. Several "learned" teachers carried Luther's body to the grave, which had been dug "not far from the pulpit," and there laid it to rest.

Hardly anyone present expected Luther to remain in the grave—but not because his remains would be stolen, although it almost happened one year later when Emperor Charles V visited his grave in person. Many of the mourners at Luther's funeral trusted St. Paul's metaphor for resurrection of the body, a rhetorical gem that could then be read in Luther's German translation: "What is sown is perishable, what is raised is imperishable; it is sown in dishonor, it is raised in glory; it is sown in weakness, it is raised in power."[79] With a condensed form of these words, which Luther steadfastly believed, Jonas and Coelius ended the account of their friend's final days. They realized he was perishable, and close friends such as Jonas and Melanchthon had observed his weaknesses and shared the disrepute that he suffered. In spite of the pedestal on which he remained, those who knew him well remembered that Luther had not displayed either perfect faith or miraculous power. Like them he was a weak and prodigious sinner. They had learned from Luther himself, however, that real sinning was a prerequisite to salvation and that a little faith was often more genuine than a lot. If that were true, then the perishable Luther would enjoy the same imperishable glory they hoped one day for themselves.

EPILOGUE

Martin Luther was survived by his wife Katharina (46) and four living children: Hans (19), Martin (14), Paul (13), and Margaret (11). The reactions of the children to his death were not recorded or, if recorded, have not survived. But seven weeks later, on April 6, 1546, Katharina divulged her grief to her sister-in-law, Christina von Bora:

> That you have a heart-felt compassion for me and my poor children I do readily believe. For who would not be fittingly saddened and concerned for such a worthy man as my dear master was, who served so well not just a town or a single country but the whole world. . . . I can neither eat nor drink. Nor again sleep. If I had owned a principality or empire I would not have felt as bad had I lost it as I did when our dear Lord God took from me—and not only from me but from the whole world—this dear and worthy man.[1]

Katharina overstated the effect of her loss on the world, but the consequences for her own life were greater than she could imagine. At first, owing to Luther's estate and the generosity of Elector John Frederick, the counts of Mansfeld, and Luther's close colleagues, there was plenty of money. Against the advice of former chancellor Brück and Melanchthon, Katharina purchased a low-lying farm at Wachsdorf, across the Elbe river, two hours by wagon from Wittenberg but closer by far than her family property at Zöllsdorf. Contrary to Luther's testament, which did not conform to Saxon law, the Elector also appointed independent guardians and new financial arrangements for the children.[2]

After one year, however, everything changed. Soon after Luther died, Emperor Charles V gave up negotiating with Protestants and attacked the

Lutheran Smalcald League. The forces of John Frederick of Saxony and Philip of Hesse were no match for the troops assembled by Charles and his brother Ferdinand, and in April of 1547 the Lutherans surrendered at Mühlberg on the Elbe river, forty-five miles (seventy kilometers) southeast of Wittenberg. Both John Frederick and Philip were taken captive and Wittenberg was quickly placed under siege. The town capitulated after only a month and shocked inhabitants, who were brave enough to emerge from hiding, watched the emperor on horseback head toward Luther's grave in the Castle Church. According to Wittenberg tradition, Emperor Charles vetoed the exhumation and burning of Luther's remains that was much anticipated by the Spanish elite in his retinue.[3]

Katharina and three of the children had already fled to the fortified city of Magdeburg, which belonged to the Smalcald League. She was joined by Melanchthon and his family, but the city was overrun by refugees and itself vulnerable to attack. Katharina begged Melanchthon to escort her to Denmark as the Lutheran king had already sent money for her support. They made it to the Lutheran territory of Lüneburg in north Germany, but it was full of hostile troops so they retreated to Braunschweig. Katharina remained there two months until she and the children could safely return to Wittenberg. The new property at Wachsdorf had been destroyed and the fields all around plundered, but the cloister was intact. To support the family, she turned the cloister into a boarding house, and, with the aid of Melanchthon, they escaped destitution. In 1549 he also arranged for Hans Luther to pursue his legal studies at Königsberg in east Prussia. The costs were covered by Duke Albert himself, who had made Prussia the first officially Lutheran territory.[4]

Katharina's troubles, however, were not over. Although the war of 1547 had ended, Emperor Charles V failed to achieve his goal of subjugating all of Germany to the pope. In 1548 the emperor agreed to an interim solution, which reimposed most Catholic rituals on Protestants while allowing them to keep a married clergy and to receive both bread and wine at mass. Lutherans split over whether or not to accept the interim agreement, and fierce resistance in north Germany in 1552 led to a rebellion of Protestant princes. For Katharina and her family, the renewed hostilities brought an unwanted gift to Wittenberg: an epidemic that might have touched her boarders and caused the university to relocate until the plague exhausted itself. Katharina and the youngest children, Paul and Margaret, fled Wittenberg for a second time. Before reaching Torgau the horses shied and Katharina jumped or fell from the wagon, landed awkwardly, and toppled into a soggy ditch. She was taken to Torgau but remained bedridden until her death three months later. She finally succumbed on December 20, 1552, three days after her daughter Margaret turned eighteen.[5]

After a dignified funeral arranged by the rector of the university in Wittenberg, her body was interred at Torgau in the town church of St. Mary. A large epitaph depicts in bas-relief the Luther and von Bora coats-of-arms above a wide-eyed Katharina who is standing and holding a Bible. Five months after the funeral and again in 1554 the children met with their guardians, among whom were Melanchthon and Luther's brother Jacob, to settle the estate. Katharina had saved enough money for each child to receive a fair portion. All the children eventually married, but Paul, who studied medicine, was the first. His engagement to Anna von Warbeck probably occurred before Katharina died because the wedding took place in Torgau little more than a month after her funeral. The offspring of Paul and Anna sustained the direct male line of Martin Luther's descendants into the eighteenth century.

Neither Martin nor Katharina lived to see the political and legal settlement of the German Reformation that was reached in 1555. The Protestant revolt of 1552 had forced Emperor Charles to agree that Catholic and Protestant regions could maintain their religious status until a new diet of the Empire resolved the impasse. The diet finally convened in 1555 at Augsburg, the same city in which Luther was interrogated by Cardinal Cajetan in 1518 and where, in 1530, Lutheran rulers presented their *Augsburg Confession* to Charles V. In 1555, however, Charles did not attend and was represented, as so often in the past, by his brother Ferdinand, who would become the next emperor. After agreeing that ending the religious schism was impossible, the diet drafted a document that granted legal status to Lutheran rulers and territories and protected Catholic territories and institutions from seizure by Lutherans. Catholic rulers and their clergy were forbidden to proselytize the subjects of Lutheran rulers and vice versa. The document, known as the Peace of Augsburg, was promulgated on September 25, 1555. It prevented religious warfare in Germany until the outbreak of the Thirty Years' War in 1618, but it divided Germany along religious lines that are still visible.

If Martin Luther had lived to see the Peace of Augsburg take effect, would he have considered the reformation a success? The answer is no and yes. No, because Luther did not think in those terms. True religion, like the true church, was always a matter of hope that could never be quantified and located on a scale from zero to one hundred. Nor was Luther's mission, based on a divine call, a professional project that he or anyone else could judge by human criteria to have failed or succeeded. Since God was behind it, the mission ultimately had to be fulfilled even if it did not happen until the Last Day. The gospel would eventually win out even though it was only a minority who kept it alive. That was Luther's vision, not the religiously divided Germany fixed in place by the Peace of Augsburg.

At the same time, Luther believed the reformation brought the possibility of true religion to Germany even if popular piety and ecclesiastical enterprise failed to recognize it. The Peace of Augsburg at least prevented that possibility from vanishing, or so Luther might have thought. Long before he died, Luther realized that he would not live to see his vision fulfilled. When deeply discouraged, he blamed it on human obduracy and his own naïvete:

> The world is the world. If I had to start over with the gospel, I would do it differently. I would let the vulgar crowd stay under the pope and privately give relief to those who are anxious and full of despair. It behooves a preacher to know the world better than I did when I was a monk. Back then I thought the world was so upright that people would rush forward as soon as they heard the gospel. What happened, however, was the contrary.[6]

In his best moments, however, Luther recognized that the gospel of faith and love, his true religion, was making headway in Germany. Although he preferred that committed Christians needing consolation would live by the gospel and preserve it to the end, he did not repudiate the new networks of Lutheran churches as long as they were agents of faith and love and not self-serving institutions.

It is not surprising that many people think of Martin Luther King, Jr. when Martin Luther is mentioned. In 2015 the reformation is almost 500 years old, but people still alive vividly remember both King and the civil rights movement in the United States. Both men placed very high in the categories chosen for them by the Pantheon project at M.I.T., but no direct comparison on that basis is possible because King ranked number one among social activists while Luther ranked number five among religious figures. Names and rankings, however, do not make them worthy of our attention. The benefit of considering them together comes instead from what they had in common, while acknowledging their obvious differences. King himself identified one feature they shared. In his famous letter from a Birmingham jail, King defended himself against the charge of extremism by citing examples of other extremists: Jesus, Amos, Paul, John Bunyan, Abraham Lincoln, Thomas Jefferson, and Martin Luther.[7]

Indeed, both King and Luther were extremists, and courageous ones, because they refused to settle for the status quo and defied the powers who were loath to have it disturbed. Both men were also dreamers who suspected they would not live to see their dreams come true. Both dreamers recognized that the organizations supporting their visions were imperfect but that their dreams would dissipate without structures to keep them vivid. Both had harsh critics—from their own ranks and from the establishments of their eras. Both men were indebted to strong women for the time and energy they devoted to the pursuit of their visions. Both men were powerful writers and orators whose flaws and mistakes became more glaring with time. And both were visionaries, who trusted that what remained unreformed at their deaths would one day be perfected.

ABBREVIATIONS

Aleander   *Depeschen des Nuntius Aleander vom Wormser Reichstage 1521*
ARC   *Acta Reformationis Catholicae*
ARG   *Archive for Reformation History/Archiv für Reformationsgeschichte*
AWA   *Archiv zur Weimarer Ausgabe der Werke Martin Luthers*
BSB   *Bayerische Staatsbibliothek Munich*
CE   *Contemporaries of Erasmus*
Clemen   *Luthers Werke in Auswahl, ed. O. Clemen*
CWE   *Collected Works of Erasmus*
DB   *Deutsche Biographie, online at www.deutsche-biographie.de*
EAS   *Erasmus Ausgewählte Schriften*
E var   *D. Martini Lutheri opera latina varii argumenti . . .*
HAB   *Herzog August Bibliothek Wolfenbüttel*
LuJ   *Lutherjahrbuch*
Luther   *Luther: Zeitschrift der Luther-Gesellschaft*
LW   *Luther's Works*
MBW.T   *Melanchthons Briefwechsel, Texte*
MD   *Melanchthon Deutsch*
ML-LDS   *Martin Luther: Lateinisch-Deutsche Studienausgabe*
MPL   *Patrologiae cursus completus, Series Latina*
MVGAE   *Mitteilungen des Vereins für die Geschichte und Altertumskunde von Erfurt*
MWA   *Melanchthons Werke in Auswahl*
NRSV   *The Bible: New Revised Standard Version*
OER   *Oxford Encyclopedia of the Reformation*

RFG   *500 Jahre Reformation: Von Frauen Gestaltet, online at www.*
           frauen-und-reformation.de
Roth   *Zur Wittenberger Stadt- und Universitäts-Geschichte in der*
           Reformationszeit: Briefe aus Wittenberg an M. Stephan Roth in
           Zwickau
SB   *Sächsische Biografie, online at www.saebi.isgv.de*
SCJ   *The Sixteenth Century Journal*
StA   *Martin Luther: Studienausgabe*
TRE   *Theologische Realenzyklopädie*
WA   *Luthers Werke: Kritische Gesamtausgabe, Schriften*
WABr   *Luthers Werke: Kritische Gesamtausgabe, Briefwechsel*
WADB   *Luthers Werke: Kritische Gesamtausgabe, Deutsche Bibel*
WATR   *Luthers Werke: Kritische Gesamtausgabe, Tischreden*
ZSSR   *Zeitschrift der Savigny-Stiftung für Rechtsgeschichte,*
           Kanonistische Abteilung
ZKG   *Zeitschrift für Kirchengeschichte*

NOTES

Preface

1. http://pantheon.media.mit.edu/methods.Cultural Production: Human Accomplishment.
2. http://pantheon.media.mit.edu/people/Martin%20Luther.
3. Junghans, "Lutherbiographien", 438.
4. For the various collections and their compilation, see Junghans, "Die Tischreden Martin Luthers," 35–50.
5. My attempt at a concise presentation of Luther's theology was published in 2009 in the series, Abingdon Pillars of Theology (see bibliography).

Chapter One: My Homeland

1. Luther to Count Albert of Mansfeld, February 23, 1542, in *WABr* 9, 626.
2. Martin Luther to Katharina Luther, February 14, 1546, in *WABr* 11, 300; *LW* 50, 311–312.
3. *Luther Handbuch*, ed. Beutel, 340.
4. Luther to Michael Coelius, March 9, 1541, in *WABr* 9, 335; Luther to Count Albert of Mansfeld, February 23, 1542, in *WABr* 9, 626; Luther to Counts Philip and Hans Georg of Mansfeld, March 14, 1542, in *WABr* 10, 10.
5. Martin Luther to Katharina Luther, February 14, 1546, in *WABr* 11, 300; *LW* 50, 312.
6. Martin Luther to Katharina Luther, February 14, 1546, in *WABr* 11, 300; *LW* 50, 311–313.
7. Schneider, "Martin Luthers Reise nach Rom," 120–127. For the traditional view, which is still plausible, see Steinmetz, *Misericordia Dei*, 7–10.
8. *WATR* 4, 583 (no. 4925); 6, 320 (no. 7005).
9. *Augsburg during the Reformation Era*, ed. Tlusty, 239–241.
10. Luther to George Spalatin, September 19, 1526, in *WABr* 4, 118.
11. Pfister & Fertig, *The Population History of Germany*, 4–7.
12. *WA* 53, 169.
13. *WA* 53, 22–184; see Kleckley, *The Supputatio Annorum Mundi and Luther's View of History*, 1985.
14. Lectures on Genesis, *WA* 42, 154; *LW* 1, 206.
15. Genesis 2:10–14.
16. *WA* 42, 74–75; *LW* 1, 98.
17. *WA* 42, 75; *LW* 1, 99.
18. *WA* 42, 76; *LW* 1, 100.
19. Crane, *Mercator*, 190, 201–203, 314, n. 15.

20. Hahn-Woernle, *Die Ebstorfer Weltkarte*, 25–40.
21. Hahn-Woernle, *Die Ebstorfer Weltkarte*, 7–11.
22. Hahn-Woernle, *Die Ebstorfer Weltkarte*, 41–78.
23. *WATR* 4, 412–413 (no. 4638); *LW* 54, 358–359.
24. Westman, "The Melanchthon Circle," 181–193.
25. Luther to George Spalatin, October 10, 1531, in *WABr* 6, 204.
26. *WA* 23, 7–12. Kurze, *Johannes Lichtenberger*, 57–62.
27. Buck, "Anatomia Antichristi," 361–368.
28. Grisar & Heege, *Luthers Kampfbilder* III, 1–23.
29. Bagchi, "Luther's Catholic Opponents," 99.
30. Murner, *Von den grossen Lutherischen Narren* . . . , 220; see Rummel, *Scheming Papists and Lutheran Fools*, 72–87.
31. Febvre, *The Problem of Unbelief in the Sixteenth Century*, 438.
32. *WA* 54, 192–194; *LW* 34, 363–366.
33. *WA* 54, 193–194; *LW* 34, 366.
34. *WA* 54, 478–496.

Chapter Two: All That I Am and Have

1. Luther to Philip Melanchthon, June 5, 1530, in *WABr* 5, 351; *LW* 49, 318–319.
2. Erikson, *Young Man Luther*, 49–97.
3. Evidence for the different dates is summarized by Bulisch, "Wie alt ist Martin Luther geworden?" and Staats, "Ist Zwingli älter als Luther?"
4. *Luther und die Reformation am Oberrhein* A3, 135–138, with illustration.
5. *WATR* 5, 76 (no. 5347).
6. Brosseder, "The Writing in the Wittenberg Sky," 557–576.
7. Scribner, "Incombustible Luther," in *Popular Culture and Popular Movements*, 301–322.
8. *WATR* 5, 95 (no. 5362).
9. Strauchenbruch, *Luthers Kinder*, 106.
10. *WATR* 3, 415–416 (no. 3566A); *LW* 54, 234–235.
11. Van Dülmen, *Kultur und Alltag in der frühen Neuzeit*, 101.
12. Martin Luther to Margaret Luder, May 20, 1531, in *WABr* 6, 103–106; *LW* 49, 17–21. Martin also inscribed for her a book by John von Staupitz; *Luther-Lexikon*, ed. Beutel, 190.
13. Luther to Melanchthon, June 5, 1530, in *WABr* 5, 351; *LW* 49, 318–319.
14. Stievermann, "Sozialer Aufstieg um 1500," *Martin Luther und der Bergbau*, 42–62.
15. *Fundsache Luther*, 165.
16. Beer, *Eltern und Kinder*, 341–342.
17. *WATR* 5, 95 (no. 5362).
18. Luther to Martin Seligmann, March 25, 1520, in *WABr* 2, 76.
19. Luther to Justus Jonas, April 19, 1529, in *WABr* 5, 56.
20. Luther to Spalatin, November 29, 1520, in *WABr* 2, 22.
21. *A Sermon on Keeping Children in School* 1530, in *LW* 46, 250–251; *WA* 30:2, 576.
22. *To the Councils of All Cities in Germany* . . . 1524, in *LW* 45, 369; *WA* 15, 46.
23. *Treatise on Good Works* 1520, trans. Hendrix, 98; *StA* 2, 68.
24. Scheel, *Martin Luther* 1, 32.
25. *LW* 45, 370; *WA* 15, 46.
26. *Instructions of the Visitors for Parish Pastors* 1528, in *WA* 26, 237; *LW* 40, 315-316.
27. *WATR* 3, 353 (no. 3490); *LW* 54, 211.
28. Springer, *Luther's Aesop*, 12–15.
29. *WATR* 5, 317 (no. 5677); *LW* 54, 476.
30. *Preface to the Wittenberg Edition of his German Writings* 1539, in *WA* 50, 660; *LW* 34, 287.
31. *Akten und Briefe* . . . *Georgs von Sachsen* 1, 768.
32. Luther to Elector Joachim II of Brandenburg, March 9, 1545, in *WABr* 11, 50.

33. Hendrix, "Brethren of the Common Life," 369.
34. Kolde, *Die deutsche Augustiner-Congregation*, 355. The conjecture is based on Luther's remark about Linck "from an early age growing up with me in the same (or comparable) course of study"; see Luther to Cajetan, October 17, 1518, in *WABr* 1, 222, n. 1.
35. Braasch, "Die Familie Schalbe in Eisenach," 268–270.
36. *Das Leben Martin Luthers 1546*, *MD* 2, 171; Henning, "Martin Luther als Lateinschüler in Eisenach," 112–113.
37. Luther to Güldenapf, April 28, 1507, *WABr* 1, 15.
38. Crotus Rubeanus to Luther, April 28, 1520, *WABr* 2, 91.
39. *WATR* 5, 657 (no. 6428).
40. *Sermon on Keeping Children in School* 1530, *LW* 46, 250; *WA* 30:2, 576.
41. Hintzenstern, "Vorspiele zur Reformation in Eisenach," 81.
42. Junghans, *Der junge Luther und die Humanisten*, 68.

Chapter Three: Holy from Head to Toe

1. Sermon on June 24, 1525, *WA* 17:1, 309; Scheel, *Dokumente*, 37 (no. 93).
2. *WATR* 4, 177 (no. 4170).
3. Kleineidam, *Universitas Studii Erffordensis* 2, 169–170.
4. Dietrich Lindemann to Stephan Roth, January 4, 1526, in Scheel, *Dokumente*, 42 (no. 106); Springer, "Luther als Student des Artes," 87.
5. *CE* 1 (1985) 362.
6. Scheel, *Dokumente*, 151 (no. 412).
7. Springer, "Luther als Student des Artes," 90–92.
8. *WATR* 2, 609–610 (no. 2710).
9. Kleineidam, *Universitas Studii Erffordensis* 2, 142.
10. Kleineidam, *Universitas Studii Erffordensis* 2, 168–169.
11. *Luther: Erfurter Annotationen*, ed. Matsuura, 711–727.
12. HAB Wolfenbüttel 72.5 Quod.
13. Bubenheimer, "Zur vorreformatorischen Rezeption des italienischen Humanismus," 3–5.
14. *Luther: Erfurter Annotationen*, ed. Matsuura, CXXXVII.
15. Bauer, "Kurfürst Johann Friedrich I von Sachsen und die Bücher," 171.
16. Höss, *Spalatin*, 17.
17. Junghans, *Der junge Luther und die Humanisten*, 55.
18. Scheel, *Dokumente*, 154 (no. 423).
19. Dörfler-Dierken, "Luther und die heilige Anna," 39–46.
20. Cf. Acts of the Apostles 9:3–4; Scheel, *Dokumente*, 15 (no. 31).
21. Luther to Gregor Rosseken, March 28, 1533, in *WABr* 6, 438–439.
22. Weiss, *Ein fruchtbar Bethlehem*, 31.
23. Kleineidam, *Universitas Studii Erffordensis* 2, 291.
24. Scheel, *Dokumente*, 53 (no. 156); Schneider, "Episoden aus Luthers Leben als Erfurter Mönch," 134–139. In monastic parlance, conversion meant "dying to the world" and rebirth to a life of perfection.
25. Oberman, *Harvest of Medieval Theology*, 9–21.
26. Zumkeller, *Erbsünde*, 457–458; Biel, *Expositio*, vol. 1, p. x.
27. Scheel, *Dokumente*, 144 (no. 391); *WATR* 3, 564 (no. 3722).
28. Luther to John Lang, mid-October 1516, in *WABr* 1, 66.
29. Luther to John Lang, mid-October 1516, in *WABr* 1, 65.
30. Scheel, *Dokumente*, 16 (no. 33) and 17 (no. 37).
31. Bell, *Divus Bernhardus*, 17–26.
32. Pascoe, *Jean Gerson*, 104–109.
33. Scheel, *Dokumente*, 174 (no. 480) and 127 (no. 342).
34. Luther to his father Hans, November 21, 1521, in *WA* 8, 574; *LW* 48, 322.
35. *Luther: Erfurter Annotationen*, ed. Matsuura, LXXVIII-LXXX.

Chapter Four: Not One of Those

1. *Preface to the First Volume of His Collected Latin Writings* 1545, in *WA* 54, 186; *LW* 34, 338.
2. Haile, *Luther*, 11–18.
3. Myconius, *Historia Reformationis*, ed. Cyprian, V, 24–26.
4. Neser, *Luthers Wohnhaus in Wittenberg*, 21–29, 32.
5. *WATR* 5, 77 (no. 5349). The *Table Talk* excerpt is, however, dated two years before the chapel was torn down.
6. Junghans, *Martin Luther und Wittenberg*, 24–25.
7. Scheurl to Henlein, June 3, 1507, in *Christoph Scheurls Briefbuch*, 1, 46.
8. *Lectures on Galatians* 1531, in *WA* 40/2, 92; *LW* 27, 73; Steinmetz, *Luther and Staupitz*, 141–144.
9. Wriedt, "Johannes von Staupitz," 174.
10. Schneider, "Episoden," 138.
11. *WATR* 5, 98 (no. 5371).
12. *WATR* 2, 379 (no. 2255).
13. *WABr* 12, 402–405.
14. The Wittenberg Augustinian cloister owned a fish pond in Leitzkau and was asked to surrender its patronage of the parish church in Herzberg. Negotiations concerning the latter were held at the residence of the Saxon electors in Torgau.
15. Luther to John Lang, October 26, 1516, in *WABr* 1, 72; *LW* 48, 27–28.
16. Winterhager, "Martin Luther und das Amt des Provinzialvikars," 707–738. In 1517 Karlstadt called Luther the "vicar" of the observant Augustinian brothers "throughout Saxony"; *Karlstadt und Augustin*, ed. Kähler, 4.
17. Winterhager, "Martin Luther und das Amt des Provinzialvikars," 718.
18. Luther to Lang, May 29, 1516, in *WABr* 1, 42; *LW* 48, 16.
19. Winterhager, "Martin Luther und das Amt des Provinzialvikars," 736–737.
20. Luther to John Lang, October 26, 1516, in *WABr* 1, 72; *LW* 48, 27–28.
21. Luther to Spalatin, August 24, 1516, in *WABr* 1, 50; *LW* 48, 17.
22. Luther to George Spenlein, April 8, 1516, in *WABr* 1, 33–36; *LW* 48, 11–14.
23. Luther to the Erfurt Faculty, December 21, 1514, in *WABr* 1, 29–33.
24. *Commentary on the Alleged Imperial Edict* 1531, in *WA* 30 III, 387; *LW* 34, 103.
25. Freiherr von Scheurl, "Martin Luthers Doktoreid," 46–52.
26. Köpf, "Martin Luthers theologischer Lehrstuhl," 80–86.
27. The old source is dated 1788 and no new evidence concerning the printshop has emerged from recent research; see Neser, *Luthers Wohnhaus*, 31.
28. *WA* 4, 463–526.
29. In vols. 3, 4, and 55 of the Weimar Edition.
30. Luther to Lang, July 16, 1517, in *WABr* 1, 100.
31. Augustine, *Confessions* X, 29, trans. Pine-Coffin, 233.
32. *WA* 54, 186; *LW* 34, 337.
33. Luther to Lang, mid-October 1516, in *WABr* 1, 65–66.
34. *WATR* 3, 192 (no. 3232b with variants 3232a & 3232c); *LW* 54, 193–194.
35. For more on the debates surrounding Luther's "discovery" and the role of his lectures on Romans, see Leppin, *Martin Luther*, 107–117; *Meilensteine der Reformation*, 48–59; Brecht, *Martin Luther* 1, 221–237.
36. *WA* 56, 271–277; *LW* 25, 260–264.
37. *WA* 56, 171–173; *LW* 25, 151–152.
38. *WA* 54, 186; *LW* 34, 337.
39. *WA* 56, 171–173; *LW* 25, 151–152; Augustine, *De spiritu et littera* 11.18, *MPL* 44, 211.
40. Steinmetz, *Misericordia Dei*, 85–86.
41. *WA* 54, 186; *LW* 34, 338.
42. Matthias, "Die Anfänge der reformatorischen Theologie des . . . Karlstadt," 96.
43. Luther to Staupitz, October 3, 1519, in *WABr* 1, 515.

Chapter Five: Quiet No Longer

1. Luther to Archbishop Albert of Mainz, October 31, 1517, in *WA* 1, 111; *LW* 48, 46.
2. *WA* 10:1:1, 136; *LW* 52, 37.
3. Luther to Lang, August 6, 1517, in *WABr* 1, 101–102.
4. *WA* 1, 158–220.
5. Luther to Christoph Scheurl, January 27, 1517, in *WABr* 1, 86.
6. Luther to Lang, May 18, 1517, in *WABr* 1, 99; *LW* 48, 42.
7. Paulus, *Die deutschen Dominikaner*, 1–3.
8. Winterhager, "Ablasskritik als Indikator," 24.
9. Köhler, *Dokumente*, 113–116.
10. *Against Hanswurst* 1541, in *WA* 51, 539; *LW* 41, 231–234; cf. nos. 28, 75, 77, 79 of the ninety-five theses, in *StA* 1, 176–185; *LW* 31, 25–33.
11. Köhler, *Dokumente*, 125.
12. Cited by Junghans, "Martin Luther, kirchliche Magnaten und Thesenanschlag," 38, 41.
13. Sermon on Luke 19:8, October 31, 1516, in *WA* 1, 99; see Rieske-Braun, "Glaube und Aberglaube," 27–30.
14. Prior to the Hebrews' escape from Egypt, the ninth plague was darkness; Exodus 10:21–29.
15. Sermon on Matthew 11:25, February 24, 1517, in *WA* 1, 141; *LW* 51, 31.
16. Bacon, "Art Patronage in Electoral Saxony," 973.
17. Kohnle, "Die Frömmigkeit der Wettiner," 136.
18. Erasmus, *Praise of Folly, CWE* 27, 114.
19. Luther to Albert of Mainz, October 31, 1517, in *WABr* 1, 111; *LW* 48, 46.
20. Luther to Albert of Mainz, October 31, 1517, in *WABr* 1, 111; *LW* 48, 47.
21. Albert of Mainz to his counselors in Magdeburg, December 13, 1517, in *Quellen zur Reformation*, 39.
22. Luther to Spalatin, early November 1517, in *WABr* 1, 118.
23. *WATR* 3, 564 (no. 3722); Moeller, "Thesenanschläge," 29.
24. Treu, "Der Thesenanschlag fand wirklich statt," 140–144.
25. Wengert, "Georg Major," 93–97.
26. *Against Hanswurst* 1541, in *WA* 51, 540; *LW* 41, 233.
27. The course began in the winter semester of 1517 and lasted through the summer semester of 1518; Bayer, *Promissio*, 205.
28. *Against Hanswurst* 1541, in *WA* 51, 540; *LW* 41, 234.
29. Luther to Lang, November 11, 1517, in *WABr* 1, 121–122.
30. Moeller, "Thesenanschläge," 25–31.
31. Scheurl to Caspar Güttel, January 8, 1518, in *Christoph Scheurls Briefbuch* 2, 43–44.
32. Scheurl to Conrad Peutinger, January 5, 1518, in *Christoph Scheurls Briefbuch* 2, 40–41.
33. Scheurl to John Eck, November 5, 1517, in *Christoph Scheurls Briefbuch* 2, 40.
34. Roman politician famous for his enormous wealth.
35. *WA* 1, 238; *LW* 31, 33.
36. Luther to Lang, March 21, 1518, in *WABr* 1, 155.
37. *Sermon von Ablass und Gnade* 1518, in *WA* 1, 246.
38. *Johann Tetzels Rebuttal*, 30–31.
39. *WATR* 3, 656 (no. 3846).
40. *E var* 1, 306.
41. Luther to Eck, May 19, 1518, in *WABr* 1, 178.
42. *E var* 1, 345.
43. *E var* 1, 348; *Luthers 95 Thesen samt seinen Resolutionen* . . . , ed. Köhler, 6.
44. Luther to Staupitz, May 30, 1518, in *WA* 1, 526; *LW* 48, 68.
45. *WA* 1, 527–529; Clemen 1, 19–21.
46. *WA* 1, 525–628; Clemen 1, 22–147; *LW* 31, 83–252.
47. Fuhrmann, *Die Päpste*, 157–159.

Chapter Six: The Best Theologians

1. *Preface to the Complete Edition of a German Theology* 1518, in *WA* 1, 379; *LW* 31, 75.
2. *Sermon Preached in the Castle at Leipzig,* June 29, 1519, in *WA* 2, 245; *LW* 51, 55.
3. *Sermon on the Raising of Lazarus,* March 19, 1518, in *WA* 1, 275–276; *LW* 51, 47.
4. *WA* 56, 271–277; *LW* 25, 260–264.
5. Luther to Staupitz, March 31, 1518, in *WABr* 1, 160.
6. *Disputation against Scholastic Theology* 1517 (thesis no. 50), in *WA* 1, 226; *LW* 31, 12.
7. Lecture on Psalm 119:147, 1515, in *WA* 4, 375; *LW* 11, 511.
8. Lang's note in Luther, *Propositiones* 1531 (courtesy of Bubenheimer); Scheible, "Luther und die Anfänge der Reformation am Oberrhein," 16.
9. The Franciscan theologian John Duns Scotus (d. 1308) taught at Oxford and Paris.
10. Martin Bucer to Beatus Rhenanus, May 1, 1518, in *Correspondance de Martin Bucer* 1, 61; *Luther's Correspondence* 1, 82.
11. *WABr* 1, 173; *LW* 48, 61.
12. *WABr* 1, 173–174; *LW* 48, 62–63.
13. *WABr* 1, 173; *LW* 48, 61–62.
14. Dölsch also served as university rector and as dean and lecturer in the philosophy faculty.
15. Lupin was an older colleague whom Luther won over in 1516.
16. Luther to Trutvetter, May 9, 1518, in *WABr* 1, 170.
17. Luther to Trutvetter, May 9, 1518, in *WABr* 1, 170.
18. Winterhager, "Martin Luther und das Amt des Provinzialvikars," 738.
19. *Preface to . . . A German Theology* 1518, in *WA* 1, 378; *LW* 31, 75.
20. Hamm, *Der frühe Luther*, 200–250.
21. *Preface to . . . A German Theology* 1518, in *WA* 1, 379; *LW* 31, 76.
22. Luther to Spalatin, October 31, 1518, in *WABr* 1, 225; *LW* 48, 91.
23. *Augsburg during the Reformation Era*, ed. Tlusty, 287.
24. *WATR* 5, 78–79 (no. 5349); cf. *WATR* 4, 533 (no. 4816).
25. *Proceedings at Augsburg* 1518, in *WA* 2, 8; *LW* 31, 262.
26. *WATR* 5, 78 (no. 5349).
27. Luther to Spalatin, October 31, 1518, in *WABr* 1, 224; *LW* 48, 90–91.
28. Luther to Spalatin, October 31, 1518, in *WABr* 1, 224; *LW* 48, 90–91.
29. Jedin, *History of the Council of Trent* 1, 114–116.
30. Luther to Spalatin, November 25, 1518, in *WABr* 1, 253; *LW* 48, 94.
31. Luther to Spalatin, December 2, 1518, in *WABr* 1, 260–261.
32. Staupitz to Luther, mid-December 1518, in *WABr* 1, 267.
33. *WATR* 5, 103 (no. 5375c).
34. *Kurzer Bericht wie der ehrwürdige Herr, unser lieber Vater und Präzeptor Philippus Melanchthon, sein Leben hie auf Erden geendet und ganz christlich beschlossen hat*, 19–20.
35. Luther to Spalatin, August 31, 1518, in *WABr* 1, 192; *LW* 48, 78.
36. *WATR* 4, 187 (no. 4187).
37. Brecht, *Martin Luther* 1, 309–316.
38. *Akten und Briefe*, ed. Gess 1, 61; *Documents*, ed. Naphy, 17.
39. Described by Sebastian Fröschel, who had just earned the Master of Arts degree and attended the debate; printed in Kohnle, "Die Leipziger Disputation und ihre Bedeutung für die Reformation," 9; Brecht, *Martin Luther* 1, 312.
40. Luther to Spalatin, July 20, 1519, in *WABr* 1, 422; *LW* 31, 322.
41. *Disputation and Defense of Brother Martin Luther* 1519, in *WA* 2, 161; *LW* 31, 318.
42. Luther to Spalatin, July 20, 1519, in *WABr* 1, 422; *LW* 31, 321–322.
43. *WA* 2, 80–130; *LW* 42, 19–91.
44. Luther to Lang, December 18, 1519, in *WABr* 1, 597; *LW* 48, 138.
45. *ARC* I (1520–1532), 107–116.
46. Luther to Spalatin, July 20, 1519, in *WABr* 1, 423; *LW* 31, 324.
47. *An Explanation of the Lord's Prayer for Simple Laity* 1519, in *WA* 2, 80; *LW* 42, 19.

Chapter Seven: The Sails of My Heart

1. Luther to Spalatin, January 14, 1520, in *WABr* 1, 611; *LW* 48, 147.
2. *Unterricht auf etlich Artikel* ... 1519, in *WA* 2, 69–73; Clemen 1, 148–153.
3. *WA* 2, 72; Clemen 1, 153.
4. Wurm, "Johannes Eck und die Disputation von Leipzig 1519," 104, 106.
5. Luther to Spalatin, January 14, 1520, in *WABr* 1, 610-611; *LW* 48, 145–146.
6. Luther to Spalatin, ca. February 14, 1520, in *WABr* 2, 42; *LW* 48, 153.
7. Luther to Spalatin, January 14, 1520, in *WABr* 1, 611; *LW* 48, 147–148.
8. Luther to Staupitz, October 3, 1519, in *WABr* 1, 514.
9. Borth, *Die Luthersache*, 71–72.
10. Köhler, *Luther und die Kirchengeschichte*, 32.
11. *Dr. Martin Luthers sämmtliche Schriften*, rev. ed., ed. Walch, 15, 1658–1659.
12. Fuhrmann, *Die Päpste*, 159.
13. Borth, *Die Luthersache*, 72, n. 1.
14. Luther to Spalatin, March 25, 1520, in *WABr* 2, 75.
15. 1 Corinthians 2:9; *The Rule of St. Benedict in English*, ed. Fry, 29.
16. *Vocabularius theologiae*, ed. Altenstaig, fol. 169b.
17. Rhegius, *Anzaygung, daß die romisch Bull mercklichen schaden* ... , Dr–Dv.
18. *Treatise on Good Works* 1520, trans. Hendrix, 16; *WA* 6, 203.
19. Luther to Spalatin, April 16, 1520, in *WABr* 2, 83; *LW* 48, 160–161.
20. Luther to Spalatin, May 1, 1520, in *WABr* 2, 96; *LW* 48, 162.
21. Smolinsky, *Augustin von Alveldt und Hieronymus Emser*, 18–23, 48–86.
22. *WA* 6, 293; *LW* 39, 65.
23. *WA* 6, 298; *LW* 39, 72.
24. *Letters of John Hus*, ed. Spinka, 178.
25. Leff, *Heresy in the Late Middle Ages* 2, 536–537.
26. Luther to Spalatin, March 13, 1518, in *WABr* 1, 359; *LW* 48, 110.
27. *WA* 6, 308; *LW* 39, 80.
28. *WA* 6, 289; *LW* 39, 60.
29. Luther to Spalatin, February 24, 1520, in *WABr* 2, 48.
30. *WA* 6, 404; *LW* 44, 123.
31. *WA* 6, 404–405; *LW* 44, 123–124.
32. 1 Corinthians 12:12–13; 1 Peter 2:9–10; Revelation 5:9–10.
33. *WA* 6, 407–408; *LW* 44, 127–129.
34. 1 Corinthians 2:15.
35. 2 Corinthians 3:17.
36. *WA* 6, 412; *LW* 44, 135.
37. *WA* 6, 417; *LW* 44, 142–143.
38. *StA* 2, 110, n. 132. 300,000 ducats was an enormous sum; a craftsman in sixteenth-century Germany might earn one ducat per week.
39. *WA* 6, 431; *LW* 44, 161.
40. Luther to Lang, August 18, 1520, in *WABr* 2, 167.
41. *Luther und Emser*, ed. Enders, 1, 16–37.
42. Not to be confused with John Lang, Luther's friend in Erfurt.
43. Luther to Staupitz, September 17, 1523, in *WABr* 3, 155–156; *LW* 49, 48.
44. Kohnle, *Reichstag und Reformation*, 50–51.
45. Melanchthon to Spalatin, March 2, 1521, in *MBW.T* 1, 262–263 (no. 128).
46. *WABr* 2, 194.
47. Luther to Spalatin, October 11, 1520, in *WABr* 2, 195.
48. Aleander, 20–21.
49. Kohnle, *Reichstag und Reformation*, 77–80.
50. Aleander, 19.
51. Aleander, 10–11.
52. Melanchthon to Spalatin, November 4, 1520, in *MBW.T* 1, 233 (no. 109).

53. Rhein, "Katharina Melanchthon, geb. Krapp," 501–518.
54. Luther to John Lang, August 18, 1520, in *WABr* 2, 168.
55. *Freedom of a Christian* 1520, in *WA* 7, 10; *LW* 31, 342.
56. *WA* 7, 21; *LW* 31, 344.
57. *WA* 7, 34; *LW* 31, 365.
58. *Eck's New Bulls and Lies* 1520, in *WA* 6, 576–594; *Against the Execrable Bull of the Antichrist* 1520, in *WA* 6, 597–612.
59. Luther to Spalatin, December 10, 1520, in *WABr* 2, 234; *LW* 48, 186–187.
60. *Quellen zur Reformation 1517–1555*, 68.

Chapter Eight: Subject to Him Alone

1. From the letter dedicating Luther's *Judgment on Monastic Vows* to his father Hans, November 21, 1521, in *WA* 8, 576; *LW* 48, 336.
2. In the Latin version (*Vulgate*) Luther used for his lectures, it was Psalm 21:30.
3. *Operationes in Psalmos*, in *WA* 5, 668.
4. Luther to Staupitz, January 14, 1521, in *WABr* 2, 245–246; *LW* 48, 191–192.
5. Kohnle, *Reichstag und Reformation*, 88–89.
6. Aleander, 44.
7. Mercurino Gattinara to Erasmus, April 5, 1521, in *CWE* 8, 195.
8. Luther to Melanchthon, April 7, 1521, in *WABr* 2, 296.
9. *WABr* 2, 296.
10. *Sermon at Erfurt on the Journey to Worms*, April 7, 1521, in *WA* 7, 810; *LW* 51, 65.
11. Luther to Lang, April 13, 1519, in *WABr* 1, 370.
12. "Edel Wasser" was brandy or schnapps.
13. Luther to Spalatin, April 14, 1521, in *WABr* 2, 298–299; *LW* 48, 198.
14. Möncke, "Editionsnachtrag," *ARG* 103 (2012) 275.
15. Möncke, "Editionsnachtrag," *ARG* 103 (2012) 275.
16. Spalatin, *Annales Reformationis*, 48–49.
17. Cochlaeus was born Johann Dobneck in 1479 at Wendelstein in southern Bavaria. "Cochlaeus" is medieval Latin for spiral, or the German word *Wendel*.
18. Cochlaeus, *Historia Martini Lutheri*, 86.
19. *WATR* 5, 73 (no. 5342b).
20. Wohlfeil, "Der Wormser Reichstag von 1521," 112–113.
21. Kohnle, *Reichstag und Reformation*, 95.
22. Moeller, "Luthers Bücher auf dem Wormser Reichstag," 122–123.
23. *Operationes in Psalmos*, Part 1; see Gerhard Hammer, "Historisch-theologische Einleitung," in *AWA* 1:1 (1991) 243–245.
24. Moeller, "Luthers Bücher auf dem Wormser Reichstag," 122.
25. *WA* 7, 838; *LW* 32, 112–113. The oft-quoted statement, "Here I stand, I cannot do otherwise," appears in only one account of the proceedings that were printed later in Wittenberg.
26. *Operationes in Psalmos* 1519–1521: Dedication to Elector Frederick, in *AWA* 1:2 (1981) 13–14; cf. *WA* 5, 23.
27. *Proceedings at Augsburg*, in *WA* 2,18; *LW* 31, 277.
28. *Defense and Explanation of All the Articles of Dr. Martin Luther Unjustly Condemned by the Roman Bull* 1521, in *WA* 7, 315; *LW* 32, 10–11.
29. Ludolphy, "Haben sie tatsächlich nie miteinander gesprochen?" 115–121; Ludolphy, *Friedrich der Weise*, 384.
30. Spalatin, *Annales Reformationis*, 49–50.
31. *Quellen zur Reformation*, 44; Kohnle, *Reichstag und Reformation*, 95.
32. Luther to Count Albert of Mansfeld, May 3, 1521, in *WABr* 2, 326.
33. *Briefwechsel des Justus Jonas* 1, 53, n. 2.
34. Wechmar, "Propst Justus Jonas: Luthers Freund," 147–148.

35. Ludolphy, *Friedrich der Weise*, 437–438; Kohnle, *Reichstag und Reformation*, 103.
36. Schilling, *Passio Doctoris Martini Lutheri*, 32, 92-93.
37. Luther to Lucas Cranach, April 18, 1521, in *WABr* 2, 305; *LW* 48, 202.
38. Luther to Spalatin, May 14, 1521, in *WABr* 2, 337–338; *LW* 48, 225–226.
39. Mennecke, "Luther als Junker Jörg," 63–99.
40. Luther to John Agricola, May 12, 1521, in *WABr* 2, 335–336; *LW* 48, 221.
41. Cochlaeus, *Historia Martini Lutheri*, 95.
42. Luther to Melanchthon, May 26, 1521, in *WABr* 2, 347–349; *LW* 48, 236.
43. Stephan, "Kulturpolitische Massnahmen," 70.
44. Born Lancellotto de' Politi in 1484 at Siena; Dominican friar, professor in Siena, and theologian at the Council of Trent 1545–1547. In 1521 he published a major work against Luther's attacks on the primacy of the pope. In another treatise Catharinus denounced Erasmus as the fount of all Protestant errors.
45. Luther to Melanchthon, May 26, 1521, in *WABr* 2, 347–349; *LW* 48, 233.
46. Luther to Melanchthon, July 13, 1521, in *WABr* 2, 357; *LW* 48, 257.
47. Luther to Spalatin, August 15, 1521, in *WABr* 2, 380–381; *LW* 48, 295.
48. Luther to Melanchthon, May 12, 1521, in *WABr* 2, 332–333; *LW* 48, 215.
49. Luther to Melanchthon, August 1, 1521, in *WABr* 2, 371; *LW* 48, 279.
50. HAB Wolfenbüttel, 68.7 Theol. (3).
51. Luther to his father Hans Luder, November 21, 1521, in *WA* 8, 573–576; *LW* 48, 329–338.
52. *WA* 8, 575–576; *LW* 48, 334–335.
53. *WA* 8, 576; *LW* 48, 336.

Chapter Nine: Master of a Thousand Arts

1. *That These Words of Christ, "This Is My Body . . ."* 1527, in *WA* 23, 71; *LW* 37, 17–18.
2. Brecht, "Andreas Bodenstein von Karlstadt," 135–150.
3. Luther to Melanchthon, May 12, 1521, in *WABr* 2, 332–333; *LW* 48, 216.
4. Karlstadt, *De legis litera sive carne et spiritu . . . Enarratio*, Bl. Ai; Kruse, *Universitätstheologie*, 282.
5. Kawerau, *Johann Agricola*, 19–20.
6. Luther to Melanchthon, May 26, 1521, in *WABr* 2, 349; *LW* 48, 236.
7. Erasmus to Jonas, May 10, 1521, in *CWE* 8, 202.
8. Jonas to Elector Frederick, June 19, 1521, in *Briefwechsel des Justus Jonas*, 1, 62–63 (no. 54).
9. Kruse, *Universitätstheologie*, 285.
10. Luther to Melanchthon, August 1, 1521, in *WABr* 2, 370; *LW* 48, 277.
11. Luther to Spalatin, November 11, 1521, in *WABr* 2, 403; *LW* 48, 328.
12. Luther to Melanchthon, August 1, 1521, in *WABr* 2, 372; *LW* 48, 280.
13. *The Misuse of the Mass*, in *WA* 8, 482–563; *LW* 36, 127–230.
14. Luther to Melanchthon, August 1, 1521, in *WABr* 2, 372; *LW* 48, 281–282.
15. *Die Wittenberger Bewegung*, 16 (no. 4); Kruse, *Universitätstheologie*, 318.
16. Kruse, *Universitätstheologie*, 319.
17. *DB* at http://www.deutsche-biographie.de/pnd12863460X.html.
18. Kruse, *Universitätstheologie*, 322.
19. Kruse, *Universitätstheologie*, 331.
20. Luther to Spalatin, November 22, 1521, *WABr* 2, 404–405; *LW* 48, 337–338.
21. Luther to Spalatin, ca. December 5, 1521, in *WABr* 2, 409–410; *LW* 48, 351.
22. Luther, *Eyn trew vormanung* 1522, Aiv^v–B^r; *LW* 45, 62–66.
23. Kruse, *Universitätstheologie*, 339–340.
24. Kruse, *Universitätstheologie*, 349–350.
25. Kruse, *Universitätstheologie*, 352; Müller, *Die Wittenberger Bewegung*, 132 (no. 61).
26. Karant-Nunn, *Zwickau in Transition*, 106–109; Bubenheimer, *Thomas Müntzer und Wittenberg*, 50; Edwards, *Luther and the False Brethren*, 9 & 24–25.

27. Luther to Amsdorf, January 13, 1522, in *WABr* 2, 423; *LW* 48, 364.
28. Luther to Melanchthon, January 13, 1522, in *WABr* 2, 425; *LW* 48, 366–367.
29. Bubenheimer, *Thomas Müntzer und Wittenberg*, 36–37.
30. Kruse, *Universitätstheologie*, 355.
31. Urban Baldwin to Stefan Roth, August 1, 1529, in Roth, 62 (no. 68).
32. Luther to Lang, December 18, 1521, in *WABr* 2, 413; *LW* 48, 356.
33. Melanchthon to Caspar Cruciger, March 6, 1522, in *MBW.T* 1, 458 (no. 219).
34. Bentley, *Humanists and Holy Writ*, 112–193.
35. Bluhm, *Luther: Translator of Paul*, 357.
36. Luther to Amsdorf, January 13, 1522, in *WABr* 2, 423; *LW* 48, 363.
37. Luther to Spalatin, March 30, 1522, in *WABr* 2, 490; *LW* 49, 4.
38. Luther to Spalatin, May 10, 1522, in *WABr* 2, 524.
39. Luther to Elector Frederick, ca. February 24, 1522, in *WABr* 2, 448; *LW* 48, 387.
40. Luther to Elector Frederick, March 5, 1522, in *WABr* 2, 454–455; *LW* 48, 389–390.
41. Schild, *Denkwürdigkeiten Wittenbergs*, 24.
42. *Receiving Both Kinds in the Sacrament* 1522, in *WABr* 10:2, 29; *LW* 36, 254.
43. *WA* 10:3, 11; *LW* 51, 74.
44. *WA* 10:3, 38; *LW* 51, 87.
45. Martin Luther to Hans Luder, November 21, 1521, in *WA* 8, 576; *LW* 48, 334–335.
46. Brecht, "Andreas Bodenstein von Karlstadt," 136–140.
47. *On the Councils and the Church* 1539, in *WA* 50, 633; *LW* 41, 154–155; *Trade and Usury* 1524, in *WA* 15, 301–302; *LW* 45, 256–257.
48. Luther to Gregor Brück, October 18, 1523, in *WABr* 3, 176–177; *LW* 49, 52–53; Kolb, *Martin Luther: Confessor of the Faith*, 185; Rieth, *"Habsucht" bei Martin Luther*, 198–213.
49. *A Brief Instruction on What to Look For and Expect in the Gospels* 1521, in *WA* 10:1:1, 16–17; *LW* 35, 123.
50. *Freedom of a Christian* 1520, in *WA* 7, 64; *LW* 31, 365.
51. *Receiving Both Kinds in the Sacrament* 1522, in *WA* 10:2, 37; *LW* 36, 262.
52. Luther to Duke John Frederick of Saxony, March 18, 1522, in *WABr* 2, 477.
53. Bubenheimer, "Andreas Bodenstein von Karlstadt," in *Querdenker*, 27.
54. *DB* at http://www.deutsche-biographie.de/pnd135647258.html.
55. Luther to Elector Frederick, November 1523, in *WABr* 3, 196–197; *LW* 49, 57–59.
56. "Lutherana," ed. Buchwald, 96.
57. Luther to Nicholas Hausmann, March 17, 1522, in *WABr* 2, 474; *LW* 48, 401.
58. Luther to Spalatin, September 20, 1522, in *WABr* 2, 598; *LW* 49, 15.
59. Holfelder, "Bugenhagen, Johannes," 356.
60. Luther to Spalatin, June 7, 1522, in *WABr* 2, 556; *LW* 49, 9.
61. Luther to Linck, March 19, 1522, in *WABr* 2, 478.
62. Luther to Staupitz, June 27, 1522, in *WABr* 2, 567; *LW* 49, 12.
63. Luther to Staupitz, June 27, 1522, in *WABr* 2, 567; *LW* 49, 13.
64. Staupitz to Luther, April 1, 1524, in *WABr* 3, 263–264.

Chapter Ten: A Famous Lover Like Me

1. Luther to Spalatin, April 16, 1525, in *WABr* 3, 475; *LW* 49, 104–105.
2. Krause, "Albrecht von Brandenburg und Halle," 312.
3. Krause, "Albrecht von Brandenburg und Halle," 317.
4. Luther to Spalatin, November 11, 1521, in *WABr* 2, 402; *LW* 48, 326.
5. *WA* 10:2, 105–158; *LW* 39, 247–299.
6. *WA* 6, 407; *LW* 44, 127.
7. *WA* 10:2, 105; *LW* 39, 247.
8. Smolinsky, *Augustin von Alveldt und Hieronymus Emser*, 275–289.
9. Cochlaeus, *Historia Martini Lutheri*, 116.
10. Smolinsky, *Augustin von Alveldt und Hieronymus Emser*, 279–282.

11. Wolgast, *Hochstift und Reformation*, 91–99.
12. Not to be confused with Archbishop Albert of Mainz.
13. *An Exhortation to the Knights of the Teutonic Order That They Lay Aside False Chastity and Assume the True Chastity of Wedlock* 1523, in *WA* 12, 232–244; *LW* 45, 131–158.
14. *Die Reformation im Ordensland Preussen 1523/24*, ed. R. Stupperich, 5–13.
15. *An Order of Mass and Communion for the Church at Wittenberg* 1523, in *WA* 12, 205–220; *LW* 53, 15–40.
16. *WA* 12, 215; *LW* 53, 32.
17. Luther to Staupitz, March 31, 1518, in *WABr* 2, 160.
18. *Personal Prayer Book* 1522, in *WA* 10:2, 375–406; *LW* 43, 3–45.
19. *WA* 10:2, 375; *LW* 43, 11–12.
20. *Open Letter to Bartholomew von Starhemberg* 1524, in *WA* 18, 5–7; *Early Protestant Spirituality*, ed. Hendrix, 205–206.
21. *Against the Falsely Named Spiritual Estate of the Pope and the Bishops* 1522, *WA* 10:2, 151–152; *LW* 39, 292.
22. Luther to Archbishop Albert of Mainz, December 1, 1521, in *WABr* 2, 408; *LW* 48, 342–343.
23. Bubenheimer, "Streit um das Bischofsamt . . . ," 198–209.
24. *Von ehelichem Leben* 1522, in *WA* 10:2, 275–304; *LW* 45, 11–49.
25. *WA* 10:2, 283; *LW* 45, 25.
26. *WA* 10:2, 276–277; *LW* 45, 21.
27. Luther to Wolfgang Stein, April 16, 1523, in *WABr* 3, 60; Moeller, "Wenzel Lincks Hochzeit," 199–200.
28. Treu, *Katharina von Bora*, 5–12.
29. *WATR* 4, 503–504 (no. 4786).
30. Luther to Spalatin, April 16, 1525, in *WABr* 3, 475; *LW* 49, 104–105.
31. Luther to Spalatin, April 16, 1525, in *WABr* 3, 475; *LW* 49, 104–105.
32. *Why Nuns May Leave Their Cloisters with God's Blessing* 1523, in *WA* 11, 387–400.
33. *WA* 11, 398.
34. Melanchthon to Jerome Baumgartner, July 14, 1523, in *MBW.T* 2, 70 (no. 280).
35. Luther to Baumgartner, October 22, 1524, in *WABr* 3, 357–358.
36. *DB* at http://www.deutsche-biographie.de/pnd116067128.html.
37. Kunze, *Das Amt Leisnig*, 326–346.
38. Council and People of Leisnig to Luther, January 25, 1523, in *WABr* 3, 21–23.
39. Luther to the Council of Leisnig, January 29, 1523, in *WABr* 3, 23–24; *LW* 49, 30–32.
40. German: *Kirchenordnung*, that is, church order or constitution.
41. *WA* 11, 409; *LW* 39, 306.
42. *Ordinance of a Common Chest: A Proposal for How to Handle Ecclesiastical Property* 1523, in *WA* 12, 11–30; *LW* 45, 159–194.
43. *WA* 12, 16; *LW* 45, 177.
44. *WA* 12, 19; *LW* 45, 179.
45. *WA* 12, 28; *LW* 45, 192.
46. *WA* 6, 461; *LW* 44, 205–206.
47. *Exposition of Psalm 127 for the Christians at Riga in Livonia* 1524, in *WA* 15, 361; *LW* 45, 318–319.
48. To the Mayors and City Councils, *WA* 15, 27; *LW* 45, 347.
49. To the Mayors and City Councils, *WA* 15, 28–30; *LW* 45, 348–350.
50. To the Mayor and City Councils, *WA* 15, 32; *LW* 45, 352–353.
51. To the Mayor and City Councils, *WA* 15, 40; *LW* 45, 363.
52. Bornkamm, *Martin Luther in der Mitte seines Lebens*, 133.
53. *Whether or Not To Proceed Slowly and Avoid Offending the Weak in Matters That Concern God's Will* 1524; Freys & Barge, *Verzeichnis*, 69 (no. 138).
54. Joestel, *Ostthüringen und Karlstadt*, 136–140; Bubenheimer, "Bodenstein von Karlstadt, Andreas," in *OER* 1, 179.

55. Joestel, *Ostthüringen und Karlstadt*, 138.
56. Luther to John Briessmann, July 4, 1524, in *WABr* 3, 315.
57. Müntzer, *Briefwechsel* 2, 285–286 (no. 84).
58. Müntzer, *Briefwechsel* 2, 287–292 (no. 86).
59. Joestel, *Ostthüringen und Karlstadt*, 100.
60. Karlstadt, *Schriften aus den Jahren 1523–1525* 1, 13–15 & 96.
61. Printed at Nuremberg in 1524.
62. *WA* 15, 334–341 & 327.
63. Bornkamm, *Luther in der Mitte seines Lebens*, 160–161; Looß, "Bodensteins Haltung zum Aufruhr," 271.
64. Luther to Spalatin, September 13, 1524, in *WABr* 3, 346; Luther to Duke John Frederick, September 22, 1524, in *WABr* 3, 353.
65. *WA* 15, 199–221; *LW* 40, 46–59.
66. *Letter to the Princes of Saxony* 1524, in *WA* 15, 213–215; *LW* 40, 52–53.
67. *Letter to the Princes of Saxony* 1524, in *WA* 15, 215; *LW* 40, 54.
68. *Letter to the Princes of Saxony* 1524, in *WA* 15, 216–217; *LW* 40, 55.
69. Melanchthon to Spalatin, end of December 1524, in *MBW.T* 2, 232 (no. 366).
70. Luther to Elector Frederick, March 23, 1524, in *WABr* 3, 258–259; *LW* 49, 75–76 & n. 8.
71. Luther to Amsdorf, March 15, 1529, in *WABr* 5, 40.
72. Luther to Elector Frederick, May 29, 1523, in *WABr* 3, 76; *LW* 49, 40.
73. Luther to Elector Frederick, May 29, 1523, in *WABr* 3, 77; *LW* 49, 41.
74. *WA* 15, 183; Smolinsky, *Augustin von Alveldt und Hieronymus Emser*, 289–301.
75. *WA* 15, 194–195.
76. Luther to Henry of Zütphen, September 1, 1524, in *WA* 3, 337.
77. Luther to Henry of Zütphen, September 1, 1524, in *WA* 3, 337.
78. Joachim Camerarius (1500–1574); *DB* at http://www.deutsche-biographie.de/sfz35406.html.
79. Scheible, "Philipp Melanchthon der bedeutendste Sohn der Stadt Bretten," 267–268; Richard, *Philip Melanchthon*, 121–122.
80. *MWA* 1, 179–189; Scheible, "Philipp Melanchthon der bedeutendste Sohn der Stadt Bretten," 268–269.
81. Luther to Spalatin, second half of January 1523, in *WABr* 3, 24.
82. Luther to Katharina Zell, December 17, 1524, in *WABr* 3, 405–406.
83. Luther to Spalatin, November 30, 1524, in *WABr* 3, 393–394; *LW* 49, 92; December 12, 1524, in *WABr* 3, 398.

Chapter Eleven: Rebellion is Intolerable

1. *Also Against the Robbing and Murdering Mobs of the Other Peasants* 1525, in *StA* 3, 147; *LW* 46, 54–55.
2. Stievermann, "Sozial- und verfassungsgeschichtliche Voraussetzungen Martin Luthers," 160–164.
3. *WABr* 3, 118–119.
4. *WA* 12, 92–93.
5. Herholt, "The Massacre of Weinsberg," 173.
6. The German name for this crater located in south-central Germany was the *Ries*.
7. Luther, *Ermanunge zum fride . . .*, in HAB 131.6 Theol. (16).
8. Müller, *Martin Luther und Weimar*, 41.
9. *Admonition to Peace* 1525, in *StA* 3, 111; *LW* 46, 18.
10. *Also Against the Robbing and Murdering Mobs of the Other Peasants* 1525, in *StA* 3, 147; *LW* 46, 54–55.
11. *Open Letter concerning the Harsh Book against the Peasants* 1525, in *StA* 3, 154; *LW* 46, 67.
12. *Open Letter . . .*, in *StA* 3, 165; *LW* 46, 79.

13. *Open Letter . . .*, in *StA* 3, 165–166; *WA* 46, 80–82.
14. Schwarz, *Die apocalyptische Theologie . . .*, 62–108.
15. *Dialogus oder ein gesprechbüchlin . . .* 1524. Freys & Barge, *Verzeichnis*, 64 (no. 126).
16. Barge, *Andreas Bodenstein von Karlstadt* 2, 150–154.
17. *Letter to the Christians at Strassburg . . .* 1524, *WA* 15, 391–397; *LW* 40, 65–71.
18. *Letter to the Christians at Strassburg . . .* 1524, *WA* 15, 394; *LW* 40, 68.
19. *Letter to the Christians at Strassburg . . .* 1524, *WA* 15, 396; *LW* 40, 70.
20. *Against the Heavenly Prophets in the Matter of Images and Sacraments* 1525, in *WA* 18, 65–214; *LW* 40, 79–223.
21. *Dialogus oder ein gesprechbüchlin . . .*, biii^v–c; *The Eucharistic Pamphlets of . . . Karlstadt*, 175–176.
22. *Against the Heavenly Prophets . . .*, *WA* 18, 202–203; *LW* 40, 212–213.
23. Dickens, *The German Nation and Martin Luther*, 60.
24. Luther to Nicholas Hausmann, November 17, 1524, in *WABr* 3, 373; *LW* 49, 88–90.
25. Luther to Amsdorf, January 23, 1525, in *WABr* 3, 428.
26. *De servo arbitrio*, in *WA* 18, 600–787; *LW* 33, 15–295.
27. Kolb, *Bound Choice . . .*, 15–66.
28. *LW* 9, ix–x.
29. Luther to Nicholas Hausmann, February 2, 1525, in *WABr* 3, 431.
30. *WA* 7, 463.
31. Luther to Nicholas Hausmann, March 14, 1524, in *WABr* 3, 256.
32. *WA* 17:2, ix, xviii.
33. *WA* 17:2, xviii.
34. Melanchthon to Camerarius, April 4, 1525, in *MBW.T* 2, 279 (no. 387).
35. *WA* 17:1, xxxi.
36. Luther to Amsdorf, April 11, 1525, in *WABr* 3, 472.
37. *WA* 17:1, xxxi.
38. *WATR* 5, 657 (no. 6429).
39. Griese, "Luthers Reise ins Aufstandsgebiet," 27.
40. In 1531: *WA* 30:3, 279; *LW* 47, 15.
41. Griese, "Luthers Reise ins Aufstandsgebiet," 34–35.
42. Luther to John Rühel, May 4, 1525, in *WABr* 3, 482; *LW* 49, 111.
43. John Eck to Giovanni Giberti, June 29, 1525, in *ZKG* 19 (1899) 213–214.
44. Luther to Spalatin, May 7, 1525, in *WABr* 3, 487.
45. *Georg Spalatins historischer Nachlaß . . .*, 69–72.
46. Höss, *Georg Spalatin*, 279–280.
47. Glaser, *Klimageschichte Mitteleuropas*, 103–104.
48. Luther to John Rühel, June 3, 1525, in *WABr* 3, 522.
49. Luther to Spalatin, June 10, 1525, in *WABr* 3, 525–527.
50. Justus Jonas to Spalatin, June 14, 1525, in *Briefwechsel des Justus Jonas*, ed. Kawerau, 1, 94 (no. 90).
51. Brecht, *Martin Luther* (German version) 2, 197–198.
52. Erasmus to Daniel Mauch, October 10, 1525, in *CWE* 11, 325, and note 3; Treu, *Katharina von Bora*, 6.
53. Melanchthon to Camerarius, June 16, 1525, in *Luther's Correspondence* 2, 325; *MWA* 7/1, 238–241.
54. Melanchthon to Camerarius, June 16, 1525, in *Luther's Correspondence* 2, 325; *MWA* 7/1, 242–243.
55. Luther to Amsdorf, June 21, 1525, in *WABr* 3, 541; *LW* 49, 117.
56. Luther to Spalatin, June 21, 1525, in *WABr* 3, 540; *LW* 49, 115–116; Höss, *Georg Spalatin*, 284.
57. Bornkamm, *Martin Luther in der Mitte seines Lebens*, 363.
58. Junghans, "Luther in Wittenberg," in *Martin Luther von 1526 bis 1546* 1, 14–15.
59. *WATR* 4, 431–432 (no. 4690).

60. Luther to Frederick Pistorius, April 22, 1527, in *WABr* 4, 194; Luther to Linck, May 6, 1529, in *WABr* 5, 62; *LW* 49, 220.
61. Karlstadt to Luther, June 12, 1525, in *WABr* 3, 529–530.
62. Barge, *Andreas Bodenstein von Karlstadt* 2, 364–365.
63. Barge, *Andreas Bodenstein von Karlstadt* 2, 371.
64. Luther to Spalatin, September 28, 1525, in *WABr* 3, 583.
65. *ML-LDS* 1, 246 & 247; *LW* 33, 35.
66. Duke George to King Henry VIII, May 1523, in *Akten und Briefe* I, 508–509 (no. 509).
67. Erasmus to Duke George, September 6, 1524, in *CWE* 10, 376–377; *Akten und Briefe* I, 734–735 (no. 723).
68. Luther to Eobanus Hessus, March 29, 1523, in *WABr* 3, 50; *LW* 49, 34.
69. Luther to Lazarus Spengler, November 17, 1520, in *WABr* 2, 217–218; *LW* 48, 185.
70. *Defense and Explanation of All the Articles* 1521, *WA* 7, 308 ff. and *LW* 32, 93.
71. *StA* 3, 207–208; *LW* 33, 65.
72. *StA* 3, 208; *LW* 33, 65–66.
73. Erasmus, *Hyperaspistes*, in *EAS* 4, 412; *LW* 33, 66, n. 71.
74. Luther to Michael Stifel, December 31, 1525, in *WA* 3, 653; *LW* 49, 140.
75. Erasmus to Luther, April 11, 1526; *WABr* 4, 47; *CWE* 12, 138.
76. *WATR* 1, 212–213 (no. 484); *LW* 54, 81.

Chapter Twelve: A Coarse and Unruly People

1. *The German Mass* . . . 1526, in *WA* 19, 75; *LW* 53, 64.
2. *The German Mass* . . . 1526, in *WA* 19, 72; *LW* 53, 61.
3. Luther to Hausmann, March 26, 1525, in *WABr* 3, 462.
4. Schlüter, *Musikgeschichte Wittenbergs*, 288–289, 335, 345.
5. "Verba des alten Johan Walters," in Praetorius, *Syntagma Musicum* 1, 451–452.
6. *The German Mass* . . . in *WA* 19, 74–75; *LW* 53, 63–64.
7. *WA* 19, 75; *LW* 53, 64.
8. *WA* 19, 75; *LW* 53, 64.
9. *WA* 19, 75; *LW* 53, 64.
10. *Commentary on 1 Corinthians 7* . . . 1523, in *WA* 12, 105; *LW* 28, 17.
11. Luther to Elector John, October 31, 1525, in *WABr* 3, 595; *LW* 53, 134, n. 15.
12. Junghans, *Martin Luther und Wittenberg*, 102, 104.
13. Schlüter, *Musikgeschichte Wittenbergs*, 288.
14. Luther to Elector John, October 31, 1525, in *WABr* 3, 595; *LW* 53, 135.
15. The pun (sun and son) also works in German (*Sonne und Sohn*).
16. Luther to John Rühel, June 8, 1526, in *WABr* 4, 87; *LW* 49, 152–153.
17. Luther to Spalatin, June 17, 1526, in *WABr* 4, 89.
18. "Lutherana," *ARG* 25 (1528) 75.
19. "Lutherana," *ARG* 25 (1528) 85.
20. Luther to Spalatin, December 6, 1526, in *WABr* 3, 635.
21. Luther to Linck, August 26, 1526, in *WABr* 4, 109–110.
22. *Notes on Ecclesiastes* 1532, in *WA* 20, 158 (Eccles. 9:1); *LW* 15, 144.
23. *Against the King of England* . . . 1522, in *WA* 10:2, 258.
24. Luther to Spalatin, March 27, 1526, in *WABr* 4, 42; *LW* 49, 146–147.
25. Weigelt, *The Schwenckfelders*, 36.
26. Weigelt, *The Schwenckfelders*, 38–39.
27. Weigelt, *The Schwenckfelders*, 37.
28. Luther to Linck, January 1, 1527, in *WABr* 4, 147–148; *LW* 49, 157–158.
29. Brigden, *London and the Reformation*, 213.
30. *WA* 10:2, 262.
31. *Akten und Briefe* 2, 352–353; *LW* 49, 119–120, n. 24.
32. *WA* 23, 33.

33. *WA* 23, 670–671.
34. Luther to John Agricola, early July 1527, in *WABr* 4, 219–220.
35. Luther to Spalatin, July 10, 1527, in *WABr* 4, 221.
36. Luther to Melanchthon, August 2, 1527, in *WABr* 4, 226–227.
37. *Briefwechsel des Jonas Justus* 1, 104–107 (no. 103).
38. *Bugenhagens Briefwechsel*, 72.
39. Elector John to Luther, August 10, 1527, in *WABr* 4, 226–227.
40. Luther to Spalatin, August 19, 1527, in *WABr* 4, 232.
41. George Rörer to Stephan Roth, August 20, 1527, in Roth, 3 (no. 3).
42. Luther to Jonas, ca. November 10, 1527, in *WABr* 4, 280; *LW* 49, 173.
43. *Whether to Flee from the Deadly Plague* 1527, in *WA* 23, 341–345, 363–367; *LW* 43, 121–123, 131–132.
44. Luther to Spalatin, August 19, 1527, in *WABr* 4, 232.
45. Mann, *1491: New Revelations of the Americas before Columbus*, 102–106.
46. Luther to Jonas, December 10, 1527, in *WABr* 4, 295; *LW* 49, 182–183.
47. Melanchthon to Spalatin, December 17, 1527, in *MBW.T* 3, 229 (no. 632).
48. Luther to Jonas, December 10, 1527, in *WABr* 4, 294; *LW* 49, 181.
49. Junghans, "Philipp Melanchthon als theologischer Sekretär," 131–139.
50. Luther to John Brenz, November 28, 1527, in *WABr* 4, 285; *LW* 49, 179.
51. Luther to Nicholas Gerbel, July 28, 1528, in *WABr* 4, 508; *LW* 49, 201–202.
52. *Bugenhagens Briefwechsel*, 67; *Briefwechsel des Justus Jonas* 1, 106 (no. 103).
53. Luther to Clemens Ursinus, March 21, 1527, in *WABr* 4, 177.
54. Nicholas Gerbel to Luther, April 2, 1527, in *WABr* 4, 189 & 190, n. 11; Gerbel to Luther, August 29, 1527, in *WABr* 4, 240.
55. Luther to Spalatin, March 11, 1527, in *WABr* 4, 175.
56. Luther to John Hess, January 27, 1528, in *WABr* 4, 372.
57. Melanchthon to Spalatin, November 12, 1527, in *MBW.T* 3, 214 (no. 624).
58. *Concerning Baptism* . . . 1528, in *WA* 26, 146–149; *LW* 40, 231–234.
59. *Concerning Baptism* . . . 1528, in *WA* 26, 154–155; *LW* 40, 240–241.
60. Luther to the mayor and council of Zerbst, December 24, 1527, in *WABr* 4, 301.
61. *Predigten D. Martin Luthers* 1, 169.
62. Luther to Jonas, December 29, 1527, in *WABr* 4, 307.
63. Luther to Jonas, December 30, 1527, in *WABr* 4, 312; *LW* 49, 186.

Chapter Thirteen: A New Song

1. *WA* 35, 411–415 & 487–488; *LW* 53, 211–216.
2. Luther to Melanchthon, July 13, 1521, in *WABr* 2, 359; *LW* 48, 262.
3. Wengert, "Caspar Cruciger (1504–1548)," 417–441.
4. Gregory, *Salvation at Stake*, 6.
5. Fabiny, *A Short History*, 3; Daniel, "Highlights," 23.
6. Kolb, *For All the Saints*, 85–102.
7. Myconius, *Original Life of Zwingli* 1532, 23.
8. *Elisabeth's Manly Courage*, 9–36.
9. Moeller, "Inquisition und Martyrdom," 229.
10. Moeller, "Inquisition und Martyrdom," 219.
11. Jacob Propst to Luther, mid-December 1524, in *WABr* 3, 400–403; Moeller, "Inquisition und Martyrdom," 243.
12. Luther to Jacob Propst, December 31, 1527, in *WABr* 4, 313–314.
13. *WATR* 4, 303 (no. 4414); *LW* 54, 338.
14. *WA* 26, 196; *LW* 40, 270.
15. *WA* 26, 200; *LW* 40, 272–73.
16. Luther to Hausmann, August 5, 1528, in *WABr* 4, 511; *LW* 49, 203.
17. Luther to Amsdorf, May 5, 1529, in *WABr* 5, 61; *LW* 49, 218–219.

18. Martin Luther to his father Hans Luther, February 15, 1530, in *WABr* 5, 241; *LW* 49, 271.
19. Duke John Frederick to Luther et al., March 12, 1529, in *WABr* 5, 36–37.
20. *LW* 53, 68; Arand, *That I May Be His Own*, 58–63.
21. *WA* 26, 230; *LW* 40, 308.
22. George Rörer to Stephan Roth, January 20, 1529, in Roth, 51 (no. 53).
23. Wengert, *Law and Gospel*, 51.
24. *WA* 26, 202; *LW* 40, 274.
25. *Book of Concord*, 353.
26. *Book of Concord*, 347–348.
27. *Die Reformation im Ordensland Preussen 1523/24*, 100–102.
28. *Book of Concord*, 454.
29. Mager, "Lied und Reformation," 25.
30. Mager, "Lied und Reformation," 26.
31. Brown, *Singing the Gospel*, 5; "Lied," in *Das Luther-Lexikon*, 386.
32. *Early Protestant Spirituality*, ed. Hendrix, 181–199.
33. For the following see Rhein, "Melanchthon und die Musik," 117–127.
34. *Kurzer Bericht . . .*, 35.
35. Leder, "Johannes Bugenhagen Pomeranus," in *Johannes Bugenhagen*, 24.
36. Spehr, "Reformatorenkinder," 212–213.
37. Hesse, "Ein Beitrag zur Vorgeschichte von Bugenhagens Braunschweiger Kirchenordnung von 1528," 65.
38. *Der Ehrbaren Stadt Hamburg Christliche Ordnung 1529*, 281–287.
39. Bugenhagen to Luther, Jonas, and Melanchthon, March 8, 1529, in *Bugenhagens Briefwechsel*, 84–85.
40. Koch, "Unser Bischof," 146.
41. Ebeling, *Luthers Seelsorge*, 143–155.
42. Luther to Hausmann, June 29, 1528, in *WABr* 4, 488.
43. Luther to Spalatin, October 20, 1528, in *WABr* 4, 586.
44. Rüttgardt, *Klosteraustritte in der frühen Reformation*, 273–276; for Ursula's defense, see *Convents Confront the Reformation*, 39–63.
45. Not the city of Freiburg in southwestern Germany.
46. *WATR* 2, 433 (no. 2359).
47. *WATR* 2, 458 (no. 2416).
48. Rüttgardt, *Klosteraustritte in der frühen Reformation*, 55–56.
49. Luther to Wenzel Linck, June 29, 1529, in *WABr* 5, 100.
50. Luther to Jonas, June 5, 1529, in *WABr* 5, 95.
51. Elector John to Luther, May 18, 1529, in *WABr* 5, 72.
52. Luther to Jonas, June 5, 1529, in *WABr* 5, 94.
53. Luther to Jonas, June 14, 1529, in *WABr* 5, 96–97.
54. Luther to Philip of Hesse, June 23, 1529, in *WABr* 5, 101–105; *LW* 49, 228–231.
55. Kohnle, *Reichstag und Reformation*, 371–375.
56. Brady, *Protestant Politics*, 68–69.
57. Luther to Justus Jonas, June 14, 1529, in *WABr* 5, 97; Melanchthon to Jerome Baumgartner, June 20, 1529, and to Philip of Hesse, June 22, 1529, in *MBW.T* 3, 532 & 537–538 (nos 797 & 802).
58. Luther to Philip of Hesse, June 23, 1529, in *WABr* 5, 102; *LW* 49, 231.
59. *Sources and Contexts of the Book of Concord*, 91.
60. Kohnle, *Reichstag und Reformation*, 377–378.
61. Köhler, *Zwingli und Luther* 2, 64–65.
62. *LW* 38, 23; *Das Marburger Religionsgespräch 1529*, 21.
63. *LW* 38, 17; *Das Marburger Religionsgespräch 1529*, 18.
64. *LW* 38, 64 & 67; *Das Marburger Religionsgespräch 1529*, 52 & 54.
65. *Confession concerning Christ's Supper 1528*, in *WA* 26, 339–340; *LW* 37, 228.

66. Luther, Jonas, Melanchthon, Osiander, Agricola, Brenz, Oecolampadius, Zwingli, Bucer, and Hedio. One of three original manuscripts that show the signatures is extant in Zurich.
67. *LW* 38, 88–89; *Das Marburger Religionsgespräch 1529*, 70.
68. *LW* 38, 35–36; *Das Marburger Religionsgespräch 1529*, 29
69. *LW* 38, 70–71; *Das Marburger Religionsgespräch 1529*, 56–57.
70. Taviner, Thwaites & Gant, "The English Sweating Sickness, 1485–1551," 96–98.
71. Melanchthon to Myconius, October 17, 1529, *MBW.T* 3, 627 (no. 833); cf. *WABr* 5, 164, n. 6.
72. Reston, *Defenders of the Faith*, 279–289.

Chapter Fourteen: Dead to the World

1. Martin Luther to Wenzel Linck, January 15, 1531, in *WABr* 6, 17.
2. The son of Luther's sister and her husband, George Kaufmann, came to live with Martin and Katharina. In November of 1530 Cyriac matriculated at the university in Wittenberg; Strauchenbruch, *Luthers Kinder*, 142–145.
3. Martin Luther to Hans Luder, February 15, 1530, in *WABr* 5, 239; *LW* 49, 268–269.
4. Martin Luther to Hans Luder, February 15, 1530, in *WABr* 5, 240–241; *LW* 49, 270–271.
5. Luther to Melanchthon, April 24, 1530, in *WABr* 5, 285–286; *LW* 49, 288–291; cf. Dietrich to Melanchthon, April 24, 1530, in *WABr* 12, 111.
6. Luther to Spalatin, April 15, 1530, in *WABr* 5, 290–291; *LW* 49, 293–294.
7. *LW* 15, viii–ix.
8. George Rörer to Stephan Roth in Zwickau, March 19, 1530, in Roth, 79 (no. 84).
9. *WA* 32, xxv–xxvi.
10. *Sermon on Cross and Suffering Preached at Coburg* 1530, in *WA* 32, 32–33; *LW* 51, 202.
11. *Exhortation to All Clergy Assembled at Augsburg* 1530, in *WA* 30:2, 279–280; *LW* 34, 15.
12. *WA* 30:2, 321; *LW* 34, 39–40.
13. *WA* 30:2, 345–346; *LW* 34, 53.
14. *WA* 30:2, 347–351; *LW* 34, 54–58.
15. *WA* 30:2, 353; *LW* 34, 59.
16. *WA* 30:2, 340–342; *LW* 34, 49–51.
17. Luther to Elector John, May 15, 1530, in *WABr* 5, 319; *LW* 49, 297–298.
18. *WA* 30:2, 68–69.
19. Martin Luther to Katharina Luther, June 5, 1530, in *WABr* 5, 347; *LW* 49, 312–316 & 312, n. 6.
20. Luther to Melanchthon, June 5, 1530, in *WABr* 5, 351; *LW* 49, 318–319.
21. Veit Dietrich to Katharina Luther, June 19, 1530, in *WABr* 5, 379; *LW* 49, 319, n. 22.
22. Luther to his son Hänschen, June 19, 1530, in *WABr* 5, 377–378; *LW* 49, 323–324.
23. Brady, *Protestant Politics*, 76 & n. 178.
24. Immenkötter, *Der Reichstag zu Augsburg*, 20–24.
25. Luther to Melanchthon, June 7, 1530, in *WABr* 5, 354; *LW* 49, 320. For a perceptive appraisal see Leppin, *Martin Luther*, 292–305.
26. *Briefe und Akten*, 90.
27. Melanchthon to Luther, June 26, 1530, in *WABr* 5, 396–397.
28. Luther to Melanchthon, June 29, 1530, in *WABr* 5, 405–406; *LW* 49, 328 & 330.
29. The text of the *Confutation* in English in *The Augsburg Confession*, 348–383.
30. See the discussion of this letter by Gottfried Krodel in *LW* 49, 345–347.
31. The NRSV renders verse 1 of Psalm 118 as follows: "O give thanks to the Lord, for he is good; his steadfast love endures forever."
32. *The Beautiful Confitemini* 1530, in *WA* 31:1, 65–66; *LW* 14, 45.
33. *The Beautiful Confitemini* 1530, in *WA* 31:1, 152; *LW* 14, 86.
34. *WABr* 5, 638, n. 4; *LW* 49, 426, n. 3; *WA* 48, 283–284 (Anhang X, no. 4).

35. Luther to Spalatin, July 15, 1530, in *WABr* 5, 481.
36. Martin Luther to Katharina Luther, August 14, 1530, in *WABr* 5, 544–545; *LW* 49, 400.
37. *Book of Concord*, 58–60.
38. Wicks, "Abuses under Indictment at the Diet of Augsburg," 285–287.
39. Peters, *Apologia*, 7.
40. Peters, *Apologia*, 15.
41. Luther to Nicholas Hausmann, September 23, 1530, in *WABr* 5, 632; *LW* 49, 422.
42. Martin Luther to Katharina Luther, September 24, 1530, in *WABr* 5, 633; *LW* 49, 425.
43. *WA* 32, 114.
44. *Koburger Predigten Martin Luthers*, ed. Buchwald, 44–45.
45. A liturgical chant with a prose text that is sung before or after a psalm.
46. Luther to Ludwig Senfl, October 1–4, 1530, in *WABr* 5, 639; *LW* 49, 428–429.
47. *LW* 30:3, 279; *LW* 47, 15.
48. George Rörer to Stephan Roth, October 17, 1530, in Roth, 85 (no. 94).
49. Cited from a Strasbourg source by Brady, *Protestant Politics*, 77, n. 190.
50. Wolgast, *Die Wittenberger Theologie*, 173–185.
51. Luther to Wenzel Linck, January 15, 1531, in *WABr* 6, 17.
52. Luther to Spengler, February 15, 1531, in *WABr* 6, 37; *LW* 50, 12.

Chapter Fifteen: True Religion

1. From Luther's *Exposition of the Second Psalm*, based on George Rörer's lecture notes from 1531, which were edited by Veit Dietrich and published in 1546; *WA* 40:2, 304; *LW* 12, 87.
2. *WA* 32, xxvi.
3. Luther to Linck, January 15, 1531, in *WABr* 6, 17.
4. Luther to Amsdorf, March 12, 1531, in *WABr* 6, 52.
5. Luther to Justus Menius, second half of March 1531, in *WABr* 6, 61.
6. *WADB* 10:2, vi.
7. *LW* 35, 206–207.
8. *WA* 38, 9; *LW* 35, 209.
9. *WA* 38, 11; *LW* 35, 213–214.
10. *WA* 38, 13; *LW* 35, 216.
11. *The Smalcald Articles*, part III, art. 4, in *Sources and Contexts of the Book of Concord*, 319.
12. *Warning to His Dear German People* 1531 in *WA* 30:3, 317; *LW* 47, 52.
13. *WA* 30:3, 318; *LW* 47, 52–53.
14. *WA* 34:1, 181–189.
15. Kohnle, *Reichstag und Reformation*, 396.
16. Luther to Gregor Brück, late May of 1531, in *WABr* 6, 107–108; *LW* 50, 22–23.
17. *Bugenhagens Briefwechsel*, 101–105; Schreiber, *Die Reformation Lübecks*, 72–73.
18. Luther to Barbara Lisskirchen, April 30, 1531, in *WABr* 6, 86–88.
19. Elector John to Luther, May 4, 1531, in *WABr* 6, 90.
20. Luther to Margaret Luder, May 20, 1531, in *WABr* 6, 103–106; *LW* 50, 17–21.
21. Luther to Elector John, June 16, 1531, in *WABr* 6, 122–123; *LW* 50, 24.
22. Luther to Linck, June 26, 1531, in *WABr* 6, 128.
23. Luther to Elector John, July 3, 1531, in *WABr* 6, 145–146.
24. Luther to John Rühel, October 30, 1531, in *WABr* 6, 220.
25. Luther to Nicholas Hausmann, November 6, 1532, in *WABr* 6, 384.
26. *WATR* 3, 535 (no. 3690).
27. Medem, *Die Universitäts-Jahre*, 29–32.
28. *WA* 40:1, 39; *LW* 26, 3.
29. *WA* 40:1, 45; *LW* 26, 6.
30. *WA* 40:1, 411–414; *LW* 26, 262–263.
31. *Exposition of the Second Psalm* 1532, in *WA* 40:2, 304; *LW* 12, 87.

32. Brady, *Protestant Politics*, 81–82.
33. Gäumann, *Reich Christi und Obrigkeit*, 87–93.
34. Martin Luther to Katharina Luther, February 27, 1532, in *WABr* 6, 270–271; *LW* 50, 48–49.
35. Höss, *Georg Spalatin*, 356.
36. Luther to Spalatin, May 20, 1532, in *WABr* 6, 311–312.
37. Luther to Duke Joachim, in *WABr* 6, 344–345; *LW* 50, 69–71.
38. *WA* 19, 623–662; *LW* 46, 87–137.
39. *WABr* 6, 345; *LW* 50, 71.
40. *WATR* 2, 197 (no. 1738).
41. Nicholas Hausmann to Valentin Hausmann, August 26, 1532, in Clemen, "Beiträge zur Lutherforschung," 94–96.
42. Both sermons in *WA* 36, 237–270; *LW* 51, 231–255.
43. Luther to Duke John Frederick, October 30, 1520, in *WABr* 2, 204–206, *LW* 48, 181–183; *Commentary on the Magnificat* 1521, *WA* 7, 544–545, *LW* 21, 297–298.
44. Luther to the Evangelicals in Leipzig, April 11, 1533, in *WABr* 6, 449–450.
45. Junghans, "Die Ausbreitung der Reformation von 1517 bis 1539," 63–64.
46. Wolgast, "Luther, Jonas und die Wittenberger Kollektivautorität," 91.
47. Melanchthon to Spalatin, ca. February 1533, in *MBW.T* 5, 394 (no. 1310).
48. *WA* 31:1, 430–431; *LW* 14, 110.
49. *WATR* 2, 573 (no. 2642b); Hofmann, "Felicitas von Selmenitz," at *RFG*: www.frauen-und-reformation.de/?s=bio&id=68.
50. Luther to Caspar Cruciger, December 21, 1532, in *WABr* 6, 396.
51. Peter von Naumarck to Stephan Roth, November 17, 1533, in Roth, 104 (no. 120).
52. Rhein, "Katharina Melanchthon, geb. Krapp," 515–518.
53. Scheible, "Melanchthon und Frau Luther," 378–391.
54. Melanchthon to Grynaeus, August 23, 1531, in *MBW.T* 5, 178–181 (no. 1180).
55. Luther to Robert Barnes, September 3, 1531, in *WABr* 6, 178–179; *LW* 50, 32–33.
56. Reinitzer, *Biblia Deutsch*, 115.
57. Luther to Amsdorf, ca. March 11, 1534, in *WABr* 7, 37.
58. Brecht, *Martin Luther* 3, 104–107.

Chapter Sixteen: To Better Account

1. *Lectures on Genesis*, in *WA* 43, 116; *LW* 3, 335–336.
2. Luther to Jacob Propst, August 23, 1535, in *WABr* 7, 239.
3. Luther to Joachim of Anhalt, December 19, 1534, in *WABr* 7, 131–132.
4. Luther to Anna Göritz, December 17, 1534, in *WABr* 7, 131.
5. *WATR* 5, 195 (no. 5503); *LW* 54, 434.
6. Sources are cited by Spehr, "Reformatorenkinder," 189, n. 16.
7. *WABr* 12, 416.
8. Luther to Jonas, October 28, 1535, in *WABr* 7, 316–317; *LW* 50, 108–109.
9. Martin Luther to Katharina Luther, July 29, 1534, in *WABr* 7, 91; *LW* 50, 81.
10. Kohnle, *Reichstag und Reformation*, 427–428.
11. Schwartz, *Geschichte der Reformation in Soest*, 176–177.
12. Haude, *In the Shadow of "Savage Wolves,"* passim.
13. Kerssenbrock, *Narrative of the Anabaptist Madness* 2, 713–716.
14. Luther to Rothmann, December 23, 1532, in *WABr* 6, 403; Melanchthon to Rothmann, December 24, 1532, in *MBW.T* 5, 365 (no. 1294); cf. *Schriften der münsterischen Täufer und ihrer Gegner* 1, 39–41.
15. Rhegius, *Rebuttal of the Münster Valentinians and Donatists* 1535, in *Schriften der münsterischen Täufer* 2, 82–137.
16. *WA* 38, 338–340; cf. *Schriften der münsterischen Täufer* 2, 83–86.
17. Rothert, "Eine Schrift gegen die Wiedertäufer," 90–91.

18. Luther to Nicholas Hausmann, February 23, 1538, in *WABr* 8, 200; *LW* 50, 176.
19. Haile, *Luther*, 14.
20. Luther to Jonas, November 10, 1535, in *WABr* 7, 322; *LW* 50, 110–111.
21. *WATR* 5, 633–635 (no. 6384); cf. *WATR* 5, 636–638 (no. 6388).
22. Haile, *Luther*, 19–29.
23. *LW* 50, 88–92.
24. Anderson, "Robert Barnes on Luther," 40.
25. Luther to Elector John Frederick, January 11, 1536, in *WABr* 7, 342; *LW* 50, 120–121.
26. Luther to Francis Burchart, January 25, 1536, in *WABr* 7, 352; *LW* 50, 131.
27. Luther to Elector John Frederick, March 28, 1536, in *WABr* 7, 383; *LW* 50, 132–134.
28. Anderson, "Robert Barnes on Luther," 59–60, n. 25.
29. MacCulloch, *Thomas Cranmer*, 161.
30. Luther to Edward Foxe, May 12, 1538, in *WABr* 8, 220; *LW* 50, 180. Foxe never received the letter. He died before the German delegates left for England.
31. MacCulloch, *Thomas Cranmer*, 69–72.
32. MacCulloch, *Thomas Cranmer*, 216–221.
33. *WA* 51, 449–450.
34. Luther to Philip of Hesse, October 17, 1534, in *WABr* 7, 109–110.
35. Luther to Philip of Hesse, January 30, 1535, in *WABr* 7, 157–158; *WA* 38, 300.
36. Luther to John Briessmann, May 1, 1536, in *WABr* 7, 405–406.
37. *WA* 41, xxxii; Luther's sermon in *WA* 41, 547–563.
38. Haile, *Luther*, 133–147; cf. Edwards, *Luther and the False Brethren*, 147–155.
39. *Wittenberger Konkordie* 1536, in *Martin Bucers deutsche Schriften* 6:1, 119–134.
40. Luther to Wolfgang Capito, July 9, 1537, in *WABr* 8, 99; *LW* 50, 173.
41. Elector John Frederick to Luther, Jonas, Bugenhagen, Melanchthon, and Cruciger, December 11, 1536, in *WABr* 7, 612–614; *Urkunden und Aktenstücke*, 26–28.
42. *Urkunden und Aktenstücke*, 33; *WATR* 5, 475 (no. 6079); *StA* 5, 329.
43. *Book of Concord*, 310.
44. Luther to Francis Burchart, January 25, 1536, in *WABr* 7, 352; *LW* 50, 131.
45. *Book of Concord*, 305–306.
46. *Book of Concord*, 326.
47. *Urkunden und Aktenstücke*, 69–77; *StA* 5, 330; Elector John Frederick to Luther, January 7, 1537, in *WABr* 8, 4–7.
48. *WABr* 8, 35; *LW* 50, 158.
49. Beutel, "Luther und Schmalkalden," 107–120.
50. Luther to Jonas, February 9, 1537, in *WABr* 8, 40.
51. Luther to Jonas, February 14, 1537, in *WABr* 8, 42.
52. *WATR* 3, 393 (no. 3543b); Beutel, "Luther und Schmalkalden," 119.
53. *WATR* 4, 684 (no. 5147); Beutel, "Luther und Schmalkalden," 119.
54. Martin Luther to Katharina Luther, February 27, 1537, in *WABr* 8, 51; *LW* 50, 167.
55. *WABr* 8, 54–56; Fabiny, *Martin Luther's Last Will and Testament*, 27–31.
56. Luther to Spalatin, March 21, 1537, in *WABr* 8, 59.
57. Schwarz, "Disputationen," in *Luther Handbuch*, 328–340.
58. *WABr* 12, 447–485.
59. Luther to Bugenhagen, July 5, 1537, in *WABr* 8, 96.
60. *WA* 42, vii.
61. *WA* 43, 112–116; *LW* 3, 330–336.
62. Maxfield, *Luther's Lectures on Genesis*, 10–18.

Chapter Seventeen: Indebted to My Papists

1. *WA* 50, 660; *LW* 34, 287.
2. Luther to Propst, September 15, 1538, in *WABr* 8, 292; *LW* 50, 182–183.
3. Melanchthon to Agricola, January 15, 1526, in *MBW.T* 2, 396 (no. 443).
4. *WA* 39:1, 571–572; *LW* 47, 104–105.

5. *WA* 50, 470; *LW* 47, 109.
6. *WATR* 6, 147 (no. 6725).
7. Koch, "Johann Agricola neben Luther," 135–137.
8. *WATR* 5, 482 (no. 4924).
9. Rogge, "Agricola, Johann," in *TRE* 2, 113.
10. *Book of Concord*, 326–327.
11. *WABr* 9, 169, n. 5; Richard, *Philip Melanchthon*, 272–274.
12. Martin Luther to Katharina Luther, July 2, 1540, in *WABr* 9, 168; *LW* 50, 208–209.
13. Schneider Ludorff, *Der fürstliche Reformator*, 194; Ebeling, *Luthers Seelsorge*, 80–83.
14. Luther and Melanchthon to Philip of Hesse, December 10, 1539, in *WABr* 8, 638–644.
15. Luther to Elector John Frederick, June 10, 1540, in *WABr* 9, 133–134; Ebeling, *Luthers Seelsorge*, 88–99.
16. *Briefwechsel Landgraf Philipps des Grossmüthigen* 1, 375; Ebeling, *Luthers Seelsorge*, 97.
17. Brecht, *Martin Luther* 3, 212.
18. Brady, *Protestant Politics*, 220–223.
19. Wartenberg, "Die Entstehung der sächsischen Landeskirche von 1539 bis 1559," 69.
20. *Sermon Preached in Castle Pleissenburg*, May 24, 1539, in *WA* 47, 776–777; *LW* 51, 309.
21. *WA* 47, 778; *LW* 51, 311.
22. Luther to Elector John Frederick, September 19, 1539, in *WABr* 8, 552.
23. *WADB* 4, xxvii–xxxi.
24. Buchwald, *Doktor Martin Luther*, 326.
25. Luther to Melanchthon, April 4, 1541, in *WABr* 9, 358–359 & n. 17.
26. *Biblia Germanica* 1545 (facsimile), LXXIIII.
27. Luther to Melanchthon, April 12, 1541, in *WABr* 9, 366–367.
28. Melanchthon to Meienburg, January 23, 1540, in *MBW.T* 9, 86 (no. 2354); Jonas to Prince George of Anhalt, January 24, 1540, in *Briefwechsel Justus Jonas* 1, 382 (no. 481).
29. Luther to Jonas, Bugenhagen, and Melanchthon, February 26, 1540, in *WABr* 9, 63–64.
30. Luther to Josel von Rosheim, June 11, 1537, in *WABr* 8, 89–91; *LW* 47, 62.
31. *That Jesus Christ Was Born a Jew* 1523, in *WA* 11, 336; *LW* 45, 229.
32. *Lectures on Genesis*, in *WA* 42, 448; *LW* 2, 362.
33. *Lectures on the Psalms* 1513–1515, in *WA* 3, 620 & 4, 344; *LW* 11, 110 (Psalm 82:8) & 11, 469 (Psalm 119:78).
34. *Martin Luther, the Bible, and the Jewish People*, 86.
35. *Lectures on Deuteronomy* 1525, in *WA* 14, 656; *LW* 9, 146.
36. Kaufmann, *Luthers "Judenschriften"*, 85–90.
37. Luke 24:26–27.
38. Rhegius, *Dialogus von der schönen predigt . . .*, Wittenberg 1537.
39. *WATR* 4, 517 (no. 4795); Kaufmann, *Luthers "Judenschriften*," 90, notes 37 & 157–158.
40. *WABr* 3, 101–104 & n. 1; *Martin Luther, the Bible, and the Jewish People*, 84–86.
41. Junghans, "Luther in Wittenberg," 126–127.
42. *WA* 52, 482; Hsia, *The Myth of Ritual Murder*, 133.
43. Hsia, *The Myth of Ritual Murder*, 136–143.
44. *WA* 50, 660; *LW* 34, 287.
45. *WA* 50, 393–431.
46. Edwards, *Luther's Last Battles*, 171.
47. Mundt, *Lemnius und Luther*, Part I.
48. Brecht, *Martin Luther* 3, 87–89.
49. Melanchthon to Elector John Frederick, ca. July 31, 1538, in *MBW.T* 8, 177 (no. 2070).
50. Edwards, *Luther's Last Battles*, 143–162.
51. Augustine, *City of God* [books] 15, ch. 28 & 16, ch. 1, in *Basic Writings of Saint Augustine* 2, 274–276; *WA* 42, 187; *LW* 1, 252.
52. *WA* 51, 477–499; *LW* 41, 194–206.
53. *WA* 51, 539–546; *LW* 41, 231–237.
54. *WA* 51, 499; *LW* 41, 206.

Chapter Eighteen: A Prodigious Sinner

1. Luther to Spalatin, August 21, 1544, in *WABr* 10, 639.
2. Spalatin, *Annales*, 655–671.
3. Edwards, *Luther's Last Battles*, 172–182.
4. Luther to Jonas, February 16, 1542, in *WABr* 9, 622; *LW* 50, 227–228.
5. Luther to Marcus Crodel, August 26, 1542, in *WABr* 10, 134; *LW* 50, 231–232.
6. Luther to Marcus Crodel, August 28, 1542, in *WABr* 10, 136–137; *LW* 50, 233–234.
7. Luther to Marcus Crodel, August 28, 1542, in *WABr* 10, 147; *LW* 50, 235.
8. *WATR* 5, 189–190 (no. 5494); *LW* 54, 430–431. The last sentence is from Romans 14:8.
9. *WATR* 5, 192 (no. 5496); *LW* 54, 431.
10. *WABr* 12, 353.
11. *WATR* 5, 193 (no. 5499); *LW* 54, 433.
12. *WATR* 4, 631 (no. 5041).
13. *WABr* 9, 572–574; *LW* 34, 295–297.
14. *WABr* 9, 579–587 (Beilage IV).
15. *WABr* 9, 573; *LW* 34, 296.
16. Luther to Lazarus Spengler, July 8, 1530, in *WABr* 5, 445; *LW* 49, 358–359.
17. Neser, *Luthers Wohnhaus in Wittenberg*, 41–48.
18. *WABr* 9, 573–574; *LW* 34, 297.
19. Luther to King Gustav I of Sweden, October 4, 1541, in *WABr* 9, 530–531.
20. Edwards, *Luther's Last Battles*, 91–114.
21. *WADB* 11:2, 13; *LW* 35, 300.
22. *WA* 51, 577–625; *LW* 43, 215–241.
23. *WA* 51, 586; *LW* 43, 219.
24. *WA* 51, 596; *LW* 43, 224.
25. *WA* 23, 427; *LW* 43, 162–163.
26. *WA* 53, 417; *LW* 47, 137.
27. *WA* 53, 446; *LW* 47, 172.
28. *WATR* 5, 198 (no. 5504).
29. Kaufmann, "Die theologische Bewertung des Judentums," 197–207.
30. Hsia, *The Myth of Ritual Murder*, 151; Kaufmann, *Luthers "Judenschriften,"* 174–175.
31. Kaufmann, *Luthers "Judenschriften,"* 96–110.
32. Burnett, "A Dialogue of the Deaf," 169.
33. *WA* 50, 318; *LW* 47, 73.
34. Kaufmann, "Die theologische Bewertung des Judentums," 210.
35. *Martin Bucers deutsche Schriften* 7, 391–393.
36. *WA* 53, 523; *LW* 47, 268.
37. *WA* 53, 523 & 526; *LW* 47, 268 & 272.
38. *WA* 53, 527; *LW* 47, 274.
39. *WA* 53, 529; *LW* 47, 276.
40. For sources and examples, see Kaufmann, *Luthers "Judenschriften,"* 180–181.
41. Writings against the Turks were not all harshly polemical. For an overview, see Henrich & Boyce, "Martin Luther—Translations of Two Prefaces on Islam."
42. Bullinger to Martin Bucer, December 8, 1543, in *Heinrich Bullinger Briefwechsel* 13, 336.
43. Bullinger, *Wahrhaffte Bekanntnuß*, 10r.
44. Detmers, "Sie nennen unseren Retter Christus einen Hurensohn und die göttliche Jungfrau eine Dirne . . .," 242–243.
45. Kaufmann, *Luthers "Judenschriften,"* 144, n. 35. For two additional so-called anti-Jewish works by Luther, see Edwards, *Luther's Last Battles*, 134–136.
46. Armstrong, *A History of God*, 279.
47. For example, *The Estate of Marriage*, in *LW* 45, 13–49; *WA* 10:2, 275–304.
48. *LW* 46, 50, 54, 80–85; *WA* 18, 358, 361, 397–401.
49. Luther to George Spenlein, June 17, 1544, in *WABr* 10, 594.

50. Luther to Claus Storm, June 15, 1522, in *WABr* 2, 56.
51. *Admonition concerning the Sacrament* 1530 in *WA* 303, 621; *LW* 38, 131.
52. Cited by Zeeden, *Martin Luther und die Reformation* I, 39.
53. *MD* 2, 161; cf. Erasmus to Melanchthon, December 10, 1524, in *MBW.T* 2, 214 (no. 360).
54. *Die Lügend von St. Johanne Chrysostomo* 1537, in *WA* 50, 62.
55. Ellwardt, *Evangelischer Kirchenbau*, 28–30.
56. Luke 14:1–11; *LW* 51, 333–354; *WA* 49, 588–615.
57. *WA* 49, 607; *LW* 51, 349.
58. *Preface to the Revelation of St. John* 1546, in *LW* 35, 410; *WADB* 7, 419–420.
59. Luther to Linck, June 20, 1543, in *WABr* 10, 335.
60. *WATR* 4, 124–125 (no. 4084); *LW* 54, 319.
61. Luther to Spalatin, August 21, 1544, in *WABr* 10, 639.
62. Luther to Propst, ca. April 17, 1544, in *WABr* 10, 554; *LW* 50, 245–246.
63. Luther to Propst, January 17, 1546, in *WABr* 11, 363–364.
64. Preuss, *Lutherbildnisse*, 6; *WATR* 2, 421 (no. 2327).
65. Preuss, *Lutherbildnisse*, 6–7.
66. Martin Luther to Katharina Luther, July 28, 1545, in *WABr* 11, 149–150; *LW* 50, 278–279.
67. Werdermann, *Luthers Wittenberger Gemeinde*, 72–76, 84–89.
68. Edwards, *Luther's Last Battles*, 163.
69. Cited by Edwards, *Luther's Last Battles*, 163.
70. The illustrations are located at the end of *WA* 54.
71. *WA* 54, 292; *LW* 41, 368.
72. Luther to Propst, January 17, 1546, in *WABr* 11, 363–364.
73. Brecht, *Martin Luther* 3, 371–372.
74. *WA* 54, 487–496.
75. *WA* 54, 490.
76. Brecht, *Martin Luther* 3, 376–377.
77. Birkenmeier, "Luthers Totenmaske?", 187–203.
78. *WA* 54, 496.
79. 1 Corinthians 15:43; *WA* 54, 496.

Epilogue

1. Smith, "Katharina von Bora through Five Centuries," 753.
2. Scheible, "Melanchthon und Frau Luther," 381–387.
3. Junghans, "Kaiser Karl V. am Grabe Martin Luthers," 254–259.
4. Scheible, "Melanchthon und Frau Luther," 387–389.
5. Treu, *Katharina von Bora*, 80–87.
6. *WATR* 2, 178 (no. 1682).
7. http://mlk-kpp01.stanford.edu:5801/transcription/document_images/undecided/630416-019.pdf

BIBLIOGRAPHY

SOURCES

Acta Reformationis Catholicae. Vol. 1: 1520–1532. Ed. G. Pfeilschifter. Regensburg 1959.
Akten und Briefe zur Kirchenpolitik Herzog Georgs von Sachsen. Ed. F. Gess. 2 vols. Leipzig 1905 & 1917.
Altenstaig, Johannes. *Vocabularius theologiae.* Hagenau 1517.
Archiv zur Weimarer Ausgabe der Werke Martin Luthers: Texte und Untersuchungen. 9 vols. Cologne, Weimar, & Vienna 1981–.
The Augsburg Confession: A Collection of Sources. Ed. J. M. Reu. Reprint. St. Louis n.d.
Augsburg during the Reformation Era. Ed. B. A. Tlusty. Indianapolis & Cambridge 2012.
Augustine of Hippo, *Confessions.* Trans. R. S. Pine-Coffin. Baltimore 1961.
Aurifaber, Johann. *Tischreden oder Colloquia Doct. Mart. Luthers.* Eisleben 1566.
Basic Writings of Saint Augustine. Ed. W. J. Oates. 2 vols. New York 1948.
Biblia Germanica 1545. Facsimile ed. Stuttgart 1967.
Briefe und Acten zu der Geschichte des Religionsgespräches zu Marburg 1529 und des Reichstages zu Augsburg 1530. Ed. F. W. Schirrmacher. Gotha 1876.
Der Briefwechsel des Justus Jonas. 2 vols. Ed. G. Kawerau. Reprint: Hildesheim 1964.
Briefwechsel Landgraf Philipps des Grossmüthigen von Hessen mit Bucer. 3 vols. Ed. M. Lenz. Stuttgart 1880–1891 (rpt. Osnabrück 1965).
Bullinger, Heinrich. *Warhaffte Bekanntnuß der Dieneren der Kilchen zu Zürych.* Zurich 1545.
Burkhardt, C. A. H. "Altes und Neues über Luthers Reisen quellenmässig mitgeteilt." *ZKG* 19 (1899) 99–105.
Christoph Scheurl's Briefbuch. Ed. F. von Soden and J. K. F. Knaake. 2 vols. Aalen 1962.
Clemen, Otto. "Beiträge zur Lutherforschung." *ZKG* 34 (1913) 93–102.
Cochlaeus, Johann. *Historia Martini Lutheri.* Trans. J. C. Hueber. Ingolstadt 1582.
Collected Works of Erasmus. Toronto 1974–.
Convents Confront the Reformation. Ed. M. Wiesner-Hanks. Milwaukee 1996.
Correspondance de Martin Bucer. Vol. 1. Ed. J. Rott. Leiden 1979.
D. Martini Lutheri opera latina varii argumenti ad reformationis historiam imprimis pertinentia. 7 vols. Frankfurt & Erlangen, 1865–1873.
Die Depeschen des Nuntius Aleander vom Wormser Reichstage 1521. Ed. P. Kalkoff. Halle 1886.
Documents on the Continental Reformation. Ed. W. G. Naphy. New York 1996.
Dokumente zum Ablassstreit von 1517. 2nd ed. Ed. W. Köhler. Tübingen 1934.
Dokumente zur Luthers Entwicklung. Ed. O. Scheel. 2nd ed. Tübingen 1929.
Dr. Martin Luthers sämmtliche Schriften. Rev. ed. Ed. J. G. Walch. 23 vols. St. Louis 1880–1910.
Early Protestant Spirituality. Ed. & trans. S. H. Hendrix. Mahwah, New Jersey 2009.

Der Ehrbaren Stadt Hamburg Christliche Ordnung 1529. Ed. A. Hübner. Hamburg 1976.

Elisabeth's Manly Courage: Testimonials and Songs of Martyred Anabaptist Women in the Low Countries. Ed. H. Joldersma & L. Grijp. Milwaukee 2001.

Erasmus, Desiderius. *Ausgewählte Schriften.* Vol. 4: *De Libero Arbitrio & Hyperastistes Diatribae.* Ed. W. Lesowsky. Darmstadt 1969.

——. *The Education of a Christian Prince.* Ed. L. Jardine. Cambridge 1997.

The Eucharistic Pamphlets of Andreas Bodenstein von Karlstadt. Trans. & ed. A. N. Burnett. Kirksville 2011.

Gabrielis Biel Canonis Misse Expositio. Ed. H. A. Oberman & W. J. Courtenay. 4 vols. Wiesbaden 1963–1967.

Georg Spalatins historischer Nachlaß und Briefe. Vol. 1: Friedrichs des Weisen Leben und Zeitgeschichte. Ed. C. G. Neudecker & L. Preller. Jena 1851.

Heinrich Bullinger Briefwechsel. Vol. 13: Briefe des Jahres 1543. Ed. R. Heinrich et al. Zurich 2008.

Johann Tetzel's Rebuttal against Luther's Sermon on Indulgence and Grace. Trans. D. W. Kramer. Atlanta 2012.

Dr. Johannes Bugenhagens Briefwechsel. Ed. O. Vogt, E. Wolgast, H. Volz. Reprint: Hildesheim 1966.

Karlstadt, Andreas Bodenstein von. *De legis litera sive carne & spiritu . . . Enarratio.* Wittenberg 1521. BSB 4 Asc. 186 (digital version).

——. *Dialogus oder ein gesprechbüchlin von dem grewlichen unnd abgöttischen mißbrauch des hochwirdigsten sacraments Jesu Christi.* Basel 1524.

——. *Schriften aus den Jahren 1523–1525.* Parts I & II. Ed. E. Hertzsch. Halle 1956 & 1957.

Karlstadt und Augustin: Der Kommentar des . . . Karlstadt zu Augustins Schrift De Spiritu et Litera. Ed. E. Kähler. Halle 1952.

Kerssenbrock, Hermann von. *Narrative of the Anabaptist Madness: the Overthrow of Münster, the Famous Metropolis of Westphalia.* Trans. C. S. Mackay. 2 vols. Leiden & Boston 2007.

Koburger Predigten Martin Luthers aus dem Jahre 1530. Ed. G. Buchwald. Leipzig 1917.

Kurzer Bericht wie der ehrwürdige Herr, unser lieber Vater und Präzeptor, Philippus Melanchthon, sein Leben hie auf Erden geendet und ganz christlich beschlossen hat. Wittenberg 1560. Facsimile edition. Ed. W. Heinsius. Munich 1960.

The Letters of John Hus. Trans. & ed. M. Spinka. Manchester 1972.

Luther: Erfurter Annotationen 1509–1510/11. Ed. J. Matsuura. Cologne, Weimar & Vienna 2009.

Luther, Martin. *Ermanunge zum fride auff die zwolff artickel der Bawer schafft in Schwaben.* Mainz 1525. HAB 131.6 Theol. (16).

——. *Eyn trew vormanung Martini Luther tzu allen Christen, sich tzu vorhuten fur auffruhr unnd Emporung.* Wittenberg 1522. HAB Li 5530 Slg. Hardt (69, 1385).

——. *Treatise on Good Works.* Trans. S. H. Hendrix. Minneapolis 2012.

——. *Wolfenbütteler Psalter.* Ed. E. Roach, R. Schwarz & S. Raeder. 2 vols. Frankfurt 1983.

"Lutherana." Ed. G. Buchwald. *ARG* 25 (1528) 1–98.

Luther, Martin. *Propositiones a Martino Luthero subin e dispvtatae.* Wittenberg 1531.

Luther und Emser: ihre Streitschriften aus dem Jahre 1521. Ed. L. Enders. 2 vols. Halle 1889 & 1892.

Luthers 95 Thesen samt seinen Resolutionen sowie den Gegenschriften von Wimpina-Tetzel, Eck und Prierias und den Antworten Luthers darauf. Ed. W. Köhler. Leipzig 1903.

Luther's Correspondence and Other Contemporary Letters. Ed. P. Smith & C. Jacobs. 2 vols. Philadelphia 1913 & 1918.

Luthers Werke in Auswahl. Ed. O. Clemen. Berlin 1912–1933; 1959–1967.

Luther's Works. Ed. C. B. Brown et al. Vols. 56–75. St. Louis 2006–.

Luther's Works. Ed. H. Lehman, J. Pelikan, et al. Vols. 1–55. St. Louis, Philadelphia, Minneapolis 1955–1986.

Das Marburger Religionsgespräch 1529. Ed. Gerhard May. Gütersloh 1970.

Martin Bucers deutsche Schriften. Ed. R. Stupperich et al. 20 vols. Gütersloh, Paris, 1960–.

Martin Luther, the Bible, and the Jewish People: A Reader. Ed. B. Schramm & K. Stjerna. Minneapolis 2012.

Martin Luther Lateinisch-Deutsche Studienausgabe. Ed. W. Härle et al. 3 vols. Leipzig 2006–2009.

Martin Luther Studienausgabe. Ed. H.-U. Delius et al. 6 vols. 1979–1999.

Medem, F. L. C. von. *Die Universitäts-Jahre der Herzoge Ernst Ludwig und Barnim von Pommern.* Anclam 1867.

Melanchthon Deutsch. Ed. M. Beyer, S. Rhein, G. Wartenberg. 2 vols. 1997.

Melanchthons Briefwechsel: Texte. Ed. C. Mundhenk, H. Scheible, R. Wetzel, et al. 14 vols. Stuttgart-Bad Cannstatt 1991–.

Melanchthons Werke in Auswahl. 7 vols. Ed. R. Stupperich et al. Gütersloh 1951–1983.

Müntzer, Thomas. "Briefwechsel." *Thomas-Müntzer-Ausgabe* 2. Ed. S. Bräuer & M. Kobuch. Leipzig 2010.

Murner, Thomas. *Von den grossen Lutherischen Narren . . .* Strasbourg 1522.

Myconius, Friedrich. *Historia Reformationis vom Jahr Christi 1517 bis 1542.* Ed. E. S. Cyprian. Leipzig 1718.

Myconius, Oswald. *Original Life of Zwingli* 1532. In *Ulrich Zwingli Early Writings.* Ed. S. M. Jackson, 1912 (rpt. Durham 1986).

Patrologiae cursus completus, Series Latina. Ed. J.-P. Migne. Paris 1844–1864.

Praetorius, Michael. *Syntagma Musicum.* Vol. 1. Wittenberg 1615.

Predigten D. Martin Luthers. Ed. G. Buchwald. 2 vols. Gütersloh 1925.

Politische Correspondenz der Stadt Strassburg im Zeitalter der Reformation, 1517–1545. Ed. H. Virck. 3 vols. Strassburg 1882–1898.

Quellen zur Reformation 1517–1555. Ed. R. Kastner. Darmstadt 1994.

A Reformation Reader. Ed. D. R. Janz. 2nd ed. Minneapolis 2008.

Die Reformation im Ordensland Preussen 1523/1524. Ed. R. Stupperich. Ulm 1966.

Rhegius, Urbanus. *Anzaygung, daß die romisch Bull mercklichen schaden in gewissin manicher menschen gebracht hab und nit Doctor Luthers leer . . .* Augsburg 1521.

——. *Dialogus von der schönen predigt die Christus Luc. 24. von Jerusalem bis gen Emaus den zweien jüngern am Ostertag aus Mose und allen Propheten gethan hat . . .* Wittenberg 1537, et al.

The Rule of St. Benedict in English. Ed. T. Fry. Collegeville 1982.

Schriften der münsterischen Täufer und ihrer Gegner. Ed. R. Stupperich. 3 vols. Münster 1970–1983.

Schubart, Christoph. *Die Berichte über Luthers Tod und Begräbnis.* Weimar 1917.

Sources and Contexts of the Book of Concord. Ed. R. Kolb & J. Nestingen. Minneapolis 2001.

Spalatin, Georg. *Annales Reformationis oder Jahr-Bücher von der Reformation Lutheri.* Ed. E. S. Cyprian. Leipzig 1718.

Urkunden und Aktenstücke zur Geschichte von Martin Luthers Schmalkaldischen Artikeln (1536–1574). Ed. H. Volz. Berlin 1957.

Vom christlichen Abschied aus diesem tödlichen leben des Ehrwirdigen Herrn D. Martin Lutheri. Ed. P. Frybe. Stuttgart 1996.

Die Wittenberger Bewegung 1521 und 1522. Ed. N. Müller. 2nd ed. Leipzig 1911.

Zur Wittenberger Stadt- und Universitäts-Geschichte in der Reformationszeit: Briefe aus Wittenberg an M. Stephan Roth in Zwickau. Ed. G. Buchwald. Leipzig 1893 (rpt. 1997).

BIBLIOGRAPHY

LITERATURE*

700 Jahre Wittenberg: Stadt—Reformation—Universität. Ed. S. Oehmig. Weimar 1995.

Algazi, Gadi. "'Geistesabwesenheit': Gelehrte zu Hause um 1500." *Historische Anthropologie* 13 (2005) 325–342.

Anderson, Charles S. "Robert Barnes on Luther." In *Interpreters of Luther.* Ed. W. Pauck. Philadelphia 1968, 35–66.

Arand, Charles P. *That I May Be His Own.* St. Louis 2000.

Armstrong, Karen. *A History of God.* New York 1993.

Arnold, Matthieu. *La Correspondance de Luther.* Mainz 1996.

——. *Les femmes dans la correspondance de Luther.* Paris 1998.

Augustijn, Cornelius. "Die Religionsgespräche der vierziger Jahre." In *Die Religionsgespräche der Reformationszeit.* Ed. G. Müller. Gütersloh 1980, 43–53.

Bacon, Paul. "Art Patronage in Electoral Saxony: Frederick the Wise Promotes the Veneration of His Patron, St. Bartholomew." *SCJ* 39 (2008) 973–1001.

Bagchi, David. "Luther's Catholic Opponents." In *The Reformation World.* Ed. A. Pettegree. London & New York 2000, 97–108.

Barge, Hermann. *Andreas Bodenstein von Karlstadt.* 2 vols. Leipzig 1905 (rpt. 1968).

Bauer, Joachim. "Kurfürst Johann Friedrich I von Sachsen und die Bücher." In *Johann Friedrich I.—der lutherische Kurfürst,* 169–189.

Bayer, Oswald. *Promissio.* Göttingen 1971.

Beer, Matthias. *Eltern und Kinder des späten Mittelalters in ihren Briefen.* Nuremberg 1990.

Bell, Theo. *Divus Bernhardus: Bernhard von Clairvaux in Martin Luthers Schriften.* Mainz 1993.

Bentley, Jerry. *Humanists and Holy Writ.* Princeton 1983.

Beutel, Albrecht. "Luther und Schmalkalden." *Luther* 84 (2013) 107–120.

Bierende, Edgar. "Demut und Bekenntnis—Cranachs Bildnisse von Kurfürst Johann Friedrich I. von Sachsen." In *Johann Friedrich I.—der lutherische Kurfürst,* 327–357.

Birkenmeier, Jochen. "Luthers Totenmaske? Zum musealen Umgang mit einem zweifelhaften Exponat." *LuJ* 78 (2011) 187–203.

Die Bischöfe des Heiligen Römischen Reiches 1448 bis 1648. Ed. E. Katz. Berlin 1996.

Bluhm, Heinz. *Luther: Translator of Paul.* New York 1984.

Boehmer, Heinrich. *Luther im Lichte der neueren Forschung.* 5th ed. Leipzig 1918.

---

* Collections with more than one essay appearing in this bibliography are listed below only once with complete bibliographical data; the essays themselves are listed by author with the title of the essay and a short title of the collection with page numbers.

Bornkamm, Heinrich. *Martin Luther in der Mitte seines Lebens.* Göttingen 1979.

Borth, Wilhelm. *Die Luthersache (Causa Lutheri) 1517–1524.* Lübeck & Hamburg 1970.

Braasch, Ernst-Otto. "Die Familie Schalbe in Eisenach." In *Mosaiksteine.* Berlin 1981, 268–270.

Brady, Thomas A., Jr. *Protestant Politics: Jacob Sturm (1489–1553) and the German Reformation.* Atlantic Highlands, New Jersey 1995.

Bräuer, Siegfried. "Bauernschaft in der Grafschaft Mansfeld—Fiktion und Fakten." In *Martin Luther und der Bergbau im Mansfelder Land,* 121–157.

——. "Die reformatorische Bewegung in Halle im Vorfeld des Wirkens von Justus Jonas." In *Justus Jonas (1493–1555) und seine Bedeutung für die Wittenberger Reformation,* 165–181.

Brecht, Martin. "Andreas Bodenstein von Karlstadt, Martin Luther und der Kanon der Heiligen Schrift." In *Querdenker der Reformation,* 135–150.

——. *Martin Luther.* 3 vols. Stuttgart 1981–1987. English trans. J. L. Schaaf. 3 vols. Minneapolis 1981–1993.

Brigden, Susan. *London and the Reformation.* Oxford 1989.

Brosseder, Claudia. "The Writing in the Wittenberg Sky: Astrology in Sixteenth-Century Germany." *JHI* 66 (2005) 557–576.

Brown, Christopher Boyd. *Singing the Gospel: Lutheran Hymns and the Success of the Reformation.* Cambridge, MA & London 2005.

Bubenheimer, Ulrich. "Andreas Bodenstein von Karlstadt und seine fränkische Heimat." In *Querdenker der Reformation,* 15–29.

——. "Bodenstein von Karlstadt, Andreas." *OER* 1, 178–180.

——. "Streit um das Bischofsamt in der Wittenberger Reformation." *ZSSR* 104:73 (1987) 155–209.

——. *Thomas Müntzer: Herkunft und Bildung.* Leiden 1989.

——. *Thomas Müntzer und Wittenberg.* Mühlhausen 2014.

——. "Zur vorreformatorischen Rezeption des italienischen Humanismus in Erfurt und Wittenberg: Martin Luther und Andreas Karlstadt." In *Anwälte der Freiheit! Humanisten und Reformatoren im Dialog.* Ed. M. Dall'Asta. Darmstadt 2015.

Buchwald, Georg. *Doktor Martin Luther: Ein Lebensbild für das deutsche Haus.* Leipzig & Berlin 1902.

——. *Luther-Kalendarium.* Leipzig 1929.

Buck, Lawrence. "Anatomia Antichristi: Form and Content of the Papal Antichrist." *SCJ* 42 (2011) 349–368.

Buckwalter, Stephen E. *Die Priesterehe in Flugschriften der Reformation.* Gütersloh 1998.

Bulisch, Jens. "Wie alt ist Martin Luther geworden? Zum Geburtsjahr 1482 oder 1484." *LuJ* 77 (2010) 29–40.

Burnett, Amy Nelson. *Karlstadt and the Origin of the Eucharistic Controversy.* New York 2011.

Burnett, Stephen G. "A Dialogue of the Deaf: Hebrew Pedagogy and Anti-Jewish Polemic in Sebastian Münster's *Messiahs of the Christians and the Jews* (1529/39)." *ARG* 91 (2000) 168–190.

Clemen, Otto. "Beiträge zur Lutherforschung." *ZKG* 34 (1913) 93–102.

Contemporaries of Erasmus. Ed. P. Bietenholz & T. Deutscher. 3 vols. Toronto 1985–1987.

Crane, Nicholas. *Mercator: The Man Who Mapped the Planet.* New York 2003.

Daniel, David. "Highlights of the Lutheran Reformation in Slovakia." *Concordia Theological Quarterly* 42 (1978) 21–34.

Detmers, Achim. "'Sie nennen unseren Retter Christus einen Hurensohn und die göttliche Jungfrau eine Dirne': Heinrich Bullingers Gutachten zur Duldung von Juden 1572." In *Die Zürcher Reformation.* Ed. A. Schindler & H. Stickelberger. Bern 2001, 229–259.

Dickens, A. G. *The German Nation and Martin Luther.* London & New York 1974.

Dörfler-Dierken, Angelika. "Luther und die heilige Anna." *LuJ* 64 (1997) 19–46.

van Dülmen, Richard. *Kultur und Alltag in der frühen Neuzeit.* Vol. 1: Das Haus und seine Menschen 16.–18. Jahrhundert. Munich 1990.

Ebeling, Gerhard. *Luthers Seelsorge.* Tübingen 1997.

Edwards, Jr., Mark U. *Luther and the False Brethren.* Stanford 1975.

——. *Luther's Last Battles.* Ithaca & London 1983.

Ellwardt, Kathrin. *Evangelischer Kirchenbau in Deutschland.* Petersberg 2008.

Erickson, Erik. *Young Man Luther.* New York 1958.

Fabiny, Tibor. *Martin Luther's Last Will and Testament.* Dublin & Budapest 1982.

——. *A Short History of Lutheranism in Hungary.* Budapest 1997.

Febvre, Lucien. *The Problem of Unbelief in the Sixteenth Century.* Cambridge, MA & London 1985.

Freiherr von Scheurl, Siegfried. "Martin Luther's Doktoreid." *Zeitschrift für bayerische Kirchengeschichte* 32 (1963) 46–52.

Freys, E. & H. Barge, *Verzeichnis der gedruckten Schriften des Andreas Bodenstein von Karlstadt.* Nieuwkoop 1965.

Fuhrmann, Horst. *Die Päpste.* Munich 1998.

Fundsache Luther: Archäologen auf den Spuren des Reformators. Ed. Harald Meller. Stuttgart 2008.

Gäumann, Andreas. *Reich Christi und Obrigkeit.* Bern 2001.

Georg Major (1502–1574). Ed. I. Dingel, G. Wartenberg & M. Beyer. Leipzig 2005.

Glaser, Rüdiger. *Klimageschichte Mitteleuropas.* 2nd ed. Darmstadt 2008.

"Gott hat noch nicht genug Wittenbergisch Bier getrunken": Alltagsleben zur Zeit Martin Luthers. Ed. Evangelisches Predigerseminar. Wittenberg 2001.

Griese, Christiane. "Luthers Reise ins Aufstandsgebiet vom 16.4.1525 bis zum 6.5.1525." *Mühlhäuser Beiträge zu Geschichte. . . .* 12 (1989) 25–35.

Grisar, Hartmann & Franz Heege. *Luthers Kampfbilder III.* Freiburg 1923, 1–23.

Hahn-Woernle, Birgit. *Die Ebstorfer Weltkarte.* 2nd ed. Stuttgart 1993.

Haile, H. G. *Luther: An Experiment in Biography.* Garden City, NY 1980.

Hamm, Berndt. *Der frühe Luther.* Tübingen 2010.

Haude, Sigrun. *In the Shadow of "Savage Wolves": Anabaptist Münster and the German Reformation during the 1530s.* Boston 2000.

Hendrix, Scott H. "Brethren of the Common Life." *Dictionary of the Middle Ages,* vol. 2. New York 1983, 366–370.

——. *Luther.* In the series Abingdon Pillars of Theology. Nashville 2009.

——. *Luther and the Papacy.* Philadelphia 1981.

——. *Martin Luther: A Very Short Introduction.* Oxford 2010.

——. *Recultivating the Vineyard: The Reformation Agendas of Christianization.* Louisville & London 2004.

Henning, Friedrich. "Martin Luther als Lateinschüler in Eisenach." *Luther* 67 (1996) 109–114.

Henrich, Sarah & James L. Boyce. "Martin Luther—Translations of Two Prefaces on Islam: Preface to the *Libellus de ritu et moribus Turcorum* (1530) and Preface to Bibliander's Edition of the *Qur'an* (1543)." *Word & World* 16 (1996) 250–266.

Herholt, Johann. "The Massacre of Weinsberg, 16 April 1525." In Janz, *A Reformation Reader,* 173.

Hesse, Otmar. "Ein Beitrag zur Vorgeschichte von Bugenhagens Braunschweiger Kirchenordnung von 1528." *Jahrbuch der Gesellschaft für niedersächsische Kirchengeschichte* 64 (1966) 62–69.

Hintzenstern, Herbert von. "Vorspiele zur Reformation in Eisenach." *Amtsblatt der Evangelisch-Lutherischen Kirche in Thüringen* 34:10 (1981) 79–85.

Hofmann, Mechthild. "Felicitas von Selmenitz: Die erste Frau der Reformation in Halle." In *RFG:* www.frauen-und-reformation.de/?s=bio&id=68.

Holfelder, H. H. "Bugenhagen, Johannes (1485–1558)." *TRE* 7 (1981) 354–363.

Höss, Irmgard. *Georg Spalatin 1484–1545.* Weimar 1956.

Hsia, R. Po-chia. *The Myth of Ritual Murder: Jews and Magic in Reformation Germany.* New Haven & London, 1988.

Immenkötter, Herbert. *Der Reichstag zu Augsburg und die Confutatio.* Münster 1979.

Das Jahrhundert der Reformation in Sachsen. Ed. H. Junghans. 2nd ed. Leipzig 2005.

Jedin, Hubert. *History of the Council of Trent.* 2 vols. London 1957.

Joestel, Volkmar. *Ostthüringen und Karlstadt.* Berlin 1996.

Johann Friedrich I.—der lutherische Kurfürst. Ed. V. Leppin, G. Schmidt & S. Wefers. Heidelberg 2006.

Johannes Bugenhagen: Gestalt und Wirkung. Ed. H.-G. Leder. Berlin 1984.

Junghans, Helmar. "Die Ausbreitung der Reformation von 1517 bis 1539." In *Das Jahrhundert der Reformation in Sachsen,* 37–67.

——. *Der junge Luther und die Humanisten.* Weimar 1984.

——. "Kaiser Karl V. am Grabe Martin Luthers in der Schloßkirche zu Wittenberg." In *Spätmittelalter, Luthers Reformation, Kirche in Sachsen,* 249–259.

——. "Lutherbiographien zum 500. Geburtstag des Reformators 1983." *Theologische Literaturzeitung* 110 (1985) 402–442.

——. "Luther in Wittenberg." In *Martin Luther von 1526 bis 1546.* 2 vols. Ed. H. Junghans. Berlin 1983, 1, 11–37.

——. "Martin Luther, kirchliche Magnaten und Thesenanschlag . . ." In *Luthers Thesenanschlag,* 33–46.

——. "Martin Luther und die Leipziger Disputation." In *Die Leipziger Disputation 1519,* 87–94.

——. *Martin Luther und Wittenberg.* Munich & Berlin 1996.

——. "Martin Luthers letzte Jahre." *Luther* 67 (1996) 114–130.

——. "Philipp Melanchthon als theologischer Sekretär." In *Der Theologe Melanchthon.* Ed. G. Frank. Stuttgart 2000, 129–152.

——. *Spätmittelalter, Luthers Reformation, Kirche in Sachsen.* Ed. M. Beyer & G. Wartenberg. Leipzig 2001.

——. "Die Tischreden Martin Luthers." In *D. Martin Luthers Werke . . . Sonderedition: Begleitheft zu den Tischreden.* Weimar 2000, 24–50.

Justus Jonas (1493–1555) und seine Bedeutung für die Wittenberger Reformation. Ed. I. Dingel. Leipzig 2009.

Kaplan, Debra. "Sharing Conversations: A Jewish Polemic against Martin Luther." *ARG* 103 (2012) 41–63.

Karant-Nunn, Susan C. *Luther's Pastors: The Reformation in the Ernestine Countryside.* Philadelphia 1979.

——. *Zwickau in Transition, 1500–1547.* Columbus 1987.

Kaufmann, Thomas. *Luthers "Judenschriften."* Tübingen 2011.

——. "Die theologische Bewertung des Judentums im Protestantismus des späteren 16. Jahrhunderts (1530–1600)." *ARG* 91 (2000) 191–237.

Kawerau, Gustav. *Johann Agricola von Eisleben.* Berlin 1881.

Kleckley, Russell C. *The Supputatio Annorum Mundi and Luther's View of History.* Lutheran Seminary at Philadelphia 1985.

Kleineidam, Erich. *Universitas Studii Erffordensis.* Part 2. 2nd ed. Leipzig 1992.

Koch, Ernst. "Johann Agricola neben Luther: Schülerschaft und theologische Eigenart." In *Lutheriana,* 131–150.

——. "Unser Bischof: Johannes Bugenhagen als Gestalt der Reformation." *Die Zeichen der Zeit* 39 (1985) 145–149.

Köhler, Walther. *Luther und die Kirchengeschichte nach seinen Schriften zunächst bis 1521.* Erlangen 1900.

——. *Zwingli und Luther.* Vol. 2. Ed. E. Kohlmeyer & H. Bornkamm. Gütersloh 1953.

Kohnle, Armin. "Die Frömmigkeit der Wettiner und die Anfänge der Reformation." *LuJ* 75 (2008), 125–141.

——. *Reichstag und Reformation.* Gütersloh 2001.

——. "Die Leipziger Disputation und ihre Bedeutung für die Reformation." In *Die Leipziger Disputation 1519,* 9–24.

Kolb, Robert. *Bound Choice, Election, and Wittenberg Theological Method*. Grand Rapids 2005.

———. *For All the Saints*. Macon, GA 1987.

———. *Martin Luther: Confessor of the Faith*. Oxford 2009.

———. *Martin Luther As Prophet, Teacher, and Hero*. Grand Rapids 1999.

———. *Nikolaus von Amsdorf (1483–1565)*. Nieuwkoop 1978.

Kolde, Theodor. *Die deutsche Augustiner Congregation und Johann von Staupitz*. Gotha 1879.

Köpf, Ulrich. "Martin Luthers theologischer Lehrstuhl." In *Die Theologische Fakultät Wittenberg 1502 bis 1602*, 71–86.

Krause, Hans-Joachim. "Albrecht von Brandenburg und Halle." In *Erzbischof Albrecht von Brandenburg (1490–1545)*. Ed. F. Jürgensmeier. Frankfurt 1991, 296–356.

Krodel, Gottfried G. "Wider den Abgott zu Halle: Luthers Auseinandersetzung mit Albrecht von Mainz im Herbst 1521." *LuJ* 33 (1966) 9–87.

Kruse, Jens-Martin. *Universitätstheologie und Kirchenreform: die Anfänge der Reformation in Wittenberg 1516–1522*. Mainz 2002.

Kunze, Jens. *Das Amt Leisnig im 15. Jahrhundert*. Leipzig 2007.

Kurze, Dietrich. *Johannes Lichtenberger (gest. 1503)*. Lübeck & Hamburg 1960.

Leben und Werk Martin Luthers von 1526 bis 1546. Ed. H. Junghans. 2 vols. Göttingen 1983.

Leff, Gordon. *Heresy in the Late Middle Ages*. 2 vols. Manchester & New York 1967.

Die Leipziger Disputation 1519. Ed. M. Hein & A. Kohnle. Leipzig 2011.

Leppin, Volker. *Antichrist und Jüngster Tag*. Gütersloh 1999.

———. *Martin Luther*. Darmstadt 2006.

Lindner, Andreas. "Was geschah in Stotternheim? Eine problematische Geschichte und ihre problematische Rezeption." In *Luther und das monastische Erbe*, 93–110.

Looß, Sigrid. "Andreas Bodensteins von Karlstadt Haltung zum Aufruhr." In *Querdenker der Reformation*, 265–276.

Ludolphy, Ingetraut. *Friedrich der Weise, Kurfürst von Sachsen, 1463–1525*. Göttingen 1984.

———. "Haben sie tatsächlich nie miteinander gesprochen?" *Luther* 53 (1982) 115–121.

Luther Handbuch. Ed. A. Beutel. Tübingen 2005.

Luther und die Reformation am Oberrhein. Ausstellungskatalog der Badischen Landesbibliothek. Karlsruhe 1983.

Das Luther-Lexikon. Ed. V. Leppin & G. Schneider-Ludorff. Regensburg 2014.

Lutheriana: Zum 500. Geburtstag Martin Luthers. Ed. G. Hammer & K.-H. zur Mühlen. Cologne & Vienna 1984.

Luther's "September Bible" in Facsimile. Ed. K. Strand. Ann Arbor 1972.

Luthers Thesenanschlag—Faktum oder Fiktion. Ed. J. Ott & M. Treu. Leipzig 2008.

MacCulloch, Diarmaid. *Thomas Cranmer: A Life*. New Haven & London 1996.

Mager, Inge. "Lied und Reformation." In *Das protestantische Kirchenlied im 16. und 17. Jahrhundert*. Ed. A. Dürr & W. Killy. Wiesbaden 1986, 25–38.

Mann, Charles C. *1491: New Revelations of the Americas before Columbus*. New York 2006.

Martin Luther und der Bergbau im Mansfelder Land. Ed. R. Knape. Eisleben 2000.

Matthias, Markus. "Die Anfänge der reformatorischen Theologie des Andreas Bodenstein von Karlstadt." In *Querdenker der Reformation*, 87–109.

Maxfield, John A. *Luther's Lectures on Genesis and the Formation of Evangelical Identity*. Kirksville 2008.

Meilensteine der Reformation: Schlüsseldokumente der frühen Wirksamkeit Martin Luthers. Ed. I. Dingel & H. Jürgens. Gütersloh 2014.

Mennecke, Ute. "Luther als Junker Jörg." *LuJ* 79 (2012) 63–99.

Moeller, Bernd. "Inquisition und Martyrdom in Flugschriften der frühen Reformation in Deutschland." In *Luther-Rezeption*, 219–244.

———. *Luther-Rezeption*. Ed. J. Schilling. Göttingen 2001.

———. "Luthers Bücher auf dem Wormser Reichstag." In *Luther-Rezeption*, 121–140.

———. "Thesenanschläge." In *Luthers Thesenanschlag*, 9–31.

———. "Wenzel Lincks Hochzeit: Über Sexualität, Keuschheit und Ehe im Umbruch der Reformation." In *Luther-Rezeption*, 194–218.

Möncke, Gisela. "Editionsnachtrag zu einer Flugschrift über Luther in Worms." *ARG* 103 (2012) 273–280.

Müller, Ernst. *Martin Luther und Weimar*. Weimar 1983.

Mundt, Lothar. *Lemnius und Luther*. Parts I & II. Bern 1983.

Neser, Anne-Marie. *Luthers Wohnhaus in Wittenberg*. Leipzig 2005.

Oberman, Heiko A. *The Harvest of Medieval Theology*. 3rd ed. Grand Rapids 2000.

———. *Luther: Man between God and the Devil*. New Haven & London 1989.

Oehmig, Stefan. "Der Wittenberger Gemeine Kasten in den ersten zweieinhalb Jahrzehnten seines Bestehens (1522/23 bis 1547)." *Jahrbuch für Geschichte des Feudalismus* 13 (1989) 133–179.

Oxford Encyclopedia of the Reformation. Ed. H. Hillerbrand. 4 vols. New York & Oxford 1996.

Pascoe, Louis. *Jean Gerson: Principles of Church Reform*. Leiden 1973.

Peters, Christian, *Apologia Confessionis Augustanae*. Stuttgart 1997.

Paulus, Nikolaus. *Die deutschen Dominikaner im Kampfe gegen Luther (1518–1563)*. Freiburg 1903.

Pfister, Ulrich & Georg Fertig. *The Population History of Germany*. Max Planck Institute of Demographic Research. Rostock 2010.

Preuss, Hans. *Lutherbildnisse*. Leipzig 1912.

Querdenker der Reformation—Andreas Bodenstein von Karlstadt und seine frühe Wirkung. Ed. U. Bubenheimer & S. Oehmig. Würzburg 2011.

Der Reichstag zu Worms von 1521. Ed. F. Reuter. Worms 1971.

Reinitzer, Heimo. *Biblia Deutsch: Luthers Bibelübersetzung und ihre Tradition*. Wolfenbüttel 1983.

Reston, James Jr. *Defenders of the Faith*. New York 2009.

Rhein, Stefan. "Katharina Melanchthon, geb. Krapp." In *700 Jahre Wittenberg: Stadt—Reformation—Universität*, 501–518.

———. "Melanchthon und die Musik." *Luther* 82 (2011) 117–127.

Richard, James W. *Philip Melanchthon: The Protestant Preceptor of Germany*. New York 1898.

Rieske-Braun, Uwe. "Glaube und Aberglaube: Luthers Auslegung des Ersten Gebotes 1516/1518." *LuJ* 69 (2002) 21–46.

Rieth, Ricardo. *"Habsucht" bei Martin Luther*. Weimar 1996.

Rogge, Joachim. "Agricola, Johann (1492/94–1566)." *TRE* 2 (1978) 110–118.

Roper, Lyndal. "'To His Most Learned and Dearest Friend': Reading Luther's Letters." *German History* 28 (2010) 283–295.

Rothert, Hermann. "Eine Schrift gegen die Wiedertäufer von 1535." *Mitteilungen des Vereins für Geschichte und Landeskunde von Osnabrück* 64 (1950) 88–97.

Rummel, Erika. *Scheming Papists and Lutheran Fools*. New York 1993.

Rüttgardt, Antje. *Klosteraustritte in der frühen Reformation*. Gütersloh 2007.

Scheel, Otto. *Martin Luther: Vom Katholizismus zur Reformation*. 2 vols. Tübingen 1916–1917.

Scheible, Heinz. *Aufsätze zu Melanchthon*. Tübingen 2010.

———. "Luther und die Anfänge der Reformation am Oberrhein." In *Luther und die Reformation am Oberrhein*. Ed. G. Römer & G. Schwinge. Karlsruhe 1983, 15–39.

———. "Melanchthon und Frau Luther." In *Aufsätze zu Melanchthon*, 373–391.

———. "Melanchthon und Luther während des Augsburger Reichstag 1530." In *Martin Luther: Reformator und Vater im Glauben*. Ed. P. Manns. Stuttgart 1985, 38–60.

———. "Philipp Melanchthon der bedeutendste Sohn der Stadt Bretten." In *Geschichte der Stadt Bretten von den Anfängen bis zur Zerstörung 1689*. Bretten 1977, 257–282.

———. "Die Universität Heidelberg und Luthers Disputation." In *Melanchthon und die Reformation: Forschungsbeiträge*. Ed. H. Scheible et al. Mainz 1996, 371–391.

Schild, Theodor. *Denkwürdigkeiten Wittenbergs*. Wittenberg 1892.

Schilling, Heinz. *Martin Luther: Rebell in einer Zeit des Umbruchs.* München 2012.

Schilling, Johannes. "Briefe." In *Luther Handbuch,* 340–346.

———. "Musicam semper amavi—Die Musik habe ich allezeit lieb gehabt: Martin Luther, Johann Walter und die Anfänge der evangelischen Musik." *Luther* 83 (2012) 133–144.

———. *Passio Doctoris Martini Lutheri.* Gütersloh 1989.

Schlüter, Marie. *Musikgeschichte Wittenbergs im 16. Jahrhundert.* Göttingen 2010.

Schneider, Hans. "Episoden aus Luthers Zeit als Erfurter Mönch." In *Luther* 81 (2010) 133–148.

———. "Martin Luthers Reise nach Rom neu datiert und neu gedeutet." In *Studien zur Wissenschafts- und Religionsgeschichte.* Ed. Akademie der Wissenschaften zu Göttingen. Berlin 2011, 1–157.

Schneider Ludorff, Gury. *Der fürstliche Reformator.* Leipzig 2006.

Schorn-Schütte, Luise. *Die Reformation: Vorgeschichte–Verlauf–Wirkung.* 5th ed. Munich 2011.

Schreiber, Heinrich. *Die Reformation Lübecks.* Halle 1902.

Schulze, Winfried. *Deutsche Geschichte im 16. Jahrhundert.* Frankfurt 1987.

Schwartz, Hubertus. *Geschichte der Reformation in Soest.* Soest 1932.

Schwarz, Reinhard. *Die apokalyptische Theologie Thomas Müntzers und der Taboriten.* Tübingen 1977.

———. *Luther.* Göttingen 1986.

Scribner, R. W. "Luther Myth" and "Incombustible Luther." In *Popular Culture and Popular Movements in Reformation Germany.* London 1987, 301–353.

Smith, Charlotte Colding. *Images of Islam 1453–1600: Turks in Germany and Central Europe.* London 2014.

Smith, Jeanette C. "Katharina von Bora through Five Centuries: A Historiography." *SCJ* 30 (1999) 745–774.

Smolinsky, Heribert. *Augustin von Alveldt und Hieronymus Emser.* Münster 1983.

Spehr, Christopher. "Reformatorenkinder." *LuJ* 77 (2010) 183–219.

Springer, Carl P. E. *Luther's Aesop.* Kirksville, MO 2011.

Springer, Klaus-Bernward. "Luther als Student der Artes und studentisches Leben in Erfurt im Spätmittelalter und zu Beginn der Frühen Neuzeit." *MVGAE* 72 (2011) 72–97.

Staats, Reinhart. "Ist Zwingli älter als Luther?" *Zwingliana* 16 (1985) 470–476.

———. "Luthers Geburtsjahr 1484 und das Geburtsjahr der evangelischen Kirche 1519." *Bibliothek und Wissenschaft* 18 (1984) 61–84.

Steinmetz, David. *Luther and Staupitz.* Durham 1980.

———. *Misericordia Dei: The Theology of Johannes von Staupitz in Its Late Medieval Setting.* Leiden 1968.

Stephan, Bernd. "Kulturpolitische Massnahmen des Kurfürsten Friedrich III., des Weisen, von Sachsen." *LuJ* 49 (1982) 50–95.

Stievermann, Dieter. "Sozialer Aufstieg um 1500: Hüttenmeister Hans Luther und sein Sohn Dr. Martin Luther." In *Martin Luther und der Bergbau im Mansfelder Land,* 43–62.

———. "Sozial- und verfassungsgeschichtliche Voraussetzungen Martin Luthers und der Reformation—der landesherrliche Rat in Kursachsen, Kurmainz und Mansfeld." In *Martin Luther: Probleme seiner Zeit.* Ed. V. Press & D. Stievermann. Stuttgart 1986, 137–176.

———. "Zum Sozialprofil der Erfurter Humanisten." In *Humanismus in Erfurt,* ed. G. Huber-Rebenich & W. Ludwig. Rudolstadt 2002, 33–53.

Strauchenbruch, Elke. *Luthers Kinder.* Leipzig 2010.

Taviner, Mark, Guy Thwaites & Vanya Gant. "The English Sweating Sickness, 1485–1551: A Viral Pulmonary Disease?" In *Medical History* 42 (1998) 96–98.

Die Theologische Fakultät Wittenberg 1502 bis 1602. Ed. I. Dingel, G. Wartenberg & M. Beyer. Leipzig 2002.

Treu, Martin. *Katharina von Bora.* 3rd ed. Wittenberg 1999.

———. *Martin Luther in Wittenberg: A Biographical Tour.* 2nd ed. Wittenberg 2008.

——. *Martin Luther und Eisleben: Ein Rundgang durch die Ausstellung im Geburtshaus.* Wittenberg 2007.

——. "Der Thesenanschlag fand wirklich statt." *Luther* 78 (2007) 140–144.

Vandiver, Elizabeth, Ralph Keen & Thomas D. Frazel. *Luther's Lives: Two Contemporary Accounts of Martin Luther.* Manchester 2002.

Walter, Peter. "Albrecht und Erasmus von Rotterdam." In *Erzbischof Albrecht von Brandenburg (1490–1545).* Ed. F. Jürgensmeier. Frankfurt 1991, 102–116.

Wartenberg, Günther. "Die Enstehung der sächsischen Landeskirche von 1539 bis 1559." In *Das Jahrhundert der Reformation in Sachsen*, 69–92.

Wechmar, Ernst. "Propst Justus Jonas, Luthers Freund." In *Genealogisches Jahrbuch* 15 (1975) 137–150.

Weigelt, Horst. *The Schwenckfelders in Silesia.* Pennsburg 1985.

Weiss, Ulman. *Ein fruchtbar Bethlehem: Luther und Erfurt.* Berlin 1982.

Wengert, Timothy J. "Caspar Cruciger (1504–1548): The Case of the Disappearing Reformer." *SCJ* 20 (1989) 417–441.

——. "Georg Major: An 'Eyewitness' to the Posting of Martin Luther's Ninety-Five Theses." In *Luthers Thesenanschlag*, 93–97.

——. *Law and Gospel.* Grand Rapids 1997.

——. "Martin Luther's Movement toward an Apostolic Self-Awareness as Reflected in His Early Letters." *LuJ* 61 (1994) 571–592.

Werdermann, Hermann. *Luthers Wittenberger Gemeinde wiederhergtellt aus seinen Predigten.* Gütersloh 1929.

Westman, Robert S. "The Melanchthon Circle, Rheticus, and the Wittenberg Interpretation of the Copernican Theory." *Isis* 66 (1975) 165–193.

Wicks, Jared. "Abuses under Indictment at the Diet of Augsburg 1530." *Theological Studies* 43 (1980) 253–302.

Winterhager, Wilhelm Ernst. "Ablasskritik als Indikator historischen Wandels vor 1517: Ein Beitrag zu Voraussetzungen und Einordnung der Reformation." *ARG* 90 (1999) 6–71.

——. "Martin Luther und das Amt des Provinzialvikars in der Reformkongregation der deutschen Augustiner-Eremiten." In *Vita Religiosa im Mittelalter.* Ed. F. J. Felten & N. Jaspert. Berlin 1999, 707–738.

Wohlfeil, Rainer. "Der Wormser Reichstag von 1521." In *Der Reichstag zu Worms von 1521.* Ed. F. Reuter. Worms 1971, 59–154.

Wolgast, Eike. *Hochstift und Reformation.* Stuttgart 1995.

——. "Luther, Jonas, und die Wittenberger Kollektivautorität." In *Justus Jonas (1493–1555) und seine Bedeutung für die Wittenberger Reformation*, 87–100.

——. *Die Wittenberger Theologie und die Politik der evangelischen Stände.* Heidelberg 1997.

Wriedt, Markus. "Johannes von Staupitz als Gründungsmitglied der Wittenberger Universität." In *700 Jahre Wittenberg*, 173–186.

Wurm, Johann Peter. "Johannes Eck und die Disputation von Leipzig." In *Die Leipziger Disputation 1519*, 95–106.

Zeeden, Ernst W. *Martin Luther und die Reformation im Urteil des deutschen Luthertums.* 2 vols. Freiburg 1950 & 1952.

Zumkeller, Adolar. *Erbsünde, Gnade, Rechtfertigung und Verdienst nach der Lehre der Erfurter Augustinertheologen des Spätmittelalters.* Würzburg 1964.

ILLUSTRATION
ACKNOWLEDGMENTS

1. Kloster Ebstorf/Germany; 2. Lucas Cranach the Elder/Wartburg-Stiftung/Eisenach; 3. S. Hendrix; 4. S. Hendrix; 5. S. Hendrix; 6. Artist unknown/St. Peter's Abbey/Salzburg/Photo: imagno/Getty Images; 7. Lucas Cranach the Elder/bpk, Berlin/Hamburger Kunsthalle, Germany/Photo: Elke Walford/Art Resource, NY; 8. S. Hendrix; 9. S. Hendrix; 10. S. Hendrix; 11. S. Hendrix; 12. The State Hermitage Museum/St. Petersburg/Photograph © The State Hermitage Museum/Photo: Leonard Kheifets; 13. Bernard van Orley (ca.1488-1541)/Museo e Gallerie Nazionale di Capodimonte/Naples/Giraudon/Bridgeman Art Library; 14. G. Schäfer/Die Wartburg und Ihre Geschichte/© 1991 I. P. Verlags-gesellschaft Munich/Photo p. 33: Ulrich Kneise; 15. Lucas Cranach the Elder/Klassik Stiftung Weimar/Schlossmuseum; 16. S. Hendrix; 17. S. Hendrix; 18. Plate at the back of WA 19/transliteration at *WA* 19, 70–71/*LW* 53, 69ff; 19. Lucas Cranach/Portrait of Katharina von Bora 1529/Museen Böttcherstrasse/Ludwig Roselius Museum/Bremen; 20. S. Hendrix; 21. Herzog August Bibliothek Wolfenbüttel: Bibel-S. 4° 11; 22. Stadtkirchengemeinde, Lutherstadt, Wittenberg; 23. North Carolina Museum of Art, Raleigh; 24. Lucas Cranach the Younger/Reproduction in Church of St. Blasius/Nordhausen/Bridgeman Art Library; 25. S. Hendrix.

INDEX